Handbook to Roman Legionary Fortresses

Frontispiece. Traditionally (but mistakenly) known as the Praetorium, this structure is actually the *groma* that stands in front of the headquarters building of *legio III Augusta* at Lambaesis (Tazoult-Lambèse, Algeria). An inscription (*AE* 1974, 723) records the restoration in AD 267/8 of this building, which was erected over the point from which the fortress was laid out. This nineteenth-century woodcut, based on a photograph, shows the western and southern facades of the structure before Cagnat's excavation of the *principia* (which lay to the right; one standing column is visible) and subsequent modern consolidation had taken place.

Handbook to Roman Legionary Fortresses

M.C. Bishop

Pen & Sword
MILITARY

First published in Great Britain in 2012
By Pen and Sword
An imprint of
Pen and Sword Books Ltd
47 Church Street
Barnsley
South Yorkshire
S70 2AS

ISBN 978-1-84884-138-3

A CIP catalogue record for this book is
available from the British Library

Typeset in 11/13pt Plantin by Mac Style, Beverley, E. Yorkshire
Printed and bound in England by CPI Group (UK) Ltd, Croydon, CRO 4YY

Pen & Sword Books Ltd incorporates the Imprints of Pen & Sword Aviation, Pen & Sword Family History, Pen & Sword Maritime, Pen & Sword Military, Pen & Sword Discovery, Wharncliffe Local History, Wharncliffe True Crime, Wharncliffe Transport, Pen & Sword Select, Pen & Sword Military Classics, Leo Cooper, The Praetorian Press, Remember When, Seaforth Publishing and Frontline Publishing.

For a complete list of Pen & Sword titles, please contact
Pen & Sword Books Limited
47 Church Street, Barnsley, South Yorkshire, S70 2AS, England
E-mail: enquiries@pen-and-sword.co.uk
Website: www.pen-and-sword.co.uk

Contents

List of Illustrations

List of Plates

Preface

This book came about for a very simple reason. I found I needed a reference book on Roman legionary fortresses, yet one did not exist.[1] Nor did anybody appear to be particularly keen to write one. It provides facts, pure and simple, with a light smattering of ideas and notions, a few mine, mostly those of other and better scholars. Not only the dimensions, dates, units garrisoning, and the like, but published references and, most importantly, a standardized series of drawings using all the available (and frequently disparate) published information.

The drawings themselves, included here as part of each gazetteer, have proved problematical for reasons readily familiar to anybody who has attempted to work with the drawn products of others. Consistency, scale and conventions are all richly varied and, at times, enviably imaginative. Plans of fortresses can be distorted in the process of drawing and publication, so that comparing two superimposed plans frequently reveals stretching in one dimension, skewing or shearing, and possibly a little rotation. Thus an element of fudging has been necessary to get the various elements to fit, a phenomenon that will be recognized by all archaeological illustrators (and not a few surveyors). A citation for a principal published plan is offered for most sites, but these are seldom the only source and in one or two cases (notably Nicopolis and Sura) I have derived my plans from (frankly, very limited) published sketches and descriptions. Nevertheless, the results reproduced here will hopefully allow the comparison of these various sites in a way not previously possible to such a degree. As has become customary with my drawings, I am making all of the fortress plans contained within the volume available with a Creative Commons license as PNGs, albeit with the caveat that these are book illustrations not surveyed plans, and derived from published plans not excavation site drawings or surveys. Open source software and data was used to create them: *Inkscape* for the master vector drawings, *The GIMP* for processing all bitmaps that have been derived from these, and the *Natural Earth* 1:10m dataset and *QGIS* to plot the overall location map. Thus I hope my making the plans available may be seen as a practical way of contributing something back to the open source 'community'.[2]

Many published fortress plans are quite clearly palimpsests, as the Koenenlager at Neuss so plainly reveals: not only are there buildings superimposed upon one another, but even within apparently homogeneous structures partitions change with phases and the composite plan is, at best, confusing. Some cannot now be unravelled without further work, usually because they were excavated long ago when stratigraphy was imperfectly understood. Others hold out more hope and, where determined work has been undertaken to separate phases, one particular manifestation has been chosen for illustration here (although others should be present on the accompanying website).[3]

Several interesting (and, frankly, perplexing) decisions have to be made about what to include and what exclude. As an example, for the bibliography of a particular site, should references that deal just with finds be included? And what exactly constitutes the catchment for a legionary fortress: the base itself (so excluding extramural features like exercise grounds or amphitheatres), the base and accompanying establishments, the *canabae*, the *territorium*, the cemeteries? And so it goes on. Whatever decision is made is bound to be open to criticism, so rather than attempt to anticipate what you want (which is probably different to what she or he wants), I have (almost) unashamedly reflected what *I* want (since the original impulse to write the book was the absence of a reference volume *I* would find of use).

An equally fraught, if seemingly trivial, dilemma is what to call a fortress. Whilst 'Vindonissa' or 'Aquincum' may be familiar to many, would 'Isca' represent Exeter or Caerleon to most readers? The European penchant for associating modern and ancient names, as with Neuss–Novaesium, is useful, but potentially tree-costly in a work that frequently rehearses the names of camps. Thus, once again, I have made arbitrary decisions in nomenclature and can only point out that the index will cross-reference alternative names and the gazetteers present both ancient and modern placenames (including ambiguities), where known. The scope of this work has been deliberately restrained to what has been published, although that term has been interpreted broadly, as this has included material that is available on the internet and not elsewhere.

For the sake of consistency, I have chosen to number legions using the subtractive principle, e.g. *Legio IV Macedonica*, rather than *Legio IIII Macedonica*, although both were evidently acceptable to the Romans.[4]

There are a number of people I should like to thank for their help with various aspects of this project. Both Jon Coulston and Duncan Campbell were kind enough to read and comment upon a draft of the text (naturally all remaining errors, idiosyncrasies, and examples of bloodymindedness remain my sole responsibility), whilst Jon also generously permitted the use of a variety of his photographs in the plates section.

I began my career as an excavator digging for Viv Metcalf and her supervisor Simon Tomson, first at Usk (Market Street) and subsequently at Caerleon (Roman Gates) and from them I learned much; thanks, too, to their planning supervisor, Andy Marvell, who later went on to run the unit which then employed him, and who taught me how to plan a legionary base on a stone-by-stone basis. My good friend and sometime PhD supervisor, Prof David Kennedy, patiently answered many niggling questions I directed at him, and he was good enough to solicit the help of Ross Burns in my initial enquiries about the then-undiscovered fortress at Raphanaea. As a former junior library assistant, it would indeed be remiss of me not to acknowledge the assistance of the staffs of the Joint Library of the Hellenic and Roman Societies and Institute of Classical Studies in London, the Robinson Library in the University of Newcastle upon Tyne, the Reid Library at the University of Western Australia, and the Library of the University of St Andrews. Additional help in obtaining badly needed literature, answering questions on specific (and sometimes obscure) points of detail, or providing guided tours of fortresses they were excavating was, over the years, kindly provided by Joaquin Aurrecoechea, Ivan Bogdanovic, David Breeze, Piotr Dyczek, Phil Freeman, Emilio Illarregui, Sonja Jilek, Lázsló Kocsis, Boštjan Laharnar, Željko Miletić, Ivan Radman-Livaja, Ángel Morillo, Tom Parker, Liviu Petculescu, Mirjana Sanader, Tadeusz Sarnowski, Guy Stiebel, Domagoj Tončinić and Willem Willems. The aerial photographs of Lejjun and Udruh courtesy of the Aerial Photographic Archive of Archaeology in the Middle East (APAAME – archive accessible from: www.classics.uwa.edu.au/Aerial_archaeology). My editor, Phil Sidnell, has shown tolerance and forbearance beyond the call of duty, as has Lorraine Marlow, who has now seen more of legionary fortresses than she probably ever dreamed was necessary (or even advisable) in the life of a normal human being. This book is for all of them, but it is also for you and, lest it be forgotten, me.

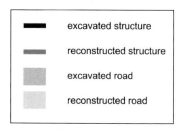

Figure 1: Conventions used in the site plans.

Chapter 1

Introduction

What was a legionary fortress? The simplest answer may be that it was the winter quarters of a legion that housed the legionary eagle standard. That is, however, an assumption. Detachments sent out from that base would march behind a *vexillum* standard (and be known as a *vexillatio*, like those based at Corbridge, Northumberland), but the core of a legion would remain where its eagle was situated. An entire legion might have campaigned in the summer with its eagle and be temporarily based in a *castra aestiva*, but it would return to its *castra hiberna*. Such a definition works well in the Principate, but what of the Dominate? Our evidence suggests that in the later Empire legions became fractured into subunits of around 1,000 men, some on frontiers, others in field armies. Did they all have their own unit standard or did they still respect one original eagle?[1]

Terminology

What should one call a legionary base? Whilst 'camp' might suffice for some, and even find resonance with modern English-language military usage, it might be thought that there are too many parallels with camping and the temporary nature of related establishments. In German, *Lager* and its specific compound noun *Legionslager* seem less controversial than 'camp'. Even the term 'legionary fortress' comes with a perceived subtext in English. It has been argued that such bases were never intended to offer the sort of defensive capabilities implied by the term 'fortress'. This is a modern meme that resurfaces in similar arguments on how Roman defensive structures like Hadrian's Wall were not intended to be defended at a tactical level. However, it might be countered that the valiant – yet ultimately futile – defence of Vetera I by *legiones V Alaudae* and *XV Primigenia* during the Batavian uprising of AD 69 negates this objection nicely, and just because legionary bases did not normally require defending this did not mean they were not capable of it. In fact, 'base' is itself a good compromise term, but it has been decided to use camp, fortress, and base interchangeably to mean the same thing.[2]

The modern scholarly terminology of Roman legionary fortresses is ultimately largely derived from the text *De Munitionibus Castrorum*, often (and probably wrongly) attributed to the writer Hyginus Gromaticus, and thus sometimes rather awkwardly known as 'Pseudo-Hyginus'. The assumption is made that the campaign camps for armies with many units that this work describes were basically the same as legionary fortresses, but it is important to understand that it is just that: an assumption, albeit a not unreasonable one. Since the Pseudo-Hyginean terms are now so deeply embedded in the subject, a short glossary has been included (as Appendix 2) to explain these and other technical (or pseudo-technical) words the reader may encounter, along with their sources.[3]

Terminology is a complex area, not helped by the Latin language's all-too-common lack of specificity. Nor is it made any easier by the fact that the substantive *castra* is a plural form, so 'a camp' is in fact 'camps' (the singular form *castrum* or *kastrum* returns to popularity in the Late Empire). In order to understand what a Roman would have called a legionary camp/fortress/base, we must turn to our sources. Historians tell of the use of *castra aestiva* and *castra hiberna*, the first being summer campaign camps, the latter winter quarters. A rhythm of occupying campaign camps with other legions and auxiliaries, then returning to their own winter quarters, is evident for the early first century AD in the writings of Tacitus. Vegetius groups *castra aestiva* and *castra hiberna* into a class together, *castra stativa*: permanent bases (thus distinguishing them from more temporary fortifications, such as those dug when on the march). The term *stativa* is also found in other writers such as Tacitus. An inscription of AD 142 from Gerze (Egypt) names the *castra Augusta hiberna*, recording *legio II Traiana Fortis* sharing its base (otherwise known as Nicopolis, near Alexandria) with *ala I Thracum Mauretana*. The sub-literary record provides confirmation in AD 157, by which time that legion was sharing with *ala Gallorum veterana*. Another inscription, this time from Mainz, identifies that fortress as the *hiberna* of *legio XXII Primigenia*.[4]

Size

Beyond terminology, there is the vexed question of dimensions. As has already been indicated, published plans can vary slightly. Moreover, the definition of the size of a site varies between scholars and many do not define what is being measured when dimensions are cited. For the purposes of this volume, dimensions are taken from the outer face of the defensive curtain wall of each fortification (thus excluding projecting towers or ditch complexes), so the area quoted for any site is the area enclosed within those defensive walls as defined by the outer face of its walls – often termed 'over the ramparts' – and this may be termed the *maximum area* of the fortress. This is very different from, say, the usable area within any rampart (or the *functional area*) that accompanies the defensive wall – the two figures for the Koenenlager at Neuss are 25.8ha and 22.9ha respectively, and if the *intervallum* is excluded and just the area available for accommodation allowed for, this drops to 20ha (this may be termed the *minimum area*, only 78% of the maximum area of the fortress).[5]

The subject of dimensions becomes even more perplexing when advocates of modular systems of layout and their critics confront each other. Those who think the Roman army used such a system have as a powerful ally the *centurio* with his *decempeda*, a ten-foot ranging pole used to check soldiers' work when digging camps. Unfortunately, there is no agreement on what sort of feet were used, whether the *pes Monetalis* or *Drusianus*. This issue can best be characterized as undecided, not least because it is plagued by the same sort of mensural uncertainties evident when trying to draw up definitive plans of fortresses. Similar complexities (and little clarity) arise over issues of orientation of camps.[6]

Sources

The source material, as with so many areas of the study of the Roman army, falls into four broad categories, each with their own particular strengths and weaknesses: the excavated, the written, the depicted, and the commemorative.

Archaeological

Archaeology provides us with both standing and excavated remains of legionary fortresses. The fact that some have been comprehensively explored (Carnuntum, Lauriacum, Lambaesis and, albeit by selective trenching, Inchtuthil) and others (most Eastern and many key Danubian sites) left virtually untouched is reflected both in the amounts of information contained within the gazetteers (see below, Chapter 9) and in the archaeological examples cited below. The quality of excavation, in terms of its practice, recording, analysis, and publication, varies widely both in time and space. The availability of any given site for examination is also dictated by circumstances. Open (or rural) sites are often easily accessible, but prone to severe stratigraphic degradation through subsequent agricultural practices. Urban sites, on the other hand, are encumbered by overlying structures, but cumulative deposition can mean that Roman military

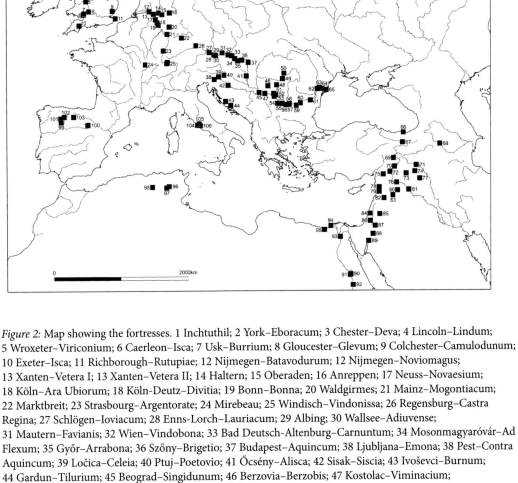

Figure 2: Map showing the fortresses. 1 Inchtuthil; 2 York–Eboracum; 3 Chester–Deva; 4 Lincoln–Lindum; 5 Wroxeter–Viriconium; 6 Caerleon–Isca; 7 Usk–Burrium; 8 Gloucester–Glevum; 9 Colchester–Camulodunum; 10 Exeter–Isca; 11 Richborough–Rutupiae; 12 Nijmegen–Batavodurum; 12 Nijmegen–Noviomagus; 13 Xanten–Vetera I; 13 Xanten–Vetera II; 14 Haltern; 15 Oberaden; 16 Anreppen; 17 Neuss–Novaesium; 18 Köln–Ara Ubiorum; 18 Köln-Deutz–Divitia; 19 Bonn–Bonna; 20 Waldgirmes; 21 Mainz–Mogontiacum; 22 Marktbreit; 23 Strasbourg–Argentorate; 24 Mirebeau; 25 Windisch–Vindonissa; 26 Regensburg–Castra Regina; 27 Schlögen–Ioviacum; 28 Enns-Lorch–Lauriacum; 29 Albing; 30 Wallsee–Adiuvense; 31 Mautern–Favianis; 32 Wien–Vindobona; 33 Bad Deutsch-Altenburg–Carnuntum; 34 Mosonmagyaróvár–Ad Flexum; 35 Győr–Arrabona; 36 Szőny–Brigetio; 37 Budapest–Aquincum; 38 Ljubljana–Emona; 38 Pest–Contra Aquincum; 39 Ločica–Celeia; 40 Ptuj–Poetovio; 41 Őcsény–Alisca; 42 Sisak–Siscia; 43 Ivoševci–Burnum; 44 Gardun–Tilurium; 45 Beograd–Singidunum; 46 Berzovia–Berzobis; 47 Kostolac–Viminacium; 48 Grădişte–Sarmizegetusa; 49 Alba Iulia–Apulum; 50 Turda–Potaissa; 51 Orşova–Dierna; 52 Kladovo–Transdrobeta; 53 Brza Palanka–Aegeta; 54 Archar–Ratiaria; 55 Gorni Tsibar–Cebrum; 56 Selanovtsi–Variniana/Valeriana; 57 Gigen–Oescus; 58 Celei–Sucidava; 59 Svištov–Novae; 60 Ruse–Sexaginta Prista; 61 Silistra–Durosturum; 62 Turcoaia–Troesmis; 63 Isaccea–Noviodunum; 64 Tulcea–Aegyssus; 65 Caraorman–Inplateypegiis; 66 Trabzond–Trapezus; 67 Sadak–Satala; 68 Artashat–Artaxata; 69 Battalgazi–Melitene; 70 Samsat–Samosata; 71 Hasankeyf–Cephae; 72 Belkis–Zeugma; 73 Ras al'Ayn–Resaina; 74 Nusaybin–Nisibis; 75 Kurus–Cyrrhus; 76 Souriyah–Sura; 77 Balad Sinjar–Singara; 78 Afamia–Apamea; 79 Barin–Raphanaea; 80 Tayibeh–Oresa; 81 Busayrah–Circesium; 82 Mehin–Danaba; 83 Tadmor–Palmyra; 84 Lajjun–Legio (Caparcotna); 85 Bosra–Bostra; 86 Jerusalem–Hierosolyma; 87 Lejjun–Betthorus (-um); 88 Udruh–Adrou; 89 Aqaba–Aila/Aelana; 90 Luxor (al-Uqsor)–Thebae; 91 Armant–Hermonthis; 92 Tukh–Ombos; 93 Old Cairo–Babylon; 94 Alexandria–Nicopolis; 95 Al-Burdan; 96 Haïdra–Ammaedara; 97 Tebessa–Theveste; 98 Tazoult-Lambèse–Lambaesis; 99 Rosinos de Vidriales–Petavonium; 100 Castillejo; 100 Dehesilla; 100 Peña Redonda; 100 Renieblas; 101 Astorga–Asturica; 102 León–Legio VII Gemina; 103 Herrera de Pisuerga–Pisoraca; 104 Ostia Castrum; 105 Roma–Castra Praetoria; 106 Albano Laziale–Castra Albana.

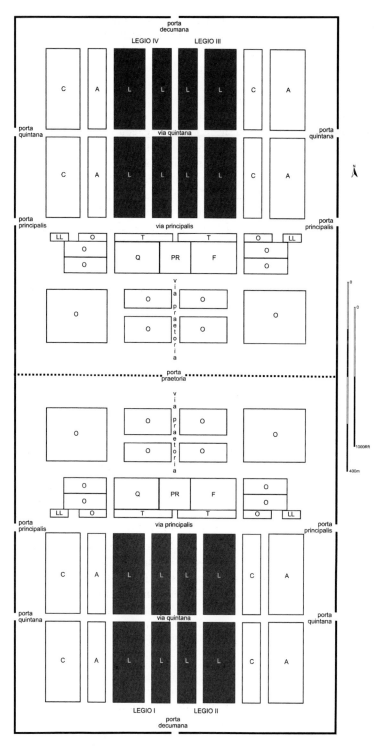

Figure 3: Camp of Polybius (after Dobson 2008), showing the mirroring of two double-legionary camps. Key: L – legions (*triarii, hastate, principes,* and cavalry); A – allied cavalry; C – allied infantry; O – other; LL – *legati*; T – *tribuni*; F – *forum*; Q – *quaestorium*; PR – *praetorium*.

levels are sometimes better preserved than is the case for their rural counterparts. Moreover, the pressures for development will nowadays normally lead to opportunities (albeit limited) to examine the archaeology. Some sites fall victim to poor placement and the dynamic behaviour of the river systems next to which they were inevitably placed, and here we might note Ptuj and Vetera II.

Archaeological data, even at its most simple, can present very complex problems to the researcher. Moreover, as archaeology has developed, the quality and quantity of that data has increased, even though the area examined at any given site tends to have reduced. So whilst it was once possible to excavate (almost) an entire legionary base over several seasons of work (e.g. the work of von Groller at Carnuntum and Lauriacum), now it takes much longer to record even a tiny fraction of one. The imperatives have changed too from pure research into mainly 'rescue'-driven scenarios where the excavation strategy is dictated not by the needs of the researcher, but all too often by the whim of a developer. Nevertheless, it is both refreshing and encouraging to note stalwart and imaginative research campaigns at Lejjun in the past, Caerleon (revived in recent times), and the continuing work at Novae.[7]

Literary
References to legionary camps in the ancient literature can range from a mere passing mention of a site (Tacitus refers to a fortress at Camulodunum, but not to its legion) to a reasonably detailed description of how one was defended against attackers (again Tacitus, but this time describing the defence of Vetera I). Indirectly applicable to the study of the castrametation of legionary fortresses is the section of Polybius' *Historiae* that describes the Roman Republican army of his day and one of its camps. This has often been used to interpret known Republican camps like those around Numantia (Spain), although recently a successful inversion has been applied by, effectively, using the archaeology to interpret the literary source.[8]

So much for the 'literary' writers, often seen as being as much driven by stylistic as by factual considerations. Authors of supposedly technical treatises are also crucial to the study of the topic and two in particular merit some attention. Vegetius' precis of earlier military writers, produced in the late Roman period – the *Epitoma Rei Militaris* – evidently contains more than one writer's take on fortification and careful analysis of his style (aided by his own – probably incomplete – list of sources) has produced some likely candidates for the relevant passages (1.21–5, Cornelius Celsus; 2.10, Tarruttienus Paternus; and 3.8, Frontinus). However, his comments on the structure of the legion (2.4–14), his *antiqua legio*, also of relevance to the study of legionary fortresses (see below, p. 39), have been called into question, so use of his work is by no means straightforward.[9]

The enigmatic Pseudo-Hyginus' description of a campaign camp for three legions and auxiliaries is similarly pivotal in any discussion of legionary fortresses (Figure 4). The nature and date of the text are unclear, but it has become fundamental both to interpreting the layout of fortifications under the Principate and, especially, to answering the question of the strength of the first cohort. There is a plausible, but by no means incontrovertible, argument for seeing the work as being Flavian in date, rather than the more traditional Antonine interpretation.[10]

Sub-literary sources such as papyri, ostraca, or writing tablets can provide titbits of information about garrison or even terminology. For example, the document already mentioned, drawn up in AD 153 at Nicopolis and recording a loan, it so happens, fortuitously also records that the legionary base was called a *castra hiberna* and that it not only housed *legio II Traiana Fortis*, but also the *ala Gallorum Veterana*.[11]

Falling half way between literary and sub-literary in its form, the *Notitia Dignitatum* is a list of military and civil officials from the Dominate with details of their commands and locations. Thus, almost incidentally, it provides a partial army list with details of postings, although there is much uncertainty over the coherence, completeness, and relative dating of the various sections. Other

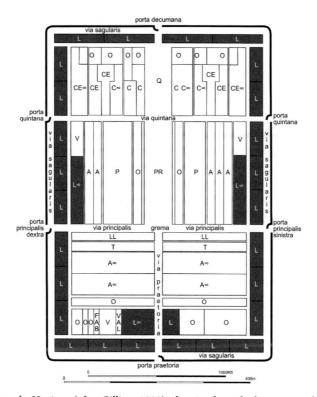

Figure 4: Camp of Pseudo-Hyginus (after Gilliver 1993), showing how the legionary cohorts (shaded) are mainly distributed around the periphery. Key: L – legionary cohort; L∞ – double-strength legionary cohort; P – Praetorian cohorts, cavalry, and *equites singulares*; A – *ala* of auxiliary cavalry; A∞ – double-strength *ala* of auxiliary cavalry; C – cohort of auxiliary infantry; C∞ – double-strength cohort of auxiliary infantry; CE – cohort of mounted auxiliary infantry; CE∞ – double-strength cohort of mounted auxiliary infantry; O – other; LL – *scamnum legati*; T – *scamnum tribunorum*; VAL – *valetudinarium*; FAB – *fabrica*; Q – *quaestorium*; PR – *praetorium*.

sources, such as Ptolemy's *Geographia* (Antonine), record unit names in association with places, occasionally anachronistically, as was the case with *legio II Augusta* placed at Exeter (an understandable slip, since the same name was given to the legion's new base at Caerleon).[12]

Representational

Depictions of Roman fortifications are not unknown, although far less common than images of soldiers themselves, and never without problems of interpretation. Whether it be the many representations of fortifications on Trajan's Column, the biases of which are much debated, the Castra Praetoria on coins, or terracotta models of gateways, their significance and accuracy is never straightforward; they play little part in what follows.[13]

Epigraphic

Epigraphy can supply incidental detail about the units associated with (but not necessarily garrisoning) a base, whether as funerary monuments or simple centurial building stones. At Colchester, for example, it was noted above that, although Tacitus does not mention which legion was based there, the tombstone of the centurion M. Favonius Facilis of *legio XX* provides a clue.

More formal commemorative inscriptions can provide insights into terminology and sometimes, importantly, vital and very specific dating evidence, such as a series of inscriptions recording the reconstruction of the British legionary bases at York, Caerleon and Chester in stone under Trajan. The great *adlocutio* inscription of Hadrian, preserved within the exercise field (*campus*) at Lambaesis, has many interesting and applicable aspects, describing exercises and construction work undertaken by various auxiliary units in ssociation with *legio III Augusta*, and, not surprisingly, the implication that the address was delivered there at the *campus* (see below, p. 36).[14]

Another class of inscribed material is the literary detritus left behind by any legion: graffiti, dipinti and stamps on a range of materials, such as pottery, wood, leather and most especially brick and tile. The army produced large amounts of fictile material at works depots associated with their bases and marked a proportion of the output with distinctive stamps. These last are amongst the most enduring testaments to the involvement of a unit with (but not necessarily present at) a site.[15]

A brief history of investigation

Antiquarian interest in fortresses concentrated, for obvious reasons, on those with significant remains – such as York, Chester or Regensburg – or large amounts of epigraphic and representational material, such as Mainz. Many fortress sites went on to become major urban centres, but a few that did not – Carnuntum, Inchtuthil, Ločica and Burnum are good examples – attracted campaigns of excavation in the late nineteenth and early twentieth centuries. The base at Novaesium, just outside Neuss, excavated between 1886 and 1900, became the most completely examined legionary fortress in the Roman Empire and its plan still dominates in the literature and on the worldwide web, thanks to its prompt and detailed publication in 1904. There were many problems with both the techniques employed and the interpretation of what was found, especially the conflation of a sequence of structures, but its importance and influence cannot be ignored. Whilst interest in the archaeology of such sites increased, it arguably took the urban devastation of the Second World War and subsequent attempts at economic regeneration to provide a major boost to the exploration of many of the sites that had seen subsequent re-use.[16]

The latter part of the twentieth century and the beginning of the twenty-first have witnessed an exciting growth in the technologies of remote sensing. Starting with aerial photography, this moved on to geophysical techniques like magnetometry, resistivity, ground-penetrating radar, lidar survey and satellite imagery, providing an arsenal of scientific techniques to supplement the established means of studying fortresses. Work at Sadak-Satala, Belkis-Zeugma and the newly identified site of Raphanaea near Barin has seen such techniques being employed to good effect.[17]

Nevertheless, we are still woefully ignorant about some legionary fortresses. Many of the Dominate fortresses of the east, particularly the series Sura/Oresa/Danaba on the *Strata Diocletiana* are either unexplored (Souriyah-Sura and Tayibeh-Oresa) or have not been identified with any certainty (?Mehin-Danaba and Aqaba-Aila). In the last case, the curious Islamic-era fortress at Aqaba is at the very least a close copy of a Dominate fortress and is approximately the same size as Sura (there is even a re-used Constantinian building inscription from it), yet does not appear to be Roman and no suitable alternative has been identified. In the west, major bases like Mainz and Strasbourg suffer (or perhaps benefit) from being beneath historic cities where developmental pressures are kept under strict control.[18]

None of this can or should be divorced from the study of other aspects of Roman military fortification, such as temporary camps and forts, since all contribute to the whole and are the better for it. That being said, the class of sites we know as legionary fortresses is readily identifiable, distinct, and can be shown to undergo evolution. With these thoughts in mind, it is time to consider the legions themselves and the origins of the legionary fortress.

Chapter 2

The Legions

There are plenty of good descriptions of the history and structure of the legion that can be referred to, both general and detailed, but this chapter aims briefly to outline the relevance of aspects of this history and development that affect the arrangement and evolution of the legionary fortress.[1]

The legion originated as a basic component of a consular field army in the Republican period, each consul being assigned two legions. The word *legio* is thought to derive from the origins of the unit as a peasant levy. Legions remained a unit raised for the campaigning season in time of war and disbanded soon after until Rome spread overseas and found itself having to provide winter quarters for armies rather than disband them. Republican citizen legions were twinned with allied legions in the field.[2]

Later Republican and early Imperial legions comprised sixty centuries (*centuriae*) of infantry, each of around eighty men commanded by a centurion (*centurio*), organized into ten cohorts (*cohortes*) numbered accordingly, the First Cohort being the most senior and occupying the coveted right wing of the battle line, as well as being commanded by the senior centurion in the legion (the *primus pilus*). The First Cohort comprised five centuries and this would give a paper strength of 4,720 (59×80) men. However, it has been argued that these were double strength from the Flavian period onwards, which yields a total of 5,120 ($(54 \times 80) + (5 \times 160)$), but the evidence for this assertion is contentious and it may well be the case that this was only true for a comparatively short period in the second half of the first century AD.[3]

After the civil wars of the later Republican period, when the number of legions rose to around sixty, the army settled down under Augustus to a more manageable twenty-eight, a fact highlighted by Tacitus in his assessment of the Empire at the death of that *princeps* and the accession of his stepson, Tiberius. Some legions were disbanded, other new ones created, but the basic number remained around thirty, raised to thirty-three by Severus, until the latter part of the third century AD. A list of legions inscribed on a pillar from Rome, dated to *c.*AD 165, records a total of thirty-three (Table 1; Plate 1). Set out in three columns, twenty-eight of them are geographically ordered clockwise around the Empire (and thus by base), starting with Britain and ending with Spain, and then the recently created legions *II–III Italica* and *I–III Parthica* are appended. At first sight, this may suggest two separate additions, one under Marcus Aurelius, the other under Septimius Severus. However, an alternative interpretation might be that, at the time of its preparation, *II* and *III Italica* had not yet been allotted bases, so the only addition is the Severan one. Notwithstanding such niceties, this is arguably the only complete list of (sadly unnamed) legionary bases we have for any period.[4]

In the later Empire, the number of legions was increased by dint of their being split into several subunits. This much is evident from the *Notitia Dignitatum*, but it is also clear that this was not a uniform or tidy process. Scholars now recognize that legions in the later Empire were smaller units than their predecessors.[5]

Table 1: The *nomina legionum* inscription (on the Colonnetta Maffei from Roma) with bases added (primary additions emboldened; secondary additions emboldened and italicized)

Column I	Base	Column II	Base	Column III	Base
		Nomina leg(ionum)			
II Aug(usta)	[Caerleon]	II Adiut(rix)	[Budapest]	IIII Scyth(ica)	[Belkis]
VI Victr(ix)	[York]	IIII Flav(ia)	[Beograd]	XVI Flav(ia)	[Samsat]
XX Victr(ix)	[Chester]	VII Claud(ia)	[Kostolac]	VI Ferrat(a)	[Caparcotna]
VIII Aug(usta)	[Strasbourg]	I Italic(a)	[Svištov]	X Frete(nsis)	[Jerusalem]
XXII Prim(igenia)	[Mainz]	V Maced(onica)	[Igliţa]	III Cyren(aica)	[Bosra]
I Min(ervia)	[Bonn]	XI Claud(ia)	[Silistra]	II Traian(a)	[Alexandria]
XXX Ulp(ia)	[Xanten]	XIII Gem(ina)	[Alba Iulia]	III Aug(usta)	[Tazoult-Lambèse]
I Adiut(rix)	[Szőny]	XII Fulm(inata)	[Eski Malatya]	VII Gem(ina)	[Leon]
X Gem(ina)	[Wien]	XV Apol(linaris)	[Sadak]	**II Italic(a)**	**[Albing]**
XIIII Gem(ina)	[Bad Deutsch-Altenburg]	III Gall(ica)	[Barin]	**III Italic(a)**	**[Regensburg]**
I Parth(ica)	*[Sinjar]*	*II Parth(ica)*	*[Albano Laziale]*	*III Parth(ica)*	*[Ra's al-'Ayn]*

It is worth noting that whilst it is the general practice of modern commentators to interpret legionary structure under the Principate in terms of the literary and epigraphic sources, this is reversed for the Dominate where the archaeology has tended to be afforded primacy. As a paper exercise, interpreting a Principate-period legion from its fortress produces rather different results. For example, the notional accommodation of *legio II Augusta* at Caerleon (fifty-four barrack blocks, each with twelve room-pairs, plus six double-strength barracks with twenty-four room-pairs) would yield a legion of 6,144 (5,184 + 960) in centuries. Such calculations are effectively meaningless, since it is unlikely that a legion would ever be up to strength (whatever that might have been) and the practise of outposting will have further diminished numbers (see below, p. 15). Moreover, since not all of these barrack blocks have been excavated, even the number of rooms is an assumption based on the excavated buildings in the Prysg Field.[6]

Chapter 3

History and Development of Legionary Bases

The Republican Period

Whilst Rome was small and its armies campaigned near home, it was a simple matter to maintain a system whereby they were disbanded at the end of each campaigning season. Fortified settlements have been identified, such as the *castrum* at Ostia – 194m by 126m, constructed around 400 BC out of tufa blocks – but appear to be exceptional and, of course, defensive (Figure 5). This particular example was rectangular, with four main streets meeting at the centre, and was provided with gate towers.[1]

Such a parochial approach to warfare changed with the advent of overseas campaigns that began to demand a prolonged presence, most notably the Punic Wars. Roman armies began to overwinter away from Italy as early as 153/2 BC, when Fulvius Nobilior rather ineptly adapted his campaign camp (possibly Renieblas, Spain) for the purpose. Most of our knowledge of the physical nature of purpose-built camps comes from excavated sites, such as Castillejo, around the hilltop Iberian town of Numantia (Figure 7), besieged by the army of Scipio Aemilianus in 134/3 BC. Other sites, like Cáceres el Viejo (probably dating to the Sertorian War of the first century BC), are known (Figure 8), and all can be compared with the (evidently idealized) contemporaneous account of a Roman campaign camp provided by the Greek writer Polybius (Figure 3), one of Scipio Aemilianus' inner circle of friends.[2]

The Numantine sites (like those at Cáceres or in Polybius' account) were field army camps, not just legionary ones, and the concept (however loosely interpreted) of unit bases had yet to evolve. It might be argued that tactical considerations dominated, such as keeping a field army together. By the Late Republic, however, the campaigns of Caesar in Gaul often saw him overwintering armies in tribal territory, and in some instances he refers to basing them by legion, suggesting that unit identity was beginning to play an important role under the warlords of the period and that it could be a determining factor in the composition of a garrison.[3]

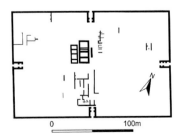

Figure 5: The castrum *at Ostia (after Calza 1953).*

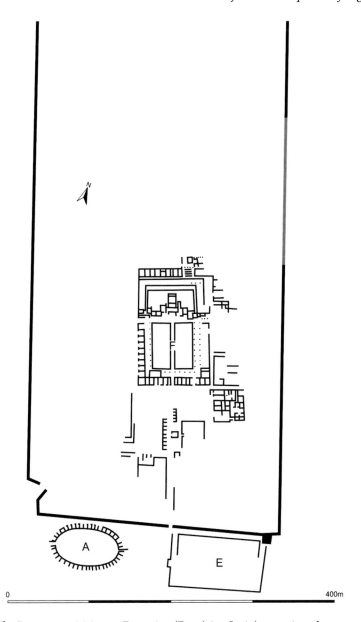

Figure 6: The Roman *municipium* at Emporion (Empúries, Spain), sometimes known as the Camp of Scipio (after Aquilué 2006).

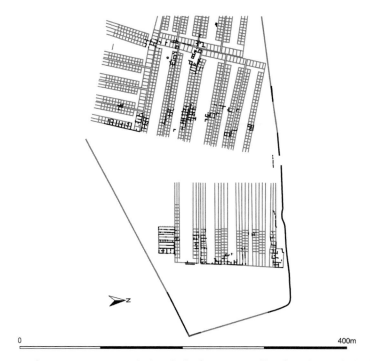

Figure 7: A modern reconstruction of The Black Phase at Castillejo based on Schulten's discoveries (after Dobson 2008).

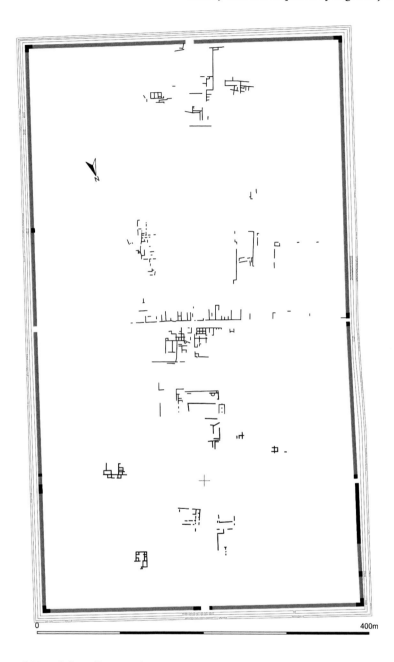

Figure 8: Cáceres el Viejo (after Ulbert 1984).

The Early Principate

From the Augustan period, a number of bases were constructed large enough to hold two legions, perhaps a reflection of that old Republican practice of campaigning with two-legion consular armies. These double-legionary camps were mainly located along the Rhine, at Xanten (Vetera I), Köln, and Mainz. Whilst they were a useful core force for a campaigning field army, they also posed a political threat, ultimately realized in AD 89 when the army commander of Germania Superior, L. Antonius Saturninus, used the combined pay chests of the Mainz-based *legiones XXI Rapax* and *XIV Gemina* to fund a revolt against Domitian. Double-legionary fortresses must also have been something of a strain on the Roman logistical system by comparison with later, smaller bases. After the suppression of the revolt of Saturninus, Domitian was said to have abolished double legionary bases, but in fact one remained at Nicopolis until at least the beginning of the second century AD.[4]

The earliest known bases in north-west Europe are those already mentioned on the Rhine, together with a series reflecting Roman penetration into Germany between the Rhine and Elbe, principally along the valley of the Lippe. Additional large bases are known at Nijmegen and suspected at Windisch, and anticipated at a number of Balkan sites, including Sisak and Ljubljana. The establishment of a binary occupation pattern (off-season in *castra hiberna*, campaigning season in *castra aestiva*) is evident from the literary sources and it is clear that both *hiberna* and *aestiva* could be shared by the same legion pairs. Camp C at Neuss has been suggested as an *aestiva* for the legions based at Xanten and Köln and scene of the infamous mutiny of AD 14. Both the locations and many of the internal structures of the more thoroughly explored Augustan camps anticipate those of later legionary fortresses, so a link seems logical and evolution from one to the other likely. In these terms, the single-legionary fortress that included auxiliary accommodation becomes more readily understandable. Moreover, the revelation that some of the Augustan bases incorporated hybrid barrack structures, with timber officers' quarters and canopies covering what are presumed to have been tented areas for the men (so-called *hibernacula*), would appear to provide a transitional form between temporary and permanent camps. In fact, the barracks of the Numantine camps already closely resembled later structures in many ways and the ability of the Roman army of the late Republic to provide itself with more-or-less permanent accommodation when needed should not be underestimated.[5]

Construction in turf and timber

When the army of Scipio Aemilianus was constructing its fortifications around Numantia, it used stone and timber. When Caesar was campaigning in Gaul, he used turf and timber, and the careful employment of available materials was a mark of the Roman army's construction projects. The early Principate saw an emphasis on construction using primarily timber for defences, employing the so-called Holz-Erde-Mauer or box rampart (a construction technique that dated back at least to the Bronze Age: see below p. 18). It is found at first-century BC sites like Dangstetten and continues in use well into the first century AD. It even occurs at some sites in Britain, although it was never as widespread there as turf and timber.[6]

Construction in stone

The fourth- or third-century BC tufa-built *castrum* at Ostia has already been mentioned (above, p. 11). It is also perhaps relevant to consider here the role of the Castra Praetoria in Rome, constructed under Tiberius in AD 23. Although not a legionary base, as such, it was a focus for the ten cohorts of the Praetorian Guard within the city and clearly shared many characteristics with fortresses intended for legions. It was also one of the first such encampments to acquire fortifications that were not made of timber (in this case brick-faced concrete). It was laid out as a rectangle with rounded corners and, although complicated by later developments and obscured for the most part by overlying structures, there seem to have been strong internal resemblances with contemporary legionary fortresses.[7]

The first legionary base in the north-western provinces to have received stone defences was probably Vetera I in the middle of the AD 40s, whilst in Britain Inchtuthil's timber defences were being replaced in stone (before it was even complete) in the 80s. However, Colchester made early and ingenious use of sun-dried clay blocks containing a sand core for its rampart, whilst a form of shuttered concrete was employed for its barrack footings. Sun-dried clay may have found widespread use in the East, but not enough sites have been excavated to be certain about this. The other British fortresses at York, Chester and Caerleon had to wait until around AD 100 to receive their reconstructions in stone.[8]

Auxiliaries

It has already been mentioned how a document of AD 153, *P. Fouad* I.45, illustrates that a legion could share its base with an auxiliary unit (above, p. 5). Other instances of the practice are known. The Koenenlager fortress at Neuss clearly contained auxiliary barracks within its walls. The discovery of auxiliary artefacts, such as a *patera* handle from Caerleon with a stamp of *ala I Thracum*, lend further weight to this practice and only help to blur the definition of a legionary fortress. It has been tentatively suggested in the past that legions had particular groups of auxiliary units associated with them and this may be a manifestation of such affiliations.[9]

Outposting and billeting

Under the Principate, legionaries were routinely and continually detached from the main parent body of the legion, a fact acknowledged by Hadrian in his address to *legio III Augusta* at Lambaesis. Small numbers went off on specific tasks and duties, whilst larger detachments, serving as part of *vexillationes*, might participate in campaigns in other areas of the Empire, such as the Dacian Wars, the Crimea or the Danube delta or in construction work. This meant that a fortress must seldom (if ever) have housed its entire designated garrison. It may also explain why detachments from other legions are sometimes attested in the base of another unit, as with *IV Flavia Felix* in *VII Claudia*'s fortress at Kostolac.[10]

It is often suggested that, in the early Principate, legionary forces were accommodated by billeting, particularly in the eastern provinces. Evidence is scarce and almost exclusively literary, some of it at best ambiguous. Billeting certainly took place, and was probably essential in small-scale outposting, but there is no good reason to think that entire units were accommodated this way and some scholars prefer to think in terms of a 'military quarter' within a city, as epitomized by Dura-Europos (Syria).[11]

The Dominate

Although many legionary fortresses continued in use from the Principate to the Dominate, some were abandoned whilst other newer bases were constructed. De novo constructions are known in the east at Lejjun and Udruh, and suspected at Sura and Tayibeh, whilst adapted sites include the pharaonic temple at Luxor under Diocletian. These new sites are all smaller than the 'standard' legionary fortress of the Principate and it has been suggested that they reflect the diminished size of the legions of the later Empire. They may also illustrate the fact that the large legionary base had become impractical and that legions were starting to function in a new way.[12]

The Notitia Dignitatum

Ostensibly just a list of officials of the later Empire, the *Notitia Dignitatum* nevertheless supplies important information about the dispositions of the Roman army under the Dominate (Appendix 3). There are many problems with it, not least the dating of its contents, but it seems clear from it that a degree of fragmentation of the legions of the Principate had taken place and that many more sites were now the bases for legions (or, strictly, part-legions). In Syria, for instance, the document only lists one legion per site (and all of the *Strata Diocletiana* sites – Sura, Oresa, Palmyra and Danaba – except Bostra were new establishments) whereas, on the lower Danube, it can be seen how units were divided between more than one base. *Legio II Adiutrix*, for example, is listed as being based at Alisca, Florentia, Aquincum, Constantia, Cirpi, Lussonium and (probably) Transaquincum (see Appendix 3).[13]

Chapter 4

Defences

Contemporary writers record that it was customary for Roman encampments to be given some form of defensive circuit, some even elaborating a scale according to purpose. At their least impressive, this might be a low bank with a shallow ditch for an overnight camp, dug whilst a detachment was on the march, becoming more substantial on campaign when troops were intending to spend more than one night in a place. The most substantial were to be constructed when an enemy was nearby, so it is clear that the scale of the defences was considered to be commensurate with the perceived level of threat. The ramparts of temporary camps, whether of the overnight or campaign type, were enhanced by a breastwork of stakes, carried by the soldiers themselves. Although reconstructions have traditionally sought to depict these as inserted vertically as a sort of fence, an alternative solution suggests that they were tied together in threes to form *chevaux de frise*, making them harder to clear than individual stakes, which could have been plucked from the ground.[1]

The defences of legionary bases were a development of those employed in cities and temporary encampments but were, in line with the role of such sites as winter quarters, more substantial. In at least one case, the defences of a temporary camp at Rhyn Park (Wales) appear to have been 'hardened' to upgrade to winter-quarters standard, enhanced with added gateways and revetted ramparts. Although they are not directly described by ancient writers, there is a considerable amount of excavated evidence to show the range of types of defences employed in legionary fortresses. As has already been discussed, 'permanent' legionary camps were generally constructed with either timber or stone defences, the former tending to be earlier than the latter.[2]

Ramparts

A site with timber defences that used an earthen or turf rampart (*vallum*) would be surrounded by a bank that was in the region of 6m wide and probably 4m high, the broad base being battered back to the top for the sake of stability, where a walkway would be provided behind a timber breastwork that provided protection for defenders. Where turf was used, turves would be cut into blocks and laid in rows. The batter was normally steeper at the front than at the rear, presenting an asymmetrical cross-section to a rampart, and was often vertical for a few courses at its base. The angles of the front and back batters have been used to deduce likely heights for the walkways of earthen banks. Clay could also be used for the rampart. Naturally, it is in the nature of archaeological evidence that the lowest component – the rampart base – should be the most certain and the upper elements (such as the breastwork and walkway) largely speculative, but there is comparative evidence available from stone fortifications to suggest that these are not unreasonable surmises. Many reconstructions, whether physical or virtual/artistic, are influenced by depictions on Trajan's Column, despite the many problems with the uncritical use of such representations. Earthen ramparts would frequently be placed on some sort of foundation, such as cobbling or a timber corduroy comprising logs laid across the width of the bank, usually to facilitate construction on difficult ground.[3]

An alternative form of defensive bank used in timber fortresses comprised a so-called box rampart (or Holz-Erde-Mauer in German), where pairs of posts were linked to their neighbours with horizontal timber shuttering, the resulting void being filled with spoil from the ditch. This form of rampart in fact dates back to the Bronze Age in both mainland Europe (such as Isingerode, Germany) and Britain (Ivinghoe Beacon, England) and was commonly used in the early prototype wooden legionary fortresses of the Lippe valley at Haltern and Oberaden. It has also been noted at other continental European sites such as Nijmegen and Marktbreit, whilst in Britain it has only been seen amongst legionary fortresses at the Flavian site of Lincoln. A box rampart had the advantage of having vertical faces and taking up less room than a purely earthen bank (typically 3m compared to the 6m mentioned above) but obviously required much greater timber resources than a turf and soil bank. The height of a box rampart presumably matched that of an earthen bank but it is more difficult to determine this just from postholes. Timbers used for the uprights of the rampart were usually scantled to between 0.25m and 0.45m, each post being set into a postpit or (more commonly) into a post trench (as at Nijmegen or Oberaden). Such defences can appear in the archaeological record as lines of posts surrounding a site or in geophysical surveys can resemble additional pairs of ditches.[4]

A variant on the full box rampart was the partially revetted timber type, as appears to have been employed at Wroxeter and York amongst British sites, although the shallow front slot at Wroxeter has been explained as a lockspit. Here, one face – typically the front – was vertical and finished in timber in the same way as a box rampart, but the rest of the rampart was a clay or turf bank, so effectively a hybrid form and one that anticipated the move to stone-fronted ramparts.[i]

One distinctive element of the defensive bank (of whatever type) of the classic legionary base, as with temporary camps, was its rounded corners. Pseudo-Hyginus describes how these should be laid out for a camp but does not say why and it has been suggested that it may be derived from the use of turf in such defences (it does not feature in the Ostia *castrum* or the early Spanish sites around Numantia). The corners were set out using the width of the *intervallum* as the radius of the arc, which in the case of the camp described in the *De Munitionibus Castrorum* was 60 Roman feet (17.8m). At Caerleon, that radius was 19.3m to the inner face of the curtain wall and 13.9m to the inner face of the rampart, whilst at Inchtuthil it was 19.5m and 15.2m respectively. Structurally, an earthen rampart, apart from its obvious function as a barrier, would also serve to absorb impact under attack, whether from artillery or rams. When used with a curtain wall it could also help to buttress it. At Nijmegen, where turf ramparts were lacking, stone buttresses were used, but often rampart-back buildings might be employed, perhaps with a truncated rampart, as at Caerleon (Figure 12).[6]

Walls

Stone fortresses substituted a defensive curtain wall (*murus*), gateways, and towers made of local stone for their timber or turf-and-timber equivalents. These often began in the first century AD by cutting back the front of the existing earthen rampart and inserting a stone wall against its front face, as at Inchtuthil and Caerleon (Figure 12); even sites that saw a stone curtain accompany the arrival of a new garrison may have retained an existing rampart. Local stone would be used preferentially (usually limestone or sandstone, although peperino – a type of tufa – was employed at Castra Albana). As such, stone walls were usually still backed with an earthen rampart but it could be removed in whole or in part for rampart-back buildings. The stone construction of such curtain walls generally consisted of facings of squared rubble with a rubble infill, which could be clay- or mortar-bonded (Plate 4), but there were clearly exceptions, like Chester, where *opus quadratum* was employed (Plate 5), or Gardun where a form of internal timber-framing has been identified. At Vindonissa, a form of cavity wall – a stone version of a box rampart – seems to have been employed. Curtain walls could range in width between 1.8m and 3.5m in just one fortress (Albing, in this instance) and surviving examples show them to have been between 4.9m and 5m high at rampart-walk height, this course perhaps being marked by a decorative (Chester) or plain (York) cornice or string course (Plates 5 and 6).[7]

Where concealed by a rampart, the inner face was less neatly finished than on the outside. A crenellated breastwork with merlons and merlon caps was employed on top of the walkway, possibly with projecting wings or traverses to provide additional protection for defenders (similar to surviving examples on the city wall at Dura-Europos: Plate 7). The merlons of the Tiberian Castra Praetoria in Rome (which, unlike any of the legionary fortresses, was constructed of brick-faced concrete) are preserved within the later city walls (Plate 8). Richmond was of the opinion that the spacing of these is in the region of 3m width for the merlon and 0.6m for the merlon gap but analysis of evidence from other sites (as well as representations) suggests a variety of alternative configurations were employed. Various forms of rendering may have been used for the stone defences, including plaster, lime wash, and flush pointing, although evidence for any of these in the context of legionary bases is sparse. Red lines on a white background, painted to simulate *opus quadratum*, are known from a number of locations at Caerleon.[8]

Curtain walls in later fortresses became thicker and could range between 2.4m (Lejjun) and 3.3m (Richborough) in width, examples surviving up to 8m in height (Richborough, with no indication of the wall-walk level). The Castra Praetoria in its later phases again suggests the continued use of crenellations (Plate 8).[9]

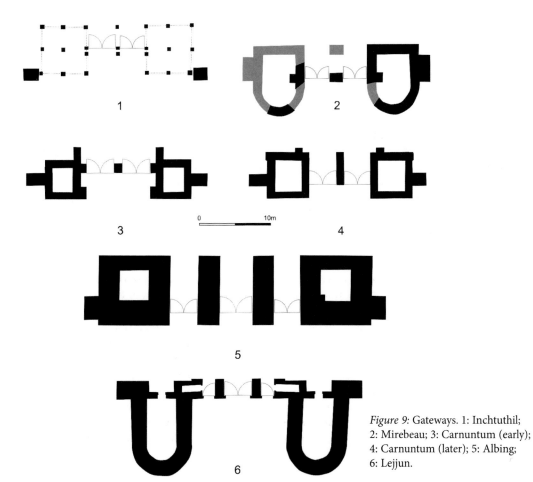

Figure 9: Gateways. 1: Inchtuthil; 2: Mirebeau; 3: Carnuntum (early); 4: Carnuntum (later); 5: Albing; 6: Lejjun.

Figure 10: Corner towers. 1: Oberaden; 2: Caerleon; 3: Albing; 4: Köln-Deutz; 5: Lejjun; 6: York.

It seems to have been considered normal practice to mount artillery on walls, in addition to in towers, during the Principate at least. Josephus comments on this practice, as does Arrian during his inspection of the cohort fort at Phasis.[10]

Towers

Every fortress was furnished with a tower on either side of the four principal gates (see below), one at each corner (the angle towers), and a varying number of regularly spaced interval towers between those angle and gate towers. In timber fortresses, interval towers were square, with four upright posts set within postpits, whilst in stone bases they started as simple square structures set flush with the front of the wall or rampart face (but often became more elaborate with time) (Figure 9 and Plates 9–11). Angle (or corner) towers were placed internally with their side-walls at a tangent to the curve of the corner of the defences and so tended to be trapezoidal rather than truly square (Figure 10 and Plates 12–13). In Dominate fortifications, interval and corner towers usually projected externally from the line of the wall, possibly to facilitate enfilading shooting by artillery and other missile weapons (Plates 33–4). However, some at least of these were evidently as much for decoration as for defence, as with the polygonal towers on the south-west side of the fortress at York (Plate 14). It is assumed towers provided shelter for those on sentry-go around the rampart walk and an elevated platform for a view above that possible from breastwork height, although not necessarily a means of access to the top of the rampart from ground level. It is uncertain how such towers were roofed, whether with a flat crenellated top as a lookout, signalling, or artillery platform, or whether they were equipped with a pitched roof (similar to that shown on a ceramic model gateway from the cohort fort at Intercisa). It is not even certain whether they were of a consistent height or of one or two storeys. Access to the rampart walk, in

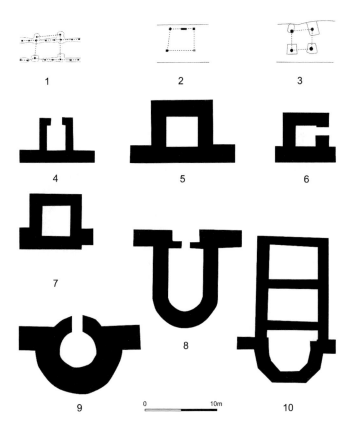

Figure 11: Interval towers.
1: Oberaden; 2: Wroxeter;
3: Exeter; 4: Caerleon;
5: Ločica; 6: Lauriacum;
7: Albing; 8: Lejjun; 9: Köln-Deutz; 10: York.

the form of a ramp or stairs (an *ascensus*), might be provided at other points nearby and elsewhere around the defences, but the bases of towers do not seem always to have been connected to the upper levels and may have been used for storage.[11]

Gateways

There were four principal gateways through the defences of a legionary base. The main or front gate was the *porta praetoria*, situated at the end of the *via praetoria* and facing the headquarters building (*principia*). The side gates – the *porta principalis sinistra* and the *porta principalis dextra* – were at either end of the *via principalis*, which ran across the front of the *principia* and formed a T-junction with the *via praetoria* at the *groma*. The rear gateway was the *porta decumana*, usually at the opposite end of the *via decumana* to the commanding officer's house (*praetorium*). The terminology is taken from the layout of temporary camps. The gateways of legionary bases were usually double-portalled, but at Albing, there was a hierarchy of gateways: the *porta praetoria* had a central road passage with flanking pedestrian passages; the *porta principalis dextra* was double-portalled; the *porta decumana* single-portalled. In classic legionary fortresses, gate towers were the only ones likely to protrude from the line of the defences, whilst the gate itself might actually be recessed inwards, adding to their defensive qualities by forcing an attacking enemy to crowd into the available space (already a defensive 'pinch point') and provide an easier target for the defenders above. For timber fortresses, the timber used for the uprights of the gate towers was usually scantled to around 0.3m square (but could be as much as 0.5m, as at Vindonissa), each post being set into a substantial postpit, usually rectangular (as at Inchtuthil) but sometimes square (as at Oberaden).[12]

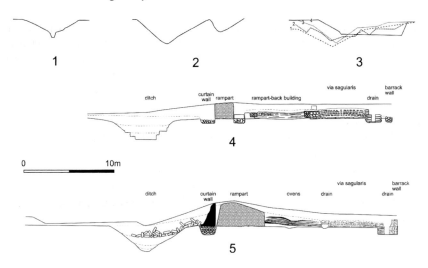

Figure 12: Ditches and defence sections. 1: Inchtuthil; 2: Carnuntum; 3: Neuss; 4–5: Caerleon.

Stone gateways, angle-towers, and interval towers all copied (but initially simplified) their timber antecedents in form, although the move to stone ultimately led to architectural elaboration of the sort evident on surviving gateways such as those at Regensburg or Aquincum (Figure 11 and Plates 16–19). The simplest form consisted of square towers on either side of the twin portals, separated by a central pier, and positioned centrally to the junction with the curtain wall, so that they protruded slightly, as at Alba Iulia. Such protrusions ultimately led to horseshoe-shaped towers like those at Mirebeau. At Windisch, the west gate unusually even had polygonal towers. Tower walls would usually (but not invariably) be of a similar thickness to the curtain wall and, again, formed from coursed dressed rubble facings with a clay- or mortar-bonded rubble core. As with timber towers, these projected above rampart-walk height, but it is also equally unclear how they were roofed (Plate 20).[13]

Ditches

The defensive value of the rampart and/or curtain wall was enhanced by the addition of a ditch (usually only one for the classic legionary fortress but occasionally more) some distance from its base, the intervening space forming the berm (Figure 12). The berm could range in width between 0.3m (Lincoln) and 6m (York) and its purpose may have been to ensure the stability of the rampart bank. Carnuntum, on the other hand, had two ditches (a smaller inner and larger outer) but no berm for much of its circuit. The 4.9m berm at Inchtuthil was metalled and probably used to afford access for vehicles during the insertion of the stone curtain wall.[14]

Ditches themselves could be between 4m and 13m wide and 1.4m to 2.9m deep, but might in fact vary even within the circuit of one fortress. Although a range of forms of ditch profile were known to (and employed by) the Roman army, including the asymmetrically profiled *fossa Punica* employed at Carnuntum, the most commonly used for legionary fortresses was the *fossa fastigata*, with a V-shaped profile, found at Caerleon (Figure 12). Ditches required regular cleaning (see below p. 40) so the original profile as dug is never likely to be preserved, but it is not unreasonable to assume that less effort was involved to preserve a V-sectioned ditch during cleaning than to modify an asymmetrical one by re-cutting. V-sectioned ditches often had an 'ankle-breaker' or basal slot, suggested as an additional hazard or merely the result of the cleaning process (see below p. 40). Ditches were normally terminated adjacent to gateways, leaving a causeway, but would occasionally provide a complete circuit that would then require to be bridged.[15]

A counterscarp could be placed beyond the ditch, effectively enhancing its depth and probably constructed from material derived from that ditch, possibly occasionally augmented as a result of its cleaning and this was noted at Neuss. That at Inchtuthil had the addition of brushwood entanglements on top of it, but at other sites, particularly those excavated in the earlier years of the twentieth century, extramural earthworks may not always have been sought or recognized.[16]

Additional defences

No legionary base has as yet produced evidence for the sort of defensive outworks found around some vexillation fortresses and cohort-sized forts in advanced areas. Such defences may have been intended to protect a work site during construction, so it could well be that, because legionary fortresses tended only to be constructed in pacified areas, they were deemed unnecessary. Nevertheless, it is not impossible that such outer defences may come to light around legionary camps.[17]

Chapter 5

The Internal Buildings

Whilst the identifications of some internal buildings in legionary fortresses are, at best, tentative, many structures like the barracks, *principia*, or granaries are easily recognized. The same is true of the *praetorium* and tribunes' houses, but there are additional courtyard and basilical structures that defy easy identification. The case for identifying *valetudinaria*, for instance, has been disputed. Thus the reader should be aware that the interpretation of the function of structures is prone to change. Nevertheless, the definitive study of internal buildings in legionary bases remains that of von Petrikovits.[1]

The administrative core

The principia (Figure 13)
The headquarters building (now known as the *principia* – like the English, a plural form – but for a long time erroneously referred to as the *praetorium*) was normally situated immediately adjacent to the *groma* at the junction of the *via principalis* and the *via praetoria*, positioned so that it was facing the latter street. The main components of the structure consisted of a forum or courtyard, a basilical cross-hall and a rear range of offices. There was some variety in the range of sizes, even allowing for the fact that the abnormally small timber *principia* at Inchtuthil (45m by 42m) was probably a temporary structure intended ultimately to be replaced, and legionary *principia* could vary between 60m by 96m (Novae) and 85m by 100m (Lambaesis). These can be compared with the structure at Vetera I (97m by 128m) designed to accommodate the headquarters contingents of two legions; economies of scale are evident, if slight. The *principia* was usually situated at the head of the T-junction formed by the intersection of the *via principalis* with the *via praetoria*, Windisch being one of the few exceptions to this. The legionary headquarters building was an intentionally monumental structure conceived as the *forum* of the fortress in every sense.[2]

  The courtyard, usually peristyled, was normally surrounded by ranges of rooms. A pit in the centre of the courtyard at Inchtuthil was interpreted as ritual in nature. These rooms are sometimes identified with the *armamentaria* recorded on inscriptions by dint of occasional finds of military equipment within them, but this is questionable. The principal feature of the cross-hall or *basilica* was a *tribunal* or raised platform at one (or sometimes both) of the ends from which a senior officer could address an assembly. The hall invariably had two rows of substantial columns (7.75m high at York) forming a nave with flanking aisles (Plates 21–2) and separated from the courtyard by an arcade (Plate 23). The rear range of offices were normally laid out symmetrically about a central shrine of the standards (*aedes* or *sacellum*), often apsidal, where the legionary eagle would be located (Plate 24). A strongroom would be provided to hold the unit savings and although this was often beneath the *aedes*, it could be to one or other side of it. The rear-range rooms would also include a *tabularium* and a *schola*. In the case of the Camp of Diocletian at Palmyra, this rear range of rooms had a second storey.[3]

Care seems to have been taken to ensure line of sight to the standards from the *porta praetoria*, along the *via praetoria*, across the *groma*, courtyard and *basilica*, and through the entrance to the *aedes* although this feature seems to have developed after the proto-fortresses (the *porta praetoria* at Oberaden did not align with the *aedes*). Similarly, the early Augustan bases show a close relationship between the *principia* and *praetorium* that may reflect their common origin.[4]

It has been argued that both the *principia* and *praetorium* evolved from the original *forum/agora* of Republican camps adjacent to the commanding general's quarters and that this can be seen in the intimate relationship between *principia* and *praetorium* at the proto-fortresses of Haltern, Marktbreit, and Oberaden.[5]

The location of the original setting-out point of the *groma* was often formally marked by a particular type of tetrapylon or *quadrifrons* from the second century AD onwards. The example at Lambaesis demonstrates from its inscription that it was known homonymously as the *groma*. Others are known from Caerleon, Aquincum, Enns-Lorch, and Lejjun, amongst others, but at Palmyra the tetrapylon at the junction of the *viae principalis* and *praetoria* was advanced away from the *principia* and so stood by itself at a crossroads. *Gromae* were evidently substantial and enduring structures. The one at Lambaesis still stands (Frontispiece), whilst those at Caerleon and Aquincum apparently survived into the medieval period. The *groma* was one of the regular locations for guard duty.[6]

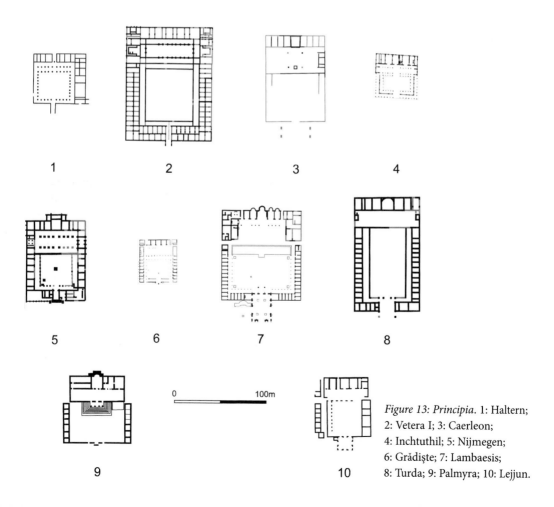

1 2 3 4

5 6 7 8

9 0 100m 10

Figure 13: Principia. 1: Haltern; 2: Vetera I; 3: Caerleon; 4: Inchtuthil; 5: Nijmegen; 6: Grădişte; 7: Lambaesis; 8: Turda; 9: Palmyra; 10: Lejjun.

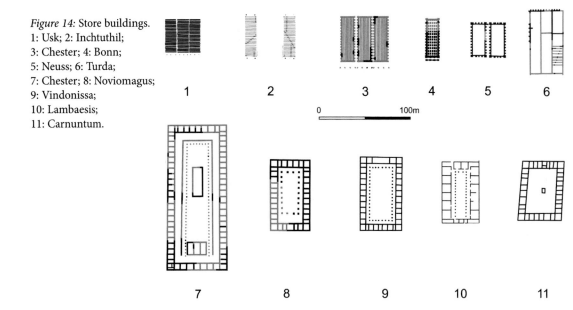

Figure 14: Store buildings.
1: Usk; 2: Inchtuthil;
3: Chester; 4: Bonn;
5: Neuss; 6: Turda;
7: Chester; 8: Noviomagus;
9: Vindonissa;
10: Lambaesis;
11: Carnuntum.

Communal facilities

Horrea (Figure 14)

Store buildings, or *horrea*, were a vital component of all fortresses, and usually described as 'granaries', although it is generally held that they contained far more than just grain. Unlike cohort-sized forts, where they were invariably placed in the central range, they were usually located close to gates in legionary camps and were provided with ample vehicular access to a loading platform at one end. None are recorded by name on inscriptions from legionary sites, although a *dispensator horreorum* is known from Kostolac in AD 252.[7]

In form they would be equipped with raised floors supported on pillars or dwarf walls (the former if of timber, either if of stone) and the outer load-bearing walls were invariably buttressed if of stone. Typical sizes were 41.5m by 12.8m at Inchtuthil (which had six granaries and was probably intended to have eight). Whilst the majority of timber granaries probably had shingle roofs, those at Inchtuthil had tiles. They were specifically designed to keep grain dry to prevent rotting, cool to prevent germination and spontaneous combustion, securely stored with minimal fire risk, and free of vermin.[8]

Valetudinarium (Figure 15)

One particular type of courtyard building has come to be identified with the *valetudinarium* of Pseudo-Hyginus and interpreted as a hospital, although this identification is not without its critics. These structures typically vary in size from 59m by 67m (Vindonissa) up to 85m by 86m (Vetera I) and consist of two concentric sets of four ranges of rooms around the central courtyard, with a circulating corridor between them. Each room is then separated from its neighbour by a corridor. The identification has been seen to be supported by finds of medical implements and the recovery of environmental evidence interpreted as belonging to plants used for medicinal purposes. Whilst the courtyard at Neuss was apparently used as a herb garden, that at Svištov housed a small shrine to Aesculapius.[9]

No structure has as yet been identified with the *veterinarium* of the *De Munitionibus Castrorum*.

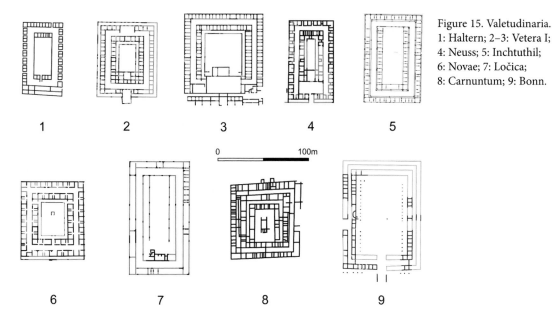

Figure 15. Valetudinaria.
1: Haltern; 2–3: Vetera I;
4: Neuss; 5: Inchtuthil;
6: Novae; 7: Ločica;
8: Carnuntum; 9: Bonn.

Balnea

The bath buildings (*balnea*) of legionary fortresses could be situated both inside and outside the defences and the reason for the differentiation between the two is unclear. Intramural baths buildings were executed on a grand scale and comprised the core elements of a changing room (*apodyterium*), cold room (*frigidarium*), warm room (*tepidarium*) and hot room(s) (*caldarium*), usually with a 'sweat' room (*laconicum*), an exercise area (*palaestra*) and a swimming pool (*piscina*). Examples have been explored in some detail in more recent times at Exeter, Caerleon and Aquincum, amongst others, and they range in size from 69m by 66m (Vindonissa) up to 146m by 117m (Aquincum). Interestingly, Inchtuthil had not had an internal baths suite constructed by the time of its abandonment, although a small example was provided in a nearby compound, presumably for the construction party, and there were vacant plots behind and next to the headquarters building there.[10]

Extra-mural baths are considered below (p. 36).

Accommodation

The praetorium (Figure 16)

The commanding officer's house (*praetorium*) was the residence for the *legatus legionis* and his *familia*, which would have included his immediate family, household slaves, and personal staff. The *praetorium* was usually placed next to the *principia*, to one side or the other (Vetera I), or behind it (Caerleon or Carnuntum). Unoccupied areas to the rear or the side at Inchtuthil were probably intended for such a structure. The twin *praetoria* (one for each legion) in Vetera I both had side doorways placed opposite corresponding entrances in the *principia*, reminiscent of the covered passage between the *praetorium* and *principia* at Oberaden.[11]

In form, *praetoria* were courtyard houses of the so-called Mediterranean type but on a grand, almost palatial, scale befitting the senatorial status of the individual. Some of these structures had what have been termed 'hippodrome' gardens, but they may also have incorporated large water features. Examples typically occupied 0.38ha (Carnuntum) to 0.67ha (Neuss) for single-legion fortresses (about 2.0 to 2.6 per cent of total area), and by comparison 0.79ha and 0.89ha for the

Figure 16: Praetoria.
1: Haltern; 2–3: Vetera I;
4: Caerleon; 5: Neuss;
6: Vindonissa.

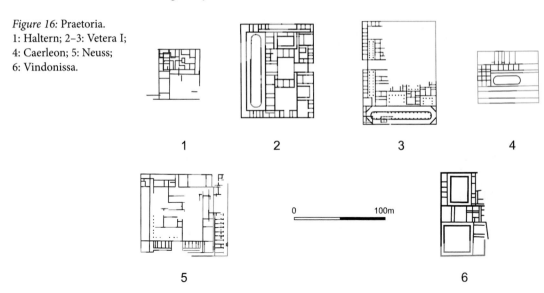

double legionary fortress at Vetera I (2.9 per cent for the two). Presumably for reasons of both practicality and dignity two *praetoria* had to be maintained in double-legionary camps, to judge from the example of Vetera I.[12]

Tribunes' houses

Additional officers' accommodation was provided for the six legionary tribunes (one *tribunus laticlavius*, five *tribuni angusticlavii*). Their ranks and respective status were reflected in the relative sizes of their dwellings. The house of the *tribunus laticlavius* was excavated at Aquincum. Measuring 39m by 59m, in its second phase it incorporated a small mithraeum in its east wing. Examination of houses of *tribuni angusticlavii* at Caerleon showed primary use for smithing in one room whilst a structure at Windisch (unsurprisingly, perhaps) incorporated a kitchen area. At Neuss, the tribunes' houses each occupied around 16 per cent of the senior officer's house and around 0.7 per cent of the total minimum area – see above, p. 2 – of a fortress. These structures were located in the *scamnum tribunorum*, normally that part of the *praetentura* facing the *via principalis* (and on the opposite side of it to the *principia*). The commanding officers' houses of any auxiliary units based within a fortress would most likely be located close to the barracks of their men, although it has been argued – not unreasonably – that they too would be located in the *scamnum tribunorum*. Once again these were Mediterranean-style courtyard houses, albeit on a much humbler scale than the *praetorium*.[13]

Further accommodation was required for the *praefectus castrorum*, although no structure has yet been convincingly identified for this purpose. Since he would rank between the junior and senior *tribune*, we might expect an accommodation provision between these two.[14]

Barracks (Figures 17–18)

Legionary barracks were arranged in *cohors quingenaria* blocks of six, reflecting the six *centuriae* forming a *cohors* (with the possible exception of the first cohort). The buildings were also known as *centuriae* and were paired to face each other (in Pseudo-Hyginian terms, a *striga*), harking back to the *manipuli* of the Republican army and earlier courtyard-style barracks. The structures comprised a large rectangular block at one end (the centurion's quarters and offices and possibly accommodation for the *principales*), a long section of accommodation for the soldiers (each unit consisting of rear room and front room, generally

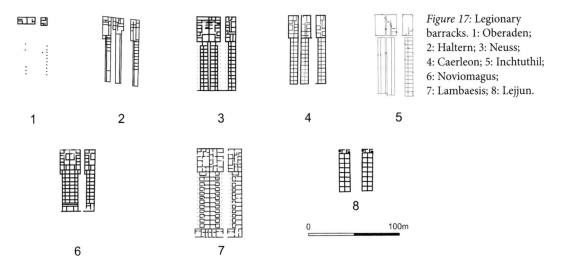

Figure 17: Legionary barracks. 1: Oberaden; 2: Haltern; 3: Neuss; 4: Caerleon; 5: Inchtuthil; 6: Noviomagus; 7: Lambaesis; 8: Lejjun.

assumed to have matched the *papilio* and *arma* of a temporary camp), whilst a colonnaded verandah, which could be paved, ran the entire length, continuing the roof line from the centurion's quarters. Apart from being used for storage, front rooms could contain a hearth, as at Vindonissa, presumably for both heating and cooking. The far end of the block could often contain additional offices or accommodation (so-called Schlußbauten), sometimes suggested as alternative accommodation for *principales* or legionary horsemen, and most blocks contained more than the theoretical minimum of ten room-pairs.[15]

Although most barracks were constructed in a limited range of styles indicative of only a single storey, it has been noted that the Praetorian barracks in the Castra Praetoria were (in at least one phase) two-storey structures, and the nature of the buttressed barracks at Gardun, built on a slope, may also indicate a de facto second floor there. Similarly, comparable vaulted ceilings at Lejjun in both defensive towers and barrack buildings might suggest a second floor in the latter.[16]

Stables

The identification of stabling was for a long time tentative, but work on auxiliary fort sites led to confident identifications of composite cavalry barrack/stable structures that have subsequently been confirmed as a modification of existing buildings in the legionary base at Usk. The presence of auxiliary cavalry within fortresses is thus confirmed archaeologically, epigraphically, and in sub-literary sources in addition to the anticipated legionary mounted component, which have proved much harder for modern writers to locate, although it is generally held that the men were

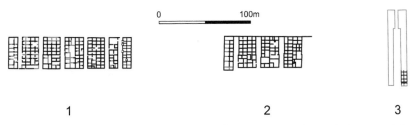

Figure 18: Auxiliary barracks. 1–2: Neuss–Novaesium (after Koenen 1904); 3: Usk–Burrium (after Marvell 1996).

held on century strength. Von Petrikovits attempted to install the legionary cavalry in *tabernae*, but this is unconvincing in the light of what we now know about stabling.[17]

Services
A number of other types of structures that do not fit easily within any of the above categories are known and these generally provided some sort of service.

Storage
A very common type of structure is that known nowadays as *tabernae*, often manifested as a series of rooms opening on to the *via praetoria* and *via principalis*, as well as some other main streets. Such locations meant they usually helped mask officer accommodation from the main roads. The function of these has been much debated, but storage is commonly suggested, when it is recalled that every legion had need of large numbers of wheeled vehicles, artillery pieces and matériel. They have also been suggested as workshops. Towers may also have been used for storage, as evidently happened with a range of military matériel at Dura-Europos.[18]

Workshops (Figure 19)
Legionary bases also contained workshops (*fabricae*) and our sources stress their self-sufficiency in manufacturing and repair under the Principate. A papyrus from Egypt even records production of various fittings in the *fabrica* of *legio II Traiana Fortis* at Nicopolis. The best known excavated example of a workshop is that at Inchtuthil, which produced a pit containing, amongst other things, a famously large hoard (ten tonnes) of nails. This structure, measuring 59.7m by 58.2m, had aisled halls 12.8m wide on three sides of a courtyard and a range of rooms, possibly offices on either side of an entrance, on the fourth. Similar courtyard structures are known from other sites, including one from Exeter, but none that are identical.[19]

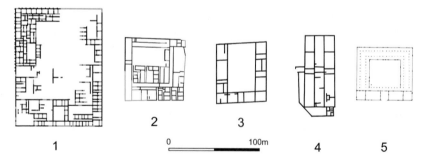

Figure 19: Quaestoria and other buildings. 1: Vetera I; 2: Caerleon; 3–4: Carnuntum; 5: Inchtuthil.

Rampart-back structures (Figure 20)
All fortresses contained buildings in the *intervallum* space between the rampart or curtain wall and the *via sagularis*. These included latrines, ovens and storage facilities.

Latrines are known from a number of sites and seem to have been distributed to serve cohort blocks. The main room of the structure in the north-west corner of the fortress at Caerleon measured 8.8m by 4.6m (compared with 9.4m by 4.9m for the famous auxiliary example at Housesteads) and, by analogy with other structures, could perhaps have seated twenty users at any one time. They are also found in hospital buildings, unsurprisingly, as well as in intramural baths facilities, and even, in the case of Palmyra, in the *principia*.[20]

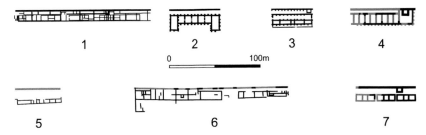

Figure 20: Rampart-back buildings. 1: Caerleon; 2: Neuss; 3: Noviomagus; 4: Aquincum; 5: Bonn;
6: Carnuntum; 7: Chester.

In Flavian fortresses, ovens were distributed around the *intervallum* area to service nearby sets
of barrack blocks, with an apparent allotment of one oven to each barrack. They were circular
with a raised paved stone floor and covered by a clay dome in the traditional style of a bread oven.
The examples at Caerleon were not discovered by excavation but during consolidation work in
the 1930s; those at Inchtuthil were between 2.1m and 2.7m (with internal diameters of between
1.5m and 1.8m). These were often replaced by more formal cookhouses, in the case of Caerleon
added onto the back of the interval and corner towers. No provision for communal messing has
ever been identified and it is assumed soldiers consumed food in their barracks.[21]

Another category of rampart-back building appears to be related to the storage of equipment.
Both at Carnuntum and at Caerleon, structures set into the rampart were found upon excavation
to have been used as weapons stores and these seem the most likely candidates for identification
as *armamentaria* (which are known in their own right from inscriptions and were thus probably
separate from headquarters buildings).[22]

Other buildings

Other buildings within a fortress are more enigmatic. A large (30m by 60m) rectangular stone
building with an oval courtyard at Chester (often now referred to as 'The Elliptical Building') was
constructed twice on the same plot with a gap of more than a century between the structures that
implied the existence of plans to which reference could be made. A fountain at the heart of the first
version was supplied by lead water pipes bearing the name of the governor Agricola. Its function
is unknown, but much speculated about. A further building at Chester has also excited attention.
Placed behind the *principia* (a position sometimes occupied by the *praetorium*), an extremely long
courtyard building (60m by 160m), surrounded on all four sides by ranges of rooms (but bearing
little resemblance to a *praetorium*) has been suggested as the palace of the governor.[23]

Similarly puzzling buildings occur at other sites and tend to be dismissed as store buildings, but
it is clear that even now we do not fully understand the workings of a legionary camp and, whilst
it is possible to identify many of the structural elements with confidence, others remain baffling.[24]

A spiritual dimension

Most of the internal structures of a fortress were believed to have a tutelary *genius*, including the
barracks (*genius centuriae*) and weapons stores (*genius armamentaria*) as well as, more generally,
the fortress (e.g. *genius Lambaesis*), and the legion itself (*genius legionis*). The water supply was in
the care of nymphs and the baths were overseen by Fortuna. Deities also watched over the exercise
ground (the Campestres, generally associated with cavalry) and of course the unit standards were
revered as deities in the own right, chief amongst which was the *aquila* or legionary eagle.
Additionally, a shrine to Aesculapius, the god of healing, was found in the courtyard of the
valetudinarium at Novae and a structure next to the *principia* at Nijmegen has been identified as
an *auguratorium*, where the auspices would have been taken.[25]

Chapter 6

Infrastructure

Roads

Each legionary fortress had an integral system of all-weather roads. These provided access between the interior and exterior of the camp by means of the four principal gates and allowed efficient movement around the interior. The two principal roads were the *via praetoria* and the *via principalis*, which met in a T-junction at the *groma* and formed one of the main divisions of the blocks within the camp, passing through the front (*porta praetoria*) and side gates (*porta principalis sinstra* and *dextra*). Secondary roads included the *via decumana*, which entered through the rear gate, the *via quintana*, which ran parallel to the *via principalis* but behind the central range (*latera praetorii*), and the *via sagularis*, which ran around the periphery of the camp, just inside the defences. A series of smaller streets ran between the blocks and between the individual barrack blocks (*viae vicinariae*).[1]

At Caerleon, the *via praetoria* and *principalis* were 7.5m wide and the *via sagularis* 5.5m, whilst at Neuss the latter dimension was 5.9m. The minor streets of a camp tended to be smaller, with a 4m-wide *via vicinaria* between Buildings 99 and 100 at Neuss. Roads were inevitably subject to resurfacing, especially in camps occupied over a long period, and that could lead to their levels being raised, a phenomenon plainly visible in the section through the defences at Caerleon (Figure 12).[2]

The roads were generally constructed of cobble foundations with tamped gravel metalling, both materials which, since most legionary bases (in temperate provinces, at least) were situated on or near the flood plains of major rivers, were not hard to find. Nevertheless, although some roads were of gravel at Colchester, others between the barracks were left unsurfaced. Repairs and resurfacing often incorporated reused building materials such as roofing tile or other substantial refuse like quernstones. Some sites were provided with more substantial slab-paved surfaces, but again these made good use of available materials.[3]

Fresh water and wastewater (Figure 21)

In the northern and western provinces of the Empire, fresh water was usually brought into a fortress by means of an aqueduct, normally drawn off upstream of the site or even from a separate water source, as at Chester. The point of entry for an aqueduct, usually in the form of a subterranean channel, would be one of the four gateways, as at Vindonissa. When excavated, the Vindonissa aqueduct was found to be still flowing. Within the fortress itself, water pipes could be of timber, ceramic, or lead, examples of the last from Chester being stamped with the governor Agricola's name. The principal destinations for such imported water were of course the baths, the commanding officer's house, and other major buildings that might have need of it (such as the hospital and workshops), but it is not clear how it was distributed to the bulk of the soldiery, although fountains located around a camp are one obvious solution and a '*nymphaeum*' was

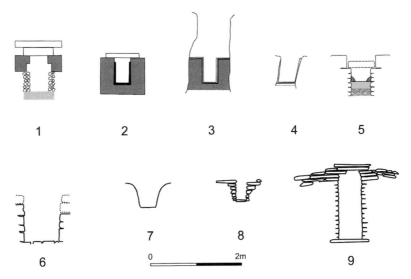

Figure 21: Aqueducts and drains. 1–2: Windisch–Vindonissa (after Hartmann 1986); 3–5: Lajjun–Legio (after Parker 1986; 2000); 6–7: Inchtuthil (after Pitts and St Joseph 1988); 8–9: Caerleon–Isca (after Nash-Williams 1931).

identified at Lambaesis immediately next to the *groma*. Existing cisterns and aqueducts may have been used at Castra Albana. Neuss contained several wells, including a 9m-deep one in one of the tribunes' houses.[4]

In eastern and southern provinces, water management was equally important but posed a different set of problems when rivers were not always available. Here fortresses had to be placed to exploit perennial springs and oases, as at Palmyra, Raphanaea, and Lejjun.[5]

The sewer beneath the *via principalis* at Caerleon was 0.5m wide and 1.3m deep, whilst that at York beneath Church Street (probably running behind the *scamnum tribunorum*) was 0.45m wide and 1.2m deep and traced for some 44m, being roofed with flat slabs and with relieving arches to support overlying buildings. Seven roof inlets or splashdowns were identified. These mostly fed into the principal sewers that also carried foul water out of the fortress and into the river, although some officers' houses were equipped with pools or basins in courtyard gardens, which could take run-off from roofs and these too were serviced by overflow drains. Such sewers were accessible for maintenance through manholes, one of which was found in the Church Street sewer at York. Waste water from latrines (see above p. 30) also drained into the sewerage system. Outfalls from the sewers were kept clear of the potable water – quite logically, since both were gravity fed – and seem to have been directly into the ditch, usually near the corners. In the case of York, environmental evidence suggests a link directly to the river Foss.[6]

Middens

Legionary bases produced vast amounts of other waste, much of it recycled during the life of a site, but – particularly at times of garrison change and in places where concealment was not a prime concern – there would often be major episodes of dumping and this would frequently occur in one place: a midden. The best-known and most comprehensively studied midden is the Schutthügel at Vindonissa, but other examples are known, including one at Carnuntum. The Vindonissa example grew up immediately next to the defences on the northern side of the fortress, where there was a steep bank down to the river Aare. It appears to have grown horizontally with successive abandonments and incorporated discarded organic and inorganic material, presumably not deemed essential for removal. In the earliest phase of occupation at Vindonissa, a series of large ditches known as the Keltengraben served as the first area for the dumping of rubbish. Middens from other sites are not as yet known and it is possible that Vindonissa and Carnuntum are unique, but this seems unlikely, and a site identified as an extramural workshop at Bonn may also actually have been such a tip.[7]

Chapter 7

Extramural Buildings

Although a detailed account of the extramural facilities of legionary bases is outwith the scope of this volume, some account needs to be given of the associated structures and facilities. Every legionary fortress was part of a complex landscape formed from various components associated with its operation (Figure 22), whether military (exercise grounds or auxiliary forts), civilian (*canabae*), economic (works depot and *prata legionis*), or possible dual-function facilities (amphitheatre and external baths).

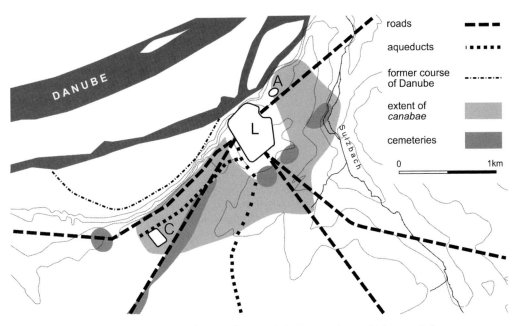

Figure 22: A fortress in its landscape (after Kandler 1986). L: fortress; A: amphitheatre; C: fort.

Amphitheatres

Amphitheatra (sometimes known by scholars as *ludi*, but not recorded as such in a military context) are so commonly associated with legionary bases that the few sites that have not yet yielded one (such as York) might be anticipated as eventually doing so. They are commonly placed close to one of the principal gates and have been variously interpreted as venues for training soldiers, for occasional gladiatorial entertainment or beast hunts, and for general assemblies of the troops, particularly on special occasions (Plate 30). Many legionary examples produce direct evidence of having been constructed by the army.[1]

Extramural baths

Some legionary bases possessed both intramural (see above, p. 27) and extramural baths buildings, although it is not clear whether there was any distinction between the two. Caerleon, with its Castle Baths, is probably the best known example, but it is matched by the Watergate Baths just west of the fortress at Chester. Again, extramural baths were normally placed close to the fortress defences and it is not inconceivable that these belong with a *mansio* as at Windisch (see below). The partly surviving baths at Castra Albana (Plate 31), immediately outside the *porta praetoria*, were built by *legio II Parthica*, to judge from the many brick stamps incorporated, so were presumably used by them too.[2]

Exercise grounds

Legionary exercise grounds (sometimes known as parade grounds) have been identified at Caerleon and Lambaesis, the *tribunal* of the latter adorned with Hadrian's famous *adlocutio* inscription. That implies that an exercise ground (*campus*) was less a place for parades and drill but rather the location for much of the soldiers' training, as the rank of *campidoctor* also suggests. Although the full dimensions are uncertain, the exercise ground at Caerleon may have measured around 220m by 145m, whilst that at Lambaesis was 200m square. Another possible site has been identified just over 300m east of the fortress at Mirebeau, measuring some 272m by 212m. The location varied: the exercise ground at Caerleon was immediately adjacent to the fortress, but that at Lambaesis was nearly 2km away, and at Caerleon, Chester and Burnum it was close to the amphitheatre. The Caerleon example was suggested as having been laid over the construction camp for the fortress, which might explain why examples like Mirebeau and Lambaesis had rounded corners and might even suggest an eventual intended use for the location of the large construction camp at Inchtuthil.[3]

Auxiliary accommodation

Some fortresses, possibly many – there is insufficient evidence to make a judgement as yet – included provision for auxiliary troops within their walls. Amongst such inclusive camps are Neuss, Caerleon, Nicopolis (the last two on epigraphic and sub-literary evidence) and possibly Svishtov and Exeter. At the same time, another type of exclusive base made do with an auxiliary fort in close proximity. Examples of this type include Bad Deutsch-Altenburg with Petronell, Wroxeter with a fort to the south, Lambaesis and its Camp de l'Est, and possibly Colchester with Stanway (although there is no obvious reason beyond its size why the last has to be auxiliary). Burnum and its neighbouring fort may fall within this group too. Some fortresses, such as the Koenenlager at Neuss, Rosinos de Vidriales and Usk, were succeeded by auxiliary forts placed over them, and it may well be the case that an auxiliary component that shared its base (or its replacement) stayed on in the same location in a reduced fort.[4]

This has important implications for assessments of what is a 'standard-sized' legionary base, and what is a 'small' one, especially if a 'small' one like Exeter can also be shown to contain auxiliaries. Clearly the flexibility of having auxiliaries within or outwith a fortress could affect (and complicate) modern calculations, not least when a fort like Petronell could occupy a minimum area of 2.7ha, but its complement, sharing the facilities of a fortress, might only have taken up 45 per cent of that area if included in a fortress.[5]

Civil settlements

Fortresses almost invariably had extramural civil settlements, commonly known as *canabae*. These generally seem to have resembled the *vici* of smaller forts, in that they provided civilian accommodation and the traditional entertainments expected by legionary troops. They are less well understood than *vici*, partly because only a handful have been excavated in anything approaching any detail.[6]

The structures of the civil settlement included strip houses fronting onto streets, as at Caerleon, Strasbourg and Alba Iulia. These presumably provided both shops and accommodation for their proprietors. A frequent (perhaps universal) feature was the *mansio*, a posting station where visitors could be accommodated and a change of horses secured. An example has been excavated just outside the east defences of the fortress at Windisch; another is suspected at Chester. Extramural bath-houses may also have played a role in civilian life, but there is no clear evidence to confirm this hypothesis.[7]

Legionary territory

There is some evidence that an area of land (*territorium*) was associated with each legionary base and territorial markers are known. This may be connected with agricultural land (*prata legionis*), *legio IV Macedonica* laying claim to over 500km^2 around Herrera de Pisuerga, but it may also have included works depots such as the tileries at Holt, Binyanei Ha'uma, Ilovica, or Rheinzabern – belonging to the legionary fortresses at Chester, Jerusalem, Ločica and Mainz respectively – or the lime kilns of *legio XXX* at Iversheim. Quarries too, like those at Inchtuthil and Chester, may have fallen within the *territorium*.[8]

Cemeteries

The final component of this legionary landscape is one or more burial grounds. As was customary, cemeteries were usually located alongside roads on the outskirts of the fortress and *canabae* settlement. They are also the principal source of the epigraphic material cited for each site in the gazetteers, with monumental inscriptions from fortresses themselves always being a minority part of the epigraphic record for a site. Gravestones from Apamea, re-used in a tower of the city wall, are the principal physical evidence for the presence of *legio II Parthica* at that site. At Haïdra, tombstones of legionaries of *III Augusta* still stand by the side of the road (Plate 32).[9]

Chapter 8

Construction and Demolition

Location

There were three principal considerations in the location of any Roman military base: the strategic, the tactical and the topographical. Both of the first two were connected to the third, topography and physical geography. Arrian's comments on the location of the auxiliary fort at Phasis are apposite here, since he noted that it was strong by virtue of the nature of the topography and well placed for its task of protecting those sailing in the area.[1]

The strategic role of bases was linked with the logistics of their supply, hence under the Principate they were habitually sited at key points in the road network and with access to a major river, both of which could be used for supply purposes. It also required that it should be more or less centrally located for its given zone of influence, once again served by access to the communications network. A key difference with cohort-sized forts is that legionary bases, like towns, were an integral part of the road system; main roads entered their gates. Smaller forts tended to be placed next to major roads, not on them. These same factors meant that many of these sites went on to become important towns and cities in Roman and post-Roman times.[2]

Tactically, fortresses were normally placed in a serviceably defensible location, accomplished by careful use of the local topography. Care was evidently taken not to permit any tactical disadvantages in the immediate vicinity (so-called *novercae*), such as dominating ground overlooking the site. In the rare cases where a site was chosen (or its location dictated) adjacent to such an obstacle, it might be incorporated within the defensive circuit, as appears to have happened at Palmyra.[3]

Topographically, fortresses in temperate regions were normally placed at the confluence of a major river and a tributary, often on a slight eminence overlooking the watercourses (such as a river terrace) and almost invariably at a bridging point. Some, particularly in frontier regions, were accompanied by a bridgehead fortification on the other side of the river (example, being Aquincum and Transaquincum). Such preferences were not peculiar to legionary bases and were frequently followed for cohort-sized forts too, although obviously a larger 'fort platform' was required for a legionary base. Castra Albana, on the other hand, was sited on disadvantageous sloping ground, at the edge of a steep slope, so that it could re-use the site of an imperial villa belonging to Domitian, part of the *nymphaeum* from the latter being incorporated within the fortress. Occasionally sites were poorly chosen, the fortress at Strasbourg displaying evidence of inundation. Similarly the sites of Vetera II at Xanten, and possibly Ptuj, were set low down and subsequently removed by changes of river course.[4]

Responsibility for the choice of site seems to have been vested in the *praefectus castrorum*, an experienced soldier who had risen through the ranks, although it was a familiar literary *topos* that great commanders chose their own sites for fortifications. The principles traditionally accepted for the location of military sites of all kinds (although arguably primarily intended for temporary sites) were laid out in Roman writers and recorded in Vegetius and Pseudo-Hyginus. Whether written manuals per se were employed is open to debate and no such texts survive, but it has been suggested that the recreation in stone of the Flavian Elliptical Building at Chester, some 150 years after its demolition, may imply the existence of plans that could be modified.[5]

Construction

The incomplete fortress at Inchtuthil is one of the few to preserve indications of how a legionary base was built. Adjacent construction camps have been identified and a neighbouring compound with internal structures has been suggested as having been inhabited by construction parties, with another small fortification being used to store materials.[6]

The first task of construction once a site had been chosen was setting out. This was done by *agrimensores*, using a cruciform surveying instrument called the *groma*, which comprised four arms on a staff, each terminated by a suspended plumb bob. This enabled straight lines, right angles and forty-five-degree angles to be set out simply, its only drawback being a vulnerability to disturbance by wind. The instrument also gave its name to the point where it was set up within the base where the principal roads, the *via praetoria* and the *via principalis*, would meet in a T-junction. As has been noted, this location was often subsequently covered with a tetrapylon or *quadrifrons*, as recorded in an inscription on the structure at Lambaesis. Once the *groma* was established, the line of the defences and the secondary roads (*via sagularis*, *via decumana* and *via quintana*) and tertiary roads (*viae vicinariae*) could be placed within the camp as offsets from the two principal alignments, thereby defining the construction *insulae*.[7]

It was stated by Pseudo-Hyginus that camps should be laid out facing the enemy, whereas Vegetius says the camp should either face east or the enemy. Where cardinal orientation is known for legionary bases (determined by the direction in which the *principia* was facing, down the *via praetoria*), the observation that a site faced hostile territory (where known) seems to hold true and is particularly clear along the Rhine and Danube (Table 2). Variations from the expected

Table 2: Orientation of the *nomina legionum* inscription legionary bases in comparison with approximate expected enemy location.

Base	Orientation	Enemy	Base	Orientation	Enemy	Base	Orientation	Enemy
Caerleon	132°	?270°–360°	Budapest	104°	105°	Belkis	?	?90°
York	219°	?270°–360°	Beograd	140°/320°	310°–15°	Samsat	?	?90°
Chester	163°	?180°–270°	Kostolac	21°	330°–360°	Caparcotna	?	?
Strasbourg	233°	90°	Svištov	5°	0°	Jerusalem	?	?
Mainz	?48°	60°	Igliţa	?	0°	Bosra	270°/90°	90°
Bonn	77°	75°	Silistra	?6°	0°	Alexandria	?	?
Nijmegen	33°	25°	Alba Iulia	101°	?	Tazoult-Lambèse	356°	?
Szőny	12°	0°	Eski Malatya	8°/188°	?	León	161°	?
Wien	43°	50°	Sadak	100°	90°	Albing	50°	25°
Bad Deutsch-Altenburg	324°	330°	Barin	?	?	Regensburg	7°	5°
Sinjar	?	?	Albano Laziale	235°	?	Ra's al-'Ayn	?	?

orientation may be due to allowances for terrain or subsequent changes in river course, although the British sites are undeniably heterodox if it is assumed the same criteria were used to lay them out.[8]

With orientation decided, barracks would be laid out *per scamnum* or *per strigas* in *insula* blocks (the latter known as *cohortes*) bordering the *via sagularis* and, in the case of the first cohort, close to the *via principalis* and usually in the *latera praetorii*, next to the *principia*. In the case of Caerleon, all of the known barrack blocks were set out *per strigas*, whilst at Inchtuthil it was half and half, and Chester and Neuss had the majority aligned *per strigas*.[9]

If a timber site, construction required either the digging of post trenches (these being preferred to individual postholes in the first centuries BC and AD) or the laying of sill beams (or sole plates), sometimes within beam slots (these invariably being shallower than post trenches). Post trenches for structures such as tribunes' houses and *valetudinaria* could range between 0.46m and 0.72m in width and 0.38m and 0.85m in depth in the case of Inchtuthil. Uprights would be inserted and then the trenches backfilled around them. Despite the additional labour involved, it seems to have been considered preferable to dig trenches rather than pits for uprights, since (besides buildings) they are also used for box ramparts, as at Oberaden, only tower posts at gates, and corner and interval towers being placed within post pits. For sill beams, uprights could then be inserted into them by means of a mortice and tenon joint, but this technique seems to have been less common for fortresses than post-in-trench construction. In both cases, panelling employed for structures would normally be of wattle and daub, despite Vitruvius' dislike of the technique. This could be formed from horizontal ledgers fixed to the main uprights with vertical rods lashed between them, or horizontal wattles woven between vertical staves. The panels would then be given a coat of daub and rendered (and probably lime washed or painted).[10]

Stone-built sites were different from, but nevertheless shared many similarities with, their timber predecessors. Whilst some structures were wholly constructed of stone (or even forms of concrete), others are generally believed to have been built on stone footings, using dwarf walls, upon which a timber and wattle-and-daub superstructure would rest. Much seems to have depended upon the location (and availability of materials) and the status of the structure in question. In the west, the army frequently favoured clay- over mortar-bonded walling, a technique that works well providing its integrity is maintained by rendering, thus retaining a degree of moisture within the fabric of the wall. In the east, straightforward stone construction was a long-standing tradition, but variations of both could be found anywhere within the Empire.

Maintenance

Once constructed, all fortifications and structures contained within required maintenance. Dendrochronology of timber structures, as well as reconstruction work on defences like those at The Lunt and Vindolanda, show just how limited the life of such bases could be without intervention. Shoddy workmanship and periods of abandonment could also take their toll on stone structures and inscriptions are found marking the restoration of buildings, such as repairs to baths 'collapsed through age' at Lambaesis or Mainz. Scholarly opinion once held that such phrases were euphemisms for enemy attack, although that view is no longer in vogue and a simple record of maintenance and reconstruction is thought more likely.[11]

In the case of ditches, it has been argued that the classic 'ankle-breaker' feature at the bottom of V-sectioned ditches, since it matched the width of a shovel blade, was formed as a result of cleaning a difficult shape in the simplest way possible and it is clear that frequent attention would be needed if the ideal defensive profile were to be maintained. Restoration of defences, including towers, is recorded at Lambaesis.[12]

Demolition

The phases that can be identified within legionary fortresses are usually thought to coincide with changes in garrison. The implication of such major programmes of reconstruction at some sites is that the interior would habitually be razed to the ground, either by the departing unit or by their replacements. Such might well be the reason for changes at sites like Vindonissa, Carnuntum and Aquincum, but single-garrison sites such as Caerleon must be for different reasons, probably to do with the lifetime of the building materials employed. Moreover, multiple-occupancy sites might be expected to exhibit more coordinated phasing across the site, since garrison change would be a reason for wholesale change. In a long-term, single-occupancy site, buildings might last longer and decay (and thus need replacing) at different rates. Thus, in the former, all the barrack blocks might be replaced at once, whereas in the latter, they will have fallen out of synchronization to be replaced or repaired at different times.

Inchtuthil is not just instructive about the construction of a legionary fortress, since it seems to have been dismantled before it was ever commissioned, and thus has much to reveal about the demolition process. It may well be that the compounds described above were also (perhaps only) connected with the demolition of the site. Certainly the collection and subsequent burial of some ten tonnes of iron nails is indicative of methodical dismantling of timber structures.[13]

The processes involved in demolition – tidying was apparently one such – can be identified from traces in the archaeological record. The removal of structural timbers could be dealt with in different ways. At Lincoln, the 178mm by 127mm uprights of the rampart were apparently rocked back and forth prior to withdrawal. The gateposts of the auxiliary fort at Carlisle, on the other hand, were sawn off just above ground level. Frequent evidence of burning shows that some at least of the organic components were destroyed whilst the curtain wall at Inchtuhil was toppled onto the berm.[14]

Chapter 9

Gazetteers

Introduction

These gazetteers provide summary details for the known legionary fortresses and their antecedents as well as plans, where the information is available. Gazetteer A lists the classic legionary fortresses alphabetically by site name, whilst Gazetteer B does the same for the fortresses of the Dominate. Additional indices list sites 1) clockwise around the Empire by modern country, starting with Britain, and 2) by Roman province.

The gazetteers may be used in tandem with the *Google Earth* and *Google Maps* data on the website (see Appendix 5) to view vertical satellite and aerial photographs of the sites (at the time of writing just one site – Inchtuthil – is still only available as a low-resolution LandSat image).

The categories in each gazetteer are as follows:

Location	The location of the *groma* of the fortress where it can be ascertained. **Emboldened** where it is known for certain, *italicized* where it is approximate, roman type where unknown and only a guess.
Situation	Most European fortress sites lie at the confluence of a major river and a tributary (and this is the order in which they are named here).[1]
Height ASL	The (present-day) approximate height of the *groma* above sea level, in metres. This is generally derived from *Google Earth*.[2]
Country	Modern country within which the base is situated.
District	Modern administrative district within which the base is situated.
Province	The Roman province (or provinces, where this changed) within which the base is situated.
Length	Dimension of the long axis of the base, measured across the wall or rampart base, in metres.
Width	Dimension of the short axis of the base, measured across the wall or rampart base, in metres.
Area	Area of the base, measured across the wall or rampart base, in hectares.
Proportion	The ratio of length to width of a fortress. As a guideline, the 1:1 proportion of a square would be 1.0 whilst an ideal 2:3 proportion (*castra tertiata*) would be 1.5.[3]
Cardinal orientation	Orientation along the *via praetoria* and through the *porta praetoria*, where known, expressed as degrees from true north.
Phases & Dating	These are broad phases and dating, not the detailed phasing of a site, together with garrison information, expressed in the form of 'constructional material – garrison unit (period of occupation)'.[4] A question mark signifies that one or the other is unknown.

Literary references	Ancient literary references to legionary presence at the site.[5]
Units attested	Epigraphic records of units mentioned at the site. This does not mean they were necessarily in garrison, since a career inscription could mention several units in which a man had served. Known garrisons are **emboldened**.[6]
Sub-literary references	Sub-literary references (e.g. papyri, writing tablets, ostraka) to legionary presence at the site.
Modern references	Publications of excavations and relevant major works of synthesis.[7]

Gazetteer A: Legionary Fortresses of the Principate

Listed in alphabetical order, these are the 'classic' legionary fortresses of the empire, many of them utilizing the familiar playing-card shape. Some have their origins at the very beginning of the Principate and some continue on into the Dominate.

Afamia–Apamea (Figure 2,78)
Location: *35° 25′ 17.75″ N, 36° 25′ 0.06″ E*
Situation: Confluence of two wadis draining into the Orontes
Height ASL: *c.*265m (GE)
Country: Syria
Region: Governorate of Hamah
Province: Syria
Length: –
Width: –
Area: –
Proportion: –
Cardinal orientation: –
Phases & Dating: ?Stone – *Legio II Parthica* (AD 215–18) … *Legio II Parthica* (AD 231–3) … *Legio II Parthica* (AD 242–4)
Literary references: Cass. Dio 79.34.2
Units attested epigraphically: *Legio II Parthica*: **AE 1971, 469; 1974, 647; 1991, 1572; 1992, 1686; 1993, 1571–5; 1579–85; 1587–8; 1597; CIL III, 187; GLISyrB 130; IGLS IV, 1357; 1359–60; 1375.** *Legio IV Flavia*: *AE* 1993, 1578. *Legio IV Scythica*: *IDRE* II, 411. *Legio XIII Gemina*: *IDRE* II, 410; *IGLS* IV, 1362. Unspecified legion: *AE* 1995, 1517. *Cohors I Praetoria*: *AE* 1995, 1516. *Equites singulares Augusti*: *Denkm* 689; 690; *IGLS* IV, 1374. *Ala I G[*: *AE* 1976, 666. *Ala I Ulpia Contariorum*: *AE* 1987, 955; 1993, 1589–93; 1596. *Ala Britannica*: *AE* 1993, 1594; *IGLS* IV, 1361; *RHP* 65–6. Unspecified cavalry unit: *AE* 2000, 1496. Unspecified infantry unit: *AE* 1974, 648. Unspecified unit: *CIL* III, 6700
Sub-literary references: –
Modern references (site): Balty 1988
Modern references (finds): Balty 1987; Balty and Rengen 1993
Notes: Open site postulated but not investigated

Alba Iulia–Apulum (Figures 2,49; 23)
Location: 46° 04′ 02.81″ N, 23° 34′ 20.57″ E
Situation: Confluence of the Mureş and Ampoi
Height ASL: 246m (GE)
Country: Romania
Region: Alba county, Transylvania
Province: Dacia

Length: *c.*425m
Width: *c.*405m
Area: *c.*17.2ha
Proportion: *c.*1.049
Cardinal orientation: 101°
Phases & Dating: Stone – *Legio XIII Gemina* (AD 109–272)
Literary references: Ptol., *Geog.* 3.8; *Tab. Peut.* 8.1; *Rav. Cosm.* 4.7
Units attested epigraphically: *Legio I Adiutrix: CIL* III, 981; 1004; 1008; 1180–2; 1206; *IDR* III.6, 1. *Legio III Italica: CIL* III, 1178; 7785. *Legio IV Flavia Felix: CIL* III, 1201; 14468; *AE* 1997, 1294. *Legio IV Scythica: CIL* III, 1044; 1178. *Legio V Macedonica: AE* 1980, 735; *CIL* III, 987; 1077; 1094. *Legio VII Claudia: CIL* III, 1180–2. *Legio XI Claudia: CIL* III, 971. **Legio XIII Gemina:** *AE* 1894, 4; 6; 1903, 62; 1910, 84; 1912, 71a; 1934, 113–16; 1944, 28; 1947, 23; 1956, 204; 1960, 244; 1962, 209a–b; 1965, +35; 38a; 1967, 385; 1972, 461; 1972, 462; 1978, 664; 1980, 738; 740–1; 743; 752; 1983, 801; 814; 1993, 1334–5; 1994, 1491a; 1494a; 1495a; 1997, 1209a3; 1290a1–2; 1290a4–5; 1290b1–2; 1290c–d; 1291; 1998, 1075a–d; 1082; 2000, 1248; 2007, 1197; 1199; 2004, 1203; *CIL* III, 981; 989–90; 993; 995; 1000; 1011–13; 1017; 1019–20; 1032; 1034; 1037–8; 1041–2; 1044–5; 1052; 1056; 1058; 1061–3; 1067; 1070–2; 1074–6; 1078; 1092–3; 1099–1101; 1111; 1118; 1125; 1129; 1142; 1155; 1158; 1163; 1169; 1171–2; 1184; 1186; 1188; 1192; 1194; 1199–1200; 1202; 1204–5; 1629,1a–c; 1629,2; 1629,5–9; 1629,11a–d; 1629,13; 1629,14a–b; 1629,18; 1629,21; 1629,22b; 1629,24b; 1629,24d; 7741–2; 7753–4; 7769–70; 7792; 8064,1c–d; 8065,6a–c; 7b; 11a–b; 14b–c; 14g; 15a; 15c; 16b; 17d; 19; 22b; 26b; 26d; 26f; 27a–b; 29c; 30a; 30c; 31b–e; 34b–c; 35b; 12608ia; 12608ia; 12610c–d; 12612g; 12613c–d; 12614a–b; 12615e–f; 12616d; 12617k–l; 12618g–h; 12619f; 12620–1; 12622a–b; 12623–6; 12627a–b; 12628–9; 14216,21–3; 14469; 14476–7; *IDR* III.2, 541,3; 5; 8–9; III.3, 36; 195,1a; 2–3; 9a–b; 10; 12; 265,4; III.4, 44; 51,1; 4; 53–4; 189; III.5.1, 3; 180; 192; 221; 236; 282; 290; 406; 408; 413; III.5.2, 508; 511; 540; 560; 579; 591; 617; 619; 622–3; 629; 697; 716; 724; III.6, 1–100; 102–3; 105–9; 111; 113–17; 119; 121–3; 125–33; 139–47; 148a–d; 151a–c; 152; 154; 156; 157–62; 165–6; 168–9; 171–3; 176; 178–82; 184; 186; 188–91; 193a–b; 194–5; 197–204; 204a; 205–11; 213; 215–17; 220–2; 224; 226; 227a; 229–42; 245–9; 251–2; 255; 258–68; 303; 310; 435–44; 455–68. *Legio XIV Gemina: CIL* III, 1158; 1196; 1615. *Legio XVI Flavia Firma: CIL* III, 1044; 1178. *Legio XXII Primigenia: CIL* III, 1481. Unspecified legion: *AE* 2007, 1197; *CIL* III, 1015; 1189; 1191; 6265; 7784; *IDR* III.5.2, 626; 717; 723. *Ala Batavorum: AE* 1987, 829; *CIL* III, 7800. *Ala Bosporanorum: CIL* III, 1197. *Ala Campagonum milliaria: CIL* III, 1193. *Ala Illyricorum: AE* 1987, 829; 1988, 947. *Cohors I Alpinorum equitata: CIL* III, 1183. *Cohors I Britannica: CIL* III, 1193; *IDR* III.5.2, 484. *Cohors I Cretum equitata: CIL* III, 1163. *Cohors VII Gallorum: CIL* III, 1193. *Cohors II Hispanorum: IDR* I, 26. *Cohors IV Pannoniorum: AE* 1894, 7. *Cohors IV Praetoria: CIL* III, 12631. *Cohors I sagittariorum Tibiscensium: IDR* III.5.1, 371. *Numerus Germanicianorum exploratorum: AE* 1972, 487. *Numerus Maurorum (Hispanorum): AE* 1978, 662; *CIL* III, 1149. *Numerus Palmyrenorum Tibiscensium: IDR* III.5.2, 559. *Numerus singularium: AE* 1891, 77a; 1962, 209c; *CIL* III, 7800; 12633a–b; 12644; *IDR* III.6, 305. *Numerus singularium Britannicorum: CIL* III, 1633,14. *Equites singulares: AE* 1962, 208; *CIL* III, 7787; 7799; 12633h. *Pedites singulares consularis: AE* 1891, 77b–d; 1903, 63; *CIL* III, 1160; 1195; 12633c–g; *IDR* III.6, 275–7; 279–81; 283–4.] *singulares: IDR* III.6, 285–6. *Veteranus: AE* 1930, 5; *CIL* III, 1203; 7736; 14481; *IDR* III.5.1, 91; 384; III.5.2, 491. Unspecified cavalry unit: *CIL* III, 7801. Unspecified infantry unit: *AE* 1944, 37b; 1995, 1290; *CIL* III, 1187; 14478. Unspecified unit: *AE* 1983, 800; 804b; *CIL* III, 1098a–b; 1138; 1173; 1179; *IDR* III.5.2, 503; 628
Sub-literary references: –

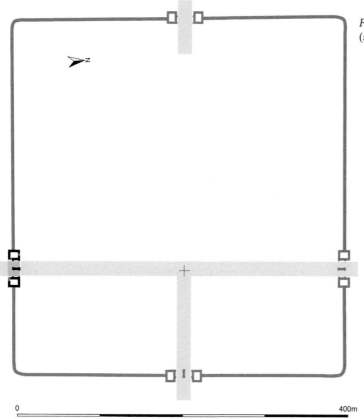

Figure 23: Alba Iulia–Apulum (after Moga 1999a).

Modern references (site): Anghel 1999; Gudea 1979, 70; Hanson and Oltean 2003; Moga 1994; 1997; 1999a; 1999b; 2002; Opreanu 1998; 1999

Modern references (finds): Băluță 1995; 1997; 2000; Ciugudean and Ciugudean 2000; Coulston 1995

Notes: Urban site, largely destroyed by later Austro-Hungarian fort. Earlier fortress of *I Adiutrix* may be on a separate site to the south (cf. Opreanu 1998; 1999)

Albano Laziale–Castra Albana (Figures 2,106; 24; Plates 11; 17; 31)

Location: 41° 43′ 46.94″ N, 12° 39′ 39.37″ E
Situation: On shore above Lago Albano
Height ASL: 404m (GE)
Country: Italy
Region: Provincia di Roma
Province: Italia
Length: 450m
Width: 240m
Area: 10.8ha
Proportion: 1.875
Cardinal orientation: 235°

Figure 24: Albano Laziale–Castra Albana (after Chiarucci 1988).

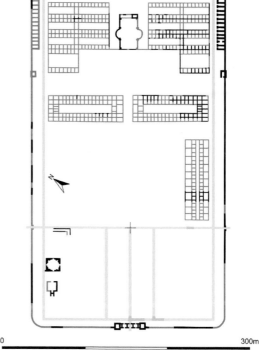

0   300m

Phases & Dating: Stone *Legio II Parthica* (AD 197–214) ... *Legio II Parthica* (AD 219–30) ... *Legio II Parthica* (AD 234–41) ... *Legio II Parthica* (AD 245–Tetrarchic)

Literary references: Cass. Dio 55.24.4

Units attested epigraphically: *Legio II Parthica: AE* 1913, 219; 1919, 72–4; 1955, 26–7; 1968, 90; 92–3; 96; 105; 1975, 153; 162–3; 166–7; 170–1; 174; 1993, 422; *CIL* VI, 793; 32878; 37261; 37263; XIV, 2269; 2273–4; 2276; 2278–81; 2283; 2285; 2289–91; 2293–4; 2296–7; 4213; *EE* IX, 975,1. Unspecified legion: *CIL* XIV, 2255; 2268; 2272; 2282. *Cohors II Praetoria: CIL* XIV, 4214. *Cohors III Praetoria: AE* 1975, 159. *Equites singulares Augusti: CIL* XIV, 2286. *Corpus veteranorum: AE* 1913, 222. Unspecified unit: *AE* 1968, 91; 95; 104; 106–7; 1975, 176; *CIL* VI, 37264; XIV, 2254; 2277; 2303?; 2348; 4215–16. *Veteranus: AE* 1975, 152; *CIL* XIV, 2270; 2284; 2292; 4217. *Evocatus: CIL* XIV, 2288

Sub-literary references: –

Modern references (site): Benario 1972; Chiarucci 1988; 1999, 68–116; Coarelli 1981; Lugli 1969; Nibby 1848; Ricci 2000, 397–406; Ricci 1787; Terenzio et al. 1972; Tortorici 1975

Modern references (finds): –

Notes: Urban site

Albing (Figures 2,29; 25)

Location: 48° 13′ 34.46″ N, 14° 32′ 59.91′ E

Situation: Confluence of the Danube and Enns (right bank)

Height ASL: 240m (GE)

Country: Austria

Region: Amstetten, Niederösterreich

Province: Noricum
Length: 568m
Width: 412m
Area: 23.3ha
Proportion: 1.379
Cardinal orientation: 50°
Phases & Dating: Stone – *Legio II Italica* (AD 173–204)
Literary references: –
Units attested epigraphically: –
Sub-literary references: –
Modern references (site): Groller 1907; Ruprechtsberger 1985; 1986b; 1996; Vetters 1989; Winkler 1971; 2003
Modern references (finds): –
Notes: Partly open site.

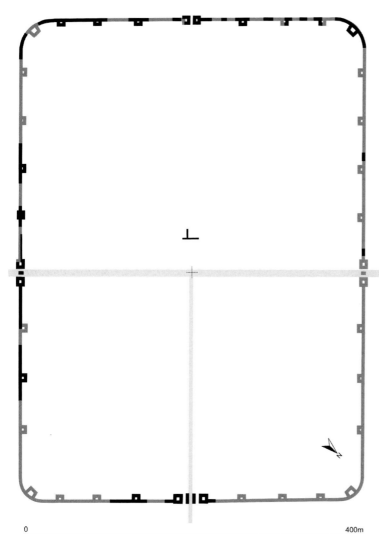

0   400m

Figure 25: Albing (after Vetters 1989).

Alexandria–Nicopolis (Figures 2,94; 70)

Location: 31° 13′ 45.57″ N, 29° 56′ 39.95″ E
Situation: On the shore of the Mediterranean, between Lake Mareotis and Lake Aboukir
Height ASL: 9m (GE)
Country: Egypt
Region: Alexandria Governorate
Province: Aegyptus
Length: –
Width: –
Area: –
Proportion: –
Cardinal orientation: –
Phases & Dating: ? – *Legiones III Cyrenaica + XXII Deiotariana* (AD 10–117); *Legiones III Cyrenaica + XXII Deiotariana* (AD 117–24); *Legiones XXII Deiotariana + II Traiana Fortis* (AD 125–36); *Legio II Traiana Fortis* (AD 137–?Tetrarchic)
Literary references: Joseph., *BJ* 2.494
Units attested epigraphically: *Legio II Traiana Fortis*: *AE* 1902, 219; 1980, 895; *CIL* III, 13; 6580; 6592–3; 6594a; 6595–6; 6604–5; 6609; 6611; 6613; 12048; 12052; 12054–7; 12058a; 13574; 14137; 14138,2; 14138,4; 14140–1; *IGLAlexa* 486; *Kayser* 113. *Legio III*: *CIL* III, 6591. *Legio III Augusta*: *CIL* III, 12057. *Legio III Cyrenaica*: *AE* 1986, 701; *CIL* III, 6599; 6602–3; 6607; 14138,3; 14138,5; *IGLAlexa* 501. *Legio III Gallica*: *CIL* III, 12053. *Legio VI Victrix*: *CIL* III, 12053. *Legio XXII Deiotariana*: *CIL* III, 6023; 6023a; 6598; 6600; 6602; 12059. Unspecified legion: *CIL* III, 6577; 6597; 12061; *IGLAlexa* 500. *Ala I Singularium*: *CIL* III, 12053. *Ala I Thracum Mauretana*: *CIL* III, 14; 14139. *Ala Veterana Gallica*: *CIL* III, 14–15. *Cohors I Breucorum*: *CIL* III, 12053. *Cohors V Gallica*: *CIL* III, 12053. *Cohors I Hispanorum*: *CIL* III, 6590. *Cohors Scutata*: *CIL* III, 6610. *Cohors II Varcianorum*: *CIL* III, 12053. Unspecified infantry unit: *CIL* III, 6576; 6594; 12064. Unspecified unit: *CIL* III, 6612; 12058; 12060; *IGLAlexa* 488; 493; 568
Sub-literary references: *P. Fouad* I,45
Modern references (site): Alston 1995, 192–3; Murray 1880, 141
Modern references (finds): –
Notes: Part of late fortress recorded during British attack on Aboukir Bay (see Gazetteer B, below). Earlier fortress not located. Urban site

Anreppen (Figures 2,16; 26)

Location: 51° 44′ 17.06″ N, 8° 35′ 31.49″ E
Situation: Adjacent to Lippe
Height ASL: 89m (GE)
Country: Germany
Region: Delbrück, Kr. Paderborn
Province: Germania Magna
Length: >723m
Width: 324m
Area: >23.4ha
Proportion: >2.231
Cardinal orientation: 59°
Phases & Dating: Timber – ? *c.*AD 4–9
Literary references: –
Units attested epigraphically: –

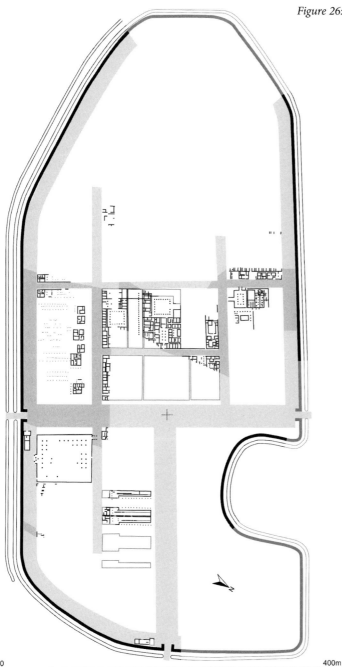

Figure 26: Anreppen (after Kühlborn 2000).

0   400m

Sub-literary references: –
Modern references (site): Doms 1970; Glüsing 2000; Kühlborn 1991; 1995; 2005; 2006; 2007; Schnurbein 2002; 1981, 29–32; Wells 1972, 222
Modern references (finds): Ilisch 1999
Notes: Open site

Archar–Ratiaria (Figure 2,54)
Location: 43° 48′ 55.35″ N, 22° 55′ 48.36″ E
Situation: Confluence of Danube and Archar
Height ASL: 31m (GE)
Country: Bulgaria
Region: Vidin Province
Province: Moesia Superior
Length: –
Width: –
Area: –
Proportion: –
Cardinal orientation: –
Phases & Dating: ? – *Legio IV Flavia Felix* (AD 86–101) … *Legio XIII Gemina* (AD 272–Tetrarchic)
Literary references: *ND Or.* 42.29
Units attested epigraphically: *Legio IV Flavia Felix: AE 1984, 742a. Legio V Macedonica: AE 1902, 129,1; 1984, 00742b2–4; CIL III, 14597,1. Legio VII Claudia: AE 1938, 103; 108; 2005, 1312a; CIL III, 6297; 12649. Legio XIV Gemina: AE 1938, 96; 1984, 742d2–3; 74db; 2005, 1312b; CIL III, 14597,4. Unspecified legion: CIL III, 6292–3. Ala milliaria?: AE 1984, 742e. Cohors I Cretum: AE 1984, 742f. Unspecified unit: AE 1979, 539.*
Sub-literary references: –
Modern references (site): Atanassova-Georgieva 1986; Georgetti 1983; Wilkes 2000, 116
Modern references (finds): –
Notes: Open site

Astorga–Asturica (Figure 2,101)
Location: 42° 27′ 17.54″ N, 6° 3′ 18.68″ W
Situation: Adjacent to the Río Tuerto
Height ASL: 870m
Country: Spain
Region: Province of León
Province: Hispania Tarraconensis
Length: –
Width: –
Area: –
Proportion: –
Cardinal orientation: –
Phases & Dating: Timber – *Legio X Gemina* (15/10 BC–AD 15/20)
Literary references: –
Units attested epigraphically: *Legio I Italica: CIL II, 2638. Legio II Adiutrix: CIL II, 2639. Legio IV Macedonica: AE 1960, 210. Legio VI Victrix: CIL II, 2637. Legio VII Gemina: CIL II, 2634; 2640–1; ERPLeon 173. **Legio X Gemina: CIL II, 5076; ERPLeon 144; 210; 216; 244; Hep VIII, 320a–b.** Ala Flavia: ERPLeon 152. Ala Flavia Lusitanorum: ERPLeon 19. Ala Sulpicia: CIL II, 2637. Cohors VI Asturum: CIL II, 2637. Cohors Thracum: ERPLeon 171*
Sub-literary references: –
Modern references (site): Morillo 2003, 86–90; Morillo and Ángeles Sevillano 2006
Modern references (finds): Finds: –
Notes: Urban site

Bad Deutsch-Altenburg–Carnuntum *(Figures 2,33; 27; Plate 30)*

Location: 48° 7′ 26.80″ N, 16° 53′ 20.15″ E
Situation: Confluence of the Danube and Sulzbach
Height ASL: 178m (GE)
Country: Austria
Region: Bruck an der Leitha, Niederösterreich
Province: Pannonia Superior
Length: *c.*505m
Width: 403m (max)
Area: c.19.4ha
Proportion: 1.253
Cardinal orientation: 324°
Phases & Dating: Timber – *Legio XV Apollinaris* (AD 14–61); *Legio X Gemina* (AD 62–8); *Legio VII Claudia* (AD 69–70); *Legio XV Apollinaris* (AD 71–114); Stone – *Legio XIV Gemina* (AD 114–?)
Literary references: Itin. Ant. 247.4; 262.8; Pliny, HN 4.80; Ptol., Geog. 2.14.3; Tab. Peut. 4.2; Vell. Pat. 2.109.5–110.2

0   400m

Figure 27: Bad Deutsch-Altenburg–Carnuntum (after Kandler 1986).

Units attested epigraphically: *Legio I: CIL* III, 12035,2. *Legio I Adiutrix: AE* 1992, 1402; 2002, 1167a; 1167b; *AEA* 1980/81, +13; 1999/00, 165; 2006, 29; *CIL* III, 4655g-h; 11221–2; 11240; 11345g-i; *Lupa* 1763. *Legio I Minervia: CIL* III, 11242b. *Legio I Vic[: CIL* III, 11367. *Legio II Italica: CIL* III, 4656; 11350a-d. *?Legio XI Claudia: CIL* III, 13500a. **Legio X Gemina: AE 1929, 193; 1997, 1252; AEA 1993/98, 133; 278; CIL III, 4659,1g-i; 4659,1k-n; 4659,2a; 4661,6a; 4661,8a; 11182; 11244; 11245a-b; 11350e; 11352g-i; 11352k-n; 11353a.** *Legio XI Claudia: CIL* III, 11239. *Legio XIII Gemina: AE* 1992, 1431. **Legio XIV Gemina: AE 1898, 32; 1905, 238; 242–3; 1907, 176; 1938, 87; 1974, 498; 1995, 1265; 1997, 1254a; 1254b; 1254c; AEA 1980/81, 29; 1982, 22; 1983/92, 206; 209; 1993/98, 272c; 277a-b; 301; 2005, 102; CIL III, 4661,1b; 11108; 11118; 11121; 11126; 11135; 11137–8; 11142; 11148; 11152; 11172; 11189–90; 11204b; 11209; 11217; 11223; 11232; 11234–7; 11243; 11245c; 11246–8; 11249a; 11362a; 14071; 14074; 14076; 15191; Lupa 4924; MaCarnuntum 126. Legio XV Apollinaris: AE 1907, 177; 1978, 622; 1992, 1402–4; 2002, 1156; AEA 1993/98, 275; 1999/00, 165; 2003, 44; CIL III, 4662a-c; 11123; 11194; 11210; 11213–15; 11218–20; 11224–5; 11228–9; 11231; 11238; 11250; 11368–9; 13479–81; 13483–6; 15193.** *Legio XXX Ulpia Victrix: CIL* III, 11370d-f. Unspecified legion: *AEA* 2005, 105b; *CIL* III, 11211; 11216; 11226; 11242a. *Equites singulares: CIL* III, 11212. *Ala Frontoniana: RHP* 213. *Ala Pannoniorum: AEA* 1993/98, 274. *Ala I Surorum: AE* 1992, 1431. *Ala I Tampiana: AEA* 1982, 23. *Ala I Thracum: RHP* 173. *Cohors V Breucorum: RHP* 268. *Cohors I Canathenorum: AE* 2005, 1237. *Cohors II Mattiacorum: AE* 1992, 1431. *Cohors VII Praetoria: AE* 1953, 00126. *Cohors I Ulpia Pannoniorum: CIL* III, 11227. *Cohors XVIII Voluntariorum: AE* 1905, 240; *RHP* 477a-b. Unspecified infantry unit: *AEA* 2004, +10; *CIL* III, 11107; 11111–12; 11114; 11233; 11252; *MaCarnuntum* 278. Unspecified unit: *CIL* III, 11144; 11180; 11206c; 11207; 11241. *Veteranus: MaCarnuntum* 274

Sub-literary references: –

Modern references (site): Domaszewski et al. 1886; 1887; Groller 1900; 1901; 1902; 1903; 1904; 1905; 1906a; 1908b; 1909a; Gugl and Kastler 2007; Hauser 1884; Hauser et al. 1888; Hirschfeld 1877; 1878; Jilek 1994; Jobst 1983; Kandler 1974; 1976; 1977; 1980; 1986; 1997; 1999; 2006; Mócsy 1962; Nowotny 1914; Pascher 1949; Stiglitz 1997; Swoboda-Milenovic 1956; 1957; Tragau 1897; Vetters 1963; 1969

Modern references (finds): Alram-Stern 1989; Beszédes and Mosser 2002; Göbl 1987; Grünewald 1981; 1983; 1986; Jilek 1991; 2005; Krüger 1967; 1970; 1972; Vorbeck 1954; 1980a; 1980b

Notes: Open site

Balad Sinjar–Singara (Figures 2,77; 28)

Location: 36° 19′ 43.13″ N, 41° 51′ 22.64″ E

Situation: In city, adjacent to wadis

Height ASL: 544m (GE)

Country: Iraq

Region: Ninawa Governorate

Province: Mesopotamia

Length: >600m

Width: 340m

Area: 15.0ha

Proportion: –

Cardinal orientation: –

Phases & Dating: Stone – *Legio I Parthica* (AD 197–360)

Literary references: Amm. Marc. 19.9.9; 20.6.8–9; 25.7.9; Cass. Dio 55.24.4; 68.22.2; Ptol., *Geog.* 5.18.2; 5.18.9

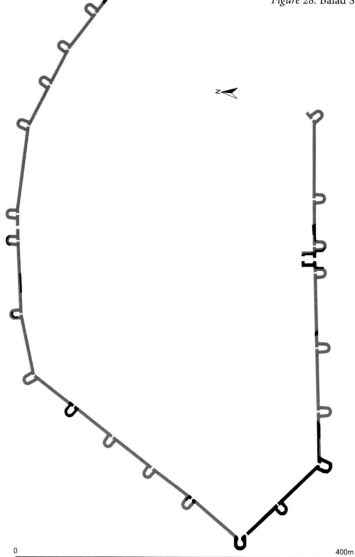

Figure 28: Balad Sinjar–Singara (after Oates 1968).

Units attested epigraphically: Speidel and Reynolds 1985
Sub-literary references: –
Modern references (site): Gregory 1995–97, vol. 2, 104–8; Gregory and Kennedy 1985, 385–91;
   Kennedy and Riley 1990, 125–31; Oates 1956; 1968, 97–106; Parker 2000, 126–7
Modern references (finds): Speidel and Reynolds 1985
Notes: A fortified city, rather than a fortress. Partly open, partly urban site

Barin–Raphanaea (Figure 2,79)
Location: 34° 56′ 28.22″ N, 36° 23′ 51.09″ E
Situation: On a plain near springs at Naba at-Tannur and Ayn Bini
Height ASL: 416m (GE)

Country: Syria
Region: Hama Governorate
Province: Syria
Length: –
Width: –
Area: –
Proportion: –
Cardinal orientation: –
Phases & Dating: ? – *Legio XII Fulminata* (AD 10–70); *Legio III Gallica* (AD 70–219)
Literary references: Joseph., *BJ* 7.18; Ptol., *Geog.* 5.14.12; Hdn. 5.3.9
Units attested epigraphically: *Legio III Gallica: AE* **1951, 148; 2007, 1610.** *Legio VI Ferrata: CIL*
III, 14165,13
Sub-literary references: –
Modern references (site): Gschwind 2006; 2007; 2008a; 2008b; Gschwind and Hasan 2008; in
press; Gschwind et al. 2009; in press; Mouterde 1949/50
Modern references (finds): –
Notes: Raphaneae in Ptolemy, Raphanaia in Josephus. Open site

Belkis–Zeugma (Figure 2,72)
Location: 37° 2′ 2.97″ N, 37° 52′ 3.82″ E
Situation: On right bank of Euphrates
Height ASL: 473m (GE)
Country: Turkey
Region: Gaziantep Province
Province: Syria
Length: –
Width: –
Area: –
Proportion: –
Cardinal orientation: –
Phases & Dating: ? – *Legio IV Scythica* (AD 66–256)
Literary references: –
Units attested epigraphically: *Legio I Adiutrix: AE* 2003, 1791b. *Legio II Adiutrix: AE* 2003,
1791c; *Speidel. Legio III Augusta: AE* 2003, 1791d. *Legio IV Flavia: AE* 2003, 1791g. *Legio IV*
Scythica: AE **1908, 25; 2003, 1785; 1791a.** *Legio VII Claudia: AE* 2003, 1789; 1791e. *Legio XIV*
Gemina: AE 2003, 1791f. *Cohors milliaria Maurorum: AE* 2003, 1790
Sub-literary references: –
Modern references (site): Gregory 1995–97, vol. 2, 129–31; Hartmann and Speidel 2001; 2002;
2003; forthcoming a; forthcoming b; Hartmann et al. 1999; 2000; 2001; Speidel 1998; 2000;
2001
Modern references (finds): Kennedy 1998b
Notes: Site uncertain. Originally thought to have been submerged, but may actually still await
discovery as an open site (cf. Hartmann and Speidel 2002)

Beograd–Singidunum (Figures 2,45; 29)
Location: 44° 49′ 19.19″ N, 20° 27′ 07.54″ E
Situation: Confluence of Danube and Sava
Height ASL: 111m (GE)
Country: Serbia

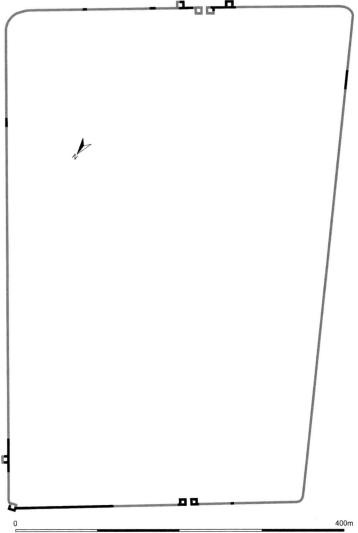

Figure 29: Beograd–Singidunum (after Bojović 1996).

Region: City of Beograd
Province: Moesia Superior
Length: 565m
Width: 415m (max.)
Area: 20.1ha
Proportion: 1.371
Cardinal orientation: 140°/320°
Phases & Dating: Stone – *Legio IV Flavia Felix* (AD 120–4th century)
Literary references: –
Units attested epigraphically: *Legio II Adiutrix: IMS* I, 25. **Legio IV Flavia:** *AE* 1952, 186; 1976, 600; 1978, 701; 1989, 632; 1997, 1302–3; 2001, 1727; *CIL* III, 1663; 1665; 6305; 6326; 8148; 8154; 8156; 8276,1a; 8276,2; 12663; *IMS* I, 4; 6; 16; 28–30; 34; 37–8; 40; 42. Unspecified legion: *ILJug* II, 507. *Cohors Flavia: CIL* III, 6334. *Cohors I Ulpia Pannoniorum: CIL* III, 6302.

Cohors XVIII Voluntariorum: CIL III, 6302. Unspecified infantry unit: *CIL* III, 6336; *IMS* I, 5; 19. Unspecified unit: *CIL* III, 6303; *IMS* I, 43. *Veteranus: IMS* I, 41

Sub-literary references: –

Modern references (site): Bikić 1997; Bojović 1996; Ivanišević and Nikolić-Đorđević 1997; Kondić 1961; Mirković 1961; 1976; Popović 1997; Wilkes 2000

Modern references (finds): Bugarski 2005; Krunić 2005; Mirković 1997; Mirković 2000; 2005a; 2005b; Nikolić-Đorđević 2005

Notes: Urban site

Berzovia–Berzobis (Figures 2,46; 30)

Location: 45° 25′ 40.51″ N, 21° 37′ 23.95″ E
Situation: Confluence of Bârzava and two streams (to E and W)
Height ASL: 136m (GE)
Country: Romania
Region: Caraş-Severin County
Province: Dacia
Length: 475m
Width: 400m

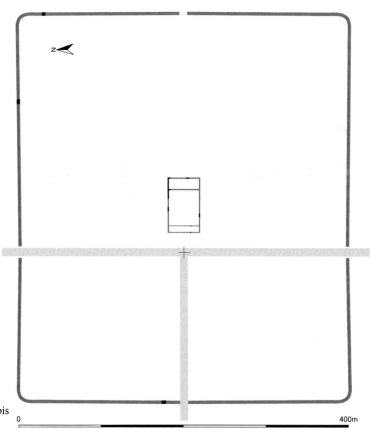

Figure 30: Berzovia–Berzobis
(after Protase 2010).

Area: 19.1ha
Proportion: 1.188
Cardinal orientation: 248°
Phases & Dating: Timber & stone – *Legio IV Flavia Felix* (AD 102–19)
Literary references: Prisc., *Inst.* 2.205.6
Units attested epigraphically: *Legio IV Flavia Felix*: AE 1912, 77; *IDR* 3.1, 113a-g. *Legio V Macedonica: AE* 1912, 73b. *Cohors Hispanorum: AE* 1967, 404. *Cohors XV Voluntariorum: ILD* 178.
Sub-literary references: –
Modern references (site): Flutur 1999–2000; 2001a; 2006; Moga 1971; Medeleţ and Petrovszky 1974; Protase 2010
Modern references (finds): Flutur 2001b; 2002–2003; Németh 1998; Protase and Petculescu 1975; Septilici and Truican 2006
Notes: Urban site

Bonn–Bonna (Figures 2,19; 31)

Location: 50° 44′ 40.30″ N, 7° 06′ 02.65″ E
Situation: Confluence of Rhine and Alte Bach
Height ASL: 63m (GE)
Country: Germany
Region: Nordrhein-Westfalen
Province: Germania Inferior
Length: 524m
Width: 528m
Area: 27.8ha
Proportion: 0.992
Cardinal orientation: 77°
Phases & Dating: Timber – *Legio I Germanica* (AD 35–69); *Legio XXI Rapax* (AD 70–82); Stone – *Legio I Minervia* (AD 82–?359)
Literary references: Ptol., *Geog.* 2.9.8; Tac., *Hist.* 4.19–20; 25; 62; 70; 77; 5.22
Units attested epigraphically: *Legio I Flavia: CIL* 13, 8062a; *Lehner* 1183. **Legio I Minervia: AE 1901, 70; 1931, 11; 1932, 12; 1935, 235; 1938, 75; 1939, +235; 1977, 576; 2004, 964; CIL XIII, 8006; 8009–10; 8014–15; 8017; 8019; 8021; 8035; 8038–41; 8050; 8053–60; 8062; 8064–78; 8086–7; 12042–3; IRheinland I, 4; II, 1; Nesselhauf 151–6; 160; 182; 186–7; 198; 200; 205–6; 213–14; Schillinger 161; 170.** *Legio III Parthica: CIL XIII,* 8065. *Legio VIII Augusta: AE* 1939, +235; *Nesselhauf* 155. *Legio XV Primigenia: AE* 1952, 17; *CIL* XIII, 8079–80. **Legio XXI Rapax: AE 1945, 9; 1977, 577–8; CIL XIII, 8032; 8081.** *Legio XXII Primigenia: AE* 1960, 160; *CIL* XIII, 8082. *Legio XXX: CIL* XIII, 8053; 8078; 8082a. *Unspecified legion: CIL* XIII, 8011; 8016; 8033; 8083–5; 8088; 8090. *Ala Frontoniana: AE* 1963, 49; *Schillinger* 162. *Ala Longiniana: CIL* XIII, 8092–6. *Ala Pomponiana: CIL* XIII, 8097. *Cohors V Asturum: CIL* XIII, 8098. *Cohors Silaucensium: GraffBonn* 155. *Cohors Thracum: CIL* XIII, 8099. *Veteranus: CIL* XIII, 8037. Unspecified infantry unit: *CIL* XIII, 8100; *GraffBonn* 140; *Schillinger* 158. Unspecified unit: *AE* 1977, 579; *CIL* XIII, 8091; 8101; *Nesselhauf* 184; 201
Sub-literary references: –
Modern references (site): Gechter 1979b; 1980; 1984; 1985; 1986; 1987; 1989a; 1989b; 2001; 2005; 2007b; Gechter and Wentscher 1989; Grewe 2001; 2002; Schaffhausen et al. 1888; Sölter 1977
Modern references (finds): Bemmann 1984; Driel-Murray and Gechter 1984
Notes: Urban site.

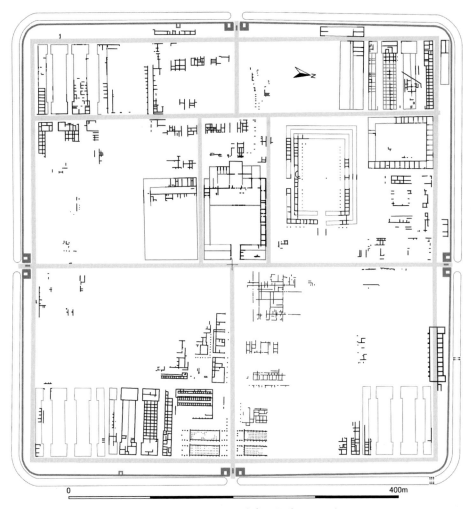

Figure 31: Bonn–Bonna (after Gechter 1986).

Bosra–Bostra (Figures 2,85; 32)

Location: 32° 31' 28.51" N, 36° 28' 59.67" E
Situation: South of wadi
Height ASL: 841m (GE)
Country: Syria
Region: Governorate of Daraa
Province: Arabia
Length: 430m
Width: 349m
Area: 15.1ha
Proportion: 1.232
Cardinal orientation: 270°/90°
Phases & Dating: Stone – *Legio III Cyrenaica* (AD 106–18); *Legio VI Ferrata* (AD 118–25); *Legio III Cyrenaica* (AD 125–4th century)

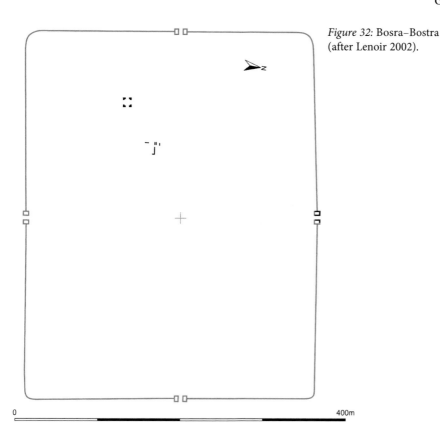

Figure 32: Bosra–Bostra
(after Lenoir 2002).

0   400m

Literary references: Ptol., *Geog.* 1.5.17

Units attested epigraphically: *Legio I Minervia*: IGLS XIII.1, 9187. *Legio I Parthica*: CIL III, 99.
Legio II Italica: IGLS XIII.1, 9187. **Legio III Cyrenaica:** *AE* **1900, 161; 1904, 69; 1973, 553;**
1987, 970; 1996, 1595; 2000, 1528–31; 2003, 1817; *CIL* **III, 89; 92; 94–7; 100–4; 14149,4;**
IGLS **XIII.1, 9033; 9035; 9050–1; 9070; 9073; 9085–7; 9095–6; 9098; 9170; 9175–6; 9178;**
9180–1; 9186–8; 9191; 9198; 9203–4; 9449–51; 9453. *Legio VI Ferrata*: IGLS XIII.1, 9179.
Legio XXII Primigenia: *AE* 1920, 73; IGLS XIII.1, 9081. Unknown legion: *IGLS* XIII.1, 9010;
9075; 9196; 9468. *Equites singulares*: CIL III, 93. *Ala Nova Firma*: CIL III, 99. *Numerus*
Maurorum Illyricianorum Constantium: IGLS XIII.1, 9174. Unknown cavalry unit: CIL III, 90;
IGLS XIII.1, 9173. Unknown infantry unit: *IGLS* XIII.1, 9185; 9193. Unknown unit: CIL III, 91;
IGLS XIII.1, 9169?; 9455

Sub-literary references: *P. Mich.* 8.466

Modern references (site): Dentzer et al. 2002; Kermorvant et al. 2000; Lenoir 1998; Leblanc and
Lenoir 1999; Lenoir 2002; Al-Mougdad et al. 1990

Modern references (finds): –

Notes: Open site

Budapest–Aquincum (Figures 2,37; 33; Plate 16)

Location: 47° 32′ 33.60″ N, 19° 2′ 26.93″ E

Situation: Adjacent to Danube

Height ASL: 108m (GE)

Country: Hungary

Region: Budapest
Province: Pannonia Inferior
Length: 526m
Width: 473m
Area: 25.0ha
Proportion: 1.112
Cardinal orientation: 104°
Phases & Dating: Timber & stone – *Legio II Adiutrix* (AD 89–?Tetrarchic)
Literary references: Ptol., *Geog.* 2.14; *It. Ant.* 245.7; 263.9
Units attested epigraphically: *Legio I Adiutrix: AE* 1962, 113; 1967, 366; *CIL* III, 3550; 3557; 4655o-r; 13372; 14341,5; *Lupa* 2880; *TitAq* I, 305. **Legio II Adiutrix: AE 1910, 127; 1933, 120; 1936, 163; 1937, 180; 183; 1948, 86; 1953, 8a; 12; 1955, 11; 1962, 114; 1965, 43–5; 47–8; 119; 46; 1969/70, 482; 1972, 375; 380a-b; 382–3; 1976, 546a; 546c; 550; 1979, 472; 1990, 812–14; 817–19; 1998, 1058; 2000, 1857; 2001, 1691; 2002, 1207; 2003, 1455; 2004, 1141; 2005, 1254–6; CIL III, 3412; 3420; 3426–7; 3433–5; 3445; 3453; 3455; 3457–8; 3460; 3462; 3464; 3466; 3469–70; 3472; 3478; 3481; 3484; 3489; 3501; 3505; 3508; 3511; 3515; 3520–1; 3525–30; 3532–4; 3538; 3540–1; 3543–4; 3548; 3553–4; 3556; 3558–61; 3563; 3565–7; 3568–9; 3571–3; 3575; 3707–8; 3750bb; 3750g-i; 3750k-x; 6456–7; 10394–5; 10403; 10406; 10411; 10419–20; 10423; 10425; 10428–9; 10435; 10501; 10660k-w; 10716; 13369–71; 13373; 13375; 14341,3; 14342; 14342,1; 14347,3; 14349; 14349,2; 14349,4; 14349,6; 14349,9; 14350; 14354,4–6; 15157; 15159–61; 15165; Lupa 2832; 2837; 2928; 2943–4; 2961; 3141; 4982; 5042; 5094; 5098; 5101; 6142; 9732; 10148; 10691–2; 10779; StudEpPann p. 169; TitAq I, 3; 40; 77; 79; 94–5; 108; 115–16; 118; 120–1; 132; 198; 336; 354; 372–3; 377; 379; 385; 387; 389; 396; 408; 410–11; 413; 421; 425; 435; 445; 452.** *Legio III Augusta: CIL* III, 10419. *Legio III Gallica: CIL* III, 14349,3. *Legio IV Flavia Felix: AE* 1962, 112; 1976, 545; 2005, 1262; *CIL* III, 3463; 3468; 3537; 3555; 3578; 3753; 10663a-b; *Lupa* 9766; *TitAq* I, 37; 333; 361. *Legio VI Herculia: CIL* III, 10665k. *Legio VII Claudia: TitAq* I, 213. *Legio X Fretensis: Lupa* 2894. **Legio X Gemina: AE 1965, 121; CIL III, 3550; 4659,1x; 15162; Lupa 2893.** *Legio XI Claudia: CIL* III, 4658a; 4658c. *Legio XII Fulminata: CIL* III, 14349,3. *Legio XIII Gemina: CIL* III, 3513; 6020, 1–2. *Legio XIV Gemina: CIL* III, 3547. *Legio XXII Primigenia: CIL* III, 14347,5. Unknown legion: *AE* 1937, 185; 1969/70, 490; 1975, 688; 1990, 820; *CIL* III, 3473; 3536; 3539; 10437; 14349,5; *Lupa* 2962; *TitAq* I, 370; 409; 456. *Ala Auriana I: CIL* III, 14349,8; *RHP* 138. *Ala Brittonum: AE* 2005, 1263; *Lupa* 3032. *Ala Frontoniana: AE* 1938, 125. *Ala I Hispanorum: AE* 1937, 216; *CIL* III, 15163. *Ala I Ituraeorum: CIL* III, 3446. *Ala I Thracum: CIL* III, 3465; *Lupa* 5085; *RHP* 185. *Ala I Tungrorum Frontoniana: RHP* 209; 215. *Cohors I B[: CIL* III, 3476. *Cohors Batavorum: RHP* 491. *Cohors VII Breucorum: AE* 1955, 14; 1972, 374; *CIL* III, 3757h-i; 3757k-n; 6472; 10668h-i; 10668k-m. *Cohors Maurorum equitata milliaria: CIL* III, 3444; 3545; 10673c-d. *Cohors X Maurorum: CIL* III, 3542. *Cohors Nova Surorum: RHP* 451. *Cohors Numidarum: RHP* 404. *Cohors I Thracum: RHP* 454. *Cohors I Ulpia Pannoniorum: CIL* III, 3756a-e. *Cohors I Vindelicorum: CIL* III, 3562. Unknown cavalry unit: *CIL* III, 3574; *TitAq* I, 402. Unknown infantry unit: *AE* 2007, 1177; *CIL* III, 3502; 3576; 3758a-i; 10401–2; *Lupa* 2868; *TitAq* I, 63; 399. Unknown unit: *CIL* III, 3413; 3422; 3549; 6461–2; 14347,1; 14347,4; *Lupa* 2836; 5102; 9882; 10147; *AE* 1937, 181; 1955, 10; *TitAq* I, 383. Veteranus: *CIL* III, 3669; 14348; *TitAq* I, 205.
Sub-literary references: –
Modern references (site): Ertel 1999; Horváth 1985; Kaba 1986; 1991; Kaba and Szentpétery 1987; Kerdő 1990; Kocsis 1990; 1991; 2001; Madarassy 1999; Nagy 1977; Németh 1976; 1986; 1990; 1991; 1993; 1994; 2005; Németh and Kerdő 1986; Pető 1976; Póczy 1976a; 1976b; 1983; 1984; 1986; Póczy et al. 1986; Polenz 1986; Szirmai 1976; 1980; 1984a; 1985; 1986; 1990; 1991a; 1991b; 1991c; 1997; Wellner 1973; 1980

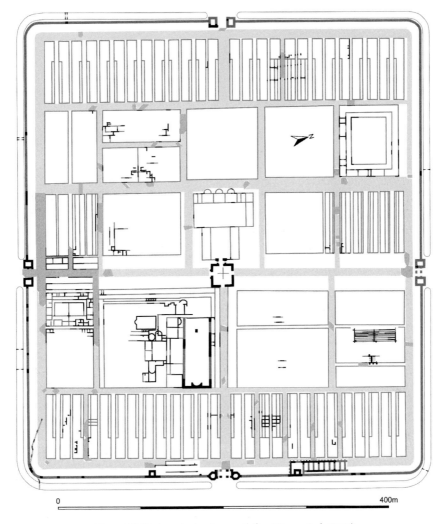

Figure 33: Budapest–Aquincum (after Póczy et al. 1986).

Modern references (finds): Bezeczky 1992; Kocsis 1986; 1989; Póczy and Zsidi 1992; Szirmai 1984b; 1996

Notes: Urban site. Fortress repositioned twice from initial location (for the late fortress, see below)

Caerleon–Isca (Augusta) (Figures 2,6; 34; Plates 4; 10; 26; 28-9)

Location: 51° 36' 37.14" N, 2° 57' 19.92" W
Situation: Confluence of Usk and Afon Lwyd
Height ASL: 18m (GE)
Country: Great Britain
Region: Newport, Wales
Province: Britannia
Length: 490m
Width: 418m

Figure 34: Caerleon–Isca
(after Boon 1972).

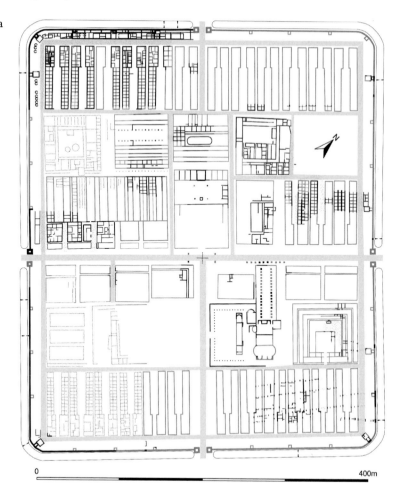

0   400m

Area: 20.5ha
Proportion: 1.172
Cardinal orientation: 132°
Phases & Dating: Timber & stone – *Legio II Augusta* (AD 74–?Tetrarchic)
Literary references: *It. Ant.* **484,4; 484,10; 485,8;** *Rav. Cosm.* **106,24**
Units attested epigraphically: *Legio II Augusta: AE* **1928, 103; 1929, 47a–b; 1960, 201c; 1965,
219b; 1966, 233; 1969/70, 312; 1971, 214; 1975, 550; 1977, 504; 1994, 1095a;** *RIB* **322; 324;
326–7; 330–1; 334; 357; 359–61; 363; 365; 368; 385.** *Legio XX Valeria Victrix: AE* 1975, 551.
Unspecified legion: *AE* 1929, 39–45; 1968, 279; 1971, 213; 1971, 216; 1975, 549; *RIB* 316; 317;
320; 336–43; 345–55; 358; 362; 369; 395; 3086–7; 3088–92. *Ala I Thracum: RIB* 2415.39.
Unknown cavalry: *AE* 1997, 981a; *RIB* 356. Unknown infantry: *AE* 1997, 981c.
Sub-literary references: –
Modern references (site): Boon 1964; 1972; 1978b; 1987; Boon and Williams 1967; Bosanquet
and King 1963; Brewer 2001; Brewer and Gardner forthcoming; Casey and Hoffmann 1995;
Chapman 2002; Evans 1991; 2002; Evans and Maynard 1997; Evans and Metcalf 1992; Fox
1940; Fox 1995; Gardner and Guest 2007; 2009; 2010; Grimes 1935; Guest and Gardner 2008;
Guest and Young 2006; Hawkes 1930; Knight 1964; 2003; Lee 1862; Mason and MacDonald
1987; Moore 1970; Murray Threipland 1965; 1967; Murray Threipland and Davies 1959;

Nash-Williams 1929; 1930; 1931; 1932a; 1933; 1936; 1939; 1953; Wheeler and Nash-Williams 1970; Wheeler and Wheeler 1928; Young 2006; Zienkiewicz 1984a; 1984b; 1986a; 1987a; 1990; 1993

Modern references (finds): Boon 1975; 1984a; 1984b; Chapman 2005; Dickinson and Webster 2002; Driel-Murray 1988; Helbaek 1964; Lewis 1957; Morgan 1866; 1877; Nash-Williams 1932b; 1932c; 1932d; 1951; Rice 1719; Webster 1990; Zienkiewicz 1986b; 1987b

Notes: Partly urban, partly open site

Chester–Deva (Figures 2,3; 35; Plates 3; 5; 13; 22)

Location: 53° 11′ 26.91″ N, 2° 53′ 35.29″ E
Situation: On a bend in the Dee
Height ASL: 31m (GE)
Country: Great Britain

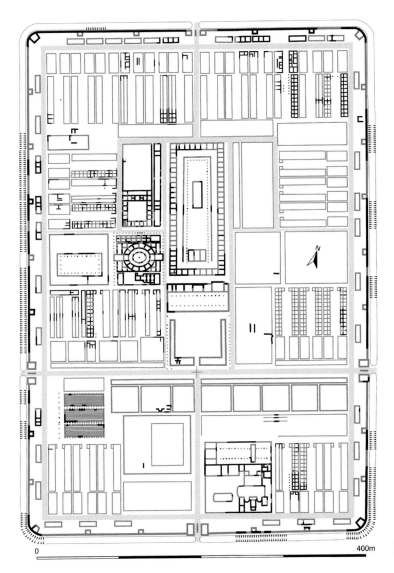

0   400m

Figure 35: Chester–Deva
(after Mason 2001).

Region: Cheshire, England
Province: Britannia
Length: 590m
Width: 410m
Area: 24.3ha
Proportion: 1.439
Cardinal orientation: 163°
Phases & Dating: Timber – *Legio II Adiutrix* (AD 78–88); stone – *Legio XX Valeria Victrix* (AD 89–4th century)
Literary references: *It. Ant.* **469.2; 482.5; 482.8;** Ptol., *Geog.* **2.3.11**
Units attested epigraphically: *Legio II Adiutrix: RIB 475–85. Legio II Augusta: RIB 488; 509. Legio VIII Augusta: RIB 509. Legio XX Valeria Victrix: AE 1892, 97; 1914, 293; 1926, 85; 1937, 109; 1947, 124a-b; 1951, 132a-c; 1952, 91a-b; 1958, 114; 1959, 165; 1964, 200a; 201; 1965, 215; 1978, 446; RIB 449–52; 460; 489–503; 505; 507–13; 515–16. Legio XXII Deiotariana: AE 1965, 215. Cohors I Delmatarum: AE 1958, 102.* Unknown legion: *AE 1977, 507; RIB 467–8; 532; 539; 545.* Unknown cavalry unit: *RIB 557.* Unknown infantry unit: *AE 1967, 253; 1968, 245; 1984, 624; RIB 446; 448; 458; 470–3; 535; 544.* Unknown unit: *RIB 504; 506; 514; 521–3; 525–6; 540; 547. Veteranus: RIB 517; 534*
Sub-literary references: –
Modern references (site): Anon 1981; Baum and Robinson 2002; Carrington 1977; 1985; 1986; 2002a; 2002b; Dunn 2006; Grimes 1930; LeQuesne 1999; McPeake et al. 1998; Mason 1982; 1987; 1988; 1996; 2000; 2001; 2002b; 2005; Matthews 1995; Newstead 1899; Newstead and Droop 1932a; 1932b; 1935; 1940; Petch 1968; 1970–71; Stephens 1986; Strickland 1980; 1982a; 1982b; 1983; 1984; 1993; 1996; Thompson 1959; 1962; 1967a; 1967b; 1967c; 1969; Thompson et al. 1976; Ward 1975; Ward and Strickland 1978; Ward 1988; Webster 1952; 1953; 1955; 1956; Wilmott et al. 2006
Modern references (finds): Jones 2003–4; Lloyd-Morgan 1987; Ward 1998
Notes: Urban site

Colchester-Camulodunum (Figures 2,9; 36)
Location: 51° 53′ 22.91″ N, 0° 53′ 52.55″ E
Situation: Adjacent to Colne
Height ASL: 37m (GE)
Country: Great Britain
Region: Essex, England
Province: Britannia
Length: 515m
Width: 422m
Area: 21.7ha
Proportion: 1.220
Cardinal orientation: 89°
Phases & Dating: Timber/mudbrick – *Legio XX Valeria Victrix* (AD 43–9)
Literary references: Tac., *Ann.* 12.32
Units attested epigraphically: *Legio XX: RIB 200; 203. Ala I Thracum: RIB 201. Cohors I Va[: RIB 205*
Sub-literary references: –
Modern references (site): Brooks 1977; 2004; Carter 1986; Crummy 1974; 1977; 1984; 1988; 1990; 1992; 1993a; 1993b; Dunnett 1967; 1971; Smith 1982

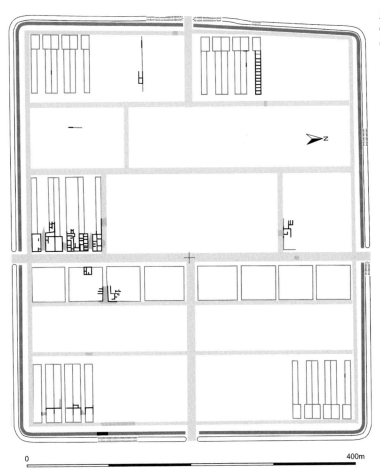

Figure 36: Colchester–Camulodunum (after Crummy 1988).

0 ⊢──────────────────────────────────────┤ 400m

Modern references (finds): Crummy, N.C. 1983; 1987; Crummy, N.C. and Winter 1987; Crummy, P.J. 1987; Phillips 1975

Notes: Urban site

Enns-Lorch–Lauriacum (Figures 2,28; 37)

Location: 48° 13′ 11.11″ N, 14° 28′ 26.09″ E
Situation: Confluence of the Danube and Enns (left bank)
Height ASL: 253m (GE)
Country: Austria
Region: Enns, Oberösterreich
Province: Noricum
Length: 539m
Width: 398m
Area: 21.7ha
Proportion: 1.354
Cardinal orientation: 52°
Phases & Dating: Stone – *Legio II Italica* (AD 205–Tetrarchic)
Literary references: *It. Ant.* 235.1; 249.1; 256.6; 258.2; *ND Occ.* 34.27; *Tab. Peut.* 4.2

Units attested epigraphically: *Legio II Italica*: *AE* 1934, 271a-b; 272a-b; 273b; *CIL* III, 5671; 5681; 5681a; 5682; 5757,1c; 5757,1e; 5757,1k-l; 5757,1n; 5757,1q-u; 11849f-h; 11853c; 13535a; 13535c; 15208; 963,11; 963,13; 964,17; *AEA* 1983/92, +63; 1979, 18; 1982, +14; 1993/98, 65; 2006, +12. *Legio XV Apollinaris*: *CIL* III, 5680. *Cohors I Aelia Dacorum*: *AEA* 2006, +12. *Cohors I equitata Antoniniana*: *AE* 2005, 1119. *Cohors I T[*: *AEA* 1999/00, 210. *Milites auxiliares Lauriacenses*: *CIL* III, 5670a (p. 1844). Unspecified unit: *CIL* III, 5757,1a; 964,18; *AEA* 1993/98, 65

Sub-literary references: –

Modern references (site): Eckhart 1984; FÖ 1, 1930–34, 15; 63f; 128; 185; 234; 2, 1935–38, 94; 4, 1940–45, 57; 8, 1961–65, 109; 13, 1974, 121f; 122; 18, 1979, 473; 33, 1994, 437; 34, 1995, 36f; 35, 1996, 43f; 36, 1997, 36f; 38f; 39; 37, 1998, 44; 38, 1999, 43; 40, 2001, 40f; 41, 2002, 37ff; 42, 2003, 38f; 39f; 43, 2004, 46; 47; 44, 2005, 39; 45, 2006, 44; 46, 2007, 39; 43; Groller 1906b; 1907b; 1908a; 1909b; 1910; 1919a; 1919b; 1924a; 1924b; 1925a; 1925b; 1925c; Genser 1986; Harreither 2003; Ruprechtsberger 1986a; 1986b; Vetters 1977; Winkler 1971; 2003

Modern references (finds): –

Notes: Partly urban, partly open site

Eski Malatya/Battalgazi–Melitene (Figure 2,69)

Location: 38° 25′ 14.35″ N, 38° 21′ 46.83″ E
Situation: On the floodplain of the Tohma river
Height ASL: 795m (GE)
Country: Turkey
Region: Malatya province
Province: Cappadocia
Length: *c.*520m
Width: *c.*390m
Area: *c.*20.6ha
Proportion: *c.*1.333
Cardinal orientation: 8°/188°
Phases & Dating: ? – *Legio XII Fulminata* (AD 70–?4th century)
Literary references: Joseph., *BJ* 7.18; Procop., *De Aedif.* 3.4.12
Units attested epigraphically: –
Sub-literary references: –
Modern references (site): Crow 1986; Gabriel 1940, 264–8; Gregory 1995–97, vol. 2, 49–53; Mitford 1980, 1186
Modern references (finds): –
Notes: Urban site. Formerly Eski Malatya, and before that Malatya

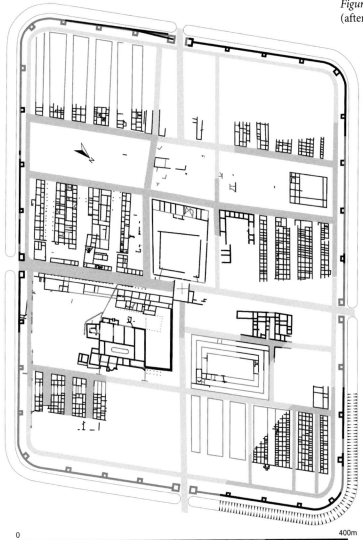

Figure 37: Enns-Lorch–Lauriacum (after Ruprechtsberger 1986a).

0   400m

Exeter–Isca (Figures 2,10; 38)
Location: 50° 43' 20.16" N, 3° 31' 55.95" W
Situation: Confluence of Exe and Taddiforde Brook
Height ASL: 42m (GE)
Country: Great Britain
Region: Devon, England
Province: Britannia
Length: 470–82m
Width: 346–9m
Area: 16.6ha
Proportion: 1.381
Cardinal orientation: 226°

Figure 38: Exeter–Isca (after Henderson 1991).

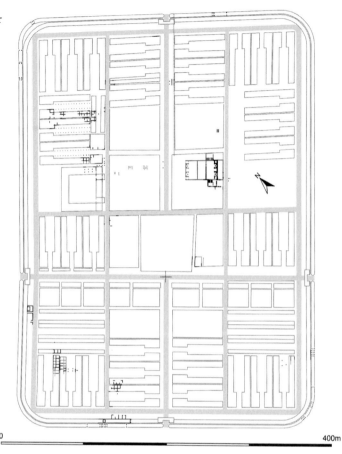

0   400m

Phases & Dating: Timber – *Legio II Augusta* (AD 49–73)
Literary references: Ptol., *Geog.* **2.3.13**
Units attested epigraphically: –
Sub-literary references: –
Modern references (site): Bidwell 1979; 1980; Blaylock and 1987; Booth 2007; Fox 1952; 1966; Frere 1983, 320–3; Henderson 1984; 1988; 1991; Holbrook and Fox 1987; Morris 1933–6; Ralegh Radford and Morris 1933–6; Rankov 1982, 382
Modern references (finds): Bidwell and Boon 1976; Holbrook and Bidwell 1991; 1992; Straker et al. 1984
Notes: Urban site

Gardun–Tilurium (Figures 2,44; 39; Plate 27)
Location: 43° 36′ 46.95″ N, 16° 42′ 56.41″ E
Situation: Adjacent to the Cetina river
Height ASL: 440m (GE)
Country: Croatia
Region: Splitsko-Dalmatinska županija
Province: Dalmatia
Length: 368–455m

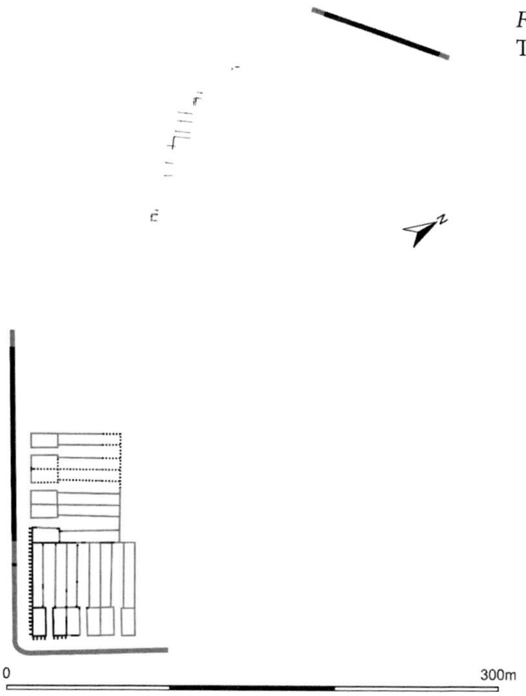

Figure 39: Gardun–Tilurium (after Sanader and Tončinić 2003).

Width: 300m
Area: 12.6ha
Proportion: 1.227
Cardinal orientation: 124°/304°
Phases & Dating: Timber and stone: *Legio VII Claudia* (AD 10–58)
Literary references: –
Units attested epigraphically: *Legio I Adiutrix: ILJug* I, 144. **Legio VII: CIL III, 2709–10; 2714–17; 9734; 9737; 9741–2; 14931–2.** *Legio XI: CIL* III, 2708; 2711; 13350. Unspecified legion: *CIL* III, 13975; 13976. *Ala Claudia Nova: CIL* III, 2712. *Ala Frontoniana: CIL* III, 9735. *Cohors III Alpinorum: CIL* III, 14935. *Cohors I Belgarum: CIL* III, 9739. *Cohors II Cyrrestarum: CIL* III, 14934. *Cohors VIII Voluntariorum: AE* 2004, 1104; *CIL* III, 2706; 9732–3; 13187; 14336,1; 14930. Unspecified infantry unit: *CIL* III, 2713; 13973; 14937. Unspecified unit: *CIL* III, 2718–19; 2721; 14936; 14938–9. *Veteranus: CIL* III, 13974; 13977
Sub-literary references: –
Modern references (site): Sanader 1998; 2000; 2001; 2002; 2003c; 2006; 2009; Sanader and Tončinić 2003; 2005; 2010a
Modern references (finds): Sanader 2003a; Sanader et al. 2007; Sanader and Tončinić 2009; 2010b; Tončinić 2007
Notes: Open site

Gigen–Oescus (Figure 2,57)
Location: 43° 42′ 36.12″ N, 24° 27′ 53.21″ E
Situation: At the confluence of the Danube and Iskăr
Height ASL: 28m (GE)
Country: Bulgaria

Region: Pleven Province
Province: Moesia Inferior
Length: –
Width: –
Area: –
Proportion: –
Cardinal orientation: –
Phases & Dating: ?Timber – *Legio V Macedonica* (AD 10–60) … *Legio V Macedonica* (AD 70–105)
   … ?stone: *Legio V Macedonica* (AD 162–167)
Literary references: Ptol., *Geog.* 3.10.10
Units attested epigraphically: *Legio I Italica: AE 1985, 736a; 736ba-bd; 2005, 1326; CIL III, 7428;*
   *12352; ILBulg 13; 17. Legio I Minervia: ILBulg 65. Legio IV Flavia Firma: CIL III, 6128. **Legio V***
   Macedonica: AE 1908, 82; 1996, 1336; CIL III, 7428; 12348; 14415; ILBulg 1; 9–10; 41; 47–8;
   52; 55; 58. *Legio VIII Augusta: ILBulg 65. Legio XI Claudia: AE 1985, 736c; CIL III, 6130; ILBulg*
   62. Unspecified legion: CIL III, 14416. Ala Gaetulorum: ILBulg 57. Ala Pansiana: ILBulg 50.
   Cohors II Flavia Brittonum: ILBulg 64. Cohors IV Gallorum: CIL III, 14417,1. Cohors I
   Praetoria: ILBulg 66. Cohors II Praetoria: ILBulg 65. Unspecified infantry unit: ILBulg 11.
   Veteranus: ILBulg 54
Sub-literary references: –
Modern references (site): Ivanov 1998; Kabakcieva 1999; Wilkes 2000, 116
Modern references (finds): –
Notes: Open site.

Gloucester–Glevum (Figures 2,8; 40)
Location: 51° 51′ 54.40″ N, 2° 14′ 45.82″ W
Situation: Between confluences of Severn and (N) River Twyver and (S) Sudbrook
Height ASL: 24m (GE)
Country: Great Britain
Region: Gloucestershire, England
Province: Britannia
Length: 490m
Width: 395m
Area: 19.3ha
Proportion: 1.241
Cardinal orientation: 39°
Phases & Dating: Timber – *Legio XX Valeria Victrix?* (AD 49–54)
Literary references: –
Units attested epigraphically: **Legio XX:** *AE 1984, 619; 1986, 464; 2005, 897; RIB 122. Cohors*
   VI Thracum: RIB 121. Unspecified infantry unit: RIB 119. Unspecified unit: AE 1975, 537
Sub-literary references: –
Modern references (site): Green 1942; Hassall 2000; Hassall and Rhodes 1974; Heighway 1983;
   Hurst 1972; 1974; 1976; 1986; 1988; Manning 2000, 72–3; O'Neil 1966
Modern references (finds): –
Notes: Urban site

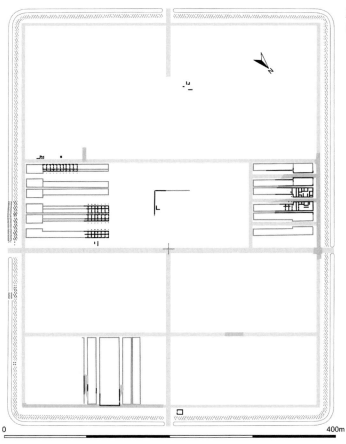

Figure 40: Gloucester–Glevum (after Hurst 1988).

0   400m

Grădişte/Sarmizegetusa–Sarmizegetusa (Figures 2,48; 41)
Location: 45° 30′ 50.83″ N, 22° 47′ 14.50″ E
Situation: Floodplain of Râu Mare
Height ASL: 502m (GE)
Country: Romania
Region: Hateg
Province: Dacia
Length: 545m
Width: 440m
Area: 24.1ha
Proportion: 1.239
Cardinal orientation: ?350°
Phases & Dating: Timber – *Legio XIII Gemina* (AD 102–8)
Literary references: Cass. Dio 68.9.7
Units attested epigraphically: *Legio I Minervia*: CIL III, 1480. *Legio II Adiutrix*: AE 1983, 824; ?*IDR* III.2, 136a; III.3, 268. *Legio II Parthica*: CIL III, 1464. *Legio II Traiana*: AE 1979, 506. *Legio III Augusta*: CIL III, 1455. *Legio IV Flavia Felix*: AE 1967, 391; 1977, 687; 1996, 1279b; 1279e; 2004, +1210; 2007, 1202; CIL III, 7904; 8070e-f; *IDR* III.2, 540c; III.3, 269b-c. *Legio V Macedonica*: AE 1913, 55; 1933, 249; CIL III, 12635. *Legio VI*: CIL III, 1427. *Legio VI Ferrata*:

Figure 41: Grădiște–
Sarmizegetusa (after
Piso 2006).

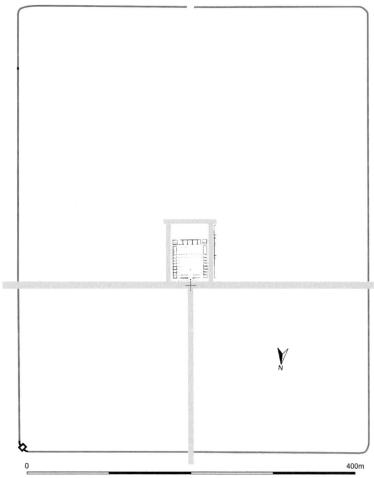

AE 1983, 825; *IDR* III.3, 270. *Legio VI Victrix:* AE 1933, 247; 1976, 571; *CIL* III, 1474; *IDR* III.2, 127. *Legio VII Claudia:* CIL III, 1480. *Legio VII Gemina:* CIL III, 1464. *Legio VIII Augusta:* CIL III, 1480. *Legio X Fretensis:* CIL III, 1455. *Legio XI Claudia:* CIL III, 1457; 1480. **Legio XIII Gemina: AE 1933, 248; 1996, 1280; 2006, 1167; CIL III, 88; 1434; 1459; 1464; 1471; 1476–7; 1479; 1485; 1629,1g; 1629,17a; 1629,24c; 7921; 8065,1h; 8065,20c; 8065,34e; IDR III.2, 243; 245; 248; 420; 541,2; 541,4; 541,10.** *Legio XV:* AE 1998, 1087; CIL III, 1478. *Legio XX Valeria Victrix:* CIL III, 1458; 1472. Unspecified legion: *IDR* III.2, 151; 495. *Equites singulares:* CIL III, 7904. *Cohors I Praetoria:* AE 1933, 248. *Ala II Pannoniorum:* CIL III, 1483. *Cohors VII Breucorum:* CIL III, 1464. *Cohors IV Delmatarum:* CIL III, 1474. *Cohors II Flavia:* CIL III, 1484. *Cohors I Pannoniorum:* CIL III, 90. *Cohors I Augusta Thracum:* IDR III.2, 348. *Cohors I Vindelicorum:* CIL III, 12587. *Numerus Maurorum:* CIL III, 1418. *Numerus Palmyrenorum:* AE 2004, 1212. Unspecified infantry unit: *AE* 2006, 1171; *CIL* III, 1482. Unspecified unit: CIL III, 7900; *IDR* III.2, 270. *Veteranus:* CIL III, 7980; *IDR* III.2, 500

Sub-literary references: –

Modern references (site): Alicu 1980; Alicu and Paki 1995; Opreanu 2006; Piso 2006

Modern references (finds): Alicu 1983; Alicu et al. 1994; Dawson 1990; Găzdac 2009; Voişan 1997

Notes: Formerly known as Grădişte. Fortress presumed to lie beneath eastern two-thirds of the *colonia*. Disagreement over whether timber 'proto-forum' (cf. Piso 2006) is in fact the *principia* (cf. Opreanu 2006)

Haïdra–Ammaedara *(Figure 2,96)*
Location: 35° 33′ 49.10″ N, 8° 27′ 15.37″ E
Situation: Adjacent to a wadi
Height ASL: 815m (GE)
Country: Tunisia
Region: Kasserine Governorate
Province: Numidia
Length: –
Width: –
Area: –
Proportion: –
Cardinal orientation: –
Phases & Dating: ? – *Legio III Augusta* (AD 14–74)
Literary references: Ptol., *Geog.* 4.3
Units attested epigraphically: *Legio III Augusta*: *AE* 1969/70, 661; 1987, 1038–41; 1043; 1994, 1842; 1995, 1652; 1997, 1622b-c; 1624; 1626; 1628–32; 1634–6; 1999, 1795; *BCTH* 1900.94; *CIL* VIII, 23251; 23253–4; 23256; 23259–60; *Haidra* 3P, 10; 15–16; *ILAfr* 153; 155a; *ILPBardo* I, 39–42; 44; 46–9; 51; 53. *Legio VII Gemina*: *AE* 1988, 1119. *Legio X Fretensis*: *AE* 1912, 205; *ILAfr* 154; 155b. *Legio XXI*: *ILAfr* 153. *Ala I Pannoniorum*: *AE* 1969/70, 661; *CIL* VIII, 23258. *Cohors XI Urbana*: *AE* 1997, 1621a. Unspecified infantry unit: *AE* 1992, 1768; 1997, 1620; 1625; 1633; 1637; 1637c; *CIL* VIII, 312; 23252; 23255. Unspecified unit: *ILPBardo* I, 43; 52
Sub-literary references: –
Modern references (site): Le Bohec 1989, 341–3, 353, and 357; Duval 1982, 643–4; Mackensen 1997
Modern references (finds): Abdallah 1990; 1992; Abdallah et al. 1997
Notes: Open site.

Haltern *(Figures 2,14; 42)*
Location: 51° 44′ 29.68″ N, 7° 10′ 13.38″ E
Situation: Confluence of Lippe and Stever
Height ASL: 58m (GE)
Country: Germany
Region: Kr. Recklinghausen
Province: Germania Magna
Length: 530m
Width: 363m
Area: 19.2ha
Proportion: 1.460
Cardinal orientation: 150°
Phases & Dating: Timber – *Legio XIX* (*c.*8 BC–AD 9)
Literary references: –
Units attested epigraphically: *Legio XIX*: Schillinger-Häfele 1977, Nr. 205
Sub-literary references: –
Modern references (site): Aßkamp 1989; 2010; Koepp et al. 1909; Pietsch 1993; Roth-Rubi et al. 2006; Schnurbein 1974; 1981

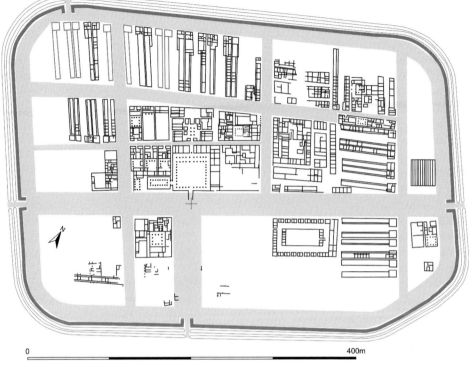

Figure 42: Haltern (after Kühlborn 2000).

Modern references (finds): Galsterer 1983; Harnecker 1997; Loeschcke 1909; Müller 2002; Rudnick 2001; Rudnick et al. 1995; Schillinger-Häfele 1977; Schnurbein 1979; 1982; Stieren 1943; Stupperich 1990; Voelling 1991–92; Wells 1972, 163–211; Westphal 1995

Notes: Mostly urban, partly open. Has been identified with the Aliso of Tac., *Ann.* 2.7 and Vell. Pat. 120.4

Herrera de Pisuerga–Pisoraca (Figure 2,103)
Location: 42° 35′ 40.84″ N, 4° 19′ 46.37″ W
Situation: Confluence of the Pisuerga and Bureja
Height ASL: 846m (GE)
Country: Spain
Region: Provincia de Palencia
Province: Hispania Tarraconensis
Length: –
Width: –
Area: –
Proportion: –
Cardinal orientation: –
Phases & Dating: ?Timber – *Legio IV Macedonica* (AD 10–43)
Literary references: Ptol., *Geog.* 2.6.51

Units attested epigraphically: *Legio IV Macedonica*: *IRPPalencia* 193,1–10. *Ala Parthorum*: *Hep* VII, 561–3; XIII, 500. *Cohors I Gallaecorum*: *CIL* II, 2913. Unspecified cavalry unit: *CIL* II, 2912; *Hep* VII, 559. Unspecified infantry unit: *AE* 2003, 966; *Hep* VII, 558.

Sub-literary references: –

Modern references (site): García-Bellido et al. 1962; González Echegaray and Solana 1975; Illarregui 1999; 2002; Morillo, Á. 2000; Morillo et al. 2006; Pérez-González 1996; Pérez-González and Illarregui 1992; 1994; 2006

Modern references (finds): Marcos Herran 2002; Morillo 1992; Morillo and Fernández Ibáñez 2001/2; Morillo and Gómez Barreiro 2006a; 2006b; Pérez-González 1989

Notes: Urban site

Igliţa–Troesmis (Figure 2,62)
Location: 45° 8′ 36.44″ N, 28° 11′ 42.42″ E
Situation: Confluence of unnamed stream and Danube
Height ASL: 39m (GE)
Country: Romania
Region: Tulcea County
Province: Moesia Inferior
Length: –
Width: –
Area: –
Proportion: –
Cardinal orientation: –
Phases & Dating: ? – *Legio V Macedonica* (AD 106–61); *Legio II Herculia* (4th century AD)
Literary references: Ptol., *Geog.* 3.10.5
Units attested epigraphically: *Legio I Italica*: *CIL* III, 6176; 6185; 6192; 6239c. *Legio II Adiutrix*: *CIL* III, 6186. **Legio II Herculia**: *CIL* III, 6174; 6194. *Legio III Cyrenaica*: *CIL* III, 6186. *Legio IV Flavia*: *CIL* III, 6186. **Legio V Macedonica**: *AE* 1957, 266; 1960, 337; 1972, 547; 1980, 818; 821; *CIL* III, 776; 6162; 6166; 6168–9; 6186; 6189–90; 6192; 6198; 6240a-c; 7499; 7501–3; 7505–7; *IScM* V, 215d; 217. *Legio X Fretensis*: *CIL* III, 6186; 6192. *Legio X Gemina*: *CIL* III, 6186. *Legio XI Claudia*: *CIL* III, 6196. *Legio XII Fulminata*: *CIL* III, 6186; 6191. Unspecified legion: *CIL* III, 6178; 6187–8. *Ala I Dardanorum*: *CIL* III, 7504. *Ala I Pannoniorum*: *CIL* III, 6242. Unspecified cavalry unit: *CIL* III, 6205. Unspecified unit: *CIL* III, 7500; *IScM* V, 204
Sub-literary references: –
Modern references (site): Poulter 1986; Wilkes 2000, 116
Modern references (finds): –
Notes: Open site

Inchtuthil (Figures 2,1; 43)
Location: 56° 32′ 27.34″ N, 3° 25′ 30.54″ W
Situation: Confluence of Tay and Millhole Burn
Height ASL: 48m (GE)
Country: Great Britain
Region: Perth and Kinross, Scotland
Province: Britannia
Length: 465m
Width: 440m
Area: 20.5ha
Proportion: 1.057

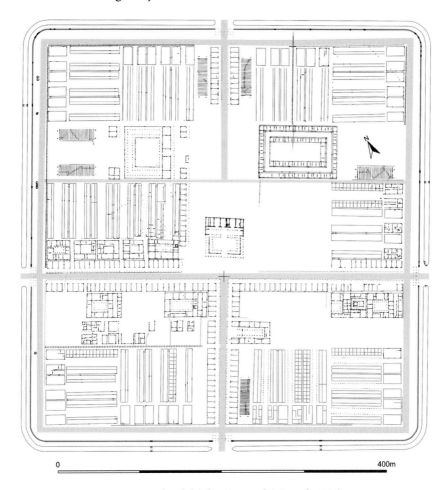

Figure 43: Inchtuthil (after Pitts and St Joseph 1988).

Cardinal orientation: 204°
Phases & Dating: Timber & stone – Under construction (*c.*AD 82–7)
Literary references: –
Units attested epigraphically: –
Sub-literary references: –
Modern references (site): Abercromby et al. 1902; Martin 1995; Pitts and St Joseph 1985; Richmond 1959; Shirley 1996; 2000; 2001; Taylor 1999
Modern references (finds): Angus et al. 1962; Kapusta and Underwood 2000; Mapelli et al. 2009
Notes: Unfinished when demolished. Open site

Ivoševci–Burnum (Figures 2,43; 44; Plate 23)
Location: 44° 1′ 2.84″ N, 16° 1′ 32.45″ E
Situation: Adjacent to the Krka
Height ASL: 252m (GE)
Country: Croatia
Region: Šibenik-Knin

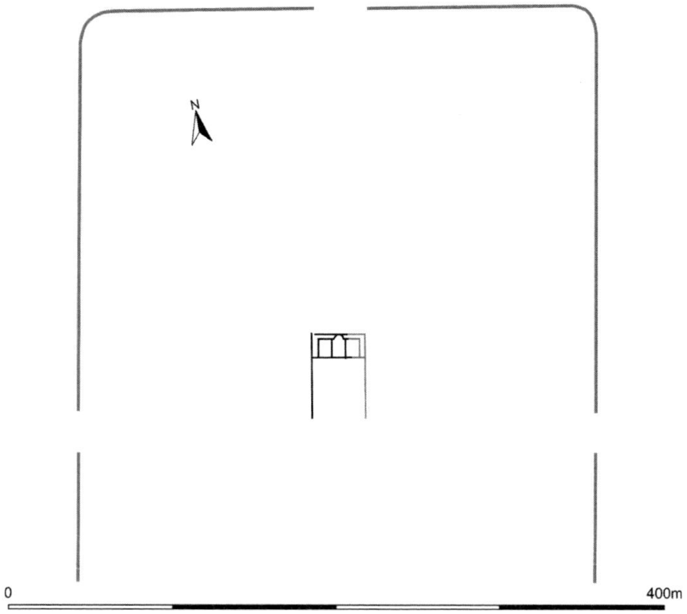

Figure 44: Ivoševci–Burnum
(after Miletić 2010a).

Province: Dalmatia
Length: >325m
Width: *c.*315m
Area: >10.2ha
Proportion: ?
Cardinal orientation: 187°
Phases & Dating: ? – *Legio XI Claudia* (AD 10–69); *Legio IV Flavia Felix* (AD 70–86)
Literary references: Pliny, *NH* 3,141; Vell. Pat. 2.112.1–2; Procop., *Goth.* 1,16
Units attested epigraphically: *Legio I Adiutrix: CIL* III, 2823; *ILJug* II, 832; III, 2808. *Legio II Augusta: CIL* III, 15024. **Legio IV Flavia Firma: CIL III, 14995; 15110a-b.** *Legio V Macedonica: ILJug* III, 2807. *Legio VII Claudia: CIL* III, 13251; 14992. *Legio VIII Augusta: ILJug* III, 2818. *Legio X Fretensis: CIL* III, 15026. **Legio XI Claudia: AE 1900, 44–5; 1979, 446; CIL III, *394,3–6; 394,8; 2832–5; 2839; 6416–18; 9903–4; 9906; 9908; 13263; 14321,13; 14321,19; 14996–7; 14997,1; 14997,2; 14998–9; 15001; 15004; 15004a; 15005; 15005,1; ILJug II, 835–40; III, 2810–12; 2814; 2816.** *Legio XIII Gemina: CIL* III, 2830. *Legio XIV Gemina: CIL* III, 2830. *Legio XV: CIL* III, 15026a. *Legio XX: CIL* III, 2836. *Legio XXI: CIL* III, 9909; 14993. Unspecified legion: *CIL* III, 6419; 9905; 9926; 13250; 14994; 15002. *Ala Hispanorum: ILJug* II, 843. *Cohors III Alpinorum: CIL* III, 9907. *Cohors I Belgarum: CIL* III, 14980. *Cohors II Cyrrhestarum: ILJug* II, 842; III, 2820. *Cohors Montanorum: CIL* III, 15003; *ILJug* II, 841. Unspecified infantry unit: *CIL* III, 14321,20–1. Unspecified unit: *CIL* III, 2838; 9899; 9911; *ILJug* II, 834; III, 2817; 2819. *Veteranus: CIL* III, 14990
Sub-literary references: –
Modern references (site): Cambi et al. 2007; Fortis 1778; Ilakovac 1984; Miletić 2010a; Reisch 1913; Zaninović 1968
Modern references (finds): Miletić 2010b; Zabehlicky et al. 1979
Notes: Open site. Also published as Kistanje or Šuplja Crkva. Famed for its standing arches, it is not clear whether these belong to one of the *principia* on the site or a later *forum.* Part of the *praetentura* of the fortress appears to have been eroded

Jerusalem–Hierosolyma (Figure 2,86)

Location: 31° 46′ 40.76″ N, 35° 13′ 45.84″ E
Situation: Within city walls
Height ASL: 775m (GE)
Country: Israel
Region: Jerusalem
Province: Judaea
Length: –
Width: –
Area: –
Proportion: –
Cardinal orientation: –
Phases & Dating: ? – *Legio X Fretensis* (AD 70–?Tetrarchic)
Literary references: Joseph., *BJ* 7.1.1; 7.1.2; 7.1.3
Units attested epigraphically: *Legio II Augusta*: *AE* 1939, 157. *Legio II Traiana Fortis*: *AE* 1904,
   91. *Legio III Cyrenaica*: *CIL* III, 13587. **Legio X Fretensis: *AE* 1889, 178a-b; 1891, 165; 1896,
   30; 46a-c; 1904, 91; 202; 1910, 208; 1939, 157; 1975, 851; 1978, 825; 1985, 831; 1995, 1581–3;
   2003, 1810; 1811a-g; *CIL* III, 6638; 6641; 6651a-g; 12081a; 12090a-c; 14155,3.** *Legio XI
   Claudia*: *AE* 1939, 157. *Legio XII Fulminata*: *AE* 1904, 91; 1939, 157. *Legio XIV Gemina*: *AE*
   1939, 157. *Legio XX (Valeria) Victrix*: *AE* 1939, 157. Unspecified legion: *AE* 1904, 201.
   Unspecified infantry unit: *AE* 1997, 1560–1; 2002, 1560b-c; 1560e-g; *CIL* III, 14383b-f.
   Unspecified unit: *AE* 1910, 209
Sub-literary references: *CIL* XVI, App. 12
Modern references (site): Arubas and Goldfus 1995; Bar 1998; Geva 1984; 1994; Isaac 1986
Modern references (finds): Eck 2009
Notes: Urban site

Köln–Ara Ubiorum (Figure 2,18)

Location: 50° 56′ 28.62″ N, 6° 57′ 24.70″ E
Situation: Adjacent to Rhine
Height ASL: *c.*59m (GE)
Country: Germany
Region: Nordrhein-Westfalen
Province: Germania Inferior
Length: –
Width: –
Area: –
Proportion: –
Cardinal orientation: –
Phases & Dating: ?Timber – *Legiones I Germanica + XX* (AD 10–35); *?Legio XV Primigenia*
   (AD 39–43)
Literary references: Tac., *Ann.* 1. 37. 2; 1.39.1
Units attested epigraphically: *Legio I Minervia*: *AE* 1984, 659; 2003, 1220c; *CIL* XIII, 8172; 8213;
   8222; 8232; 8239; 8267a-b; 8275–82; 12048; 12111,99, 12120,1–9; *IKoeln* 75; 270; 302; 308.
   Legio III Augusta: *CIL* XIII, 8269. *Legio V*: *AE* 2004, 974; *CIL* XIII, 12059. *Legio V Alaudae*:
   IKoeln 311. *Legio V Macedonica*: *CIL* XIII, 12146,1–3. *Legio VI Victrix*: *AE* 2003, 1220b; *CIL*
   XIII, 8174; 12155,1–9. *Legio VII Gemina*: *CIL* XIII, 8282. *Legio X Gemina*: *CIL* XIII, 8283;
   12530,11–12; *IKoeln* 314. *Legio XIV Gemina*: *CIL* XIII, 8270. **Legio XV Primigenia: *CIL* XIII,
   8209; 8284; 12264,1–2; *IKoeln* 249.** *Legio XVI*: *AE* 1938, 77e; *CIL* XIII, 8285; 10027,219; 12272;

IKoeln 319. **Legio XIX: *AE* 1975, 626. Legio XX: *CIL* XIII, 8286–8.** *Legio XXI Rapax: IKoeln* 324–5. *Legio XXII Primigenia: AE* 2003, 1220a; 1220j; *CIL* XIII, 8175; 8289–90; 12372,1–10; *IKoeln* 328. *Legio XXX Ulpia Victrix: AE* 1888, 158; 1981, 662; *CIL* XIII, 8201; 8203; 8219; 8233; 8291–4; 12387,1–9; 12544,1; *IKoeln* 331; 334–6. *Legio X[: IKoeln* 316. Unspecified legion: *CIL* XIII, 8272; 8295–6; 8298; 8300; *IKoeln* 339; 347–8. *Ala Afrorum: CIL* XIII, 8223; 8303–5. *Ala I Asturum: AE* 1990, 732. *Ala Classiana: CIL* XIII, 8306. *Ala Fida Vindex: CIL* XIII, 8307. *Ala Noricorum: CIL* XIII, 8243; 8308–9. *Ala Praetoria: CIL* XIII, 8310. *Ala Sulpicia: CIL* XIII, 8185; 8311–12. *Ala I Thracum: CIL* XIII, 12058. *Cohors II Alpinorum: IKoeln* 373. *Cohors II Asturum: CIL* XIII, 12530,13; *IKoeln* 374. *Cohors IV Breucorum: IKoeln* 375. *Cohors VIII Breucorum: CIL* XIII, 8313. *Cohors I Classica: CIL* XIII, 8325; 12061. *Cohors III Delmatarum: CIL* XIII, 8271. *Cohors I Flavia: IKoeln* 379. *Cohors I Hispanorum: AE* 1984, 667. *Cohors VI Ingenuorum: CIL* XIII, 8314–15. *Cohors I Latabicorum: AE* 1990, 727; *CIL* XIII, 8316. *Cohors III Lusitanorum: CIL* XIII, 8317. *Cohors I Raetorum: CIL* XIII, 8319. *Cohors I Thracum: CIL* XIII, 8318. *Cohors II Varcianorum: AE* 1929, 109; *CIL* XIII, 8188. *Cohors I Vindelicorum: CIL* XIII, 8320. *Cohors IV Vindelicorum: CIL* XIII, 12484. *Cohors XV Voluntariorum: AE* 2002, 1037. *Numerus Germanicianorum: CIL* XIII, 8329. Unspecified cavalry unit: *CIL* XIII, 8399; 12060; *IKoeln* 369. Unspecified infantry unit: *AE* 2004, 982a-b; 1938, 77d; 1938, 77f; *CIL* XIII, 8166; 8274; *IKoeln* 390–1. Unspecified unit: *CIL* XIII, 8324; 8326. *Veteranus: CIL* XIII, 8302

Sub-literary references: –
Modern references (site): Filtzinger 1962–63; 1980; Hellenkemper 1972–73; 1983; LaBaume 1973; 1980; Päffgen and Zanier 1995; 1998; Petrikovits 1960; Precht 1971; Wells 1972, 134–6
Modern references (finds): –
Notes: Urban site

Kostolac-Viminacium (Figure 2,47)

Location: 44° 44′ 7.90″ N, 21° 13′ 21.03″ E
Situation: Confluence of Danube and Mlava
Height ASL: 77m (GE)
Country: Serbia
Region: Braničevo
Province: Moesia Superior
Length: *c.*445m
Width: *c.*385m
Area: 17.1ha
Proportion: 1.131
Cardinal orientation: 21°
Phases & Dating: ?Timber – *Legio V Macedonica* (AD 10–58); stone – *Legio VII Claudia* (AD 59–68) … *Legio VII Claudia* (AD 71–?4th century)
Literary references: Ptol., *Geog.* 3.9.3
Units attested epigraphically: *Legio III Gallica: AE* 1905, 157. *Legio IV Flavia: AE* 1903, 292–3; 1905, 159; *CIL* III, 1646 (p 1448); 1648; 1649 (p 1021, 1448); 1652; 1653 (p 1021); 1659; 6300; 8123; 14511; 14597; *IMS* II, 16; 59; 87–8; 90; 96. **Legio VII Claudia: *AE* 1903, 294–6; 1905, 160–1; 1910, 90; 1913, 172; 1971, 418; 1973, 471; 1991, 1356; *CIL* III, 1650; 1700,1a; 1700,2; 6324a; 6325,2–3; 8103–4; 8110; 8112; 8115–19; 8121–2; 8124; 12658–9; 13806–7; 14217,4; 14506–7; 14509; 14509,1; 14510; 14512; 14514–15; *ILJug* II, 483; *IMS* II, 45; 54; 100; 104; 117; 119–20; 125–6; 128; 133–5; 137; 155; 231.** *Legio XV Apollinaris: IMS* II, 138. Unspecified legion: *CIL* III, 1651 (p 1021); 8125; 14518; *IMS* II, 105; 148. *Equites singulares: CIL* III, 14513. *Equites Dalmatae: AE* 1903, 297. *Equites sagittarii: AE* 1903, 298. *Cohors I Aquitanorum: CIL* III, 12659. *Cohors VI Breucorum: AE* 1905, 162. *Cohors VII Breucorum: AE* 2004, 1224. *Cohors*

Hemesenorum sagittariorum: *IMS* II, 144. *Cohors I Lusitanorum*: *AE* 1982, 839; 1986, 616. Unspecified infantry unit: *IMS* II, 146. Unspecified unit: *CIL* III, 8126; *IMS* II, 112; 149. *Veteranus*: *CIL* III, 13808; *IMS* II, 147; 153–4

Sub-literary references: –
Modern references (site): Korać and Pavlović 2004; Wilkes 2000, 116
Modern references (finds): Dušanić 1997; Mirković 1999; Redžić 2008
Notes: Open site. Excavations (awaiting publication) are underway on the north gate (*porta praetoria*). Dimensions courtesy of the excavator

Kurus–Cyrrhus (Figure 2,75)
Location: 36° 44′ 55.96″ N, 36° 57′ 39.37″ E
Situation: Adjacent to the river Sabun
Height ASL: 423m (GE)
Country: Syria
Region: Aleppo Governorate
Province: Syria
Length: –
Width: –
Area: –
Proportion: –
Cardinal orientation: –
Phases & Dating: ? – *Legio X Fretensis* (pre-AD 10–70)
Literary references: Tac., *Ann.* 2.57.2
Units attested epigraphically: *Legio I Adiutrix*: *CIL* III, 6706. *Legio IV Flavia*: *CIL* III, 195. *Legio VII Claudia*: *CIL* III, 194–5. *Legio VIII Augusta*: *CIL* III, 193
Sub-literary references: –
Modern references (site): Berchem 1954, 267–8; Dabrowa 2000, 318; Parker 2000, 124
Modern references (finds): –
Notes: Open site

Lajjun–Legio (Caparcotna) (Figure 2,84)
Location: 32° 34′ 35.92″ N, 35° 11′ 14.08″ E
Situation: Adjacent to the Qeini
Height ASL: 121m (GE)
Country: Israel
Region: Jenin District
Province: Judaea
Length: –
Width: –
Area: –
Proportion: –
Cardinal orientation: –
Phases & Dating: Stone – *Legio II Traiana* (AD 117–25); *Legio VI Ferrata* (AD 125–c.303)
Literary references: Ptol., *Geog.* 5.15.3
Units attested epigraphically: ***Legio II Traiana***: *AE* 2007, 1627a. ***Legio VI Ferrata***: *AE* 2007, 1627b
Sub-literary references: –
Modern references (site): Isaac and Roll 1979; Tepper 2002; 2007; Tepper and Di Segni 2005; Tsuk 1988/9
Modern references (finds): Eck and Tepper 2001; Rahmani 1981
Notes: Open site

León–Legio VII Gemina (Figures 2,102; 45)

Location: 42° 35' 55.11" N, 5° 34' 5.28" W
Situation: Confluence of Bernesga and Torío
Height ASL: 844m (GE)
Country: Spain
Region: León
Province: Hispania Tarraconensis
Length: 570m
Width: 350m
Area: 19.2ha
Proportion: 1.629
Cardinal orientation: 161°
Phases & Dating: Timber & stone – *Legio VII Gemina* (AD 74–4th century)
Literary references: *It. Ant.* 387.7; 395; Ptol., *Geog.* 2.6.28

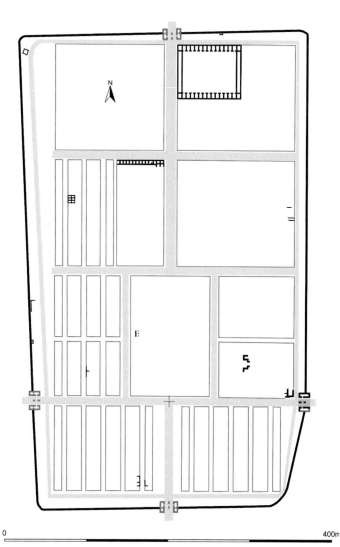

0   400m

Figure 45: León–Legio VII Gemina (after Morillo and García-Marcos 2009).

Units attested epigraphically: *Legio VII Gemina*: *AE* 1916, 70; 1971, 207; 1974, 411; 1993, 1032–4; 2006, 667; *CIL* II, 2660a-de; 2663–4; 2667a-l; 2669; 5083–4; 5676; 5681; *ERPLeon* 38; 54; 86; 113; 126; 129; 165; *IRPLeon* 20. *Ala II Flavia*: *CIL* II, 5682. Unspecified unit: *CIL* II, 2668

Sub-literary references: –

Modern references (site): Abascal 1986; Campomanes Alvaredo 1997; Garcia y Bellido 1968; 1970a; 1970b; García Marcos 2002; García Marcos and Miguel 1997; García Marcos and Morillo 2000/1; 2002; Liz and Amaré 1993; Morillo 1996; 2002; 2003; 2007; Morillo and García-Marcos 2003; 2004; 2005; 2006a; 2006b; 2009; Morillo et al. 2002; Vidal 1986; Vidal and García-Marcos 1996

Modern references (finds): Aurrecoechea 2006; Aurrecoechea and Muñoz Villarejo 2001–2; Morillo 1999; Morillo and Gómez-Barreiro 2006

Notes: Urban site

Lincoln–Lindum (Figures 2,4; 46)
Location: 53° 14′ 7.98″ N, 0° 32′ 18.72″ W
Situation: Confluence of Witham and Till (now canalized as Fossdyke)
Height ASL: 71m (GE)
Country: Great Britain
Region: Lincolnshire, England
Province: Britannia

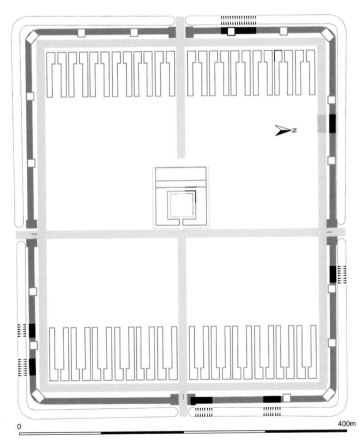

Figure 46: Lincoln–Lindum (after Jones 1988).

0   400m

Length: 440m
Width: 360m
Area: 16.0ha
Proportion: 1.222
Cardinal orientation: 93°
Phases & Dating: Timber – *Legio IX Hispana* (AD 60–70); *Legio II Adiutrix* (AD 71–7)
Literary references: Ptol., *Geog.* 2.3.11; *It. Ant.* 475.3; 476.7; 477.9; 478.10
Units attested epigraphically: *Legio II Adiutrix*: *RIB* **253; 258.** *Legio VI Victrix*: *RIB* 252. **Legio IX Hispana:** *AE* **1950, 124;** *RIB* **254–7; 260.** *Legio XIV Gemina*: *RIB* 249. Unspecified legion: *RIB* 261. *Ala II Asturum*: *RIB* 266. *Cohors IV Breucorum*: *RIB* 2415,41. Unspecified unit: *RIB* 259
Sub-literary references: –
Modern references (site): Burnham et al. 2005, 424; Jones 1980; 1988; Jones and Gilmour 1980; Jones et al. 2003; Petch 1962; Steane 2006; Thompson and Whitwell 1973; Webster 1949; Whitwell 1967
Modern references (finds): –
Notes: Urban site

Ljubljana–Emona (Figure 2,38)

Location: 46° 2′ 40.20″ N, 14° 30′ 34.56″ E
Situation: On an island in the Ljubljanica
Height ASL: 295m (GE)
Country: Slovenia
Region: Osrednjeslovenska region
Province: Dalmatia
Length: –
Width: –
Area: –
Proportion: –
Cardinal orientation: –
Phases & Dating: Timber – *Legio XV* (AD 10–13)
Literary references: Ptol., *Geog.* 8.15.7
Units attested epigraphically: *Legio II Adiutrix*: *CIL* III, 3846. *Legio II Traiana*: *CIL* III, 3846. *Legio VIII*: *CIL* III, 3845. *Legio X Fretensis*: *CIL* III, 3846. *Legio XIII Gemina*: *AE* 1950, 43; *AIJ* 157; *CIL* III, 3844; 14354,10. **Legio XV Apollinaris:** *CIL* **III, 3835; 3845; 3847; 10769.** *Ala Britannica*: *AE* 1980, 496. *Cohors II Praetoria*: *AE* 1958, 1. Unspecified unit: *AIJ* 173. *Veteranus*: *CIL* III, 3848
Sub-literary references: –
Modern references (site): Anon 2008; Šašel Kos 1995; 1998; Vičič 2008
Modern references (finds): Vičič 2002
Notes: Urban site opposite (not under) the *colonia*

Ločica–Celeia (Figures 2,39; 47)

Location: 46° 16′ 9.17″ N, 15° 5′ 42.73″ E
Situation: Adjacent to old course of Savinja
Height ASL: 284m (GE)
Country: Slovenia
Region: Polzela
Province: Noricum
Length: 515m

Figure 47: Ločica–Celeia
(after Kandler 1979).

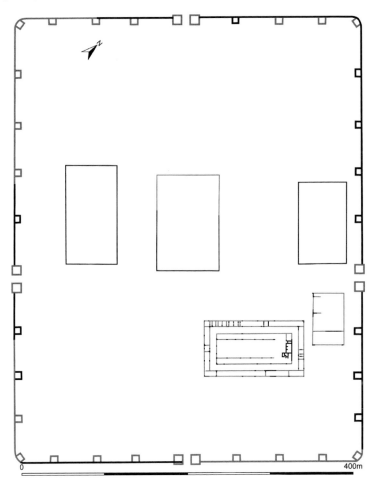

Width: 425m
Area: 21.9ha
Proportion: 1.266
Cardinal orientation: 130°
Phases & Dating: Stone – *Legio II Italica* (AD 170–2)
Literary references: –
Units attested epigraphically: *Legio II Italica*: *CIL* III, 14369,2a–i; k–q
Sub-literary references: –
Modern references (site): Lorger 1919; Kandler 1979; Lazar 2006; Winkler 1971, 88–91
Modern references (finds): –
Notes: Also known by its old Austro-Hungarian name of Lotschitz. Dimensions (revised from
Lorger 1919) from Kandler 1979, 185. Open site

Mainz–Mogontiacum (Figures 2,21; 48)
Location: 49° 59′ 40.83″ N, 8° 15′ 41.48″ E
Situation: Adjacent to Rhine
Height ASL: 125m (GE)
Country: Germany

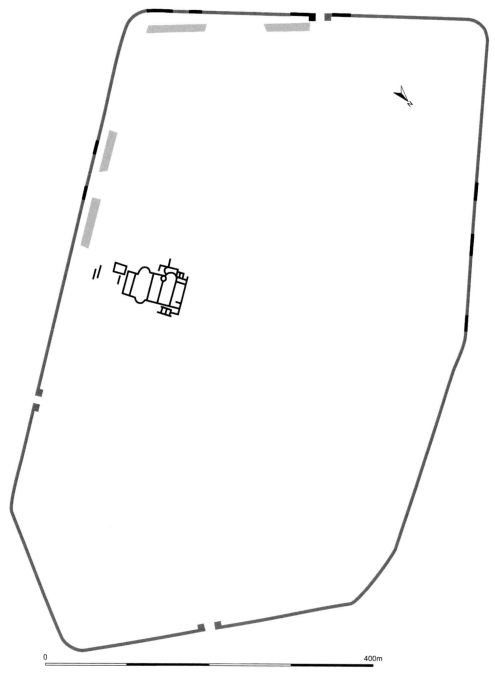

Figure 48: Mainz–Mogontiacum (after Baatz 1962).

Region: Rheinland-Pfalz
Province: Germania Superior
Length: 700m
Width: 520m

Area: 33.3ha

Proportion: 1.346

Cardinal orientation: ?48°

Phases & Dating: Timber – *Legiones XIV Gemina + XVI Gallica* (AD 10–43); *Legiones IV Macedonica + XXII Primigenia* (AD 43–69); *Legio XIV Gemina + Legio I Adiutrix* (AD 70–82); *Legio XIV Gemina* (AD 82–92); stone – *Legio XXII Primigenia* (AD 92–4th century)

Literary references: Tac., *Hist.* 4.15; 24–5; 33; 37; 59; 61–2; 70–1; Amm. Marc. 15.11.8; Eutrop. 7.13; Ptol., *Geog.* 2.8

Units attested epigraphically: *Legio I: CIL* XIII, 11845. [*Legio —*] *Adiutrix: AE* 2005, 1702. **Legio I Adiutrix: AE 1900, 71; 1911, 233; 235; 1924, 85; 1962, 293; 1978, 561; 1979, 428; 2007, 1054i; CIL XIII, 6739; 6778; 6825–34a, 6835–48f; 6948a–f; 11838a–d; 11839; 11846–7; Finke 209. Legio I Germanica: CIL XIII, 6781.** *Legio I Minervia: CIL* XIII, 6763. *Legio I[: CIL* XIII, 7237. *Legio II: CIL* XIII, 6852; 7234. *Legio II Adiutrix: CIL* XIII, 6850. *Legio II Augusta: AE* 1965, 240. *Legio II Pannonica: CIL* XIII, 6849. *Legio II Traiana: CIL* XIII, 6883. **Legio IV Macedonica: AE 1965, 242–3; 248; 252–3; 2007, 1054j; CIL XIII, 6700; 6812; 6853–78; 6880; 11848–50.** *Legio VII Claudia: CIL* XIII, 6823; 6881. *Legio VIII Augusta: AE* 1934, 131; 1976, 494; *CIL* XIII, 6721; 6728; 6738; 6783; 6803; 6882–3; 11824. *Legio X: CIL* XIII, 7097. *Legio X[: AE* 1940, 112; *CIL* XIII, 6809; 6931; 7010. *Legio XI: CIL* XIII, 6706. *Legio XI[: CIL* XIII, 7016. *Legio XIII: CIL* XIII, 6824; 6884; 6887; 6952. **Legio XIV Gemina: AE 1901, 157; 1908, 32; 1940, 113; 1951, 135; 1953, 113; 1962, 291; 1965, 254–5; 1977, 586; 1979, 428; 437–8; CIL XIII, 6885–6; 6888–917; 6919–30a; 6932–5; 6952; 7236; 7255; 11840; 11851–2; Ness-Lieb 164; 166–7; Schillinger 88. Legio XV Primigenia: 11853–6. Legio XVI: AE 1908, 256; 1909, 73; 1965, 256; CIL XIII, 6936–48; 11837; 11857–9; Finke 210.** *Legio XX[: AE* 1965, 260a. *Legio XX: CIL* XIII, 6780. *Legio XXI Rapax: AE* 1900, 154; *CIL* XIII 6949–51b; 11800. **Legio XXII Primigenia: AE 1901, 76; 1904, 106; 1923, 36; 1940, 118; 1941, 107; 1956, 86; 1964, 148; 1965, 240; 244; 257; 1976, 498–9; 502–3; 1979, 425; 1990, 744; AmphMainz-Dipinti 22; CIL XIII, 6661 (4, p 107); 6667; 6669–72; 6679; 6682; 6686; 6686a; 6690; 6694; 6704; 6708; 6710; 6712; 6714; 6716; 6720; 6726; 6728; 6730; 6732; 6740; 6740b; 6741; 6749; 6752; 6762–3; 6769; 6800–2; 6804; 6808; 6813; 6817; 6819; 6949–51b; 6952–69a; 6970–96a; 6999; 7077; 7210; 7213; 7217–18; 7244; 7248; 7256; 11801; 11811; 11815; 11834–6; 11841–3; 11860–3; 11864a; Finke 211; Ness-Lieb 168; Nesselhauf 119; Schillinger 76; 87.** *Legio XXX Ulpia Victrix: AE* 2004, 1028; *CIL* XIII, 6763; 6952. Unspecified legion: *AE* 1910, 63; 1916, 125; 1956, 171; 1979, 435; 1990, 747; 1994, 1311; *AmphMainz-Dipinti* 77; *CIL* XIII, 6668; 6672; 6677; 6681; 6683; 6685; 6691–2; 6696; 6810; 6818; 6997–8; 7009–9a; 7014; 7022; 7232; 11864. *Equites singulares: AE* 1962, 289; *CIL* XIII, 7057. *Ala Claudia: CIL* XIII, 7023. *Ala I Flavia: CIL* XIII, 7024. *Ala II Flavia: CIL* XIII, 7025. *Ala Gallorum Petriana: CIL* XIII, 6820. *Ala Hispanorum: CIL* XIII, 7026–7. *Ala Indiana: AE* 1940, 116; *CIL* XIII, 7028; 7257. *Ala Noricorum: CIL* XIII, 7029–30; *Finke* 212. *Ala Parthorum: AE* 1959, 188; 1976, 495. *Ala Picentiana: AE* 1962, 290; *CIL* XIII, 11869. *Ala Rusonis: CIL* XIII, 7031. *Ala I Scubulorum: CIL* XIII, 7032. *Cohors IV Aquitanorum: CIL* XIII, 6742. *Cohors I Asturum: CIL* XIII, 7036–7. *Cohors I Belgarum: CIL* XIII, 6687; 7038. *Cohors [—] Bituricum: Finke* 350. *Cohors II Bituricum: CIL* XIII, 6812. *Cohors I Cyrenaica: CIL* XIII, 6812. *Cohors V Dalmatarum: CIL* XIII, 7039. *Cohors I Ituraeorum: AE* 1901, 86; 1929, 131; *CIL* XIII, 6817; 7040–4. *Cohors I Lucensium: CIL* XIII, 7045. *Cohors I Noricorum: AE* 1965, 251. *Cohors II Praetoria: CIL* XIII, 6677a. *Cohors II Raetorum: CIL* XIII, 7246. *Cohors VII Raetorum: CIL* XIII, 11868. *Cohors Raetorum et Vindelicorum: AE* 1940, 115; *CIL* XIII, 7047–8; *Nesselhauf* 114; 114a. *Cohors Surorum: AE* 1938, 120. *Cohors IV Thracum: AE* 1965, 258; *CIL* XIII, 7049–50. *Cohors VI Thracum: CIL* XIII, 6812; 7052. *[Cohors —] Thracum: CIL* XIII, 7051. *Cohors XXIV Voluntariorum: Nesselhauf* 115. Unspecified cavalry unit: *CIL* XIII, 7033–4; *DefMainz* 8. Unspecified infantry unit: *AE* 1898, 19; 1990, 746; 2005, 1129; *CIL*

XIII, 6703; 6711; 6794; 7006; 7015; 7017; 7053; 7060–60a; 11801a; 11831; 11866; 11870; 11873; *ZPE* 173, 295. Unspecified unit: *AE* 1962, 292; 1979, 422; *CIL* XIII, 6680; 7012–13; 7018–20; 7046; 7056; 11867; 11871. *Veteranus*: *AE* 1941, 110; *CIL* XIII, 7055
Sub-literary references: –
Modern references (site): Baatz 1962; Decker and Selzer 1976; Esser 1972; Haensch 2003; Jacobi 1996; Oldenstein 2001; Schumacher 2003; Wells 1972, 138–46; Witteyer 1999; Ziethen 1999
Modern references (finds): Ehmig 2000; Heising 2007; Panter 2007; Pelgen 2004; Selzer et al. 1988
Notes: Urban site

Marktbreit (Figures 2,22; 49)
Location: 49° 40′ 15.55″ N, 10° 9′ 18.81″ E
Situation: Confluence of Main and Breitbach
Height ASL: 266m (GE)
Country: Germany
Region: Ldkr. Kitzingen
Province: Germania Magna
Length: 742m
Width: 600m
Area: 34.7ha
Proportion: 1.237
Cardinal orientation: 322°
Phases & Dating: Timber – ? (AD 5/6)
Literary references: –
Units attested epigraphically: –
Sub-literary references: –
Modern references (site): Herrmann 1992; Pietsch 1989; 1990; 1991a; 1991b; 1992; 1993; 2003; Pietsch et al. 1991; Wamser 1991
Modern references (finds): –
Notes: Open site

Mirebeau (Figures 2,24; 50)
Location: 47° 23′ 29.16″ N, 5° 19′ 52.41″ E
Situation: Confluence of the Bèze and an unnamed stream
Height ASL: 204m (GE)
Country: France
Region: Cote d'Or
Province: Germania Superior
Length: 580m
Width: 385m
Area: 22.4ha
Proportion: 1.506
Cardinal orientation: 212°
Phases & Dating: Stone – *Legio VIII Augusta* (AD 70–92)
Literary references: –
Units attested epigraphically: *Legio I*: D 2285. **Legio VIII: D 2285.** *Legio XI*: D 2285. *Legio XIV*: D 2285. *Legio XXI*: D 2285
Sub-literary references: –
Modern references (site): Boudot 1835; Goguey 1967; 1971; 1973; 1977; 2008; Goguey and Reddé 1995; Héron de Villefosse 1908; Reddé 1996; 2006

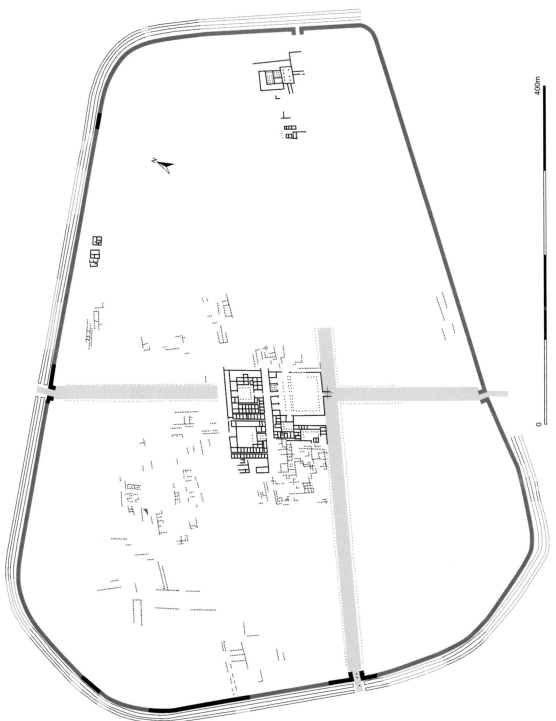

400m

0

Figure 40. Mirebeau (after Kühlborn 2000)

Figure 50: Mirebeau (after Goguey and Reddé 2005).

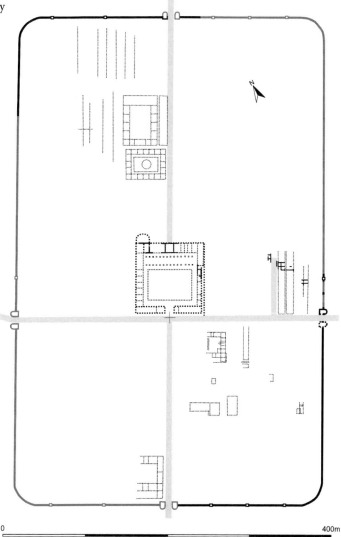

0   400m

Modern references (finds): –
Notes: Open site

Neuss–Novaesium ('Camp C') (Figure 2,17)

Location: 51° 11′ 9.98″ N, 6° 42′ 37.07″ E
Situation: Confluence of Rhine and Erft
Height ASL: 42m (GE)
Country: Germany
Region: Kr. Neuss, Nordrhein-Westfalen
Province: Germania Inferior
Length: >1070m
Width: >900m
Area: >81.0ha
Proportion: –

Cardinal orientation: 26°
Phases & Dating: Timber – four-legion *aestiva* (AD 14)
Literary references: –
Units attested epigraphically: *Legio V: AE* **2000, 1002**
Sub-literary references: –
Modern references (site): Noelke 1975a; Petrikovits 1961; Rüger 1984; Wells 1972, 127–34
Modern references (finds): Simpson 2000
Notes: Urban site. Associated by some writers with the *castra aestiva* 'apud finibus Ubiorum' of Tac., *Ann.* 1.31

Neuss–Novaesium ('Camp G') (Figures 2,17; 51)

Location: 51° 10′ 58.25″ N, 6° 43′ 29.40″ E
Situation: Confluence of Rhine and Erft
Height ASL: 42m (GE)
Country: Germany
Region: Kr. Neuss, Nordrhein-Westfalen

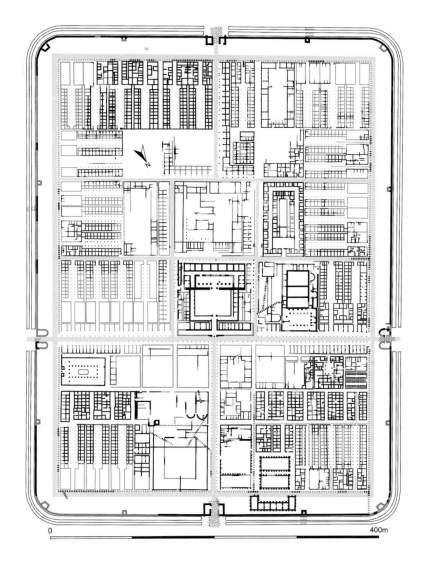

Figure 51: Neuss–Novaesium (after Koenen 1904).

0   400m

Province: Germania Inferior
Length: 571m
Width: 438m
Area: 25.8ha
Proportion: 1.304
Cardinal orientation: 28°
Phases & Dating: Timber – *Legio XX* (AD 35–43); stone – *Legio XVI Gallica* (AD 43–69); *Legio VI Victrix* (AD 70–92)
Literary references: Tac., *Hist.* 5.26; 33; 35–6; 57; 62; 70; 77; 79; 5.22
Units attested epigraphically: *Legio I Minervia*: *AE* 1905, 142. *Legio V*: *AE* 2000, 1002; *GraffNeuss* 91. *Legio VI Victrix*: *AE* 1905, 135; *CIL* XIII, 8549–51; *Lehner* 1190–1. *Legio X Gemina*: *AE* 1905, 139. *Legio XVI*: *AE* 1905, 134; *CIL* XIII, 8552; *Ness-Lieb* 242. *Legio XX*: *CIL* XIII, 8553–5. *Legio XXI*: *CIL* XIII, 8556. *Legio XXII Primigenia*: *AE* 1905, 140. *Legio XXX Ulpia Victrix*: *AE* 1905, 141. Unspecified legion: *CIL* XIII, 8557. *Ala Afrorum*: *AE* 1924, 21. *Ala Frontoniana*: *CIL* XIII, 8558. *Cohors Lusitanorum*: *Ness-Lieb* 244. Unspecified cavalry unit: *GraffNeuss* 711; ?918. Unspecified infantry unit: *CIL* XIII, 8560; GraffNeuss 626; *Lehner* 1304. Unspecified unit: *CIL* XIII, 8561. *Veteranus*: *CIL* XIII, 8559
Sub-literary references: –
Modern references (site): Chantraine et al. 1984; Gechter 1985; 2007a; Kaiser 1994; Koenen 1904; Müller et al. 1979; Nissen 1904; Noelke 1975a; Petrikovits 1961; Rüger 1984
Modern references (finds): Chantraine 1968; 1982; Ettlinger 1983; Filtzinger 1972; Kaiser 2005; Knörzer 1970; Kütter 2008; Kütter and Pause 2006; Lehner 1904; Mary 1967; Neuffer 1951; Noelke 1975b; 1977; Oxé 1925; Vega 1966
Notes: Urban site. Also known as the 'Koenenlager'

Nijmegen–Batavodurum (Figures 2,12; 52)
Location: 51° 50′ 25.40″ N, 5° 53′ 4.44″ E
Situation: Confluence of the Waal and Het Meer
Height ASL: 50m (GE)
Country: Netherlands
Region: Gelderland
Province: Germania Inferior
Length: >660m
Width: 640m
Area: >42.8ha
Proportion: >1.031
Cardinal orientation: ?32°
Phases & Dating: Timber – ? (19/18–15/14 BC)
Literary references: –
Units attested epigraphically: *Legio I G[ermanica?]*: *AE* 1976, 515; 2000, 1011. *Legio XIII*: *AE* 2000, 1012.
Sub-literary references: –
Modern references (site): Bogaers et al. 1979; Franzen 2009; Haalebos 1991; 1995; 1999; 2002; 2006; Wells 1972, 116–23
Modern references (finds): Enckevort and Zee 1999; Kemmers 2005
Notes: Urban site. Beneath Flavian fortress of Noviomagus (see below)

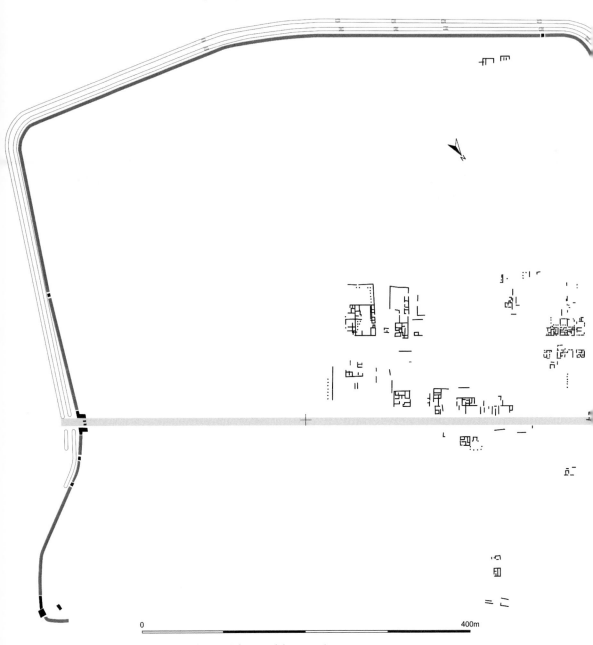

Figure 52: Nijmegen–Batavodurum (after Haalebos 2002).

Nijmegen–Noviomagus (Figures 2,12; 53)

Location: 51° 50' 23.27" N, 5° 53' 7.72" E
Situation: Confluence of the Waal and Het Meer
Height ASL: 46m (GE)
Country: Netherlands
Region: Gelderland

Province: Germania Inferior
Length: 465m
Width: 340–400m
Area: 16.8ha
Proportion: 1.163–1.368
Cardinal orientation: 33°
Phases & Dating: Timber – *Legio II Adiutrix* (AD 70); *Legio X Gemina* (AD 71–105); stone – *Legio IX Hispana* (?AD 106–?)
Literary references: Tac., *Hist.* **5.20** (as Batavodurum)
Units attested epigraphically: *Legio I Minervia: CIL* XIII, 8728. *Legio VIII Augusta: AE* 1998, 966. *Legio IX Hispana: AE* **1977, 541; 1996, 1107.** *Legio X Gemina: AE* **1968, 404; 1979, 415–16;** *CIL* **XIII, 8713; 8715; 8732–6.** *Legio XX: CIL* XIII, 8737. *Legio XXX Ulpia Victrix: AE* 2000, 1013; *CIL* XIII, 8719; 8723; 8730. Unspecified infantry unit: *AE* 1968, 405; 2000, 1014; *CIL* XIII, 8738; 12086; *Finke* 310–11. *Veteranus: CIL* XIII, 8718
Sub-literary references: –
Modern references (site): Bogaers et al. 1979; Driessen 2009; Enckevort 1997; Enckevort and Zee 1996; Enckevort et al. 2000; Haalebos 1995; 1999; 2006; Willems and Kooistra 1991; Willems 1996; Willems and Enckevort 2009

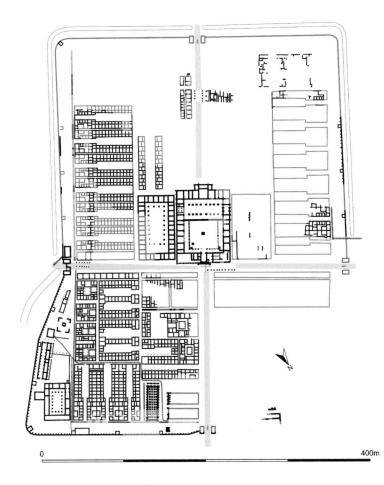

0   400m

Figure 53: Nijmegen–Noviomagus (after Driessen 2009).

Modern references (finds): Brunsting and Steures 1995; 1997; Enckevort and Thijssen 2001–2; Enckevort and Willems 1994; Enckevort van and Zee 1999; Peters 1970; Willems 1991; 1994; Willems and Enckevort 1996

Notes: Urban site

Oberaden (Figures 2,15; 54)

Location: 51° 36′ 36.64″ N, 7° 34′ 53.52″ E
Situation: Confluence of the Sesecke and Lippe
Height ASL: 62m (GE)
Country: Germany
Region: Kr. Unna, Nordrhein-Westfalen
Province: Germania Magna
Length: 695m
Width: 850m
Area: 54.1ha
Proportion: 0.818
Cardinal orientation: 185°
Phases & Dating: Timber – ? (11–8 BC)
Literary references: –
Units attested epigraphically: –
Sub-literary references: –
Modern references (site): Albrecht 1938; 1942; Aschemeyer 1963; Kühlborn 1989; 1990; 1991; 1992; 1995; 1999; 2005; 2008; Schnurbein 1981; 2002; Schwemin 1998
Modern references (finds): Böhn 1924; García Bellido 1996; Kropatscheck 1909; Kucan 1981; 1984; 1992; Roth-Rubi (ed.) 2006; Rudnick 1995; Wells 1972, 211–20
Notes: Partly urban, partly open site. Has been identified with the Aliso of Tac., *Ann.* 2.7 and Vell. Pat. 120.4

Ptuj – Poetovio (Figure 2,40)

Location: 46° 24′ 50.46″ N, 15° 51′ 48.86″ E
Situation: Adjacent to the Drava
Height ASL: *c.*220m (GE)
Country: Slovenia
Region: Lower Styria
Province: Pannonia
Length: –
Width: –
Area: –
Proportion: –
Cardinal orientation: –
Phases & Dating: ?Timber – *Legio VIII Augusta* (AD 10–43); *Legio XIII Gemina* (AD 44–88)
Literary references: Tac., *Hist.* 3.1; Ptol., *Geog.* 2.15.4
Units attested epigraphically: *Legio I Adiutrix: AIJ* 365; 374–5; *CIL* III, 10880. *Legio II: CIL* III, 11371a1. *Legio II Adiutrix: CIL* III, 4057. *Legio II Italica: CIL* III, 15184,6. *Legio IV Flavia: CIL* III, 4056; *ILJug* I, 340. *Legio V Macedonica: AE* 1936, 54–7. **Legio VIII Augusta: AE 1978, 646; CIL III, 4060; 10878–9.** *Legio X Gemina: AE* 1950, 40; *AIJ* 273; *CIL* III, 4030. *Legio XI: AE* 1920, 63. **Legio XIII Gemina: AE 1934, 225; 1936, 54–7; 1977, 629; 1986, 562; 570; AIJ 385; CIL III, 4061; 4660,1a-b; 4660,25c; 10877; 10881; 10887; 14355,2–3; ILJug I, 345; II, 1134; 1152.** *Legio XIII[: CIL* III, 4058. *Legio XIV Gemina: AIJ* 378; *CIL* III, 14065. Unspecified legion:

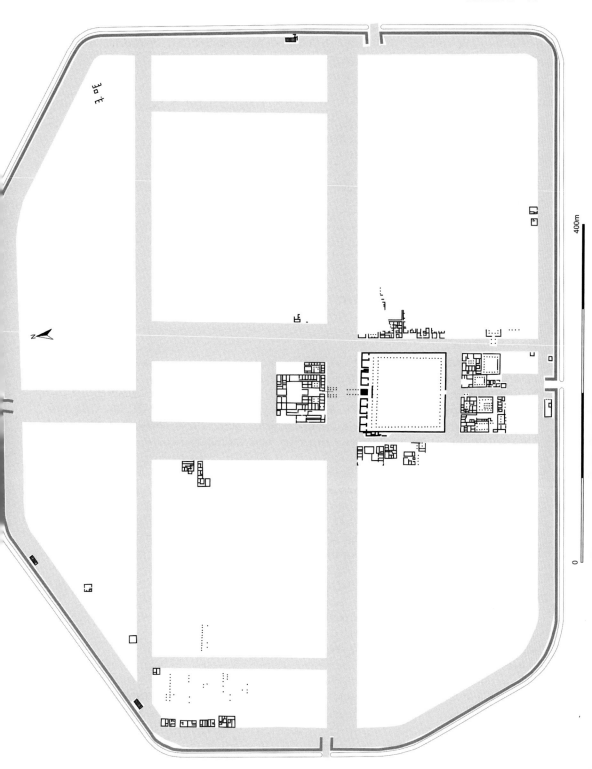

Figure 54: Oberaden (after Kühlborn 2000).

AIJ 267; *CIL* III, 4055. *Ala I Thracum: ILJug* I, 339. *Cohors X Praetoria: CIL* III, 4037. *Cohors II Aurelia Dacorum: CIL* III, 15184,16. *Cohors I Germanorum: AE* 1993, 1285. *Cohors II Hispanorum: AE* 1993, 1285. Unspecified infantry unit: *CIL* III, 14355,5; 14360,12. Unspecified unit: *AIJ* 384; *CIL* III, 14063. *Veteranus: AIJ* 383

Sub-literary references: –

Modern references (site): Abramić 1925a; 1925b; Gojković 2009; Pahič 1996, 139; Sanader 2003b; Saria 1974, 225; Wilkes 2000, 116

Modern references (finds): Tragau 1909

Notes: Probably destroyed by the River Drava

Regensburg–Castra Regina (Figures 2,26; 55)

Location: 49° 1′ 4.96″ N, 12° 5′ 54.00″ E

Situation: Adjacent to the Danube

Height ASL: 346m (GE)

Country: Germany

Region: Bayern

Province: Raetia

Length: 515m

Width: 450m

Area: 23.2ha

Proportion: 1.144

Cardinal orientation: 7°

Phases & Dating: Stone – *Legio III Italica* (AD 179–?5th century)

Literary references: *Tab. Peut.* 4.4

Units attested epigraphically: *Legio I Minervia: IBR* 497a. ***Legio III Italica: AE* 1906, 183a; 1986, 532; 2004, 1062; *CIL* III, 5942; 5947; 5949–50; 5953; 5955; 5956–8; 6000a-c; 6000k; 6531-2; 6571; 11965–6; 11968–70; 11988a-i; *IBR* 496c; 496k-l; 496n; *Lupa* 6540; *Wagner* 101.** *Legio IV Macedonica: IBR* 498b-e. *Legio VIII Augusta: IBR* 498. Unspecified legion: *AE* 1906, 183b; *CIL* III, 5946; 5952; 14370,12 (p 2328,201). *Ala Auriana: IBR* 499. *Ala II Flavia: IBR* 500a-b. *Ala I Singularium: CIL* III, 11995a-b; *IBR* 500. *Cohors II Aquitanorum: CIL* III, 6537; *IBR* 503. *Cohors III Britannorum: Lupa* 6539. *Cohors I Canathenorum: CIL* III, 11992d-e; *IBR* 502a-c. *Cohors I Noricorum: CIL* III, 14370,13. *Cohors I Ulpia Pannoniorum: AE* 1986, 535. Unspecified cavalry unit: *CIL* III, 11972. Unspecified infantry unit: *CIL* III, 14371,3. Unspecified unit: *CIL* III, 5945; 5951. *Veteranus: CIL* III, 5948; 14370,9

Sub-literary references: –

Modern references (site): Dietz 2000; Dietz and Fischer 1996; Dietz et al. 1979; Fink 1885; Gauer 1981; Konrad 2005; 2006; 2009; Lewis 1891; Ohlenschlager 1885; Osterhaus 1972; 1974; Reinecke 1958; Schmidts 2001; Spindler 1978; Strobel 1965; Stroh 1953; 1958; 1963; 1971; Waldherr 2001

Modern references (finds): Bogaers 1986; Dietz 1984; Ohlenschlager 1874

Notes: Urban site.

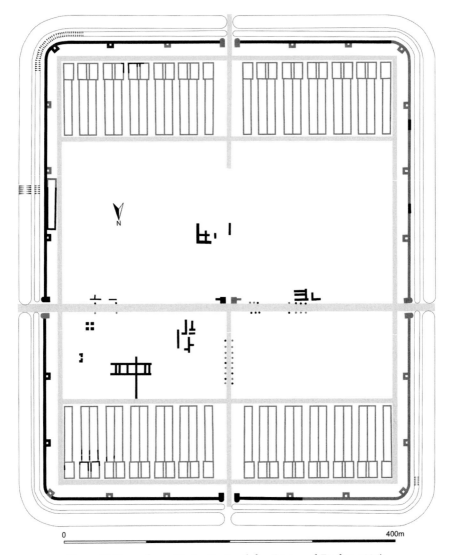

Figure 55: Regensburg–Castra Regina (after Dietz and Fischer 1996).

Roma–Castra Praetoria (Figures 2,105; 56)

Location: 41° 54′ 24.32″ N, 12° 30′ 23.47″ E
Situation: North-eastern edge of the City
Height ASL: 61m
Country: Italy
Region: Provincia di Roma
Province: Italia
Length: 470m
Width: 395m
Area: 17.9ha
Proportion: 1.190
Cardinal orientation: 159°

Figure 56: Roma (after Coulston 2000).

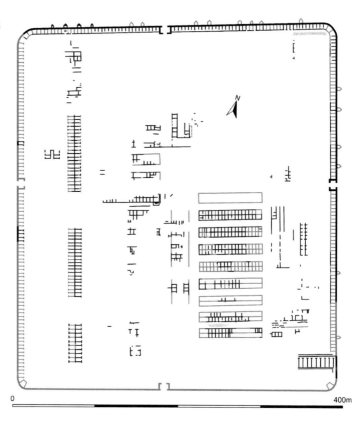

0   400m

Phases & Dating: Brick-faced concrete – *Praetoriani* (AD 23–312)

Modern references (site): Cf. Coulston 2000

Notes: Not a legionary base but included for the purposes of comparison. Praetorian cohorts moved to Roma in AD 23. Urban site

Rosinos de Vidriales–Petavonium (Figure 2,99)

Location: 42° 5' 17.65" N, 5° 59' 51.72" W

Situation: Confluence of Arroyo de la Almucera and Regato de los Moros

Height ASL: 736m (GE)

Country: Spain

Region: Provincia de Zamora

Province: Hispania Tarraconensis

Length: 560m

Width: 325m

Area: 19.1ha

Proportion: 1.723

Cardinal orientation: 119°

Phases & Dating: Timber – *Legio X Gemina* (AD 15/20–62)

Literary references: –

Units attested epigraphically: *Legio X Gemina: AE* 1928, 179–80; 1976, 289; 1984, 555; 1997, 867–8. Unspecified cavalry unit: *AE* 1937, 166

Sub-literary references: –

Modern references (site): Carretero Vaquero 1999a; Carretero Vaquero and Romero Carnicero 1999; 2004; Carretero Vaquero et al. 1999; Romero Carnicero and Carretero Vaquero 2006

Modern references (finds): Carretero Vaquero 1999b; 2000; 2001; Martin Valls et al. 2002; Martinez Garcia 1999

Notes: Open site

Sadak–Satala (Figures 2,67; 57)

Location: 40° 1′ 37.89″ N, 39° 35′ 54.16″ E
Situation: Between two unnamed minor tributaries of the Kelkit
Height ASL: 1673m (GE)
Country: Turkey
Region: Gümüşhane
Province: Armenia Minor
Length: 495m
Width: 410m
Area: 20.3ha
Proportion: 1.207
Cardinal orientation: 100°

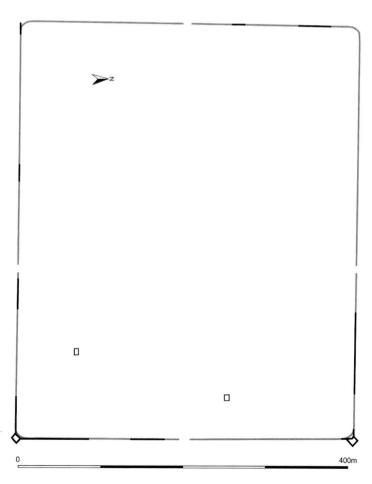

0   400m

Figure 57: Sadak–Satala (after Mitford 1980).

Phases & Dating: Stone – *Legio XVI Flavia Firma* (AD 70–117); *Legio XV Apollinaris* (AD 117–4th century)

Literary references: Cass. Dio 68.19.2; Ptol., *Geog.* 5.7.3; Procop., *De Aedif.* 3.4.2–5; *ND Or.* 38.13

Units attested epigraphically: *Legio IV Flavia*: *AE* 1988, 1044; *LegioXVApo* 101. **Legio XV Apollinaris: *AE* 1975, 818; 1988, 1044; *CIL* III, 13647a-d; *LegioXVApo* 101; 123; 143. Legio XVI Flavia Firma: *AE* 1971, 465; 1972, 665; 1975, 817; 1997, 1509.** Unspecified infantry unit: *AE* 1997, 1511

Sub-literary references: –

Modern references (site): Crow 1986; Drahor et al. 2004; 2008; Gregory 1995–97, vol. 2, 39–42; Lightfoot 1990a; 1990b; 1998; Mitford 1974a; 1980

Modern references (finds): Mitford 1974b; 1997

Notes: Partly open, partly urban site. Listed by Farnum (2005, 28) as Kelkit

Samsat–Samosata (Figure 2,70)

Location: 37° 33′ 47.12″ N, 38° 30′ 6.73″ E

Situation: Adjacent to the Euphrates

Height ASL: *c.*530m (GE)

Country: Turkey

Region: Adıyaman Province

Province: Syria

Length: –

Width: –

Area: –

Proportion: –

Cardinal orientation: –

Phases & Dating: ?Stone – *Legio VI Ferrata* (AD 70–117); *Legio XVI Flavia Firma* (AD 117–?Tetrarchic)

Literary references: Cass. Dio 55.24.3; Ptol., *Geog.* 5.14.8; Amm. Marc. 14, 8, 7; 18, 4, 7

Units attested epigraphically: *Legio IV Scythica*: *CIL* III, 6048. **Legio XVI Flavia: *AE* 1903, 254; *CIL* III, 13609; 13615**

Sub-literary references: –

Modern references (site): French 1994; Gregory 1995–97, vol. 2, 124–8; Parker 2000, 123

Modern references (finds): –

Notes: Never identified during excavations, the site is now flooded

Silistra–Durostorum (Figures 2,61; 58)

Location: 44° 6′ 49.68″ N, 27° 16′ 13.78″ E

Situation: On bend in the Danube

Height ASL: 27m (GE)

Country: Bulgaria

Region: Silistra Province

Province: Moesia Inferior

Length: 510m

Width: 430m

Area: 19.1ha

Proportion: 1.186

Cardinal orientation: ?6°

Phases & Dating: Stone – *Legio XI Claudia* (AD 106–4th century)

Literary references: Ptol., *Geog.* 3.10.10

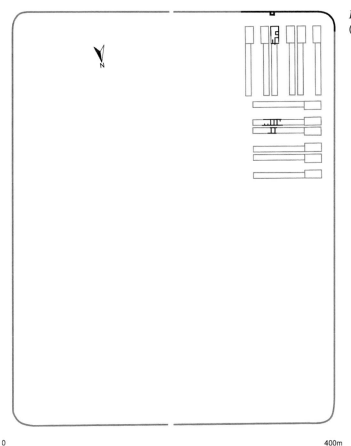

Figure 58: Silistra–Durosturum (after Donevski 2004).

0 ———————————————— 400m

Units attested epigraphically: *Legio I Italica: AE* 1936, 16. *Legio VII Claudia: AE* 1902, 133b; *CIL* III, 14597,2–3. **Legio XI Claudia: *ADBulgar* 457–8; *AE* 1895, 59; 1902, 133a; 1925, 108–9; 1936, 12–15; 1974, 570–1; 2004, 1268; 2005, 1335; *CIL* III, 7474–7; 7619a; 12458–9; 12525; 14436.** Unspecified legion: *CIL* III, 14213,2; 14435. Unspecified infantry unit: *CIL* III, 12460; *IGBR* II, 865

Sub-literary references: –
Modern references (site): Donevski 1990a; 1990b; 1991; 2004; 2009; Gerov 1977; Ivanov 1993
Modern references (finds): Elefterescu and Muşeţeanu 1990
Notes: Dimensions from Donevski 2009, 105; Urban site

Sisak–Siscia (Figure 2,42)
Location: 45° 29′ 3.44″ N, 16° 22′ 29.00″ E
Situation: Confluence of Kupa and Sava
Height ASL: 100m (GE)
Country: Croatia
Region: Sisak-Moslavina county
Province: Pannonia Superior
Length: –
Width: –
Area: –

Proportion: –
Cardinal orientation: –
Phases & Dating: ?Timber – *Legio IX Hispana* (AD 10–43)
Literary references: Strabo 7.5.3; Vell. Pat. 2.113; Cass. Dio 49.37–8
Units attested epigraphically: *Legio X Gemina: AE* 1901, 234; *CIL* III, 15180. *Legio XIV Gemina: CIL* III, 3970; 3972; 15181,1. *Legio XV Apollinaris: CIL* III, 10853. *Cohors XXXII Voluntariorum: CIL* III, 10854
Sub-literary references: –
Modern references (site): Durman 1992; Mócsy 1974, 37–41; Radman-Livaja 2004b; 2010a; Wilkes 2000, 116
Modern references (finds): Buzov 2006; Koščević 2003; Radman-Livaja 2004a; 2010b
Notes: Urban site

Strasbourg–Argentorate (Figures 2,23; 59)
Location: 48° 34′ 58.08″ N, 7° 45′ 3.51″ E
Situation: On island in Ill
Height ASL: 151m (GE)
Country: France

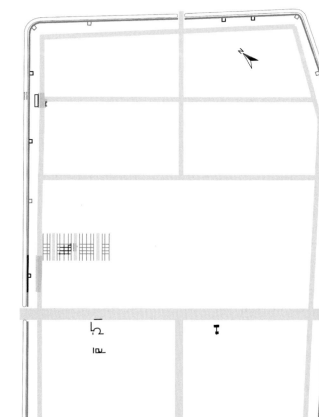

Figure 59: Strasbourg–Argentorate
(after Schnitzler and Kuhne 2010).

0   400m

Region: Région Alsace
Province: Germania Superior
Length: 530m
Width: 275m
Area: 21.0ha
Proportion: 1.927
Cardinal orientation: 233°
Phases & Dating: Timber – *Legio II Augusta* (AD 10–43) … stone – *Legio VIII Augusta* (AD 92–?5th century)
Literary references: Ptol., *Geog.* **2.8**
Units attested epigraphically: *Legio II*: *AE* 1906, 179; 1998, 983; *CIL* XIII, 5975–8. **Legio II Augusta: AE 1902, 248.** *Legio VII[*: *CIL* XIII, 11625. **Legio VIII Augusta: AE 1906, 180a; 1951, 69a; 70a-b; *CIL* XIII, 5979; 5982; 11608–9; 11621; 11624; 11627; Finke 136; 332; ILTG 420; 494–5.** *Legio XXI Rapax*: *AE* 1906, 180b; *CIL* XIII, 12310,1–4; *Wiegels* 118–20. *Legio XXII Primigenia*: *AE* 1906, 180c. Unspecified legion: *AE* 1902, 247; 1907, 76; *CIL* XIII, 5970; 11626; *ILTG* 422. *Ala Petriana*: *AE* 1907, 77; *CIL* XIII, 11605. *Numerus militum Pacensium*: *AE* 1976, 490. Unspecified unit: *AE* 1907, 75; *CIL* XIII, 11628–9. *Veteranus*: *CIL* XIII, 5983
Sub-literary references: –
Modern references (site): Forrer 1927; Gissinger 2002; Hatt 1949a; 1949b; 1949c; 1953; 1956; 1980; 1993; Reddé 1997; Schnitzler and Kuhnle 2010; Wells 1972, 147–8
Modern references (finds): Straub 1879
Notes: Urban site

Svištov–Novae (Figures 2,59; 60)

Location: 43° 36′ 48.62″ N, 25° 23′ 40.47″ E
Situation: Confluence of Danube and Dermen-dere
Height ASL: 50m (GE)
Country: Bulgaria
Region: Veliko Tarnovo Province
Province: Moesia Inferior
Length: 477m
Width: 360m
Area: 16.9ha
Proportion: 1.325
Cardinal orientation: 5°
Phases & Dating: Timber – *Legio VIII Augusta* (AD 44–69); stone – *Legio I Italica* (AD 70–4th century)
Literary references: Ptol., *Geog.* **3.10.5**
Units attested epigraphically: Legio I Italica: ADBulgar 451a-e; 453; AE 1932, 51–2; 1939, 121; 1944, 14; 1965, 134; 135a; 1966, 345; 347; 1968, 454a; 1972, 526; 528; 1973, 480a-b; 1975, 754a; 1982, 849; 1983, 878; 1987, 863; 866a-b; 1988, 984; 1990, 863; 1991, 1373–4; 1993, 1363; 1364a; 1366–7; 1995, 1334; 1996, 1340a; 1998, 1130; 1132–3; 1136; 1999, 1332–3; 1335; 2004, 1243; 1249; CIL III, 750 (p 992, 1338); 756 (p 993, 1338); 785,1; 7438; 7441; 7617; 1932, 52; IGLNovae 10; 17–18; 31; 40; 82; 85; 165; ILBulg 277; 279a. *Legio I Minervia*: *AE* 1987, 861; 865. *Legio III Gallica*: *CIL* III, 755. **Legio VIII Augusta: AE 1914, 93; 1999, 1331.** *Legio XI Claudia*: *AE* 1965, 135b; 136; 1975, 754b; *IGLNovae* 117. *Legio XX Valeria Victrix*: *AE* 1985, 735. Unspecified legion: *AE* 1982, 848; 1987, 862; 1995, 1333; 1998, 1129; 2005, 1328; 1330; *IGLNovae* 49; 51; 154. *Ala I Asturum*: *IGLNovae* 78. *Cohors V Asturum*: *AE* 1999, 1333. *Cohors I Montanorum*: *AE* 1976, 609. Unspecified infantry unit: *AE* 1999, 1334; 2004, 1248; *CIL*

Figure 60: Svištov–Novae
(after Press 1981).

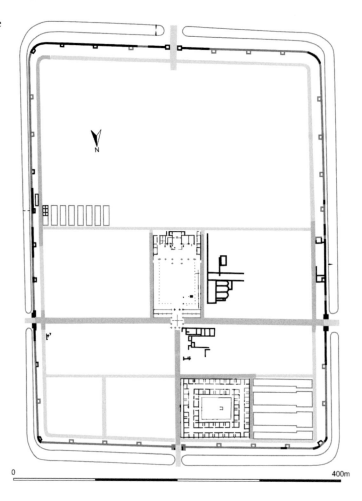

III, 12366; *ILBulg* 322. Unspecified unit: *AE* 1978, 707; 1998, 1127; 1135; 2004, 1250; *IGLNovae* 19; 90

Sub-literary references: –

Modern references (site): Derda et al. 2008; Dimitrova-Milceva 1991; Donevski 1998; Dyczek 1997; 1999; 2001; 2007; Dyczek et al. 1993; Genčeva 2003; Parnicki-Pudełko 1990; Press and Sarnowski 1987; Sarnowski 1977; 1981; 1983b; 1984; 1991; 1992; 1995; 1996a; 1999; 2000; 2002; 2003; Sarnowski and Kaniszewski 2007; Sarnowski et al. 2005; Sarnowski and Press 1990

Modern references (finds): Biernacka-Lubanska 1998; Bunsch 2000; 2002; 2003; 2006; Bunsch et al. 2003; Daszkiewicz et al. 2000; Dimitrova-Milceva 2006; Dobrowolski and Piasecki 2003; Genčeva 1998a; 1998b; 2000; Gręzak and Piątkowska-Małecka 2006; Kolendo 1980; 1988; 2001; 2002; 2003; Kovalevskaja et al. 2000; Kunisz 1987; Sarnowski, T. 1979a; 1979b; 1980; 1983a; 1985; 1989; 1993a; 1993b; 1993c; 1995; 1996b; 2005; Sarnowski and Gacuta 1982; Sarnowski and Trynkowski 1990

Notes: Ptolemy places *legio I Italica* near Durosturum, not at Novae. Open site

Szőny–Brigetio (Figures 2,36; 61)

Location: 47° 44′ 1.54″ N, 18° 11′ 38.28″ E
Situation: Confluence of Danube and Korpás ér/Fekete ér
Height ASL: 109m (GE)
Country: Hungary
Region: Közép-Dunántúl Region
Province: Pannonia Superior
Length: 540m
Width: 430m
Area: 23.2ha
Proportion: 1.256
Cardinal orientation: 12°
Phases & Dating: Timber & stone – *Legio I Adiutrix* (AD 82–4th century)
Literary references: Amm. Marc. 17.12.21; *ND Occ.* 33.29

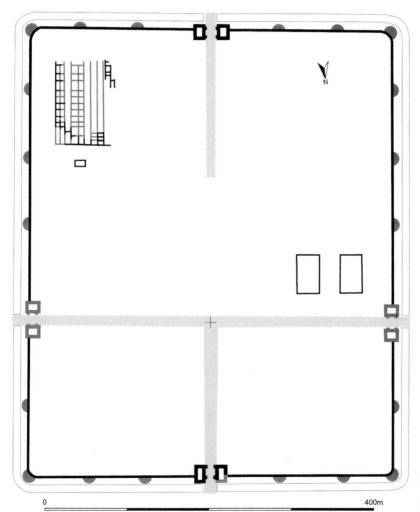

0   400m

Figure 61: Szőny–
Brigetio (after
Számadó and
Borhy 2003).

Units attested epigraphically: *Legio Adiutrix*: CIL III, 11032. *Legio* [—] *Adiutrix*: CIL III, 11038.
   Legio I Adiutrix: *AE* 1890, 14; 1935, 98; 1937, 137; 1974, 503; 1977, 625; 1994, 1395; 2006,
   1044; 1047–9; *CIL* III, 4275; 4277–9; 4285–6; 4289; 4297–8; 4300; 4306; 4308; 4310–13;
   4315; 4317; 4321–2; 4324; 4326; 4328; 4357; 4655a-b; 4655i; 4655k; 10960; 10976; 10979;
   10983–4; 10987–8; 10992; 10994; 10996; 11002–3; 11008; 11017–19; 11021; 11024–6;
   11030–1; 11034–7; 11039; 11041; 11326; 11345a-b; 11346a-e; 11348; 11424; 14355,21–3;
   IPSSTA 22; *RIU* II, 390; 399; 436; 441; 451–3; 456; 464; 485; 487; 506; 512; 527; 545–6; 552;
   561; 580; 582; 584; 590; 596; III, 656; 663–4; 671; 677; 680; 718–20; 764; 772; 792; *RIU-S,*
   95–6. *Legio II Adiutrix*: *CIL* III, 3750z; 4311; 10594; 11033; *RIU* III, 794. *Legio IV Flavia*: *CIL*
   III, 4327. *Legio X Gemina*: *CIL* III, 4659,1a; 4659,1b-c; 11352a-c. *Legio XI Claudia*: *CIL* III,
   4658b. *Legio XIII Gemina*: *AE* 1966, 293. *Legio XIV Gemina*: *AE* 1944, 105; *CIL* III, 4299; 11029;
   11363a; 11365a-b; *IPSSTA* 1; *RIU* II, 505; III, 672; 764. *Legio XV*: *CIL* III, 11365a-b. *Legio XXX*
   Ulpia Victrix: *CIL* III, 4663a-c; 10974; 11370a-c. Unspecified legion: *AE* 2003, 1376; 4292–3;
   4307; 13437; *RIU* II, 382; 417; 438; 626; *RIU-S,* 111. *Ala Flavia Britannica*: *RIU* III, 711. *Ala III*
   Thracum: *CIL* III, 4270; 4625; 11020; 11327; 11333. *Cohors I Aelia*: *CIL* III, 11373,1a-c. *Cohors*
   I Alpinorum: *CIL* III, 4284. *Cohors I Batavorum*: *RIU-S,* 126. *Cohors IV Breucorum*: *CIL* III,
   3756f. *Cohors VII Breucorum*: *CIL* III, 3757o-v; 3757w-x; 10668n-x; *RIU* II, 424. *Cohors III*
   Brittonum: *RIU-S,* 113. *Cohors Hemesenorum*: *CIL* III, 10318. *Cohors I Hispanorum*: *RHP* 370.
   Cohors Augusta Ituraeorum: *RIU-S,* 115–16. *Cohors I Ulpia Pannoniorum*: *RIU* III, 721; 782.
   Cohors Nova Severiana: *RIU-S,* 123. *Cohors I Thracum*: *CIL* III, 4316; *RHP* 457a-b; *RIU* III, 640.
   Cohors IV Voluntariorum: *RHP* 469a-b. Unspecified cavalry unit: *RIU* III, 707; 729. Unspecified
   infantry unit: *CIL* III, 3758k; 4276; 4287 (p 1045); 4329; 10971; 11040; *RIU* II, 386; 460; *RIU-S,*
   99. Unspecified unit: *CIL* III, 4323 (p 1757); *RIU* II, 457; 461; 504; *RIU-S,* 97. Veteranus: *CIL*
   III, 4318 (p 1757); 10982; *RIU* III, 641; 761; 766

Sub-literary references: –

Modern references (site): Barkóczi 1949; 1951; 1961; 1965; Berkovics 1886; 1887; Borhy 1998;
   2004; 2009; Borhy et al. 2003; Lőrincz 1975; Paulovics 1934; 1941; Rómer 1861; 1862; Számadó
   and Borhy 2003

Modern references (finds): Kuzmová 1999

Notes: Partly open, partly urban site

Tazoult-Lambèse–Lambaesis (Figures 2, 98; 62)

Location: 35° 29′ 24.78″ N, 6° 15′ 17.02″ E
Situation: On a plain (no permanent watercourse)
Height ASL: 1166m (GE)
Country: Algeria
Region: Aurès
Province: Numidia
Length: 505m
Width: 445m
Area: 22.5ha
Proportion: 1.135
Cardinal orientation: 356°
Phases & Dating: Stone – *Legio III Augusta* (AD 122–4th century)
Literary references: Ptol., *Geog.* 4.3.29
Units attested epigraphically: *Legio I Adiutrix*: *CIL* VIII, 2741; 2788; 3005; 18270. *Legio I Italica*:
   CIL VIII, 2582; 2744; 2747; 2786; 3005; 18273. *Legio II Adiutrix*: *CIL* VIII, 3001. *Legio III*
   Adiutrix (sic): *CIL* VIII, 3066. *Legio II Augusta*: *CIL* VIII, 2586; 2877; 2907; 2938; 3001. *Legio*
   II Italica: *AE* 1956, 123. *Legio II Traiana Fortis*: *CIL* VIII, 2891. **Legio III Augusta**: *AE 1895,*

204; 1898, 11–13; 108; 1899, 60; 1900, 33–4; 1902, 11; 1904, 71; 1906, 7; 10; 1908, 10; 1909, 3; 1916, 22; 1917/18, 50–1; 1920, 36; 1928, 106; 1942/43, 37–9; 1954, 137–8; 1955, 134–5; 137; 1956, 123; 1957, 83; 85; 88; 1968, 646; 1971, 508; 1973, 644; 1982, 956; 1985, 872; 1989, 872–3; 1992, 1860; 1870; *CIL* VIII, 2527–9; 2532; 2534–6; 2546–8; 2550–2; 2557; 2564; 2571; 2571a; 2572; 2576–7; 2579c; 2582; 2587; 2593; 2603; 2609–10; 2616; 2621–2; 2623; 2625; 2627–8; 2630; 2634; 2637; 2639; 2647; 2650; 2652; 2654; 2658; 2665–6; 2671; 2675–6; 2685–6; 2694; 2698–9; 2705–6; 2718; 2728; 2730; 2731; 2736–8; 2742; 2744; 2747; 2749; 2752–4; 2756; 2760; 2762–4; 2766–71; 2774; 2778; 2781–3; 2785–6; 2788–90; 2791–5; 2797–8; 2801–2; 2805; 2807–9; 2813–15; 2817–18; 2820–1; 2824–6; 2828–32; 2834; 2837; 2839–40; 2841–5; 2848; 2850–3; 2855–60; 2863; 2864–6; 2869; 2871–4; 2877–9; 2881–6; 2890–1; 2893–7; 2899; 2903–4; 2907–10; 2912; 2919; 2921–2; 2924–7; 2929; 2931–2; 2934; 2935–6; 2939–41; 2943–6; 2948; 2950; 2951–6; 295–60; 2964; 2967–71; 2973–6; 2979–80; 2983–5; 2987–9; 2992; 2994–5; 2997; 3000–4; 3007; 3012; 3014–16; 3018; 3020; 3022; 3026–8; 3033; 3037; 3039; 3041; 3043–7; 3049; 3052–7; 3059; 3062; 3064–5; 3067–8; 3071; 3076–82; 3084–5; 3087–8; 3090; 3092–3; 3096–100; 3102–3; 3106–7; 3113–17; 3125–8; 3131; 3133–7; 3140; 3143; 3146; 3148; 3150–1; 3153–4; 3156–9; 3161; 3163–5; 3167; 3171–2; 3174–5; 3177–8; 3185–6; 3188; 3193; 3198–9; 3201; 3205; 3207–9; 3211; 3214; 3216–18; 3221;

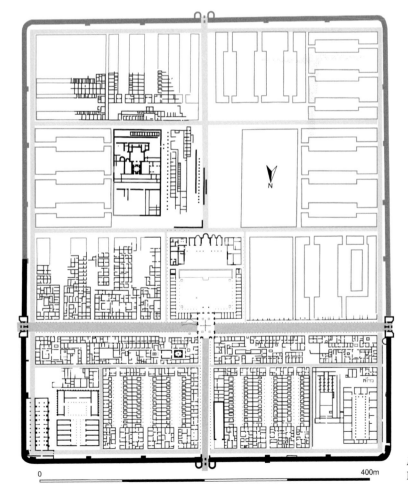

0   400m

Figure 62: Tazoult-Lambèse–Lambaesis (after Cagnat 1908) .

3223–5; 3229–30; 3232–3; 3236–7; 3241; 3243–4; 3246–7; 3249–51; 3254–6; 3258–9; 3261; 3266; 3269–70; 3272; 3274–6; 3280; 3282–5; 3288–9; 3291; 10474,1a-e; 10474,2; 10474,4a; 10474,5; 10474,6a-b; 10474,7; 10474,8a-b; 10474,9–10; 17890a; 18065; 18068; 18214; 18217; 18222–4; 18231; 18234; 18239; 18243; 18245; 18269; 18280; 18282; 18287; 18289; 18292–3; 18295–6; 18302; 18305; 18311; 18314; 18317; 18319–20; 22631,2c-i; 22631,2k-t; 22631,2v; 22631,2x; 22631,3a; 22631,5; 22631,6a-b; 22631,7a-e; 22631,8a-d; 22631,14a-e; 22631,15a-c; 22631,17b; 22631,18; 22631,21–2; 22631,23a-c; 22631,25; 22631,26a-c; 22631,26e-f; 22631,28–9; 22631,31; D 9102b. *Legio III Gallica: AE* 1898, 13; *CIL* VIII, 2627; 2904; 3157. *Legio III Parthica: CIL* VIII, 2877; 2891. *Legio IV Flavia: CIL* VIII, 2582; 2744; 3001. *Legio IV Scythica: CIL* VIII, 2627. *Legio V Macedonica: CIL* VIII, 2627; 2867. *Legio VI Victrix: CIL* VIII, 2877; 2907; 3001. *Legio VII Claudia: CIL* VIII, 2786; 3001. *Legio VII Gemina: AE* 1934, 36; *CIL* VIII, 2938; 3075; 3182; 3226; 3245; 3268; 10474,12a; 22631,32c-e. *Legio VIII Augusta: AE* 1967, 579; *CIL* VIII, 3001. *Legio IX Hispana: CIL* VIII, 2747; 18273. *Legio X Gemina: CIL* VIII, 2806; 2808; 18270. *Legio XI Claudia: AE* 1912, 17; 1954, 138; *CIL* VIII, 2741; 3005. *Legio XII Fulminata: CIL* VIII, 2582; 2744; 3001. *Legio XIII Gemina: CIL* VIII, 2582; 2744; 2891. *Legio XIV Gemina: AE* 1967, 579; *CIL* VIII, 3007. *Legio XV Apollinaris: CIL* VIII, 2582; 2744; 3001. *Legio XVI Flavia: CIL* VIII, 2627. *Legio XX Valeria Victrix: CIL* VIII, 2638; 2786; 2877; 2907; 3005. *Legio XXII Primigenia: AE* 1957, 123; *CIL* VIII, 2627; 2888–9; 2891. Unspecified legion: *AE* 1904, 70; 1911, 97; 1917/18, 29; 1989, 883b; 884; 887a; *CIL* VIII, 2537–41; 2543; 2554–5; 2560; 2565; 2567–9; 2598; 2626; 2640; 2649; 2739; 2750; 2765; 2780; 2784; 2796; 2816; 2819; 2822–3; 2827; 2838; 2846–7; 2861–2; 2868; 2875; 2876; 2892; 2906; 2914–17; 2923; 2928; 2930; 2933; 2957; 2961; 2962–3; 2965; 2972; 2982; 2986; 2990–1; 2993; 3006; 3019; 3060; 3083; 3095; 3111; 3141; 3145; 3166; 3179–80; 3191; 3200; 3213; 3219; 3227; 3260; 3271; 18281; 18291; 18321; 22631,1a-b. *Equites singulares: AE* 1957, 122; 1978, 890; *CIL* VIII, 3050. *Pedites singulares: CIL* VIII, 2911. *Ala Flavia: AE* 1914, 40; 1917/18, 74–5. *Cohors I Asturum: CIL* VIII, 2766. *Cohors III Bracaraugustanorum: CIL* VIII, 3005. *Cohors VI Brittonum: CIL* VIII, 2741. *Cohors VI Commagenorum: AE* 1969/70, 706; *CIL* VIII, 18248. *Cohors I Flavia: CIL* VIII, 2844. *Cohors II Hispanorum: CIL* VIII, 2787. *Cohors VII Lusitanorum: CIL* VIII, 2887; 3101. *Cohors I Syrorum: AE* 1892, 13. *Cohors II[: CIL* VIII, 2623. Unspecified cavalry unit: *CIL* VIII, 2776; 3197. Unspecified infantry unit: *AE* 1989, 881a; *CIL* VIII, 2531; 2553; 2563; 2618; 2683–4; 2804; 2810; 2942; 2947; 3010; 3017; 3038; 3069; 3155; 3222; 3235; 3262; 18067; 18084–7; 18286; 18290; 18315; 18318; 18418; D 9102; 9102a. Unspecified unit: *AE* 1899, 91–2; 1902, 10; 148a-b; 1908, 9; 1912, 18; 1914, 234; 1917/18, 57; 1957, 87; 1967, 580; 1987, 1063; 1989, 879; 880a; *CIL* VIII, 2561–2; 2596; 2635; 2660; 2714; 2799; 2811; 2880; 2898; 2900; 2913; 2918; 2920; 2949; 2999; 3122; 3202; 3206; 3318; 18294; 18326–7. *Veteranus: CIL* VIII, 2597; 2800; 2833; 2836; 2902; 3011; 3013; 3021; 3023–5; 3030–2; 3034–6; 3040; 3042; 3048; 3051; 3058; 3061; 3063; 3070; 3072–4; 3086; 3091; 3094; 3104–5; 3110; 3112; 3119–21; 3123–4; 3129; 3132; 3142; 3144; 3149; 3152; 3160; 3162; 3168–70; 3173; 3176; 3179; 3183–4; 3187; 3189–90; 3192; 3194–6; 3203–4; 3210; 3212; 3215; 3228; 3231; 3234; 3239; 3248; 3252–3; 3257; 3263; 3265; 3267; 3273; 3277–8; 3370; 3647; 18297–8; 18306–10; 18325. *Evocatus: CIL* VIII, 2636

Sub-literary references: –

Modern references (site): Benseddik 2001; 2003; Cagnat 1893; 1901; 1908; Golvin and Janon 1978; Janon 1973; 2005; Le Bohec 1977; 1989; 2008; Rakob 1979; 2001; Storz and Rakob 1974; Wilmanns 1884

Modern references (finds): Le Bohec 2003; Speidel 2006

Notes: Partly urban, partly open site

Tebessa–Theveste (Figure 2,97)

Location: 35° 24′ 12.05″ N, 8° 7′ 17.88″ E
Situation: Southern edge of the Oued Chabro
Height ASL: 876m (GE)
Country: Algeria
Region: Tebessa
Province: Numidia
Length: –
Width: –
Area: –
Proportion: –
Cardinal orientation: –
Phases & Dating: ? – *Legio III Augusta* (AD 75–121)
Literary references: –
Units attested epigraphically: *Legio I Adiutrix*: CIL VIII, 27851. *Legio I Minervia*: AE 1995, 1710. *Legio II Adiutrix*: CIL VIII, 16553. **Legio III Augusta**: **AE 1888, 148a; 148aa-ai; 148ak-al; 148b-i; 148k-q; 148s-z; 1969/70, 662–4; 669; 1995, 1704; 1715; 1724; 1729; CIL VIII, 1839; 1851; 1875–6; 10114; 10165; 10626; 10629; 16544–5; 16547–8; 16550; 16553–4; 22631,2b; 22631,2u; 27852–5; ILAlg I, 3098b-c; 3103; 3121.** *Legio XIV Gemina*: CIL VIII, 1858. *Legio [—] Claudia*: CIL VIII, 1874. Unspecified legion: AE 1888, 148r; CIL VIII, 27874; ILAlg I, 3114. Unspecified cavalry unit: CIL VIII, 27856. Unspecified unit: AE 1995, 1721; CIL VIII, 1856; 1879; 16552; 27850; ILAlg I, 3108; 3126. *Veteranus*: CIL VIII, 1877; 16655; 27857
Sub-literary references: –
Modern references (site): Le Bohec 1989, 360–1; de Pachtère 1916
Modern references (finds): –
Notes: Urban site

Turda–Potaissa (Figures 2,50; 63)

Location: 46° 34′ 13.03″ N, 23° 46′ 24.04″ E
Situation: Confluence of Arieș and Pârâul Racilor
Height ASL: 367m (GE)
Country: Romania
Region: Cluj
Province: Dacia
Length: 595m
Width: 415m
Area: 24.8ha
Proportion: 1.434
Cardinal orientation: 113°
Phases & Dating: Stone – *Legio V Macedonica* (AD 168–4th century)
Literary references: Ptol., *Geog.* 3.8.4
Units attested epigraphically: *Legio I Italica*: CIL III, 889. *Legio V D(acica)*: AE 1909, 34. **Legio V Macedonica**: **AE 1960, 229; 1984, 739; 1992, 1470; CIL III, *38; 875; 878–9; 881; 892; 899; 902; 904–5; 909; 7694; 8066e-f; 12645; ILD 474–5; 482; 486; 488; 494; 498; 507; 523; 526a-c; 527; 530a-d.** *Legio VII Claudia*: ILD 499. *Legio XIII Gemina*: CIL III, 1629,1k; 1629,17b; 1630a-e; 8064,01v; 8065,22e. Unspecified legion: CIL III, 887; 894; 906; 910; 6255; 7680; 7688; 7692; ?13767; ILD 504. *Cohors I Batavorum*: CIL III, 13760; 13766. *Cohors VIII Palmyrenorum*: CIL III, 13764. *Numerus Palmyrenorum*: CIL III, 907. Unspecified cavalry unit: CIL III, 886;

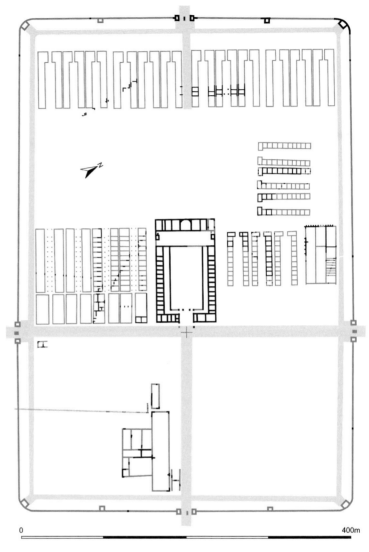

Figure 63: Turda–Potaissa
(after Bărbulescu 1987).

0   400m

12546. Unspecified infantry unit: *CIL* III, 908; 7672; *ILD* 501–2. Unspecified unit: *CIL* III, 895; 911; 7684; 7686; *ILD* 503. *Veteranus: ILD* 511

Sub-literary references: –

Modern references (site): Bărbulescu, C. 2004 ; Bărbulescu, M. 1987; 1990; 1991; 1994; 1997; 1998; Bărbulescu and Bărbulescu 2004a; 2004b; Bărbulescu et al. 1978

Modern references (finds): Bărbulescu, C. 2004; Cătinaş 1996; 1997; Grec 1998; Pîslaru 2001; 2004

Notes: Open site

Usk–Burrium (Figures 2,7; 64)

Location: 51° 42′ 0.21″ N, 2° 54′ 2.38″ W
Situation: Confluence of Usk and Olway Brook
Height ASL: 16m (GE)

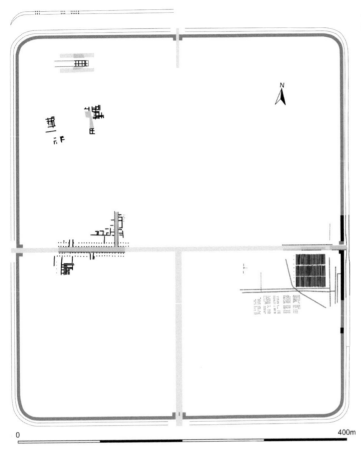

Figure 64: Usk–Burrium
(after Marvell 1996).

0   400m

Country: Great Britain
Region: Monmouthshire, Wales
Province: Britannia
Length: 455m
Width: 405m
Area: 18.4ha
Proportion: 1.123
Cardinal orientation: 156°
Phases & Dating: Timber – ?*Legio XX Valeria Victrix* (AD 55–65); Unknown (AD 65–74)
Literary references: –
Units attested epigraphically: *Legio II Augusta: RIB* 396
Sub-literary references: –
Modern references (site): Evans and Metcalf 1989; Manning 1977; 1981; 1997; 2000, 74–5; Manning and Scott 1989; Marvell 1990; 1996; Marvell and Maynard 1998; Nash-Williams 1969, 116–8; Selkirk 1987
Modern references (finds): Marvell et al. 1998
Notes: Partly urban, partly open site

Wien-Vindobona (Figures 2,32; 65)

Location: 48° 12′ 40.82″ N, 16° 22′ 15.98″ E
Situation: Confluence of the Danube and Wienfluß
Height ASL: 190m (GE)
Country: Austria
Region: Wien
Province: Pannonia Superior
Length: 535m
Width: 448m
Area: *c.*22.5ha
Proportion: 1.194
Cardinal orientation: 43°
Phases & Dating: Timber – *Legio XIII Gemina* (AD 89–102); stone – *Legio XIV Gemina* (AD 106–13); *Legio X Gemina* (AD 114–4th century)
Literary references: Ptol., *Geog.* 2.14.3; *Tab. Peut.* 4.1; *It. Ant.* 233.8; 261.4a; 266.4; 266.7; *ND Occ.* 34.25

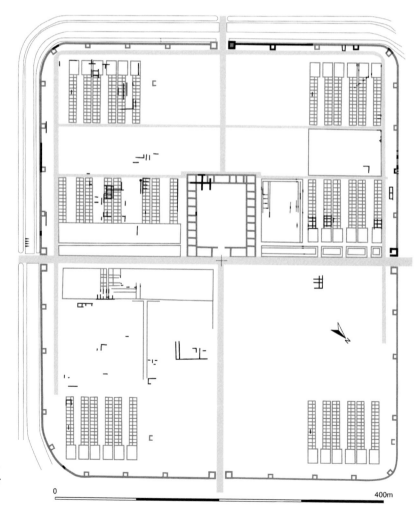

Figure 65: Wien–
Vindobona (after
Harl 1986).

0   400m

Units attested epigraphically: *Legio I Adiutrix: CIL* III, 11347a-b; 11347f. *Legio I[: CIL* III, 14359,27. *Legio II Italica: CIL* III, 5757,1h. **Legio X Gemina:** *AE* 1892, 37a; 1956, 239b; *AEA* 2001/02, 104a; 105a; 2003, 62c; *CIL* III, 4556; 4558; 4560; 4567; 4572; 4574; 4577; 4659,1ha; 4659,1ma; 4659,1maa; 4659,1qa; 4659,1ra; 4659,2b-c; 4659,3a-b; 4659,6a-e; 4660,3a-c; 6485a; 11309-10; 11350m; 11353b; 13497; 14359,26; 14359,28; 14360; *Hild* 408-9; 415; 418-19; *Lupa* 4788; 8940; 11406. *Legio X[: AE* 1973, 420c. *Legio XII: CIL* III, 12035,3. *Legio XII[: AE* 1973, 420d. **Legio XIII Gemina:** *AE* 1892, 37b; 2002, 1172; 1173a; 2005, 1238; *AEA* 2001/02, 104b; 105b; 107; 2003, 62b; *CIL* III, 4660,4a-c; 4660,5a-c; 4660,6; 4660,7a-c; 4660,8a-b; 4660,09a-e; 4660,10; 4660,11a-e; 4660,12a-b; 4660,13a-b; 4660,14; 4660,15a-b; 4660,16a-b; 4660,17a-d; 4660,18a-d; 4660,19-21; 4660,22a-b; 4660,23-4; 4660,25a-b; 4660,26; 11355a-b; 11356; 11357a-b; 11358e-h; 11359b; 14100,1a-c; 14100,2; *Hild* 405. *Legio XIV Gemina: AE* 1892, 37c; 1973, 420a-b; *CIL* III, 4563; 4578; 4661,1d-f; 4661,2b; 4661,3; 4661,4i; 4661,4k; 4661,6b-d; 4661,7b; 4661,8c-d; 4661,08i; 4661,08k-l; 4661,9a; 4661,10b; 4661,12b-c; 4661,13-15; 11361a-b; 11362d; *Hild* 404; *Lupa* 4791-2. Legio XV *Apollinaris: AEA* 2001/02, 105d; 2003, 62a; *CIL* III, 4570; 11366i; 11366k; *Hild* 412. *Legio XXX Ulpia Victrix: AEA* 2001/02, 105c. Unspecified legion: *CIL* III, 14359,26a; *Lupa* 4783. *Ala I Flavia Britannica: AE* 1903, 78; *CIL* III, 4575-6; 15197. *Ala I Thracum Victrix: AEA* 2003, 62d. *Cohors I Aelia sagittariorum: CIL* III, 4664a-c; 11373. *Cohors equitata sagittariorum: CIL* III, 11456; 14360,6. *Cohors II Vindelicorum: CIL* III, 15204,6. Unspecified cavalry unit: *CIL* III, 4586. Unspecified infantry unit: *AE* 1956, 239a; 1973, 419; *Hild* 429

Sub-literary references: –

Modern references (site): Chmelar and Heigart 1998; Gaisbauer and Mosser 2001; Genser 1986; Gietl et al. 2004; Harl 1979; Jandl and Mosser 2008; Kandler 1978; Ladenbauer-Orel 1984; Mosser 1998; 1999; 2001; 2002a; 2002b; 2004; 2005a; 2005b; Neumann 1967

Modern references (finds): –

Notes: Urban site

Windisch–Vindonissa (Figures 2,25; 66)

Location: 47° 28′ 49.14″ N, 8° 13′ 15.76″ E
Situation: Confluence of the Aare and Reuss
Height ASL: 362m (GE)
Country: Switzerland
Region: Aargau
Province: Germania Superior
Length: 595m
Width: 440m
Area: 20.9ha
Proportion: 1.352
Cardinal orientation: 262°
Phases & Dating: ?Timber – *Legio XIII Gemina* (AD 10–43); *Legio XXI Rapax* (AD 43–70); stone – *Legio XI Claudia* (AD 70–101)
Literary references: Tac., *Hist.* 4.61; 70
Units attested epigraphically: *Legio I Minervia: AE* 1946, 261; *Ness-Lieb* 83c. *Legio I[: CIL* XIII, 5198. *Legio VIII Augusta: AE* 1935, 8; *Nesselhauf* 62. **Legio XI Claudia:** *AE* 1914, 97; 1924, 9; 1926, 69; 1946, 259-60; 265; 267; 1991, 1260; 1996, 1124; 1136; *CIL* XIII, 5197; 5207; 5209-17; 5219; 11501; 11506-9; 11525; *Finke* 100; *Ness-Lieb* 59; 77; 82n; 83a-b; *Nesselhauf* 58; 61; *SVindonissa* 66. *Legio XIII Gemina: AE* 1925, 6; 1926, 6; 1996, 1126; *CIL* XIII, 5206; *Finke* 116; *Ness-Lieb* 79. *Legio XXI Rapax: AE* 1934, 18; 1953, 247; 249; 2007, 1039l; *CIL* XIII, 5201; 5208; 5218; 11510; 11514; *Ness-Lieb* 83d. Unspecified legion: *AE* 1946, 269; *CIL*

XIII, 5193; 11524; *Ness-Lieb* 82b. *Cohors Hispanorum*: AE1953, 246a. *Cohors III Hispanorum*:
   AE 1909, 139. ?*Cohors VII Raetorum*: *AE* 1992, 1272. Unspecified cavalry unit: *AE* 1953, 244;
   SVindonissa 24. Unspecified infantry unit: *AE* 1907, 148; 1926, 4–5; 9; 11; 71; 1930, 15; 1946,
   262; 1961, 266; 1996, 1125; 1127; 1132; 2001, 1523; *CIL* XIII, 5220; 11523; 11525a-d; *Finke* 104;
   112; 115; *Ness-Lieb* 60; 66–70; 72; 78; 82c; 82g; 82j-k; *SVindonissa* 12; 14; 20–1; 23; 25–30; 33;
   71; 73; 81; 84; 87a. Unspecified unit: *AE* 1925, 7–9; 1926, 3; 1953, 248; ?1996, 1131; ?*CIL* XIII,
   11504. *Veteranus*: *AE* 1946, 264; *Ness-Lieb* 82d

Sub-literary references: *AE* 1996, 1124–5

Modern references (site): Bellettati 1994; Ebnoether and Schucany 1998; Ettlinger 1961; Ettlinger
   and Gonzenbach 1955–56; Fellmann 1953/54; 1954/55; 1956/57; 1958; Frey and Pauli-Gabi
   2006; Gonzenbach 1976; Handendorn 1998; Hartmann 1973a; 1973b; 1979/80; 1980; 1983;
   1986; Hartmann and Speidel 1991; Heierli 1905; Heuberger 1909; Hintermann 1998; Lieb 1998;

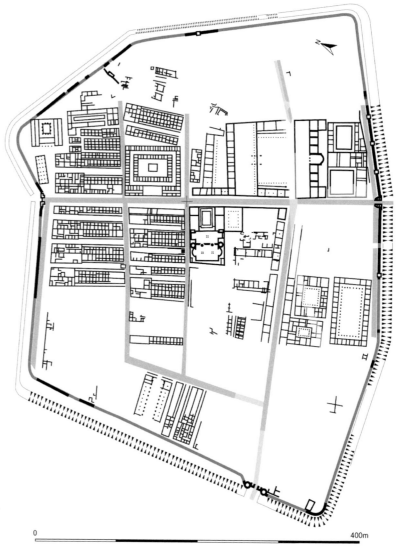

Figure 66: Windisch–
Vindonissa (after
Hartmann 1986).

0   400m

Maier 1993; 1995; 1996; 1997; 1998; 1999; Maier-Osterwalder and Widmer 1990; Meyer-Freuler 1989; 1998; Pauli-Gabi 2002; 2005a; 2005b; 2007; Pauli-Gabi et al. 2004; 2005; Pauli-Gabi and Trumm 2003; Simonett 1937; 1939; 1940; 1941; Wells 1972, 49–53

Modern references (finds): Bossert 1999; Deschler-Erb 1996; Deschler-Erb et al. 2004; Ettlinger 1998; Ettlinger and Doppler 1986; Ettlinger and Fellmann 1955; Ettlinger and Hartmann 1984; Ettlinger and Simonett 1952; Gansser-Burckhardt 1942; 1947–48; 1948–49; 1952; Ginella et al. 1999; Gonzenbach 1963; 1965; 1966; Hartmann 1982; Hartmann, T. 1991; Loeschcke 1919; Meyer-Freuler 2003; Pekáry 1971; Schaer 2005; Schneider and Wirz 1991; Simonett 1935; Ulbert 1962; 1972; 1973; Unz and Deschler-Erb 1997; Volken and Volken 2005

Notes: Iregular shape dictated by terrain. Urban site

Wroxeter–Viriconium (Figures 2,5; 67)
Location: 52° 40′ 24.16″ N, 2° 38′ 33.38″ W
Situation: Confluence of Severn and Bell Brook
Height ASL: 64m (GE)
Country: Great Britain
Region: Shropshire, England
Province: Britannia
Length: 440m
Width: 397m
Area: 17.5ha

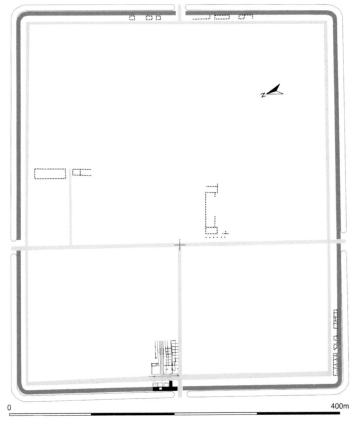

0   400m

Figure 67: Wroxeter–Viriconium (after Webster and Chadderton 2002).

Proportion: 1.108
Cardinal orientation: 287°
Phases & Dating: Timber – *Legio XIV Gemina* (AD 59–65); *Legio XX Valeria Victrix* (AD 66–88)
Literary references: –
Units attested epigraphically: *Legio XIV Gemina: RIB 292; 294; 296. Legio XX: RIB 293. Cohors [—] Thracum: RIB 291*
Sub-literary references: –
Modern references (site): Bushe-Fox 1913; 1914; 1916; Manning 2000; Tomlin 1992; Webster 1962; 1969; 1977–8; 1988b; 1991; Webster and Chadderton 2002
Modern references (finds): –
Notes: Open site

Xanten–Vetera I (Figures 2,13; 68)

Location: 51° 38' 28.55" N, 6° 28' 8.20" E
Situation: Adjacent to Rhine (old course)
Height ASL: 49m (GE)
Country: Germany
Region: Nordrhein-Westfalen
Province: Germania Inferior
Length: 933m
Width: 628m
Area: 57.8ha
Proportion: 1.486
Cardinal orientation: 172°
Phases & Dating: Timber – *Legiones V Alaudae + XXI Rapax* (AD 10–43); stone – *Legiones V Alaudae + XV Primigenia* (AD 43–69)
Literary references: Tac., *Hist.* 4.22; 28–30; 34–6; 60; 5.14–18
Units attested epigraphically: *Legio I Flavia: Lehner 1179. Legio I Minervia: AE 1898, 117a; 1905, 231. **Legio V:** AE 1914, 124a-u; CIL XIII, 8644. Legio V[: CIL XIII, 12078. **Legio VI Victrix:** AE 1903, 280a; 1905, 232; CIL XIII, *1328; 8645. Legio VIII Augusta: AE 1995, 1126. Legio X Gemina: AE 1899, 8; 1905, 234; CIL XIII, 8646. **Legio XV Primigenia:** AE 1903, 280b; 1905, 225; 1914, 124v-w; 1994, 1278c; CIL XIII, 8647. Legio XVIII: CIL XIII, 8648. **Legio XXI:** CIL XIII, 8649–51. Legio XXII Primigenia: AE 1898, 117b; 1903, 280c; 1994, 1278a; CIL XIII, 8652; 12079. Legio XXX Ulpia Victrix: AE 1898, 117c; 1903, 280d; 1905, 233; 1914, 124x; 1968, 401; 1977, 568; 1994, 1278b; CIL XIII, 8607; 8609–10; 8616; 8619–20; 8622; 8625–6; 8631–2; 8634; 8638–41; 8654; Schillinger 209; 212. Unspecified legion: AE 2002, 1041; CIL XIII, 8627. Ala Vocontiorum: CIL XIII, 8655. Cohors II Brittonum: AE 1903, 280e. Cohors VI Ingenuorum: AE 1981, 689. Unspecified cavalry unit: AE 2006, 904; CIL XIII, 10024,34. Unspecified infantry unit: AE 1938, 76a-b; 1977, 565; 1981, 688; 2006, 880; 2006, 903. Veteranus: AE 1905, 228; CIL XIII, 8636*
Sub-literary references: –
Modern references (site): Detten 1999; Gechter 1979a, 106–10; 2002; 2008; Hanel 2008; Hanel and Song 2007; Lehner 1926; 1927; 1930; 1936; Petrikovits 1958; Schultze 1925; Wells 1972, 123–7
Modern references (finds): Allison et al. 2004; Hanel 1995; Houben 1839; Reddé 1995; Rüger et al. 1979; Schalles 1996; 1999
Notes: The proximity of Vetera I and II renders it almost impossible to separate the epigraphic record for the two sites. Tombstone *CIL* XIII, 8648 is that of M. Caelius, a *centurio* killed in the Varian disaster and thus from the Augustan fortress. Open site

1. The *nomina legionum* column (the Colonnetta Maffei) from Roma: *CIL* VI, 3492 (photo J.C.N. Coulston).

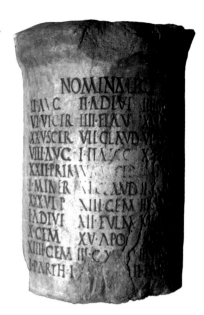

2. Brick courses on the north-west curtain wall at York (photo M.C. Bishop).

3. Eastern fortress curtain wall at Chester, constructed in *opus quadratum*, with the medieval city wall behind it (photo M.C. Bishop).

4. North-western curtain wall at Caerleon showing core and some remaining facing stones (photo M.C. Bishop).

5. Northern curtain wall at Chester with in-situ string course (photo M.C. Bishop).

6. Curtain wall at York, still standing to the height of the string course, at the eastern corner of the fortress (photo M.C. Bishop).

7. Rampart walk on the west wall at Dura-Europos, adjacent to Tower 15, with intact merlon traverses (photo M.C. Bishop).

9. Interval tower behind the north-eastern curtain wall at York, looking towards the eastern corner tower of the fortress (photo M.C. Bishop).

8. Crenellations and string course belonging to the Tiberian defences of the Castra Praetoria in Roma embedded within the later city wall (photo M.C. Bishop).

10. Interval tower behind south-western curtain wall at Caerleon (photo M.C. Bishop).

11. Interval tower from outside the eastern curtain wall at Albano (photo J.C.N. Coulston).

12. Eastern corner tower at York (photo M.C. Bishop).

13. The south-eastern corner tower at Chester (photo M.C. Bishop).

14. The late western corner tower (or Multangular Tower) at York (photo M.C. Bishop).

15. Interior of the northern corner tower at Lejjun (photo M.C. Bishop).

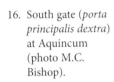

16. South gate (*porta principalis dextra*) at Aquincum (photo M.C. Bishop).

17. South-east gate (*porta principalis sinistra*) at Albano (photo J.C.N. Coulston).

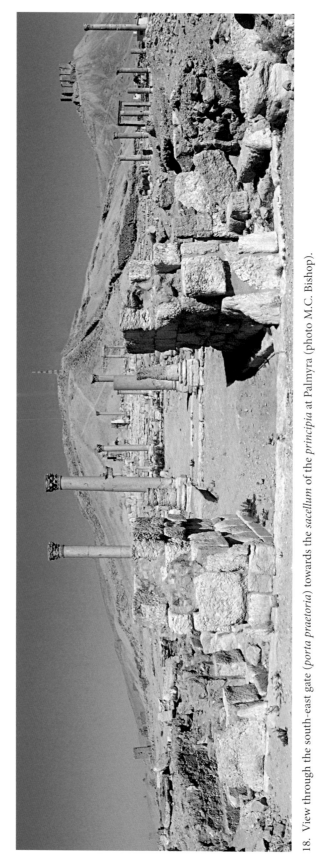

18. View through the south-east gate (*porta praetoria*) towards the *sacellum* of the *principia* at Palmyra (photo M.C. Bishop).

19. West gate (*porta decumana*) at Udruh (photo M.C. Bishop).

20. Reconstructed single-portalled gateway with horseshoe towers at Weißenburg, Germany (photo Creative Commons/Brego).

22. Column from the *principia* at Chester (photo M.C. Bishop).

21. Reassembled *principia* column outside the minster at York (photo M.C. Bishop).

23. Standing arches thought to belong to the *principia* crosshall at Burnum (photo M.C. Bishop).

24. The *sacellum* in the rear range of the *principia* at Palmyra (photo M.C. Bishop.

25. The *principia* at Lejjun (photo M.C. Bishop).

27. Buttressed barracks at Gardun (photo M.C. Bishop).

26. The Prysg Field barracks at Caerleon (photo M.C. Bishop).

28. Rampart-back ovens at Caerleon (photo M.C. Bishop).

29. Rampart-back latrine at Caerleon (photo M.C. Bishop).

30. The military amphitheatre at Carnuntum (photo M.C. Bishop).

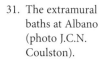

31. The extramural baths at Albano (photo J.C.N. Coulston).

32. Haïdra legionary roadside cemetery (photo J.C.N. Coulston).

33. Lejjun from the air looking south-west (photo David L. Kennedy, APAAME_20020930_DLK-0072.tif).

34. Udruh from the air looking south-east (photo David L. Kennedy, APAAME_20090930_DLK-0281.tif).

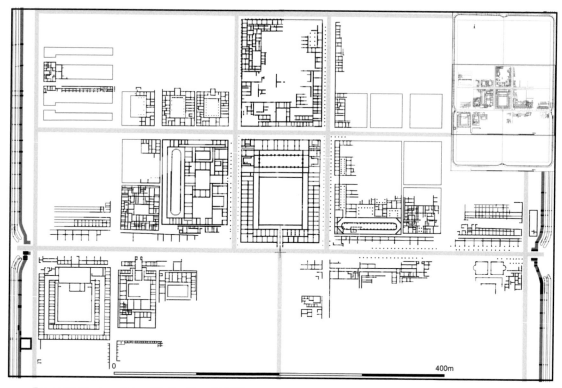

Figure 68: Xanten–Vetera I (after Hanel 1995).

Xanten–Vetera II (Figure 2,13)

Location: 51° 38′ 46.97″ N, 6° 28′ 48.62″ E
Situation: Adjacent to Rhine (old course)
Height ASL: ?17m (GE)
Country: Germany
Region: Nordrhein-Westfalen
Province: Germania Inferior
Length: –
Width: –
Area: –
Proportion: –
Cardinal orientation: –
Phases & Dating: ?Stone – *Legio XXII Primigenia* (AD 71–92); *Legio VI Victrix* (AD 93–121); *Legio XXX Ulpia Victrix* (AD 122–4th century)
Literary references: Ptol., *Geog.* 2.8
Units attested epigraphically: See Vetera I above
Sub-literary references: –
Modern references (site): Gechter 2002; Petrikovits 1958; 1959; Schmitz 2008
Modern references (finds): Reddé 1995; Rüger et al. 1979; Schalles 1994a; 1994b; 1996; 1999; Schalles and Schreiter 1993
Notes: Destroyed by the Rhine

York–Eboracum (Figures 2,2; 69; Plates 2; 6; 9; 12; 14; 21)

Location: 53° 57′ 41.35″ N, 1° 4′ 57.29″ W
Situation: Confluence of Ouse and Foss
Height ASL: 24m (GE)
Country: Great Britain
Region: North Yorkshire, England
Province: Britannia
Length: 470m
Width: 425m
Area: 20.0ha
Proportion: 1.106
Cardinal orientation: 219°
Phases & Dating: Timber & stone – *Legio IX Hispana* (AD 71–?106); *Legio VI Victrix* (AD 122–4th century)
Literary references: Ptol., *Geog.* 2.3.16; *It. Ant.* 466.
Units attested epigraphically: *Legio VI Victrix: AE* 1954, 124a; 1959, 164; 1964, 170b; 1965, 219c; 1967, 267; 1968, 260; 1971, 220; 1977, 511; 1998, 834a-c; *RIB* 653; 658; 669a-b; 670–1; 675; 679; 685; 690. *Legio IX Hispana: AE* 1975, 558a-c; *RIB* 659; 665; 673; 680. Unspecified

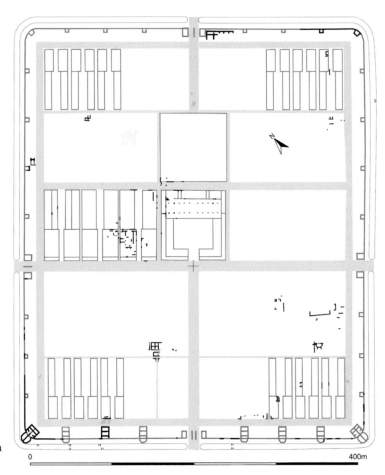

Figure 69: York–Eboracum (after Ottaway 2004).

0   400m

legion: *AE* 1971, 219; *RIB* 668. Unspecified infantry unit: *AE* 1958, 96–7; *RIB* 649; 669c-e; 669g; 669i. *Veteranus*: *RIB* 654

Sub-literary references: –

Modern references (site): Brinklow 1987; Dyer and Wenham 1967; Evans 1998; 2000; Hall 1997; Macnab 2000; Miller 1925; 1928; Ottaway 1985; 1991; 1992; 1996; 1997; 2004; Pearson 1986; 1990; Phillips and Heywood 1995; Radley 1966; 1970; 1972; Ramm 1956; RCAHME 1962; Stead 1958; 1968; Stockwell 1990; Sumpter and Coll 1977; Wenham 1961; 1962; 1968; 1972; Whitwell 1976; Wood 1995

Modern references (finds): Buckland 1976; Cool et al. 1995; Kenward et al. 1986; MacGregor 1976; Monaghan 1993; 1997; Wright 1976; 1978

Notes: Urban site

Other sites

Other sites that may have acted as or even incorporated legionary bases, and which are either too insubstantial or not located archaeologically, include Aquileia (Aquileia), Antakya (Antioch), Osijek (Mursa), Petrijevci (Mursella), Ra's al 'Ayn (Resaina) and Sremska Mitrovice (Sirmium). More information on these sites can be found on the accompanying website (see Appendix 5).

Gazetteer B: Legionary fortresses of the Dominate

These are some of the principal legionary fortresses added under the Dominate, all of them much smaller than their predecessors and constructed using the newer methods of fortification, and many of them listed within the *Notitia Dignitatum*. It is likely that that document is incomplete and thus this gazetteer could never be complete. It must also be remembered that many of the earlier, larger, fortresses continued in use alongside these newcomers.

Alexandria–Nicopolis (Figures 2,94; 70)

Location: 31° 17' 20.24" N, 30° 0' 55.46" E

Situation: On the shore of the Mediterranean, between Lake Mareotis and Lake Aboukir

Height ASL: 9m (GE)

Country: Egypt

Region: Alexandria Governorate

Province: Aegyptus

Length: *c.*290m (291 paces)

Width: *c.*265m (266 paces)

Area: *c.*7.69ha

Proportion: *c.*1.094

Cardinal orientation: *c.*45° / 225°

Phases & Dating: Stone – *Legio II Traiana Fortis* (?Tetrarchic–?)

Literary references: *ND Or.* 28.7

Units attested epigraphically: See Gazetteer A

Sub-literary references: –

Modern references (site): Alston 1995, 192–3; Murray 1880, 141

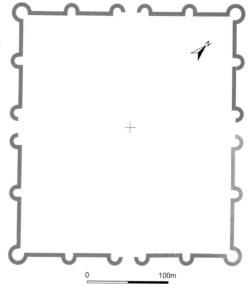

Figure 70: Alexandria–Nicopolis.

Modern references (finds): –

Notes: Urban site. Fortress paced out and described in Murray. Also known as Parembole

Aqaba–Aila/Aelana (Figures 2,89; 71)

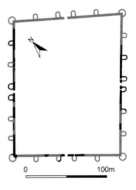

Location: 29° 31′ 50.38″ N, 34° 59′ 59.91″ E
Situation: On the shore of the Red Sea
Height ASL: 9m (GE)
Country: Jordan
Region: Aqaba Governorate
Province: Arabia
Length: *c.*170m
Width: 135m
Area: *c.*2.2ha
Proportion: 1.259
Cardinal orientation: 42°/222°

Figure 71: Aqaba–Aila/Aelana (after Whitcomb 1990).

Phases & Dating: ?Stone – *Legio X Fretensis* (*terminus post quem* AD 293)
Literary references: ND *Or.* 34,30; Eusebius, *Onom.* 6.17–21; 7.25–8
Units attested epigraphically: ?: *IGLS* XXI.4 no.150
Sub-literary references: –
Modern references (site): Gregory 1995–97, vol. 2, 412–13; Kennedy 2000, 194–7; Macadam 1989; Parker 1996; 1997; 1998; 2000; Whitcomb 1990
Modern references (finds): –
Notes: Urban site. Islamic fortress resembling Roman examples known, but no indication that it is in fact Roman in origin other than size, form, and a building inscription

Budapest–Aquincum (Figures 2,37; 72)

Location: 47° 32′ 29.56″ N, 19° 2′ 38.61″ E
Situation: Adjacent to the Danube
Height ASL: 107m (GE)
Country: Hungary
Region: Budapest
Province: Pannonia
Length (m): –
Width (m): –
Area (ha): –
Proportion: –
Cardinal orientation: –
Phases & Dating: Stone – *Legio II Adiutrix* (?Tetrarchic–?)
Literary references: Amm. Marc. 19.11.8; *It. Ant.* 245.7; 263.9; *ND Occ.* 33.32
Units attested epigraphically: See Gazetteer A
Sub-literary references: –
Modern references (site): Facsády 1976; Nagy 1976; Póczy 1976b; 1977; 1990; Wellner 1990
Modern references (finds): –
Notes: Urban site

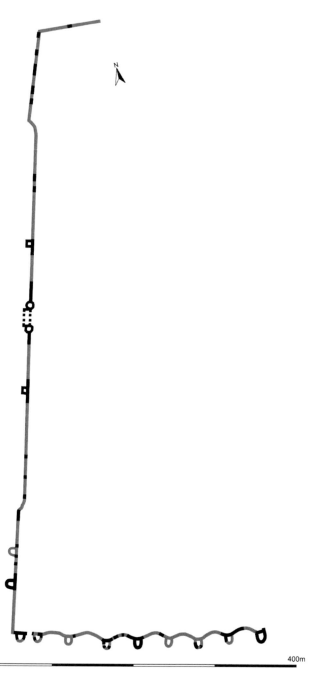

Győr–Arrabona (Figures 2,35; 73)
Location: 47° 41′ 20.38″ N, 17° 37′ 53.38″ E
Situation: Confluence of Mosoni-Duna and Rába
Height ASL: 122m (GE)
Country: Hungary

Region: Győr-Moson-Sopron County
Province: Pannonia
Length: *c.*175m
Width: *c.*150m
Area: 2.6ha
Proportion: 1.167
Cardinal orientation: 16°/196° or 106°/286°
Phases & Dating: Stone – *Legio X Gemina* + *Legio XIV Gemina* (?Tetrarchic–?)
Literary references: *ND Occ.* 34.5; *It. Ant.* 246.6
Units attested epigraphically: *Legio I Adiutrix*: CIL III, 4363–4; 4375; 4655l. *Legio II Adiutrix*: AE 1995, 1259d-e. **Legio X Gemina: CIL III, 4659,1w; 4659,07a-b.** *Ala I Aravacorum*: CIL III, 4373. *Ala III Augusta Thracum*: CIL III, 4380. *Ala Augusta Ituraeorum*: CIL III, 4367–8; 4371; 11083. *Ala Pannoniorum*: CIL III, 4372; 4376–7. *Ala I Ulpia Contariorum*: CIL III, 4359–62; 4369–70; 4378–9; *RHP* 94; 103; 105; 120a-b. *Cohors* [—] *Alpinorum equitata*: CIL III, 4374. Unknown cavalry unit: *RHP* 109

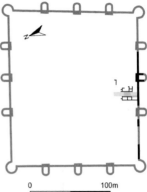

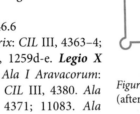

Figure 73: Győr–Arrabona (after Szőnyi 2003).

Sub-literary references: –
Modern references (site): Szőnyi 2003
Modern references (finds): –
Notes: Urban site

Köln-Deutz–Divitia (Figures 2,18; 74)

Location: 50° 56′ 15.93″ N, 6° 58′ 10.00″ E
Situation: Adjacent to Rhine
Height ASL: 47m (GE)
Country: Germany
Region: Nordrhein-Westfalen
Province: Germania Magna
Length: 140m
Width: 135m
Area: 1.89ha
Proportion: 1.037
Cardinal orientation: 88°
Phases & Dating: Stone – ? (*c.*AD 315–401)
Literary references: –
Units attested epigraphically: *Legio I Minervia*: AE 1935, 100; CIL XIII, 8495. *Legio XXX Ulpia Victrix*: AE 1935, 100. Unspecified legion: CIL XIII, 8503. *Pedites singulares*: AE 1935, 100. *Ala Felix Moesica*: CIL XIII, 8503. *Numerus Brittonum*: CIL XIII, 8492

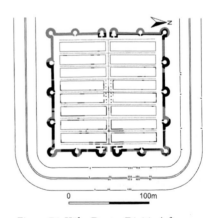

Figure 74: Köln-Deutz–Divitia (after Caroll-Spillecke 1997).

Sub-literary references: –
Modern references (site): Carroll-Spillecke 1993; 1997; Precht, G. 2002; Precht 1972/3; Wolff, G. 2000
Modern references (finds): Gechter 1991; Hanel and Verstegen 2005; 2006; Scheithauer and Wesch-Klein 1990
Notes: Urban site. A legionary connection is suggested by the *Legio II Italica Divitiensium* (*AE* 1982, 258)

El-Lejjun–Betthorus (-um?) (Figures 2,87; 75; Plates 15; 25; 33)
Location: 31° 14′ 13.50″ N, 35° 52′ 6.74″ E
Height ASL: 696m (GE)
Country: Jordan
Region: Kerak Governorate
Province: Arabia
Length: 242m
Width: 190m
Area: c.4.6ha
Proportion: 1.300
Cardinal orientation: 71°
Phases & Dating: Stone – *Legio IV Martia* (late 3rd/early 4th); stone (4th century)
Literary references: *ND Or.* 37, 22
Units attested epigraphically: –
Sub-literary references: –
Modern references (site): Kennedy 2000, 146–50; Kennedy and Riley 1990, 131; Lander and Parker 1982; Parker 1986, 58–74; 1987; 1988; 1990; 1991; 2006
Modern references (finds): –
Notes: Open site

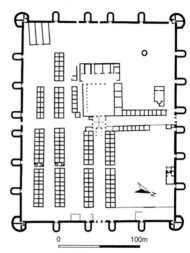

Figure 75: El-Lejjun–Betthorus (-um?) (after Parker 2000).

Luxor (al-Uqsor)–Thebae (Figures 2,90; 76)
Location: 25° 41′ 56.38″ N, 32° 38′ 22.26″ E
Situation: Adjacent to Nile
Height ASL: 79m (GE)
Country: Egypt
Region: Luxor Governate
Province: Aegyptus
Length: 249–68m NS
Width: 202–7m EW
Area: 5.0ha
Proportion: 1.233
Cardinal orientation: 35°
Phases & Dating: Stone – *Legio III Diocletiana* (Tetrarchic)
Literary references: *ND Or.* 30.38
Units attested epigraphically: *Legio* [: *AE* 1987, 975b. Unknown legion: *IGLAlexa* 69. Cohors [—] *Augusta equitata*: *IGLAlexa* 69. Cohors II *Thracum*: *AE* 1987, 975d; *CIL* III, 12074
Sub-literary references: –
Modern references (site): El-Saghir et al. 1986; Golvin and Reddé 1986
Modern references (finds): Deckers 1979
Notes: Open site

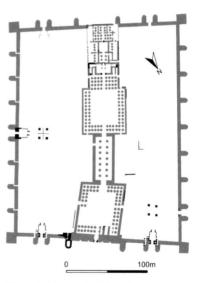

Figure 76: Luxor (al-Uqsor)–Thebae (after Golvin and Reddé 1986).

Mehin–Danaba? (Figure 2,82)

Location: 34° 14′ 31.23″ N, 37° 3′ 33.05″ E
Height ASL: *c.*923m
Country: Syria
Region: Homs Governorate
Province: Syria
Length (m): –
Width (m): –
Area (ha): –
Proportion: –
Cardinal orientation: –
Phases & Dating: ?Stone – *Legio III Gallica* (Tetrarchic)
Literary references: *ND Or.* 32.15
Units attested epigraphically: –
Sub-literary references: –
Modern references (site): Dussaud 1927, 266; 1929, 60
Modern references (finds): –
Notes: Urban site

Old Cairo–Babylon (Figures 2,93; 77)

Location: 30° 0′ 21.37″ N, 31° 13′ 50.47″ E
Situation: Adjacent to Nile
Height ASL: 24m (GE)
Country: Egypt
Region: Cairo Governorate
Province: Aegyptus
Length: 260m
Width: 215m
Area: 5.1ha
Proportion: –
Cardinal orientation: 43.5° / 223.5°
Phases & Dating: Stone – *Legio XIII Gemina* (?Tetrarchic–?)
Literary references: *ND Or.* 28.3
Units attested epigraphically: –
Sub-literary references: –
Modern references (site): Alston 1995, 204; Butler 1978, 238–44; Grossmann et al. 1988; 1994; Murray 1880, 226–7; Sheehan 1996
Modern references (finds): –
Notes: Open site

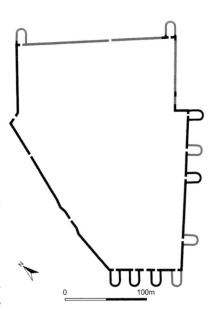

Figure 77: Old Cairo–Babylon (after Butler 1902).

Richborough–Rutupiae (Figures 2,11; 78)

Location: 51° 17′ 38.31″ N, 1° 19′ 56.96″ E
Situation: Confluence of Stour and Goshall Stream
Height ASL: 11m (GE)
Country: Great Britain
Region: Kent, England
Province: Britannia

Length: *c.*170m
Width: 150m
Area: 2.6ha
Proportion: 1.1
Orientation: 283°
Phasing & Date: Stone – *Legio II Augusta* (?Tetrarchic–?)
Literary references: *ND Occ.* 28.19
Units attested epigraphically: –
Sub-literary references: –
Modern references (site): Blagg 1989; Brown 1971; Bushe-Fox 1926; 1928; 1932; 1949; Cunliffe 1968; Johnson 1970; 1979, 48–51; 1981; Pearson 2002, 26–8; Philp 1981; Roach Smith 1850
Modern references (finds): Cobbett 2008; Lyne 1994; 1999
Notes: Open site

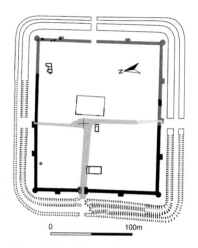

Figure 78: Richborough–Rutupiae (after Blagg 1989).

Schlögen–Ioviacum (Figures 2,27; 79)

Location: 48° 25′ 27.28″ N, 13° 52′ 14.88″ E
Situation: Confluence Danube and Freyentalerbach
Height ASL: 284m (GE)
Country: Austria
Region: Oberösterreich
Province: Pannonia
Length: 110m
Width: 70m
Area: 0.7ha
Proportion: 1.571
Cardinal orientation: 62°
Phases & Dating: Stone – *Legio II Italica* (?Tetrarchic–?)
Literary references: *ND Occ.* 34.25
Units attested epigraphically: *Legio II: CIL* III, 5757,1b. *Legio II Italica: CIL* III, 5757,1m.
Sub-literary references: –
Modern references (site): Eckhart 1969; Schwanzar 1989
Modern references (finds): Bender and Moosbauer 2003
Notes: Urban site

Figure 79: Schlögen–Ioviacum (after Schwanzar 1986).

Souriyah–Sura (Figures 2,76; 80)

Location: 35° 53′ 48.79″ N, 38° 46′ 46.39″ E
Situation: Adjacent to Euphrates
Height ASL: 260m
Country: Syria
Region: Ar-Raqqah Governorate
Province: Syria
Length: 145m
Width: 145m
Area: 2.1ha
Proportion: 1.000
Cardinal orientation: 214°/34° or 123°/303°

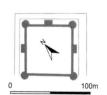

Figure 80: Souriyah–Sura.

Phases & Dating: Stone – *Legio XVI Flavia Firma* (Tetrarchic)
Literary references: *ND Or.* 33.6, 28
Units attested epigraphically: –
Sub-literary references: –
Modern references (site): Chapot 1907, 285–8, fig. 7; Honigmann 1931; Kennedy and Riley 1990, 115–16; Moritz 1889; Poidebard 1934, 83–4, pl. LXXIX–LXXX; Sarre-Herzfeld 1911, 153, fig. 66
Modern references (finds): –
Notes: Unexplored. Dimensions from Chapot 1907, 287. Open site

Tadmor–Palmyra (Figures 2,83; 81; Plates 18; 24)
Location: 34° 33′ 19.07″ N, 38° 15′ 45.47″ E
Situation: In oasis city
Height ASL: 417m (GE)
Country: Syria
Region: Homs Governorate
Province: Syria
Length: 341m
Width: 268m
Area: 7.0ha
Proportion: 1.272
Cardinal orientation: 121°
Phases & Dating: Stone – *Legio I Illyricorum* (?Tetrarchic–?)
Literary references: *ND Or.* 32.14
Units attested epigraphically: *Legio IV Scythica*: AE 1947, 172. *Legio VI Ferrata*: AE 1947, 172. *Legio X Fretensis*: AE 1933, 204. *Legio XXX Gallica*: AE 1947, 172. *Ala Flavia Agrippiana*: AE 1933, 212. *Ala Herculiana*: AE 1933, 209. *Ala Ulpia singularis*: AE 1933, 210–11. *Cohors I Flavia Chalcidenorum*: AE 1933, 216; 1969/70, 610–11; 1991, 1573–4. *Cohors Sebastena*: AE 1947, 172. *Cohors II Thracum*: AE 1911, 124. Unspecified cavalry unit: *AE* 1933, 213; 2001, 1961. Unspecified infantry unit: AE 2002, 1515–16. Unspecified unit: *SEG* 34, 1456. *Veteranus*: AE 2002, 1518

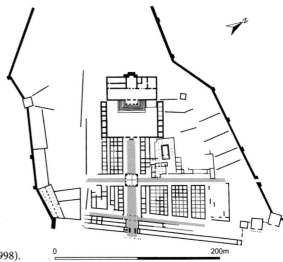

Figure 81: Tadmor–Palmyra (after Kowalski 1998).

0   200m

Sub-literary references: –
Modern references (site): Baranski 1994; Fellmann 1976; Gawlikowski 1968; 1970; 1974; 1976a; 1976b; 1977; 1978; 1979a; 1979b; 1983; 1984; 1985a; 1985b; 1986; 1987a; 1987b; Gregory 1995–97, vol. 2; Kowalski 1994; 1998; Michałowski 1960; 1962; 1963; 1964; 1966
Modern references (finds): –
Notes: Open site

Tayibeh–Oresa (Figure 2,80)
Location: 35° 5′ 29.28″ N, 38° 54′ 49.18″ E
Height ASL: 468m (GE)
Country: Syria
Region: Homs Governorate
Province: Syria
Length: *c.*150m
Width: *c.*150m
Area: *c.*2.25ha
Proportion: 1.000
Cardinal orientation: *c.*0°/180° or 90°/270°
Phases & Dating: ?Stone – *Legio IV Scythica* (?Tetrarchic–?)
Literary references: *ND Or.* 33.9
Units attested epigraphically: –
Sub-literary references: –
Modern references (site): Kennedy and Riley 1990, 137, Fig. 84; Poidebard 1934, 79, pl. LXXI
Modern references (finds): –
Notes: Unexplored. Partly urban, partly open site

Udruh–Adrou (Figures 2,88; 82; Plates 19, 34)
Location: 30° 19′ 45.05″ N, 35° 45′ 45.39″ E
Situation: Adjacent to perennial spring
Height ASL: 1309m (GE)
Country: Jordan
Region: Ma'an Governorate
Province: Arabia
Length: 245m
Width: 185m
Area: *c.*4.7ha
Proportion: 1.324
Cardinal orientation: 79°
Phases & Dating: Stone – *Legio VI Ferrata* (*c.*AD 304–?)
Literary references: –
Units attested epigraphically: *Legio VI Ferrata*: Kennedy and Falahat 2008
Sub-literary references: –
Modern references (site): Brünnow and Domaszewski 1904, 431–63; Gregory 1995–97, vol. 2, 383–9; Kennedy 2000, 168–70; Kennedy and Riley 1990, 131–4; Killick 1982; 1983a; 1983b; 1986a; 1986b; 1989; Parker 1986, 94–8
Modern references (finds): Kennedy and Falahat 2008
Notes: Open site

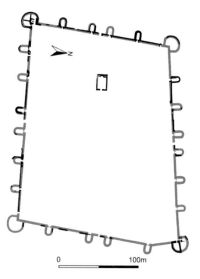

Figure 82: Udruh–Adrou (after Killick 1983b).

Wallsee–Adiuvense (Figures 2,30; 83)

Location: 48° 10′ 1.22″ N, 14° 42′ 56.62″ E
Situation: Adjacent to Danube
Height ASL: 276m (GE)
Country: Austria
Region: Melk, Niederösterreich
Province: Pannonia Prima
Length: 200m
Width: 160m
Area: 3.2ha
Proportion: 1.250
Cardinal orientation: 78/258°
Phases & Dating: Stone – *Legio I Noricorum* (?Tetrarchic–?)
Literary references: *ND Occ.* 34.28
Units attested epigraphically: *Legio X Gemina*: *CIL* III,
   4659,1s. *Ala I[*: *AE* 1990, 785.
Sub-literary references: –
Modern references (site): Friesinger and Krinzinger 1997, 195–202; Ruprechtsberger 2006;
   Tscholl 1977/78; 1986; 1989; 1990
Modern references (finds): Tscholl 2002
Notes: Urban site

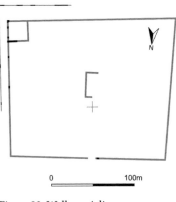

Figure 83: Wallsee–Adiuvense (after Tscholl 1986).

Other sites

Other sites mentioned in the *Notitia Dignitatum* are either too insubstantial or not located archaeologically and these include Armant (Hermonthis), Banostor (Bononia), Begeč (Onagrinum), ?Brza Palanka (Aegeta), Burghöfe bei Mertingen (Submontorium), Caraorman (Inplateypegiis), Celei (Sucidava), Dalj (Teutoburgium), Dunabogdány (Cirpi), Dunakömlőd (Lussonium), Dunaszekcső (Florentia), ?Felsőgöd (Constantia), Füssen (Foetibus), Golubatz (Cuppi), Gorni Tsibar (Cebro), Hasankeyf (Cepha), Isaccea (Noviodunum), Kladovo (Transdrobeta), Linz (Lentia), Mautern (Favianis), Novi Banovci (Burgena), Nusaybin (Nisibis), Orşova (Zernis), Pest (Contra Aquincum), Ruse (Sexaginta Prista), Schabur (?Andro), Seone (Aureus Mons), Selanovtsi (Variniana), Őcsény (Alisca), Trabzon (Trapezus), Tulcea (Aegyssus), Kom Ombos (Ombos), Tutrakan (Transmarisca). More information on these sites can be found on the accompanying website (see Appendix 5).

Figure 84: Pest–Contra Aquincum (after Visy 2003).

Appendix 1

Timeline of Legionary Movements

This appendix provides a brief outline of legionary movements (listed by legion) between bases around the Empire during the first to third centuries AD, so far as it is currently possible to reconstruct them. As such it draws on a number of previous attempts and can make no pretence at being either complete or any better than any of the others. However, it did seem like a necessary adjunct to the main body of the text. It should act as a corollary to the listings by site in Chapter 9.

This is not of course an attempt to reconcile all movements of the legions, but only their main home camp locations.

Legio I Adiutrix Mainz–Mogontiacum (AD 70–82); Szőny–Brigetio (AD 82–4th century)

Legio I Germanica Köln–Ara Ubiorum (AD 10–35); Bonn–Bonna (AD 35–69) [AD 70 reformed with *VII Galbiana* as *VII Gemina*]

Legio I Italica Svištov–Novae (AD 70–4th century)

Legio I Minervia Bonn–Bonna (AD 82–?359)

Legio I Parthica Balad Sinjar–Singara (AD 197–360)

Legio II Adiutrix Nijmegen–Noviomagus (AD 70); Lincoln–Lindum (AD 71–7); Chester–Deva (AD 78–88); Budapest–Aquincum (AD 89–?Tetrarchic)

Legio II Augusta Strasbourg–Argentorate (AD 10–43); Exeter–Isca (AD 49–73); Caerleon–Isca (Augusta) (AD 74–?Tetrarchic)

Legio II Italica Ločica–Celeia (AD 170–2); Albing (AD 173–204); Enns-Lorch–Lauriacum (AD 205–Tetrarchic)

Legio II Parthica Albano Laziale–Castra Albana (AD 197–214); Afamia–Apamea (AD 215–18); Albano Laziale–Castra Albana (AD 219–30); Afamia–Apamea (AD 231–3); Albano Laziale–Castra Albana (AD 234–41); Afamia–Apamea (AD 242–4); Albano Laziale–Castra Albana (AD 245–Tetrarchic)

Legio II Traiana Fortis Lajjun–Legio (Caparcotna) (AD 117–125); Alexandria–Nicopolis (AD 125–?Tetrarchic)

Legio III Augusta Haidra–Ammaedara (AD 14–74); Tebessa–Theveste (AD 75–121); Tazoult-Lambèse–Lambaesis (AD 122–4th century)

Legio III Cyrenaica Alexandria–Nicopolis (AD 10–106); Bosra–Bostra (AD 106–18); Alexandria–Nicopolis (AD 119–24); Bosra–Bostra (AD 125–4th century)

Legio III Gallica Barin–Raphanaea (AD 70–219)

Legio III Italica Regensburg–Castra Regina (AD 179–?5th century)

Legio III Parthica Ra's al-'Ayn–Resaina (AD 197–?Tetrarchic)

Legio IV Flavia Felix Ivoševci–Burnum (AD 70–86); Archar–Ratiaria (AD 86–101); Berzovia–Berzobis (AD 102–19); Beograd–Singidunum (AD 120–4th century)

Legio IV Macedonica Herrera de Pisuerga–Pisoraca (AD 10–43); Mainz–Mogontiacum (AD 43–69) [AD 70 reformed as *IV Flavia Felix*]

Legio IV Scythica Belkis–Zeugma (AD 66–256)

Legio V Alaudae Xanten–Vetera (I) (AD 10–69)

Legio V Macedonica Kostolac–Viminacium (AD 10–58); Gigen–Oescus (AD 10–60); Gigen–Oescus (AD 70–105); Igliţa–Troesmis (AD 106–61); Gigen–Oescus (AD 162–7); Turda–Potaissa (AD 168–4th century)

Legio VI Ferrata Samsat–Samosata (AD 70–117); Bosra–Bostra (AD 118–25); Lajjun–Legio (Caparcotna) (AD 125–c.303)

Legio VI Victrix Neuss–Novaesium (AD 70–92); Xanten–Vetera (II) (AD 93–121); York–Eboracum (AD 122–4th century)

Legio VII Claudia Gardun–Tilurium (AD 10–58); Kostolac–Viminacium (AD 59–68); Bad Deutsch-Altenburg–Carnuntum (AD 69–70); Kostolac–Viminacium (AD 71–?4th century)

Legio VII Gemina León–Legio VII Gemina (AD 74–4th century)

Legio VIII Augusta Ptuj–Poetovio (AD 10–43); Svištov–Novae (AD 44–69); Mirebeau (AD 70–92); Strasbourg–Argentorate (AD 92–?5th century)

Legio IX Hispana Sisak–Siscia (AD 10–43); Lincoln–Lindum (AD 60–70); York–Eboracum (AD 71–?106); Nijmegen–Noviomagus (?AD 106–?)

Legio X Fretensis Kurus-Cyrrhus (pre-AD 10–70); Jerusalem–Hierosolyma (AD 70–?Tetrarchic)

Legio X Gemina Astorga–Asturica (15/10 BC–AD 15/20); Rosinas de Vidriales–Petavonium (AD 15/20–62); Bad Deutsch-Altenburg–Carnuntum (AD 62–8); Nijmegen–Noviomagus (AD 71–105); Wien–Vindobona (AD 114–4th century)

Legio XI Claudia Ivoševci–Burnum (AD 10–69); Windisch–Vindonissa (AD 70–101); Silistra–Durosturum (AD 106–4th century)

Legio XII Fulminata Barin–Raphanaea (AD 10–70); Eski Malatya (Battalgazi)–Melitene (AD 70–?4th century)

Legio XIII Gemina Windisch–Vindonissa (AD 16–43); Ptuj–Poetovio (AD 44–88); Wien–Vindobona (AD 89–102); Grădişte–Sarmizegetusa (AD 102–8); Alba Iulia–Apulum (AD 109–272); Archar–Ratiaria (AD 272–Tetrarchic)

Legio XIV Gemina Mainz–Mogontiacum (AD 10–43); Wroxeter–Viriconium (AD 59–65); Mainz–Mogontiacum (AD 70–92); Wien–Vindobona (AD 106–13); Bad Deutsch-Altenburg–Carnuntum (AD 114–?)

Legio XV Apollinaris Ljubljana–Emona (AD 10–13); Bad Deutsch-Altenburg–Carnuntum (AD 14–61); Bad Deutsch-Altenburg–Carnuntum (AD 71–114); Sadak–Satala (AD 117–4th century)

Legio XV Primigenia ?Köln–Ara Ubiorum (AD 39–43); Xanten–Vetera (I) (AD 43–69)

Legio XVI Flavia Firma Sadak–Satala (AD 70–117); Samsat–Samosata (AD 117–?Tetrarchic)

Legio XVI Gallica Mainz–Mogontiacum (AD 10–43); Neuss–Novaesium (AD 43–69) [AD 70 reformed as *XVI Flavia Firma*]

Legio XVII destroyed AD 9

Legio XVIII destroyed AD 9

Legio XIX destroyed AD 9

Legio XX Valeria Victrix Köln–Ara Ubiorum (AD 10–35); Neuss–Novaesium (AD 35–43); Colchester–Camulodunum (AD 43–9); ?Gloucester–Glevum (AD 49–54); ?Usk–Burrium (AD 55–65); Wroxeter–Viriconium (AD 66–88); Chester–Deva (AD 89–4th century)

Legio XXI Rapax Xanten–Vetera (I) (AD 10–43); Neuss–Novaesium (AD 21–43); Windisch–Vindonissa (AD 43–70); Bonn–Bonna (AD 70–82)

Legio XXII Deiotariana Alexandria–Nicopolis (AD 10–136)

Legio XXII Primigenia Mainz–Mogontiacum (AD 43–69); Xanten–Vetera (II) (AD 70–92); Mainz–Mogontiacum (AD 92–4th century)

Legio XXX Ulpia Victrix Xanten–Vetera (II) (AD 122–4th century)

Unknown Usk–Burrium (AD 66–74)

Appendix 2

Glossary

In writing about Roman castrametation, jargon often gets bandied around by modern scholars as if it was (literally) set in stone by the Roman army. This is far from the case and there is no guarantee that some of the terms used here would have been recognized by all members of the army, since they derive from so few (and, it has to be said, such questionable) sources. Nevertheless, in order to fit in with contemporary and past scholarship, the terms have been used in the text, and this glossary is offered as a handy vade mecum with simple definitions, together with sources for the terms cited where appropriate.

aedes (principiorum)	shrine of the standards, in the centre of the rear range of rooms in the *principia* (*RIB* 3027). See also *sacellum*
amphitheatrum	amphitheatre (*AE* 1955, 135)
arma	that area in front of a tent set aside for the storage of weapons. Usually equated with the front room of a barrack room-pair. Literally 'weapons' (*De Mun. Cast.* 1)
armamentarium	a structure that served as an armoury (*RIB* 1092; *AE* 1984, 703)
balneum	baths (*CIL* III, 10489)
basilica	cross-hall in the *principia* (*RIB* 3027)
canabae	term often applied to the civil settlement outside a legionary base (*CIL* III, 6166)
campus	usually translated as 'parade ground' but probably more accurately 'exercise ground' or 'training area' (*CIL* VIII, 2532)
centuria	barrack block (*RIB* 334)
cohors quingenaria	cohort of six centuries (480 men) (*De Mun. Cast.* 28)
cohors milliaria	cohort of ten centuries (800 men) (*De Mun. Cast.* 28)
fabrica	workshops (*De Mun. Cast.* 4)
fossa	defensive ditch. Might be described as a *fossa fastigata* (symmetrically V-shaped) or *fossa Punica* (asymmetrically V-shaped) (*De Mun. Cast.* 49)
groma	point from which the camp was laid out, named after the surveying instrument of the same name. Also the name of a quadrifrons arch (or tetrapylon) sometimes erected over the junction of the *via praetoria* and *via principalis*, at the entrance to the *principia* (*De Mun. Cast.* 12; *AE* 1974, 723)
hemistrigium	space allotted for a *centuria* (*De Mun. Cast.* 1)
horrea	granaries or store buildings (*RIB* 1151)
intervallum	area between the rampart and the internal structures, so including rampart-back structures. Literally 'within the ramparts' (*De Mun. Cast.* 14)

latera praetorii	the central range, comprising the *principia* and accompanying structures on the opposite side of the *via principalis* to the *scamnum tribunorum* (and so between the *retentura* and *praetentura*) (*De Mun. Cast.* 23)
murus	stone wall, but see also *vallum* (*CIL* VIII, 2532)
papilio	tent (literally, 'pupa', referring – it is presumed – to the similarity between a rolled leather tent and the pupa case of a butterfly's larval stage). Usually equated with the rear room of a barrack room-pair (*De Mun. Cast.* 1)
per scamnum	aligned parallel with the *via principalis* (inferred from *De Mun. Cast.* 15)
per strigas	aligned parallel with the *via praetoria* (inferred from *De Mun. Cast.* 15)
porta decumana	the gate on the *via decumana*, in the *retentura* (*De Mun. Cast.* 18)
porta praetoria	the gate on the *via praetoria* immediately in front of the *principia*. in the *praetentura* (*De Mun. Cast.* 3)
porta principalis dextra	the gate on the *via principalis* to the right of the *principia*, when standing at the *groma*, facing the *porta praetoria* (*De Mun. Cast.* 14)
porta principalis sinistra	the gate on the *via principalis* to the left of the *principia*, when standing at the *groma*, facing the *porta praetoria* (*De Mun. Cast.* 14)
praetentura	literally 'the front tented area' on the opposite side of the *via principalis* to the *principia* (*De Mun. Cast.* 3)
praetorium	the *legatus legionis*' (commanding officer's) house (but the combined headquarters area of a campaign camp) (*De Mun. Cast.* 3; *AE* 1964, 148)
prata legionis	agricultural land belonging to a legionary base. See also *territorium* (*CIL* III, 13250)
principales	junior officers in a century, such as the *signifier* and *optio* (*AE* 1965, 18)
quaestorium	area where booty, prisoners, and hostages were kept in a campaign camp, in the *retentura*, immediately behind the *principia* (*De Mun. Cast.* 17)
retentura	literally 'the rear tented area', behind the *principia* (*De Mun. Cast.* 17)
sacellum	shrine of the standards, in the centre of the rear range of rooms in the *principia* (*CIL* VIII, 2741 and 18126; *AE* 2007, 1070). See also *aedes*
scamnum tribunorum	that part of the *praetentura* fronting onto the *via principalis* that contained the six tribunes' houses. Literally 'the bench of the tribunes' (*De Mun. Cast.* 15)
striga	the space occupied by two *centuriae*, thus two adjacent *hemistrigia* (*De Mun. Cast.* 1)
tabularium (legionis)	legionary record office (*AE* 1898, 108–9)
territorium	land belonging to a legionary base (*CIL* III, 10489). See also *prata legionis*
tribunal	platform at one end of the crosshall of the *principia* (*De Mun. Cast.* 11) or on a *campus* (*AE* 1933, 214)
tribunus angusticlavius	literally 'narrow stripe' tribune, of equestrian rank (Suet., Otho 10)
tribunus laticlavius	literally 'broad stripe' tribune, of senatorial rank (*AE* 1912, 17)
valetudinarium	hospital (*De Mun. Cast.* 4; Veg., *Epit. Rei Mil.* 2.10; 3.2; *Digest* 50.6.6; *CIL* III, 14537)
vallum	defensive rampart or wall (*De Mun. Cast.* 14). Hadrian's Wall, built of stone, was referred to as a *vallum* (*ND Occ.* 40; *RIB* 2034)

veterinarium	veterinary facility (*De Mun. Cast.* 4)
via decumana	rear road into the fortress, passing through the *porta decumana*, in the *retentura* (*De Mun. Cast.* 18)
via praetoria	main street running between the *porta praetoria* and the junction with the *via principalis*, directly in front of the *principia* (*De Mun. Cast.* 14)
via principalis	main street running between the *porta principalis sinistra* and *porta principalis dextra* (*De Mun. Cast.* 10)
via quintana	road parallel with the *via principalis* which forms a T-junction with the *via decumana*. In legionary camps, this was not usually associated with *portae quintanae* (*De Mun. Cast.* 17)
via sagularis	road running around the periphery of the camp within the defences. Literally 'the cloaked street' (*De Mun. Cast.* 3)
via vicinaria	street between buildings, especially barracks. Literally 'local street' (*De Mun. Cast.* 17)

Appendix 3

Late Fortresses in the *Notitia Dignitatum*

Reference	Command	Officer	Unit(s)	Location in text	Identification	Modern site
Occ. 28.19	*Comes litoris Saxonici per Britanniam*		*legio II Augusta*	Rutupis	Rutupiae	Richborough
Occ. 32.24	*Dux Pannoniae*	*Praefectus*	*legio V Iovia (cohortes V pars superior)*	Bononiae	Bononia	Banostor
Occ. 32.25	*Dux Pannoniae*	*Praefectus*	*legio VI Herculea (cohortes V pars superior)*	Aureo monte	Aureus Mons	Banovo Brdo?
Occ. 32.26	*Dux Pannoniae*	*Praefectus*	*legio V Iovia*	Burgenas	Burgena	Novi Banovci
Occ. 32.27	*Dux Pannoniae*	*Praefectus*	*legio VI Herculea*	Teutiborgio	Teutoburgium	Dalj
Occ. 32.28	*Dux Pannoniae*	*Praefectus*	*legiones V Iovia & VI Herculea*	in castello Onagrino	Onagrinum	Begeč
Occ. 33.29	*Dux provinciae Valeriae*	*Praefectus*	*legio I Adiutrix (cohortes V partis superioris)*	Bregtione	Brigetio	Komaróm-Szőny
Occ. 33.30	*Dux provinciae Valeriae*	*Praefectus*	*legio II Adiutrix (cohortes V pars superior)*	Aliscae	Alisca	Őcsény
Occ. 33.31	*Dux provinciae Valeriae*	*Praefectus*	*legio II Adiutrix (pars inferior)*	Florentiae	Florentia	Dunaszekcső
Occ. 33.32	*Dux provinciae Valeriae*	*Praefectus*	*legio II Adiutrix (pars superior)*	Acinco	Aquincum	Budapest
Occ. 33.33	*Dux provinciae Valeriae*	*Praefectus*	*legio II Adiutrix*	in castello contra Tautantum	Constantia?	Felsőgöd?
Occ. 33.34	*Dux provinciae Valeriae*	*Praefectus*	*legio II Adiutrix*	Cirpi	Cirpi	Dunabogdány
Occ. 33.35	*Dux provinciae Valeriae*	*Praefectus*	*legio II Adiutrix*	Lussonio	Lussonium	Dunakömlőd-Paks
Occ. 33.43	*Dux provinciae Valeriae*	*Praefectus*	*legio [II Adiutrix?]*	Transiacinco	Transaquincum	Budapest
Occ. 34.13	*Dux Pannoniae primae*	*Praefectus*	*legio X Geminae*	Vindomarae	Vindomora	Wien?
Occ. 34.14	*Dux Pannoniae primae*	*Praefectus*	*legio XIV Gemina, milites liburnariorum (cohortes V pars superior)*	Carnunto	Carnuntum	Bad Deutsch-Altenburg
Occ. 34.15	*Dux Pannoniae primae*	*Praefectus*	*legiones X & XIV Gemina, milites liburnariorum*	Arrabonae	Arrabona	Győr

Reference	Command	Officer	Unit(s)	Location in text	Identification	Modern site
Occ. 34.37	Dux Pannoniae primae	Praefectus	legio II Italica, milites liburnariorum	Ioviaco	Ioviacum	Schlögen
Occ. 34.26	Dux Pannoniae primae	Praefectus	legio II Italica (pars inferior)	Lentiae	Lentia	Linz
Occ. 34.27	Dux Pannoniae primae	Praefectus	legio II Italica	Lauriaco	Lauriacum	Enns
Occ. 34.40	Dux Pannoniae primae	Praefectus	legio I Noricorum milites liburnariorum (cohortes V pars superior)	Adiuuense	Adiuvense	Wallsee-Sindelburg
Occ. 34.29	Dux Pannoniae primae	Praefectus	legio I Noricorum liburnariorum	Fafianae	Favianis	Mautern
Occ. 35.5	Dux Raetiae	Praefectus	legio III Italica (pars superior)	Castra Regina, nunc Vallato	Castra Regina, now Vallatum	Regensburg, now Manching/ Weltenburg
Occ. 35.6	Dux Raetiae	Praefectus	legio III Italica (pars superior, deputatae ripae primae)	Submuntorio	Submontorium	Burghöfe bei Mertingen
Occ. 35.7	Dux Raetiae	Praefectus	legio III Italica (pro parte media praetendentis)	Vimania Cassiliacum usque, Cambidano	Vimania, Cassiliacum, Cambodunum	Isny im Allgäu, Memmingen, Kempten
Occ. 35.9	Dux Raetiae	Praefectus	legio III Italica (transvectioni specierum deputatae)	Foetibus	Foetibus	Füssen
Occ. 35.10	Dux Raetiae	Praefectus	legio III Italica (transvectioni specierum deputatae)	Teriolis	Teriolis	Zirl bei Innsbruck
Occ. 40.2	Dux Britanniarum	Praefectus	legio VI	–	[Eboracum]	[York]
Occ. 42.25	Item praepositurae magistri militum praesentalis a parte peditum	Praefectus	legio VII Gemina	Legione	Legio	Leon
Or. 28.2	Comes limitis Aegypti	?	legio V Macedonica	Memfi	Memphis	Memphis

Reference	Command	Officer	Unit(s)	Location in text	Identification	Modern site
Or. 28.3	*Comes limitis Aegypti*	?	*legio XIII Gemina*	Babilona	Babylon	Old Cairo
Or. 28.6	*Comes limitis Aegypti*	?	*legio III Diocletiana*	Andro	Ambo	Kom Ombo
Or. 28.7	*Comes limitis Aegypti*	?	*legio II Traiana*	Parembole	Parembole/Nicopolis	Alexandria
Or. 31.10	*Dux Thebaidos*	?	*legio III Diocletiana*	Ombos	Ombos	Tukh
Or. 31.11	*Dux Thebaidos*	?	*legio II Flavia Constantia Thebaeorum*	Cusas	Cusae	el-Qusiya
Or. 31.12	*Dux Thebaidos*	?	*legio II Traiana*	Apollonos superioris Apollinopolis Magna	Coptus	Edfu
Or. 31.14	*Dux Thebaidos*	?	*legio I Valentiniana*	Copto	Coptus	Qift
Or. 31.15	*Dux Thebaidos*	?	*legio I Maximiana*	Filas	Philae	Anas el Wagud
Or. 31.16	*Dux Thebaidos*	?	*legio III Diocletiana*	Thebas	Thebae	Luxor?
Or. 31.17	*Dux Thebaidos*	?	*legio II Valentiniana*	Hermunthi	Hermonthis	Armant
Or. 32.14	*Dux Foenicis*	*Praefectus*	*legio I Illyricorum*	Palmira	Palmyra	Tadmor
Or. 32.15	*Dux Foenicis*	*Praefectus*	*legio III Gallica*	Danaba	Danaba	Mehin?
Or. 33.9	*Dux Syriae*	*Praefectus*	*legio IV Scythica*	Oresa	Oresa	Tayibeh
Or. 33.14	*Dux Syriae*	*Praefectus*	*legio XVI Flavia Firma*	Sura	Sura	Soura
Or. 34.15	*Dux Palaestinae*	*Praefectus*	*legio X Fretensis*	Ailae	Aila	Aqaba
Or. 35.11	*Dux Osrhoenae*	*Praefectus*	*legio IV Parthica*	Circesio	Circesium	Busayrah
Or. 36.12	*Dux Mesopotamiae*	*Praefectus*	*legio I Parthica*	Nisibenae, Constantina	Nisibis, Constantina	Nusaybin
Or. 36.13	*Dux Mesopotamiae*	*Praefectus*	*legio II Parthica*	Cefae	Cepha	Hasankeyf
Or. 37.9	*Dux Arabiae*	*Praefectus*	*legio III Cyrenaica*	Bostra	Bostra	Bosra
Or. 37.10	*Dux Arabiae*	*Praefectus*	*legio IV Martia*	Betthoro	Betthorus	Lejjun
Or. 38.4	*Dux Armeniae*	*Praefectus*	*legio XV Apollinaris*	Satala	Satala	Saddak
Or. 38.5	*Dux Armeniae*	*Praefectus*	*legio XII Fulminata*	Melitena	Melitena	Battalgazia

Reference	Command	Officer	Unit(s)	Location in text	Identification	Modern site
Or. 38.7	*Dux Armeniae*	*Praefectus*	*legio I Pontica*	Trapezunta	Trapezus	Trabzon
Or. 39.19	*Dux Scythiae*	*Praefectus*	*legio II Herculia*	Trosmis	Troesmis	Igliţa
Or. 39.20	*Dux Scythiae*	*Praefectus*	*legio II Herculia (cohortes quintae pedaturae inferioris)*	Axiupoli	Axiopolis	Cernavodă
Or. 39.21	*Dux Scythiae*	*Praefectus*	*legio II Herculia (cohortes quintae pedaturae inferioris)*	Iprosmis	Troesmis	Igliţa
Or. 39.22	*Dux Scythiae*	*Praefectus*	*legio I Iovia*	Nouioduno	Noviodunum	Isaccea
Or. 39.23	*Dux Scythiae*	*Praefectus*	*legio I Iovia (cohortes quintae pedaturae superioris)*	Nouioduno	Noviodunum	Isaccea
Or. 39.24	*Dux Scythiae*	*Praefectus*	*legio I Iovia (cohortes quintae pedaturae inferioris)*	Accisso	Aegyssus	Tulcea
Or. 39.25	*Dux Scythiae*	*Praefectus*	*legiones I Iovia (cohortes) et II Herculia (musculorum Scythicorum) et classis*	Inplateypegiis	Inplateypegiis	Caraorman
Or. 40.21	*Dux Moesiae secundae*	*Praefectus*	*legio I Italica*	Nouas	Novae	Svištov
Or. 40.22	*Dux Moesiae secundae*	*Praefectus*	*legio I Italica (cohortes quintae pedaturae superioris)*	Nouas	Novae	Svishtov
Or. 40.23	*Dux Moesiae secundae*	*Praefectus*	*legio I Italica (cohortes quintae pedaturae inferioris)*	Sexagintaprista	Sexagintaprista	Ruse
Or. 40.24	*Dux Moesiae secundae*	*Praefectus*	*legio XI Claudia*	Durostoro	Durostorum	Silistra
Or. 40.25	*Dux Moesiae secundae*	*Praefectus*	*legio XI Claudia (cohortes quintae pedaturae superioris)*	Transmariscae	Transmarisca	Tutrakan
Or. 40.26	*Dux Moesiae secundae*	*Praefectus*	*legio XI Claudia (cohortes quintae pedaturae inferioris)*	Transmariscae	Transmarisca	Tutrakan
Or. 41.20	*Dux Moesiae primae*	*Praefectus*	*legio IV Flavia*	Singiduno	Singidunum	Beograd
Or. 41.21	*Dux Moesiae primae*	*Praefectus*	*legio VII Claudia*	Cuppis	Cuppae	Golubatz

Reference	Command	Officer	Unit(s)	Location in text	Identification	Modern site
Or. 42.22	*Dux Daciae ripensis*	*Praefectus*	*legio V Macedonica*	Variniana	Variniana	Selanovtsi
Or. 42.23	*Dux Daciae ripensis*	*Praefectus*	*legio V Macedonica*	Cebro	Cebrus	Gorni Tsibar
Or. 42.24	*Dux Daciae ripensis*	*Praefectus*	*legio V Macedonica*	Oesco	Oescus	Gigen
Or. 42.25	*Dux Daciae ripensis*	*Praefectus*	*legio XIII Gemina*	Aegeta	Aegata	Brza Palanka
Or. 42.26	*Dux Daciae ripensis*	*Praefectus*	*legio XIII Gemina*	Transdrobeta	Transdrobeta	Kladovo
Or. 42.27	*Dux Daciae ripensis*	*Praefectus*	*legio XIII Gemina*	Burgo Novo	Burgum Novum	?
Or. 42.28	*Dux Daciae ripensis*	*Praefectus*	*legio XIII Gemina*	Zernis	Zernis	Orşova
Or. 42.29	*Dux Daciae ripensis*	*Praefectus*	*legio XIII Gemina*	Ratiaria	Ratiaria	Archar
Or. 42.30	*Dux Daciae ripensis*	*Praefectus*	*legio V Macedonica*	Sucidaua	Sucidava	Celei

Appendix 4

Sites Excluded

A number of categories of site have been excluded from this volume on the grounds that they do not meet the criteria set out above (p. 2) for a legionary base. These include the following:

Insufficient evidence

Suggested fortresses such as Resaena (Ras al'Ayn, Syria) that lack literary references, inscriptions, or archaeological remains have not been included. This does not mean that they might not subsequently be shown to have been legionary bases.[1]

Vexillation forts

Many sites have now been identified that held legionary detachments and many more certainly await discovery. Most of the former have never been claimed as legionary bases, although at least one site, which from its size might traditionally be considered as a vexillation fortress, has been proposed at Alchester. Corbridge is a famous example where multiple legionary detachments were attested and an attempt to identify one structure there as a legionary *principia* caused some awkward moments in the relationship of at least two of the principal archaeologists working there. Others, like Waldgirmes, although claimed as a civil site in usage, closely resemble a military site in form, and thus pose questions of whether one is seeing a civil site built by the military or a military site converted to civil use.[2]

Missing sites

Some scholars have argued for a legionary fortress at Leicester during the first century AD. Apart from a few desultory pieces of artefactual evidence, this has yet to be found. Since there is no excavated, epigraphic, or literary evidence for it, it is not included here. The same is true of the putative legionary base at Augsburg-Oberhausen, which Colin Wells so eloquently argued against and which now appears to have been just a fort. Other sites show tentative indications that might be interpreted as military. The 'proto-forum' at Silchester is a good example, resembling a *principia* (the similarity between early *fora* and legionary *principia* has been noted elsewhere), although not enough to merit inclusion, not least because it may represent military involvement in a civilian project; this despite interesting finds of early military equipment from the site.[3]

Appendix 5

The Website

There is an inevitable and developing relationship between the internet (particularly the world wide web) and the book. There are things a book can do that the web cannot match; at the same time, there are things the web can do that can powerfully enhance book content. Thus it is natural to provide additional material relating to a book on a website. However, it is important that each component should function independently, as well as working together. Thus a reader should not need the internet to use this book, but access to it will be an advantage. The website that accompanies this volume – www.legionaryfortresses.info – contains a variety of such complementary features.

1. A **literature review** that mirrors and complements the content of the text.
2. A detailed **bibliography** by subject and site. This in many ways echoes what is to be found in the gazetteers but without the need to refer backwards and forwards between reference and bibliography. Moreover, as more material becomes available, it will be added.
3. Fortress **plans**. This is probably the first time so many newly drawn plans of fortresses have been available in one place and certainly the first time that they have been made available for download and non-commercial use under the conditions of a Creative Commons (CC-BY-NC-SA) licence. For enquiries about commercial use, contact the author at the email address below. In addition, one particular bitmap manifestation of these drawings is being made available for use on the web with a dual GFDL/Creative Commons (CC-BY-SA) licence (which will hopefully go some way to getting rid of all those repetitive versions of the Neuss plan that turn up when searching online for plans of legionary fortresses).
4. There are **links** to other websites of relevance. Superb digital reconstructions of fortresses like those of Chester or Neuss are included (along with an actual physical model of the latter), together with visitor information for legionary base museums at sites like Caerleon, Budapest or Haltern.
5. A brief illustrated **guide** to visible fortress remains around the Roman Empire.
6. An online **atlas** of all the known legionary camps that uses *Google Earth* and *Google Maps* to enable anybody with computer access to study the site locations. This includes simple outlines to show the locations of the camps, L-marks for the *groma* position (where known, **?** where uncertain) of each site, placemarks for significant associated features (like amphitheatres, exercise grounds, or neighbouring auxiliary forts), and superimposed versions of the plans from this book.

Comments (preferably helpful) and suggestions for inclusion should be sent to the author at **mcbishop@pobox.com** (but beware the many-layered spam traps).

Notes

Preface

1. For an excellent general introduction (far better than I can provide here), the reader is directed to Campbell 2006.
2. Previous plan comparisons: Boon and Williams 1967; Petrikovits 1975. Creative Commons licence: <http://creativecommons.org/licenses/>. *The GIMP*: <http://www.gimp.org> accessed 6.12.10; *Inkscape*: <http://www.inkscape.org> accessed 6.12.10. *Natural Earth*: <http://www.natural earthdata.com/> accessed 11.2.11. *QGIS*: <http://www.qgis.org/> accessed 11.2.11. Drawings: <http://www.legionaryfortresses.info/drawings>.
3. Website: <http://www.legionaryfortresses.info>.
4. *Legio IV Macedonica*: AE 2007, 01054j. *Legio IIII Macedonica*: AE 1997, 765.

Chapter 1: Introduction

1. Corbridge *vexillationes*: RIB 1125; 1127; 1130; 1132; 1136–7; 1154; 1162–3. Moving between *hiberna* and *aestiva*: Tac., *Ann.* 1.37. Fragmented legions: Casey 1991, 12–16; Tomlin 2000, 162–6.
2. Camp: cf. Lepper and Frere 1988, 260. Legionslager: Domaszewski 1921, 178. Hadrian's Wall: Collingwood 1921. Legionary fortress: Salvatore 1996, 147 n.4.
3. Pseudo-Hyginus: Frere 1980; Gilliver 1993b.
4. *Castra*: Lewis and Short 1879, *s.v. castrum* II. *Castrum/kastrum*: Lewis and Short 1879, *s.v. castrum* I; CIL XIII, 8502; VIII, 4354 (not legionary). *Castra aestiva/hiberna*: De Mun. Cast. 45; 48; Veg., *Epit. Rei Mil.* 2.11; Suet., *Claud.* 1. Tacitus and campaigns: *Ann.* 1.16; 31; 37. *Castra stativa*: Veg., *Epit. Rei Mil.* 3.8; Tac., *Ann.* 3.21. 'Marching' camps: Veg., *Epit. Rei Mil.* 3.8. Nicopolis: AE 1948, 120; ChLA 42, 1207. Mainz: AE 1964, 148.
5. Dimensions: e.g. Pitts and St Joseph 1988, 57.
6. Modular layout: Crummy 1988, 29; 1993b. *Decempeda*: Veg., *Epit. Rei Mil.* 3.8; Suet., *Aug.* 24.2. *Pes Monetalis/Drusianus*: Walthew 1981; Millett 1982. Orientation: Richardson 2005.
7. Carnuntum: Groller 1900; 1901; 1902; 1903; 1904; 1905; 1906a; 1908b; 1909a. Lauriacum: Groller 1907b; 1908a; 1909b; 1910; 1919a; 1919b; 1924a; 1924b; 1925a; 1925b; 1925c. Lejjun: Parker 2006. Caerleon: Gardner and Guest 2007; 2009; 2010; Guest and Gardner 2008; Guest and Young 2006. Novae: Derda et al. 2008; Dyczek 2007.
8. Camulodunum-Colchester: Tac., *Ann.* 12.32. Defence of Vetera: Tac., *Hist.* 4.22; 28–30; 34–6; 60; 5.14–18. Polybius: 6.27–41. Interpreting camps: Schulten 1927; 1929; Dobson 2008, 1–4. Interpreting the archaeology: Dobson 2008.
9. Vegetius: Milner 1996. Late Roman: Goffart 1977. Analysis: Schenk 1930, 26–39; 8–26; 39–64. *Antiqua legio*: Baatz 2000.
10. Pseudo-Hyginus: Gilliver 1993b. First cohort: Frere 1980; Baatz 2000, 155–6.
11. Alexandria-Nicopolis document (*P. Fouad.* I, 45): ChLA 42, 1207, <http://papyri.info/ddbdp/chla;42;1207> accessed 6.12.10.
12. *Notitia Dignitatum*: Seeck 1962. Dating: Tomlin 2000, 175 n.7. Isca: Ptol., *Geog.* 2.3.13.
13. Trajan's Column: Lepper and Frere 1988, 260–6. Castra Praetoria: RIC 1.7. Models: Aumüller 2002, D92–5.

14. Tacitus: *Ann.* 12.32. Facilis: *RIB* 200. British inscriptions: *RIB* 330 (Caerleon), 665 (York), 464 (Chester). *Adlocutio*: Speidel 2006.
15. Stamps: Boon 1984b; Wesch-Klein 2000; Warry 2010.
16. Novaesium: Koenen 1904; Lehner 1904; Nissen 1904; Chantraine et al. 1984, 171–82.
17. Sadak-Satala: Lightfoot 1990a; 1990b; 1998; Drahor et al. 2004; 2008. Belkis-Zeugma: Hartmann and Speidel 2001; 2002; 2003; Hartmann et al. 1999; 2000; 2001. Barin-Raphanaea: Gschwind 2006; 2007; 2008a; 2008b; Gschwind and Hasan 2008; Gschwind et al. 2009.
18. Souriyah: Poidebard 1934, 83–4, pl. LXXIX–LXXX. Tayibeh: ibid. 79, pl. LXXI. Mehin: Dussaud 1927, 266. Aqaba: Whitcomb 1993. Inscription: MacAdam 1989. Mainz: Baatz 1962. Strasbourg: Hatt 1993.

Chapter 2: The Legions
1. General: Parker 1958; Webster 1985; Le Bohec 1994. Detailed: Ritterling 1925; Le Bohec and Wolff 2000.
2. Two consular legions: Keppie 1984, 19. *Legio*: ibid. 15. Twinning with allied legions: Dobson 2008, 51–2.
3. Sixty centuries: Gell., *NA* 16.4.6. Eighty men: *De Mun. Cast.* 1. Ten cohorts: *CIL* III, 6178; Gell., *NA* 16.4.6; Veg., *Epit. Rei Mil.* 2.6. First cohort seniority: Veg., *Epit. Rei Mil.* 2.6. First cohort five centuries: *CIL* VIII, 18072. Double strength: *De Mun. Cast.* 3; Frere 1980.
4. Sixty legions: Keppie 1984, 145. Tacitus: *Ann.* 4.5. List: *CIL* VI, 3492.
5. Late legion size: Tomlin 2000, 169–73.
6. Legionary structure: Speidel 1992; Baatz 2000. Accommodation: Boon 1987, 47–50.

Chapter 3: History and Development of Legionary Bases
1. Ostia *castrum*: Meiggs 1973, 20–3; 116–17.
2. Nobilior: App., *Ib.* 197; cf. Dobson 2008, 43–5. Numantia: ibid. 1–6. Cáceres: Ulbert 1984.
3. Distributing legions: Caes., *BGall.* 5.24. Basing by legion: ibid. 5.25; 5.46.
4. Saturninus: Syme 1978. Logistical strain: Bishop 1999, 111. Abolition of double camps: Suet., *Dom.* 7,3. Alexandria: Keppie 1984, 196.
5. Germany: Schnurbein 2004, 26. Legion pairs: Tac., *Ann.* 1.37. Sisak: Radman-Livaja 2010a; 2010b. Ljubljana: Vičič 2002; 2008. Camp C: Wells 1972, 128–32, esp. 132 n.1. Augustan camps and later successors: Schnurbein 2000. *Hibernacula*: Baatz 1985. Numantine camps: Dobson 2008.
6. Numantia: Dobson 2008, 122–3. Caesar: *BGall.* 7.72–3; cf. Reddé and Schnurbein 1997. Holz-Erde-Mauer: Jones 1975, 14–18; 82–6. Turf and timber: ibid. 78–82.
7. Castra Praetoria: Richmond 1927; Durry 1938, 45–58; Coulston 2000, 82–4. Date of construction: Richmond 1927, 12. Brick-faced concrete: ibid. 13.
8. Inchtuthil: Pitts and St Joseph 1985, 61–8. Colchester defences: Crummy 1988, 29–30. Colchester concrete: ibid. 31. York: *RIB* 665. Chester: *RIB* 464. Caerleon: *RIB* 330.
9. Neuss: Koenen 1904, 143–5. Caerleon *patera*: *RIB* 2415.39. Associated auxiliaries: Nash-Williams 1969, 14–18.
10. Outposting: Speidel 2006, 8. Dacian Wars: *AE* 1983, 825. Crimea: *AE* 1997, 1332. Danube delta: *AE* 1990, 868. Construction work: *AE* 1922, 53. Kostolac: *AE* 1903, 292–3; 1905, 159; *CIL* III, 1646; 1648–9; 1652–3; 1659; 6300; 8123; 14511; 14597; *IMS* II, 16; 59; 87–8; 90; 96.
11. Billeting: Webster 1985, 35. Literary evidence: Veg., *Epit. Rei Mil.* 3.8. Ambiguous: Tac., *Ann.* 13.35. Military quarter: Parker 2000, 121. Dura-Europos: James 2004, 16–20.
12. Lejjun: Kennedy and Riley 1990, 131. Udruh: ibid. 131–4. Sura: ibid. 115–16. Tayibeh: ibid. 137. Luxor: Golvin and Reddé 1986.
13. *Notitia Dignitatum*: Seeck 1962.

Chapter 4: Defences
1. Ramparts: Veg., *Epit. Rei Mil.* 1.24; 3.8; *De Mun. Cast.* 50. Stakes: Veg., *Epit. Rei Mil.* 1.24; 3.8; *De Mun. Cast.* 51–2; Gilliver 1993a.
2. Rhyn Park: Jones 1982. Defences: Jones 1975; Manning and Scott 1979.

3. Defences: Jones 1975, 74–8. Trajan's Column: ibid. 4. Cobbling: ibid. 186–7 (York). Timber corduroys: Nash-Williams 1931, 103 (Caerleon); Mason 2001, 56 (Chester); Jones 1975, 186 (York).

4. Isingerode: Steinmetz 2006. Ivinghoe Beacon: Cotton and Frere 1968, 200–3. Lincoln: Jones 1975, 160–1. Oberaden: Kühlborn 1992. Nijmegen: Haalebos 1991. Marktbreit: Pietsch 1991b. Chester: Jones 1975, 142.

5. Wroxeter: Webster and Chadderton 2002, 22 and Fig. 2.9. York: Jones 1975, 186.

6. Rounded corners: *De Mun. Cast.* 54. Origins with turf construction: Gregory 1989, 170–1. Caerleon: Nash-Williams 1930, Fig.2. Inchtuthil: Pitts and St Joseph 1985, 195.

7. Squared rubble: Hill 2006, 41. Inchtuthil: Pitts and St Joseph 1985, 61. Caerleon: Nash-Williams 1931, 107–8. Castra Albana: Chiarucci 2006, 56. Chester: Strickland 1996, 104–13. Gardun: Sanader 2003b, 22. Vindonissa: Hartmann 1983, 76. Albing: Groller 1907a, 160. Chester: Strickland 1996, 106. York: Ottaway 1992, 58.

8. Dura-Europos: pers. obs. Castra Praetoria: Richmond 1927, 14. Merlons: Bidwell et al. 1988; Strickland 1996, 104–12. Rendering: cf. Bidwell and Watson 1996, 23–6. Red lines: Nash-Williams 1931, 110; Wheeler and Wheeler 1928, 121.

9. Lejjun: Parker 1986, 69. Richborough: Blagg 1989, 143; Johnson 1979, 49. Later Castra Praetoria crenellations: Richmond 1927, 16; 17.

10. Josephus: *BJ* 3.5.2. Phasis: Arr., *Peripl. P. Eux.* 12.

11. Artillery: Parker 1986, 69. York: Ottaway 1992, 97–101. *Ascensus*: Jones 1975, 89. Storage: cf. James 2004, 38.

12. Gateways: Manning and Scott 1979. Scantling: Manning and Scott 1979, 30–61. Inchtuthil: Pitts and St Joseph 1985, 71. Oberaden: Manning and Scott 1979, 54–5.

13. Towers: Jones 1975, 89–97. Alba Iulia: Moga 1999a. Mirebeau: Goguey 2008, Fig. 6. Vindonissa: Hartmann 1986, Abbn. 64–5.

14. Berm: Jones 1975, 105. Carnuntum: Groller 1904, 41–2. Inchtuthil: Pitts and St Joseph 1985, 62.

15. *Fossa Punica*: *De Mun. Cast.* 49; Groller 1904, 41–2. *Fossa fastigata*: loc. cit. Cleaning slot: Jones 1975, 36–7; 109.

16. Counterscarp: Jones 1975, 106. Neuss: Koenen 1904, 216. Inchtuthil: Pitts and St Joseph 1985, 71.

17. Outworks: Wilson 1984.

Chapter 5: The Internal Buildings

1. Petrikovits 1975.

2. *Principia*: Fellmann 1958; 1989; Petrikovits 1975, 68–75; Blagg 2000. Inchtuthil: Pitts and St Joseph 1985, 79–81. Vetera I: Lehner 1930. Windisch: Hartmann 1986, 44; 55. *Forum*: Petrikovits 1975, 68.

3. Ritual pit: Pitts and St Joseph 1985, 81 and Pl. XIII,B. *Armamentaria*: Blagg 2000, 139. Columns at York: Blagg 2000, 142. Second storey: Gawlikowsky 1984, 17–19.

4. Alignment: Blagg 2000, 142. Relationship: Schnurbein 2000, 33–4.

5. *Forum/agora*: Petrikovits 1975, 140–1; Blagg 2000, 139–40. Proto-fortresses: Schnurbein 2000, 33–5.

6. Lambaesis: Kolbe 1974; Rakob 1971–74; 1979; 2001. Caerleon: Zienkiewicz 1993, 140. Aquincum: Szirmai 1986, 427. Enns-Lorch: Groller 1910, 23. Lejjun: Parker 1988, 136–7; 1990, 92; 1991, 119. Palmyra: Kowalski 1998, 199–200. Caerleon survival: Howell 2000. Aquincum survival: Wellner 1990. Guard duties: Fink 1971, 128 and 136.

7. Granaries: Petrikovits 1975, 82–5; Manning 1975; Gentry 1976. Kostolac: *AE* 1973, 471. Store buildings: Petrikovits 1975, 85–8.

8. Contents stored: Gentry 1976, 26. Buttresses: ibid. 15. Inchtuthil: Pitts and St Joseph 1985, 117–22. Tiles: Pitts and St Joseph 1985, 121.

9. Hospital: Schultze 1925; Petrikovits 1975, 98–102, Bild 27; Watermann 1978. Criticisms: Baker 2002; 2004; n.d. Medical implements: Koenen 1904: 180–2; Dyczek 1997: 202–3. Aesculapius: Dyczek 1999; Künzl 2005.

10. Baths: Petrikovits 1975, 102. Exeter: Bidwell 1979. Caerleon: Zienkiewicz 1986a; 1986b. Aquincum: Kaba 1986; 1991; Kaba and Szentpétery 1987. Inchtuthil: Pitts and St Joseph 1985, 187–8.

11. Nature of the *praetorium*: Petrikovits 1975, 67–8.
12. Mediterranean-type houses: Petrikovits 1975, 67. Form of the *praetorium*: ibid. 67–8. 'Hippodrome' gardens: ibid. 170 n. 65.
13. *Tribuni*: Petrikovits 1975, 64. Aquincum: Kocsis 1990; 1991. Caerleon: Zienkiewicz 1993, 54. Windisch: Pauli-Gabi 2005b. Auxiliary commanders' houses: Koenen 1904, 145–7. *Scamnum tribunorum*: Zienkiewicz 1993, 75.
14. *Praefectus castrorum*: Petrikovits 1975, 64–7.
15. *Centuria*: *RIB* 334. *Striga*: *De Mun. Cast.* 1. Courtyard barracks: cf. Salvatore 1996, 149. Centurion's quarters: Hoffmann 1995; 1997. *Principales*: Petrikovits 1975, 59–61. *Papilio* and *arma*: *De Mun. Cast.* 1. Verandah: Casey and Hoffmann 1995, 71. Hearths: Hartmann 1983, 59. Schlußbauten: Petrikovits 1975, 59–61.
16. Praetorian barracks: Kennedy 1978. Gardun: Sanader 2009. Lejjun: Parker 1986, 68; 69.
17. Auxiliary fort stables: Sommer 1999; Hodgson 2002. Usk: Marvell 1996, 79–86. Epigraphic evidence: *RIB* 2415.39. Sub-literary evidence: *AE* 1948, 120; *ChLA* 42, 1207. Location of legionary cavalry: Petrikovits 1975, 51–4, Bild 6.
18. Storage: Petrikovits 1975, 58; 96. Workshops: ibid. 96–7.
19. Workshops and self-sufficiency: Bishop 1985. Inchtuhil *fabrica*: Pitts and St Joseph 1985, 105–15. Other *fabricae*: Petrikovits 1974; 1975, 88–97; Bishop 1985. Exeter: Bidwell 1980, 31–5.
20. Caerleon latrine: Nash-Williams 1931, 133–5. Housesteads: Bosanquet 1904, 249–51. Hospitals: Petrikovits 1975, 101. Bath-houses: ibid. 106. Palmyra: Kowalski 1998, 200.
21. Ovens: Hoffmann 2002b. Caerleon: Boon 1972, 124 n.53. Inchtuthil: Pitts and St Joseph 1985, 195–200. Cookhouses: Nash-Williams 1931, 115–20.
22. Carnuntum: Groller 1901, 39–44. Caerleon: Nash-Williams 1931, 126–33; Chapman 2002. Inscriptions: Cagnat 1913, 496. Separate from *principia*: Bishop and Coulston 2006, 263–6; Bishop forthcoming.
23. Elliptical building: Mason 1996; 2000. Agricola pipes: Mason 2002b, 40–1. Governor's palace: ibid. 45–6.
24. Storebuildings: Petrikovits 1975, 82–8.
25. *Genius centuriae*: *CIL* VIII, 2531. *Genius armamentaria*: *AE* 2004, 01195; cf. Speidel and Dimitrova-Milčeva 1978. *Genius Lambaesis*: *CIL* VIII, 2611–12. *Genius legionum*: *AE* 1935, 98. Nymphs: *RIB* 460. *Fortuna*: *AE* 1937, 166. *Campestres*: *CIL* III, 14355,21. *Aquila* and standards: *AE* 1993, 1571; *CIL* III, 6224. Novae: Dyczek 1999. Nijmegen: Bogaers et al. 1979, 43.

Chapter 6: Infrastructure

1. *Via principalis*: *De Mun. Cast.* 10. *Via praetoria*: *De Mun. Cast.* 14. *Groma*: *De Mun. Cast.* 12; *AE* 1974, 723. *Via decumana*: *De Mun. Cast.* 18. *Via quintana*: *De Mun. Cast.* 17. *Via sagularis*: *De Mun. Cast.* 3.
2. Caerleon: Boon 1972, 25. Neuss: Koenen 1904, 204. *Via vicinaria*: ibid. Taf. IV. Resurfacing: Boon 1972, 25.
3. Structure: e.g. Boon 1972, 25. Colchester: Crummy 1992, 49. Tile and quernstone: Evans and Metcalf 1992, 7.
4. Aqueducts: Petrikovits 1975, 105–6. Chester: Mason 2002a, 98–100. Vindonissa: Hartmann 1986, 90–2. Wooden pipes: Bidwell 1979, 35–6. Ceramic pipes: Mason 2001, 86. Lead pipes: ibid. 44–6. Baths and workshop: Bidwell 1979, 60. *Nymphaeum*: Rakob 1979. Castra Albana: Chiarucci 2006, 61. Neuss: Koenen 1904, 214.
5. Palmyra: Kennedy and Riley 1990, 134–7. Raphanaea: Gschwind 2006; 2007; 2008a; 2008b. Lejjun: Kennedy and Riley 1990, 131.
6. Caerleon sewer: Boon 1972, 25. York sewer: Whitwell 1976. Outfall in Foss: Buckland 1976, 15.
7. Windisch: Hartmann 1973b; 1986, 92. Bad-Deutsch Altenburg: Grünewald 1983. Keltengraben: Hartmann 1986, 92. Other middens: Inveresk fort (Bishop 2004, 9–15, 183–5). Bonn: Driel-Murray and Gechter 1984.

Chapter 7: Extramural Buildings
1. *Amphitheatra*: *AE* 1955, 135; 137. York: Ottaway 1992, 33–4. Use: Coulston 1998, 7–9.
2. Caerleon: Boon 1972, 102–5. Chester: Mason 1987, 146–9. Castra Albana: Chiarucci 2006, 61–3.
3. Exercise grounds: Le Bohec 1999. Caerleon: Boon 1972, 31–2. Lambaesis: Le Bohec 1977; Speidel 2006. *Campus*: *AE* 2002, 1514. *Campidoctor*: Veg., *Epit. Rei Mil.* 1.13; 2.23; *CIL* II, 4083. Caerleon dimensions: Boon 1972, folding plan. Lambaesis: Le Bohec 1977, 71. Mirebeau: Goguey 2008, 236. Burnum: Miletić 2010a, 139.
4. Neuss: Koenen 1904, 143–5. Caerleon: *RIB* 2415.39. Nicopolis: *AE* 1948, 120; *ChLA* 42, 1207. Svishtov: Donevski 1998. Exeter: Henderson 1988, 103–5. Petronell: Stiglitz 1997. Wroxeter: Webster and Chadderton 2002, 3–4. Lambaesis: Le Bohec 1989, 363–4. Colchester/Stanway: Wilson 1977. Burnum: Miletić 2010a, 130–6. Neuss: Koenen 1904, 239–41. Rosinos de Vidriales: Romero Carnicero and Carretero Vaquero 2006. Usk: Marvell 1996, 86–9.
5. 'Standard-sized fortresses': Hoffmann 2002a, 84; Bidwell 1980, 20. Exeter: Henderson 1988, 94–5. Petronell minimum area: Kandler 1986, 209 figure.
6. *Canabae*: Mason 1987, 143; *AE* 1955, 9; 97 (Budapest-Aquincum); *CIL* III, 6166; 6175 (Iglita-Troesmis); *CIL* III, 14509 (Kostolac-Viminacium); *CIL* XIII, 5967 (Strasbourg-Argentorate).
7. Caerleon: Evans, E.M. 2000. Strasbourg: Baudoux 2010. Alba Iulia: Hanson and Oltean 2003, 109. Windisch *mansio*: Hartmann 1986, 105–6. Chester: Mason 1987, 149–50.
8. *Territorium*: Schulten 1894. Territorial markers: Rippon 1996, 32–5. *Prata legionis*: Mason 1988, 163–8. Holt: Grimes 1930. Binyanei Ha'uma: Arubas and Goldfus 1995. Ilovica: Lazar 2006. Rheinzabern: Ludowici 1927; Brandl 1996; Wesch-Klein 2000. Iversheim: Sölter 1983; 2005. Inchtuthil: Pitts and St Joseph 1988, 45, 61, 255. Chester: Mason 2001, 107–8.
9. Burial grounds: Boon 1972, 106–12; Hartmann 1986, 95–6; Chantraine et al. 1984, 162–70. Apamea: Balty 1987; 1988; Balty and Rengen 1993. Haïdra: Mackensen 1997.

Chapter 8: Construction and Demolition
1. Phasis: Arr., *Peripl. P. Eux.* 9.
2. Fortresses becoming towns and cites: Watkins 1983.
3. *Novercae*: *De Mun. Cast.* 57. Tadmor-Palmyra: Kowalski 1998, 195–6; pers. obs.
4. Castra Albana: Chiarucci 2006, 52–65. Strasbourg: Hatt 1993, 13. Vetera II: Petrikovits 1959. Ptuj: Gojković 2009, 1461.
5. *Praefectus castrorum*: Veg., *Epit. Rei Mil.* 2.10. *Topos*: cf. S.H.A., *Hadr.* 10.6. Vegetius: *Epit. Rei Mil.* 1.22–5; 3.8. Pseudo-Hyginus: *De Mun. Cast.* 48–58. Written manuals: Campbell 1987. Elliptical building plans: Mason 2002b, 40–6.
6. Inchtuthil: Shirley 1996; 2000; 2001. Construction camps: Pitts and St Joseph 1985, 223–34.
7. Setting out: Shirley 2001, 38–40; cf. Polyb. 6.41. *Agrimensores*: Veg., *Epit. Rei Mil.* 3.8. *Groma*: *De Mun. Cast.* 12; Dilke 1974, 569–73. Lambaesis inscription: Kolbe 1974.
8. Facing enemy: *De. Mun. Cast.* 56. Facing east or the enemy: Veg., *Epit. Rei Mil.* 1.23.
9. *Cohortes*: *De Mun. Cast.* 54.
10. Post trenches: Davison 1989, 225–7. Oberaden: Kühlborn 1992, Abb. 14. Sill beams: Davison 1989, 218. Mortice and tenon: cf. Howard-Davis 2009, 791–7. Wattle and daub: Vitr., *De Arch.* 2.8.20.
11. Lunt: Hobley 1967. Vindolanda: Birley 1977, 160–2. Lambaesis: CIL VIII, 2706. Mainz: CIL XIII, 6804.
12. Ditch cleaning: Jones 1975, 36–7; 109. Lambaesis: CIL VIII, 2546; 2548.
13. Inchtuthil nails: Angus et al. 1962; Kapusta and Underwood 2000; Mapelli et al. 2009; cf. Pitts and St Joseph 1985, 109–13.
14. Tidying: Pitts and St Joseph 1985, 52. Lincoln: Webster et al. 1949, 63. Carlisle: Charlesworth 1980, Pl. 14.3. Burning: Pitts and St Joseph 1985, 52. Wall: ibid. 68.

Chapter 9: Gazetteers
1. In some cases, minor watercourses have been removed by urban development or canalization, but their influence on the topography will have been sufficient to provide the preferred raised platform. Topographical 'chunks' are provided in the accompanying website showing terrain with draped plans for selected fortresses.

2. *Google Earth* (GE) (and indeed *Google Maps* – GM) height data is generally derived either from NASA Shuttle Radar Topography Mission (SRTM) or ASTER GDEM data. The former is only available for the area of the Roman Empire in 90m-square tiles (with a 30m vertical margin of error), whereas the later ASTER GDEM has a notional accuracy of 20m vertically (Bailey et al. 2009, 27), although this has been questioned (e.g. <http://www.terrainmap.com/rm51.html> accessed 12.12.10). Smoothing or interpolation has been applied to the data for use in GE or GM. Neither, then, is as accurate as the height data many traditional terrestrial mapping agencies provide. Where GE readings have been used, this is indicated.

3. For the *castra tertiata*, see *De Mun. Cast.* 21.

4. The most noteworthy attempt being Farnum 2005, for which the review of Probst 2007 should be borne in mind. Whilst there are a number of errors, it is still a valuable attempt at a difficult task that a mere appendix in a book such as this cannot hope to match. Nevertheless, it would seem remiss not to at least explore the potential. Other attempts are less ambitious than that of Farnum and include Szilágyi (1986) on legionary movements on the Rhine and Hassall (2000) on the pre-Hadrianic British legions.

5. By no means exhaustive and principally intended to show references that link a site name to legionary use (such references are **emboldened**; those that just supply the site name are not).

6. Inscriptions have been harvested using the Clauss-Slaby online epigraphic database (<http://www.manfredclauss.de/gb/index.html>) and then selected manually. Some sites are better served than others, but that is a reflection on a) the body of retrieved inscriptions and b) the level of data entry by original researchers, rather than the database itself. Note that only one instance per entry has been used, where a search produces multiples results from corpora.

7. Whilst every attempt to be comprehensive has been made, this is clearly impossible to achieve, particularly where small regional publications are concerned.

Appendix 4: Sites Excluded

1. Resaena: Farnum 2005, 29 (as Rhesenae).

2. Alchester: Sauer 2005, 116. Corbridge: Freeman 2007, 288; 292. Waldgirmes: Rasbach and Becker 2000.

3. Leicester: Webster 1980, 125–7. Augsburg-Oberhausen: Wells 1970. Military involvement: Fulford and Timby 2000, 573. *Fora* and *principia*: Opreanu 2006. Military equipment: Fox and St John Hope 1901, 245.

Bibliography

A version of this bibliography is available online at www.legionaryfortresses.info which is grouped by subject and by site and includes keywords to make it more readily accessible.

Ancient sources

Amm. Marc.	Ammianus Marcellinus
App., *Ib.*	Appian, *Iberica*
Arr., *Peripl. P. Eux.*	Arrian, *Periplus Ponti Euxini*
Caes., *BGall.*	Caesar, *Bellum Gallicum*
Cass. Dio	Cassius Dio
De Mun. Cast.	*De Munitionibius Castrorum*
Eusebius, *Onom.*	Eusebius, *Onomasticon*
Eutrop.	Eutropius, *Breviarium*
Gell., *NA*	Aulus Gellius, *Noctes Atticae*
Hdn.	Herodian
It. Ant.	*Itineraria Antonini Augusti*
Joseph., *BJ*	Josephus, *Bellum Judaicum*
ND Occ.	*Notitia Dignitatum … Occidentis*
ND Or.	*Notitia Dignitatum … Orientis*
Pliny, *HN*	Pliny the Elder, *Naturalis Historia*
Polyb.	Polybius, *Historiae*
Prisc., *Inst.*	Priscian, *Institutio de arte grammatical*
Procop., *Goth.*	Procopius, *De Bello Gothico*
Procop., *De Aedif.*	Procopius, *De Aedificiis*
Ptol., *Geog.*	Ptolemy, *Geographia*
Rav. Cosm.	*Ravenna Cosmography*
Strabo	Strabo, *Geography*
Suet., *Aug.*	Suetonius, *Divus Augustus*
Suet., *Claud.*	Suetonius, *Divus Claudius*
Suet., *Dom.*	Suetonius, *Domitianus*
Suet., *Otho*	Suetonius, *Otho*
Tab. Peut.	*Tabula Peutingeriana*
Tac., *Ann.*	Tacitus, *Annales*
Tac., *Hist.*	Tacitus, *Historiae*
Veg., *Epit. Rei Mil.*	Vegetius, *Epitoma Rei Militaris*
Vell. Pat.	Velleius Paterculus
Vitr., *De Arch.*	Vitruvius, *De Architectura*

Abbreviations

Abbreviations for both the epigraphic references (following those used by the *Epigraphik Datenbank Clauss-Slaby*) and the bibliography are as follows:

AA	*Archaeologia Aeliana*
ADBulgar	Kalinka 1906
AE	*L'Année épigraphique*
AEA	*Annona Epigraphica Austriaca*
AIJ	Hoffiller and Saria 1938
AmphMainz-Dipinti	Ehmig 2000
AnzWien	*Anzeiger der phil.-hist. Klasse der Österreichischen Akademie der Wissenschaften*, Wien
ArchAnz	*Archäologischer Anzeiger*
BCTH	*Bulletin archéologique du Comité des travaux historiques et scientifiques*
BRGK	*Bericht der Römisch-Germanischen Kommission*
ChLA	*Chartae Latinae Antiquiores*
CIL	*Corpus Inscriptionum Latinarum*
CSIR	*Corpus Signorum Imperii Romani*
D	Dessau 1892–1916
DefMainz	Blänsdorf 2008
Denkm	Speidel 1994
EE	*Ephemeris Epigraphica*
ERPLeon	Rabanal Alonso and García Martínez 2001
ES	*Epigraphische Studien*
Finke	Finke 1927
FÖ	*Fundberichte aus Österreich*
GLISyrB	Prentice 1908
GraffBonn	Bakker and Galsterer-Kröll 1975
Haidra 3P	Abdallah 2009
Hep	*Hispania Epigraphica*
Hild	Hild 1968
IBR	Vollmer 1915
IDR	*Inscriptiones Daciae Romanae*
IDRE	Petolescu 1996–
IGBR	Mihailov 1958–1970
IGLAlexa	Breccia 1911
IGLNovae	Kolendo and Bozilova 1997
IGLS	*Inscriptions Grecques et Latines de la Syrie*
IKoeln	Galsterer and Galsterer 2010
ILAfr	Cagnat et al. 1923
ILAlg	*Inscriptions latines d'Algérie*
ILBulg	Gerov 1989
ILD	Petolescu 2005
ILJug	*Inscriptiones Latinae quae in Iugoslavia … repertae et editae sunt*, Ljubljana 1963–1986
ILPBardo	Abdallah 1986
ILTG	Wuilleumier 1963
IMS	*Inscriptions de la Mésie Supérieure*
IPSSTA	Ceska and Hosek 1967
Irheinland I	Rüger 1981
IRPLeon	Diego Santos 1986
IRPPalencia	Hernandez Guerra 1994
IscM	*Inscriptiones Scythiae Minoris Graecae et Latinae II*
JRMES	*Journal of Roman Military Equipment Studies*
JRS	*Journal of Roman Studies*
Kayser	Kayser 1994
LegioXVApo	Mosser 2003

Lehner	Lehner 1918
Lupa	<http://www.ubi-erat-lupa.org/> (accessed 17.2.11)
MaCarnuntum	Vorbeck 1980a
Nesselhauf	Nesselhauf 1937
Ness-Lieb	Nesselhauf and Lieb 1959
PSAS	*Proceedings of the Society of Antiquaries of Scotland*
RHP	Lörincz 2001
RIB	*Roman Inscriptions of Britain*
RIC	*Roman Imperial Coinage*
RIU	*Die römischen Inschriften Ungarns*
Schillinger	Schillinger-Häfele 1977
SEG	*Supplementum Epigraphicum Graecum*
Speidel	Speidel 2010
StudEpPann	Kovács and Szabó 2009a
SVindonissa	Speidel 1996
TitAq	Kovács and Szabó 2009b
Wagner	Wagner 1956/57
ZPE	*Zeitschrift für Papyrologie und Epigraphik*

Modern references

Abascal, J.M. 1986: 'La Legio VII Gemina. Balance de la investigación y perspectivas', in *Actas I Congreso Internacional Astorga Romana, I*, Astorga, 317–28

Abdallah, Z. Ben 1986: *Catalogue des Inscriptions Latines Paiennes du musée du Bardo*, Roma

Abdallah, Z. Ben 1990: 'Sur une épitaphe d'Ammaedara relative à un soldat de la IIIe Légion Auguste, originaire de Naples', in Mastino, A. (ed.), *L'Africa romana. Atti del VII Convegno di studio, Sassari, 15–17 dicembre 1989*, 763–7

Abdallah, Z. Ben 1992: 'Nouveaux aspects de la vie religieuse à Ammaedara, premier camp de la IIIe Légion Auguste, puis colonie de Vespasien en Afrique romaine', *Comptes-rendus des séances de l'Académie des Inscriptions et Belles-Lettres* 136, 11–27

Abdallah, Z. Ben 2009: 'Inventaire des inscriptions païennes découvertes lors des fouilles franco-tunisiennes (1994–2001)', in Baratte, F., Bejaoui, F. and Abdallah, Z. Ben (eds.), *Recherches archéologiques à Haïdra 3*, Rome, 283–323

Abdallah, Z. Ben and Le Bohec, Y. 1997: 'Nouvelles inscriptions d'Haïdra concernant l'armée romaine', *Mélanges de l'Ecole française de Rome, Antiquité* **109**, 41–82

Abercromby, J., Ross, T., and Anderson, J. 1902: 'Account of the excavation of the Roman station at Inchtuthil, Perthshire, undertaken by the Society of Antiquaries of Scotland in 1901', *PSAS* **36** (1901–02), 182–242

Abramić, M. 1925a: *Poetovio. Vodnik po muzeju in stavbnih ostankih mesta*, Ptuj

Abramić, M. 1925b: *Poetovio. Führer durch die Denkmäler der römischen Stadt*, Wien

Absil, M. 2000: 'Legio I Italica', in Le Bohec and Wolff 2000, 227–38

Albrecht, C. (ed.) 1938: *Das Römerlager in Oberaden und das Uferkastell in Beckinghausen an der Lippe. Heft 1, Bodenbefund, Munzen, Sigillaten und Inschriften*, Veröffentlichungen aus dem Städtischen Museum für Vor- und Frühgeschichte Dortmund **2,1**, Dortmund

Albrecht, C. (ed.) 1942: *Das Römerlager in Oberaden und das Uferkastell in Beckinghausen an der Lippe. Heft 2, Die römische u. d. belgische Keramik: Die Gegenstände aus Metall nach d. Funden d. Ausgrabungen v. Albert Baum*, Veröffentlichungen aus dem Städtischen Museum für Vor- und Frühgeschichte Dortmund **2,2**, Dortmund

Alicu, D. 1980: 'Le camp legionnaire de Sarmizegetusa', *Potaissa* **2**, 23–8

Alicu, D. 1983: 'Elemente de echipament militar descoperite la Ulpia Traiana Sarmizegetusa (I)', *Acta Musei Napocensis* **20**, 391–6

Alicu, D., Cocis, S., Ilies, C. and Soroceanu, A. 1994: *Small Finds from Ulpia Traiana Sarmizegetusa*, Sarmizegetusa Monograph **4**, Cluj-Napoca

Alicu, D. and Paki, A. 1995: *Town-Planning and Population in Ulpia Traiana Sarmizegetusa*, BAR **S605**, Oxford

Allison, P.M., Fairbairn, A.S., Ellis, S.J.R., and Blackall, C.W. 2004: 'Extracting the social relevance of artefact distribution in Roman military forts', *Internet Archaeology* 17, <http://intarch.ac.uk/journal/issue17/allison_toc.html> accessed 13.1.10

Alram-Stern, E. 1989: *Die römischen Lampen aus Carnuntum*, Der römische Limes in Österreich 35, Wien

Alston. R. 1995: *Soldier and Society in Roman Egypt. A Social History*, London

Anghel, D. 1999: 'Continuitatea unei fortificaţii de la castrul roman Apulum la cetăţile medievale din Alba Iulia (La continuité d'une fortification du castrum romain Apulum aux cités médiévales d'Alba Iulia)', in AANTIM, 1999, 175–80

Angus, N.S., Brown, G.T., and Cleere, H.F. 1962: 'The iron nails from the Roman legionary fortress at Inchtuthil, Perthshire', *Journal of the Iron and Steel Institute* 200, 956–68

Anon 1981: 'Chester', *Current Archaeology* 8, 6–12

Anon 2008: 'Ljubljana-Tribuna', <http://www.zvkds.si/en/novice/nova-odkritja/53-/> accessed 27.1.11

Aquilué, X. 2006: 'Empuriés camp', in Morillo and Aurrecoechea 2006, 242–5

Arubas, B. and Goldfus, H. 1995: 'The kilnworks of the Tenth Legion Fretensis', in Humphrey, J.H. (ed.), *The Roman and Byzantine Near East: Some Recent Archaeological Research*, Journal of Roman Archaeology Supplement 14, Ann Arbor, 95–107

Aschemeyer, H. 1963: 'Neue Untersuchungen im Römerlager Oberaden', *Prähistorische Zeitschrift* 41, 210–12

Aßkamp, R. 1989: 'Haltern', in Trier, B. (ed.), *2000 Jahre Römer in Westfalen*, Mainz, 21–43

Aßkamp, R. 2010: *Haltern, Stadt Haltern am See, Kreis Recklinghausen*, Römerlager in Westfalen 5, Münster

Atanassova-Georgieva, J. 1986: 'Résultats des fouilles de la ville antique de Ratiaria au cours des années 1976 à 1982', in Unz 1986, 437–40

Aumüller, T. 2002: *Die Porta Praetoria und die Befestigung des Legionslagers in Regensburg*, Dr.-Ing. Dissertation <http://deposit.ddb.de/cgi-bin/dokserv?idn=971034141> accessed 26.3.11

Aurrecoechea, J. 2006: 'Talleres dedicados a la producción de equipo militar en los campamentos romanos de León, con especial referencia a los restos de lorica segmentata', in Morillo, Á. (ed.), *Arqueología Militar Romana en Hispania. Producción y abastecimiento en el ámbito military*, León, 309–34

Aurrecoechea, J. and Muñoz Villarejo, F. 2001–2: 'A legionary workshop of the 3rd century AD pecialising in *loricae segmentatae* from the Roman fortress in León (Spain)', *JRMES* 12–13, 15–28

Baatz, D. 1962: *Mogontiacum. Neue Untersuchungen am römischen Legionslager in Mainz*, Limesforschungen 4, Berlin

Baatz, D. 1985: 'Hibernacula', *Germania* 63, 147–54

Baatz, D. 2000: 'Vegetius' legion and the archaeological facts', in Brewer 2000, 149–58

Bailey, G.B., Danielson, J., Bliss, N., Gesch, D., Duda, K.A., Evans, G. and Zhang, Z. 2009: *ASTER Global DEM Validation Summary Report* <http://tinyurl.com/38pfa7n> accessed 12.12.10

Baker, P. 2002: 'The Roman Military Valetudinaria: Fact or Fiction', in Arnott, R. (ed.), *The Archaeology of Medicine. Proceedings of the Theoretical Archaeology Group 1998*, Oxford, 69–80

Baker, P. 2004: *Medical Care for the Roman Army on the Rhine, Danube and British Frontiers from the First through Third Centuries AD*, BAR International Series 1286, Oxford

Baker, P. n.d.: 'Archaeological remains as a source of evidence for Roman Medicine', *Medicina Antiqua* <http://www.ucl.ac.uk/~ucgajpd/medicina%20antiqua/sa_ArchaeologicalRemains.pdf> accessed 2.1.10

Bakker, L. and Galsterer-Kröll, B. 1975: *Graffiti auf römischer Keramik im Rheinischen Landesmuseum Bonn*, Bonn

Balty, J.-C. 1987: 'Apamée (1986): nouvelles données sur l'armée romaine d'Orient et les raids sassanides du milieu du IIIe siècle', *Comptes-rendus des séances de l'Académie des inscriptions et belles-lettres* 131, 213–42

Balty, J.-C. 1988: 'Apamea in the Second and Third Centuries AD', *JRS* 78, 91–104

Balty, J.-C. and Rengen, W. van 1993: *Apamea in Syria: The Winter Quarters of Legio II Parthica: Roman Gravestones from the Military Cemetery*, Bruxelles

Băluță, C.L. 1995: 'Ştampile tegulare militare inedite descoperite la Apulum. Ştampile cu antroponim', *Apulum* **32**, 205–29

Băluță, C.L. 1997: 'Tipuri de ştampile tegulare militare inedite descoperite la Apulum. Ştampile fără antroponim', *Apulum* **34**, 133–68

Băluță, C.L. 2000: 'Inscripții tegulare militare descoperite recent la Apulum-Partoş', *Apulum* **37**, 351–67

Bar, D. 1998: 'Aelia Capitolina and the location of the camp of the Tenth Legion', *Palestine Exploration Quarterly* **130**, 8–19

Baranski, M. 1994: 'The Roman Army in Palmyra: A case of adaptation of a pre-existing city' in Dabrowa, E. (ed.), *The Roman and Byzantine Army in the East: Proceedings of a Colloquium held at the Jagiellonian University, Krakow in September 1992*, Krakow, 9–17

Bărbulescu, C. 2004: *Arhitectura militară şi tehnica de construcție la romani. Castrul de la Potaissa*, Cluj-Napoca

Bărbulescu, C. and Bărbulescu, M. 2004a: 'Poarta principală a basilicii castrului de la Potaissa', in *Studia Historica et Archaeologica in honorem Magistrae Doina Benea*, Timişoara, 27–34

Bărbulescu, M. 1987: *Din istoria militară a Daciei romane. Legiunea V Macedonica şi castrul de la Potaissa*, Cluj-Napoca

Bărbulescu, M. 1990: 'Les principia du camp légionaire de Potaissa', in Vetter and Kandler 1990, 821–31

Bărbulescu, M. 1991: 'Römische Legionslager von Potaissa (Rumänien)', *Antike Welt* **22**, 22–30

Bărbulescu, M. 1994: *Potaissa. Studiu monografic*, Turda

Bărbulescu, M. 1997: *Das Legionslager von Potaissa (Turda) / Castrul legionar de la Potaissa (Turda)*, Zalău

Bărbulescu, M. 1998: 'La Legio V Macedonica e lo scavo del castrum di Potaissa', *Messana* **19**, 195–214

Bărbulescu, M. 2004: 'Inscriptions votives pour les génies protecteurs dans le camp légionnaire de Potaissa', in *Orbis Antiquus. Studia in honorem Ioannis Pisonis, Cluj-Napoca*, 375–9

Bărbulescu, M. and Bărbulescu, C. 2004b: *Turda. Castrul roman de la Potaissa. Le camp légionnaire de Potaissa. The Roman legionary fortress of Potaissa (ghid turistic)*, Turda

Bărbulescu, M., Milea, Z., Cătinaş, A., and Hopârtean, A. 1978: 'Principalele rezultate ale săpăturilor arheologice în castrul roman de la Turda (1971–1976)', *Potaissa* **1**, 5–15

Barkóczi, L. 1949: 'A brigetio tábor és canabae topographiája', *Antiquitas Hungarica* **3**, 67–77

Barkóczi, L. 1951: *Brigetio*, Dissertationes Pannonicae **2.22**, Budapest

Barkóczi, L. 1961: 'Adatok Brigetio későrómai tőténetéhez', *Folia Archaeologica* **13**, 95–115

Barkóczi, L. 1965: 'New data on the history of late Roman Brigetio', *Acta Antiqua Academiae Scientiarum Hungaricae* **13**, 215–57

Barnea, I. 1950: 'O inscripție de la Aegyssus', *Studi şi cercetări de istorie veche* **1**, 175–84

Baudoux, J. 2010: 'Une maison logitudinale des *canabae legionis* au 30, rue de la Mésange', in Schnitzler and Kuhnle 2010, 63–5

Baum, J. and Robinson, D.J. 2002: 'Deva Victrix restored: the application of computer 3-D modelling techniques in the reconstruction of Roman Chester', in Carrington 2002a, 113–17

Bechert, T. 1971: 'Römische Lagertore und ihre Bauinschriften. Ein Beitrag zur Entwicklung und Datierung kaiserzeitlicher Lagergrundrisse von Claudius bis Severus Alexander', *Bonner Jahrbücher* **171**, 201–87

Bellettati, R. 1994: 'Vindonissa: Sanierungen am Nord- und Westtor 1994', *Gesellschaft Pro Vindonissa. Jahresbericht*, 39–48

Bemmann, H. 1984: 'Terra sigillata aus Abfallschichten des Bonner Legionslager', in *Beiträge zur Archäologie des römischen Rheinlands 4*, Rheinische Ausgrabungen **23**, Köln, 109–62

Benario, H.W. 1972: 'Albano and the Second Parthian Legion', *Archaeology* **25:4**, 256–63

Bender, H. and Moosbauer, G. 2003: *Das römische Donaukastell Schlögen in Oberösterreich. Die Funde aus den Grabungen 1957–59, 1984 und die Altfunde*, Passauer Universitätsschriften zur Archäologie **8**, Rahden

Benseddik, N. 2001: 'Lambèse: l'archéologie de bulldozer', *ZPE* **135**, 287–95

Benseddik, N. 2003: 'Lambaesis (Lambèse): des soldats et des dieux (Lambaesis (Lambèse): soldiers and gods)', *Les Dossiers d'archéologie* **286**, 32–7

Berchem, D. van 1954: 'Recherches sur la chronologie des enceintes de Syrie et Mésopotamie', *Syria* **31**, 254–70

Berkovics, B.M. 1886: 'Ásatásom az Ó Szőnyi római táborban', *Archaeologia Értesítő* **6**, 392–7

Berkovics, B.M. 1887: 'Ásatásom az Ó Szőnyi római táborban', *Archaeologia Értesítő* **7**, 30–8

Beszédes, J. and Mosser, M. 2002: 'Die Grabsteine der Legio XV Apollinaris in Carnuntum', *CarnuntumJb*, 9–98

Bezeczky, T. 1992: 'Amphorák. A tribunus laticlaviusok háza az aquicumi 2–3. századi legiotáborban (Amphoren aus dem Haus der tribuni laticlavii aus dem Legionslager des 2./3. Jhs.)', *Budapest égiségei* **28**, 133–4, 155–8

Bidwell, P.T. 1979: *The Legionary Bath-House and Basilica and Forum at Exeter*, Exeter Archaeological Reports **1**, Exeter

Bidwell, P.T. 1980: *Roman Exeter: Fortress and Town*, Exeter

Bidwell, P.T. and Boon, G.C. 1976: 'An antefix type of the Second Augustan Legion from Exeter', *Britannia* **7**, 278–80

Bidwell, P.T., Miket, R. and Ford, B. 1988: 'The reconstruction of a gate at the Roman fort of South Shields', in Bidwell, P.T., Miket, R. and Ford, B. (eds.), *Portae cum Turribus. Studies of Roman Fort Gates*, BAR **206**, Oxford, 155–231

Bidwell, P.T. and Watson, M. 1996: 'Excavations on Hadrian's Wall at Denton, Newcastle upon Tyne, 1986–89', *AA*[5] **24**, 1–56

Biernacka-Lubanska, M. 1998: 'Roman lead pipe production technology', *Novensia* **10**, 31–46

Bikić, V. 1997: 'Rezultati zaštitnih arheoloških iskopavanja u Knez Mihailovoj Ulici Br. 46–48 (Results of rescue excavations at the 46–48 Knez Mihailova Street site)', *Singidunum* **1**, 157–68

Birley, E. 1986: 'The Flavian colonia at Scupi', *ZPE* **64**, 209–16

Birley, R. 1977: *Vindolanda. A Roman Frontier Post on Hadrian's Wall*, London

Bishop, M.C. 1985: 'The military fabrica and the production of arms in the early principate', in Bishop, M.C. (ed.), *The Production and Distribution of Roman Military Equipment. Proceedings of the Second Roman Military Equipment Research Seminar*, BAR **S275**, Oxford, 1–42

Bishop, M.C. 1990: 'On parade: status, display, and morale in the Roman army', in Kandler and Jobst 1990, 21–30

Bishop, M.C. 1999: 'Praesidium: social, military, and logistical aspects of the Roman army's provincial distribution during the early principate', in Goldsworthy, A. and Haynes, I. (eds.), *The Roman Army as a Community*, JRA Supplementary Series **34**, Portsmouth RI, 111–18

Bishop, M.C. 2004: *Inveresk Gate: Excavations in the Roman Civil Settlement at Inveresk, East Lothian, 1996–2000*, STAR Monograph **7**, Edinburgh

Bishop, M.C. forthcoming: 'Von Groller's Waffenmagazin', *JRMES* **17**

Bishop, M.C. and Coulston, J.C.N. 2006: *Roman Military Equipment from the Punic Wars to the Fall of Rome*, ed. 2, Oxford

Blagg, T.F.C. 1989: 'Richborough', in Maxfield, V.A. (ed.), *The Saxon Shore. A Handbook*, Exeter, 140–5

Blagg, T.F.C. 2000: 'The architecture of the legionary principia', in Brewer 2000, 139–47

Blänsdorf, J. 2008: 'Die defixionum tabellae des Mainzer Isis- und Mater-Magna-Heiligtums', in Hainzmann, M. und Wedenig, R. (eds.), *Instrumenta Inscripta Latina II*, Aus Forschung und Kunst **36**, Klagenfurt, 47–70

Blaylock, S.R. and Henderson, G.C. 1987: *Exeter Archaeology 1985/6*, Exeter

Böhn, O. 1924: 'Die Zenturieninschriften auf den Holzspeeren von Oberaden', *Germania* **2**, 66–8

Bogaers, J.E. 1986: 'Regensburger Rätsel', in Unz 1986, 127–34

Bogaers, J.E., Bloemers, J.H.F. and Haalebos, J.K. (eds.) 1979: *Noviomagus. Op het spoor der Romeinen in Nijmegen*, Nijmegen

Bojović, D. 1996: 'Le camp de la légion IV Flavia à Singidunum', in Petrovic, P. (ed.), *Roman Limes on the Middle and Lower Danube*, Cahiers des Portes de Fer **2**, Beograd, 53–68

Boon, G.C. 1964: 'Three small excavations at Caerleon', *Archaeologia Cambrensis* **113**, 16–40

Boon, G.C., 1972: *Isca, the Roman Legionary Fortress at Caerleon*, Mon., Cardiff

Boon, G.C. 1975: 'Three Caerleon sculptures', *Bulletin of the Board of Celtic Studies* **26**, 227–30

Boon, G.C. 1978a: *Roman Sites*, Cambrian Archaeological Association Monographs & Collections 1, Cardiff

Boon, G.C. 1978b: 'Excavations on the site of a Roman quay at Caerleon and its significance', in Boon 1978a, 1–24

Boon, G.C. 1984a: 'A trulleus from Caerleon with a stamp of the First Cavalry Regiment of Thracians', *Antiquaries Journal* **64**, 403–7

Boon, G.C. 1984b: *Laterarium Iscanum: the Antefixes, Brick & Tile-stamps of the Second Augustan Legion*, Cardiff

Boon, G.C. 1987: *The Legionary Fortress of Caerleon-Isca*, Cardiff

Boon, G.C. and Williams, C. 1967: *Plan of Caerleon, Isca, Legio II Augusta: Discoveries to December 1966, with Restoration Commentary and Comparative Plans*, Cardiff

Booth, P. 2007: '8. South-western counties', in Burnham et al. 2007, 294–6

Borhy, L. 1998: 'Brigetio accampamento dei legionari e municipium sul Danubio', in Popescu, G.E. (ed.), *Traiano ai confini dell'Impero*, Ancona, 88–9, 246–8

Borhy, L. 2004: 'Brigetio. Ergebnisse der 1992–1998 durchgeführten Ausgrabungen (Munizipium, Legionslager, Canabae, Gräberfelder)', in Šašel Kos, M., Scherrer, P., Kuntić-Makvić, B. and Borhy, L. (eds.), *The Autonomous Towns of Noricum and Pannonia – Die autonomen Städte in Noricum und Pannonien. Pannonia II*, Situla **42**, Ljubljana, 231–51

Borhy, L. 2009: *Brigetiói amphitheatrumok?*, Budapest

Borhy, L., Kuzmová, K., Rajtár, J., and Számadó, E. 2003: *Kelemantia – Brigetio. Auf dem Spuren der Römer an der Donau*, Trnava

Bosanquet, R.C. 1904: 'Excavations on the line of the Roman Wall in Northumberland. 1: The Roman camp at Housesteads', *AA* **25**, 193–300

Bosanquet, R.C. and King, F. 1963: 'Excavations at Caerleon 1909', *The Monmouthshire Antiquary* **1**, 1–10

Bossert, M. 1999: *Die figürlichen Skulpturen des Legionslagers von Vindonissa*, Brugg

Boudot M. 1835: 'Essai sur le camp romain de Mirebeau', *Mémoires de la Commission des Antiquités de Côte-d'Or* **2**, 135–53

Breccia, E. 1911: *Catalogue général des antiquités Égyptiennes du musée d'Alexandrie, Iscrizioni Greche e Latine*, Leipzig

Brewer, R.J. (ed.) 2000: *Roman Fortresses and their Legions: Papers in Honour of George C Boon, FRHistS, FSA*, Cardiff

Brewer, R.J. 2001: 'Caerleon and the Archaeologists: Changing Ideas on the Roman Fortress', *The Monmouthshire Antiquary* **17**, 9–34

Brewer, R.J. and Gardner, A. forthcoming: *The Roman Fortress at Caerleon*, Stroud

Brinklow, D. 1987: 'Fortress wall in bus lay-by', *Interim: the Archaeology of York* **12**, 16–18

Brooks, H. 1977: *Report on a Watching Brief: 3 Church Street, Colchester, Essex*, CAT Report 411 <http://cat.essex.ac.uk/reports/CAT-report-0411.pdf> accessed 13.1.10

Brooks, H. 2004: *Archaeological Excavation at 29–39 Head Street, Colchester, Essex: May-September 2000*, CAT Report **268** <http://cat.essex.ac.uk/reports/CAT-report-0268.pdf> accessed 13.1.10

Bruckner, A. and Vegas, M. 1975: *Die Augustische Gebrauchskeramik von Neuss*, Limesforschungen **14**, Berlin

Brünnow, R.E. and Domaszewski, A. von 1904: *Die Provincia Arabia*, Strassburg, vol. I, 431–63

Brandl, U. 1996: 'Bemerkungen zu einem Ziegelstempeltyp der Legio XIV Gemina aus der Germania Superior und Carnuntum', *ZPE* **112**, 224–8

Brown, P.D.C. 1971: 'The church at Richborough', *Britannia* **2**, 225–31

Brunsting, H. and Steures, D.C. 1995: 'De backsteenstempels van Romeins Nijmegen, I. Opgravingen Castra 1950–1967; Opgravingen Kops Plateau c.a. 1986–1994', *Oudheidkundige Mededelingen* **75**, 85–117

Brunsting, H. and Steures, D. C. 1997: 'The brick stamps and the occupation history of the legionary fortress at Nijmegen', in Groenman-van Waateringe et al. 1997, 323–9

Bryer, A. and Winfield, D. 1985: *The Byzantine Monuments and Topography of the Pontos*, vol. I, Dumbarton Oaks Studies **20**, Washington D.C.

Buckland, P.C. 1976: *The Environmental Evidence from the Church Street Roman Sewer System*, Archaeology of York **14/1**, York

Bugarski, I. 2005: 'Fragment of a Late Roman parade helmet from Singidunum', *Singidunum* **4**, 137–46

Bunsch, E. 2000: 'Pomnik Urbi Romae Aeternae – rozważania nad technologią wykonania', *Novensia* **12**, 7–22

Bunsch, E. 2002: 'Badanie sladów warstw barwnych na obiektach kamiennych na przykladzie trzech zabytków epigraficznych z Novae', *Novensia* **13**, 25–34

Bunsch, E. 2003: 'Four small votive altars from the valetudinarium in Novae. Remarks of execution technique', *Novensia* **14**, 77–86

Bunsch, E. 2006: 'Roman inscriptions painted on stone – technique reconsidered. Results of the conservation work on a *titulus pictus* from *Novae* in Lower Moesia *I. Gr. Lat. Novae* 57', *Novensia* **17**, 63–71

Bunsch, E., Kolendo, J. and Zelazowski, J. 2003: 'Inscriptiones découvertes entre 1998 et 2002 dans les ruines du valetudinarium à Novae', *Archeologia* **54**, 43–64

Burnham, B.C., Hunter, F., Fitzpatrick, A.P., Worrell, S., Hassall, M.W.C. and Tomlin, R.S.O. 2005: 'Roman Britain in 2004', *Britannia* **36**, 383–498

Burnham, B.C., Hunter, F., Booth, P., Worrell, S., Hassall, M.W.C., and Tomlin, R.S.O. 2007: 'Roman Britain in 2006', in *Britannia* **38**, 241–365

Busch, A.W. and Schalles, H.-J. (eds.) 2009: *Waffen in Aktion. Akten der 16. Internationalen Roman Military Equipment Conference (ROMEC), Xanten, 13.-16. Juni 2007*, Xantener Berichte 16, Mainz

Bushe-Fox, J.P. 1913: *Excavations on the Site of the Roman Town at Wroxeter, Shropshire*, Society of Antiquaries of London, Research Committee Rept. **1**, London

Bushe-Fox, J.P. 1914: *Excavations on the Site of the Roman Town at Wroxeter, Shropshire*, Society of Antiquaries of London, Research Committee Rept. **2**, London

Bushe-Fox, J.P. 1916: *Excavations on the Site of the Roman Town at Wroxeter, Shropshire*, Society of Antiquaries of London, Research Committee Rept. **4**, London

Bushe-Fox, J.P. 1926: *First Report on the Excavation of the Roman Fort at Richborough, Kent*, Reports of the Research Committee of the Society of Antiquaries of London **6**, Oxford

Bushe-Fox, J.P. 1928: *Second Report on the Excavations of the Roman Fort at Richborough, Kent*, Reports of the Research Committee of the Society of Antiquaries of London **7**, Oxford

Bushe-Fox, J.P. 1932: *Third Report on the Excavations of the Roman Fort at Richborough, Kent*, Reports of the Research Committee of the Society of Antiquaries of London **10**, Oxford

Bushe-Fox, J.P. 1949: *Fourth Report on the Excavations of the Roman Fort at Richborough, Kent*, Reports of the Research Committee of the Society of Antiquaries of London **16**, Oxford

Butler, A.J. 1978: *The Arab Conquest of Egypt and the Last Thirty Years of Roman Dominion*, (1st. ed. 1902), Oxford

Butler, R.M. 1971: 'The defences of the fourth-century fortress at York', in Butler, R.M. (ed.), *Soldier and Civilian in Roman Yorkshire*, Leicester, 97–106

Buzov, M. 2006: 'Lucernae from Siscia', *Histria antiqua* **14**, 167–90

Cagnat, R. 1893: *Lambèse*, Paris

Cagnat, R. 1901: 'Découvertes sur l'emplacement du camp de Lambèse', *Comptes-rendus des séances de l'Académie des Inscriptions et Belles-lettres* **45**, 626–34

Cagnat, R. 1908: *Les deux camps de la légion IIIe Auguste à Lambèse d'après les fouilles récentes*, Paris

Cagnat, R. 1913: *L'armée romaine d'Afrique et l'occupation militaire de l'Afrique sous les empereurs*, Paris

Cagnat, R., Merlin, A. and Chatelain, L. 1923: *Inscriptions latines d'Afrique (Tripolitaine, Tunisie, Maroc)*, Paris

Calza, G. 1953: *Scavi di Ostia I, Topografia generale*, Roma

Cambi, N., Glavičić, M., Maršić, D., Miletić, Ž., and Zaninović, J. 2007: *Rimska vojska u burnumu (L'esercito romano a Burnum)*, Burnum: katalozi i monografije / NP Krka **2**, Šibenik

Campbell, D.B. 2006: *Roman Legionary Fortresses 27 BC–AD 378*, Oxford

Campbell, J.B. 1987: 'Teach yourself how to be a Roman general', *JRS* **77**, 13–29

Campomanes Alvaredo, E. 1997: 'Algunas cuestiones en torno a la primera muralla de la Legio VII Gemina', *Lancia* **2**, 129–48

Carretero Vaquero, S. 1999a: 'El ejército romano del noroeste peninsular durante el altoimperio. Estado de la cuestión', *Gladius* **19**, 143–56

Carretero Vaquero, S. 1999b: 'Objetos de hueso trabajado del campamento del Ala II Flavia en Petavonium (Rosinos de Vidriales, Zamora)', *Lancia* **3**, 47–70

Carretero Vaquero, S. 2000: *El campamento romano del Ala II Flavia en Rosinos de Vidriales (Zamora): la cerámica*, Zamora

Carretero Vaquero, S. 2001: 'El abastecimiento de productos cerámicos a la guarnición de la legio X Gemina en Petavonium (Rosinos de Vidriales, Zamora, España), in *XXII Congreso Internacional del Rei Cretariae Romanae Fautorum, Lyon, 2000*, 157–62

Carretero Vaquero, S. and Romero Carnicero, M.V. 1999: 'Petavonium: un núcleo civil surgido al abrigo del ejército', in *Actas de Mesa Redonda Emèrgencia e desenvolvimento das cidades romanas no Norte da Península Ibérica*, Porto, 157–70

Carretero Vaquero, S. and Romero Carnicero, M.V. 2004: 'Castra Petavonium', in Illarregui Gómez, E. and Pérez González, C. (eds.), *Arqueología militar romana en Europa*, Salamanca, 219–30

Carretero Vaquero, S., Romero Carnicero, M.V. and Martínez García, A.B. 1999: 'Las estructuras defensivas del campamento del Ala II Flavia en Petavonium (Rosinos de Vidriales, Zamora)', in Ramírez, P. and Balbín Behrmann, R. de (eds.), *II Congreso de Arqueología Peninsular: Zamora, del 24 al 27 de septiembre de 1996, Vol. 4*, Madrid, 183–94

Carrington, P. 1977: 'The planning and date of the Roman legionary fortress at Chester', *Journal of the Chester Archaeological Society* **60**, 35–42

Carrington, P. 1985: 'The plan of the legionary fortress at Chester: a reconsideration', *Journal of the Chester Archaeological Society* **68**, 23–51

Carrington, P. 1986: 'The plan of the legionary fortress at Chester: further comparisons', *Journal of the Chester Archaeological Society* **69**, 7–17

Carrington, P. (ed.) 2002a: *Deva Victrix: Roman Chester Re-assessed: Papers from a Weekend Conference Held at Chester College 3–5 September 1999*, Chester

Carrington, P. 2002b: 'Exploration of Roman Chester 1962–1999' in Carrington 2002a, 7–23

Carroll-Spillecke, M. 1993: 'Das römische Militärlager Divitia in Köln-Deutz', *Kölner Jahrbuch* **26**, 321–444

Carroll-Spillecke, M. 1997: 'The late Roman frontier fort Divitia in Cologne-Deutz and its garrisons', in Groenman-van Waateringe 1997, 143–9

Carter, G.A. 1986: 'The end of the road for Britain's first street?', *Essex Journal* **21**, 3–8

Casey, J. 1991: *The Legions in the Later Roman Empire, The Fourth Annual Caerleon Lecture in Honorem Aquilae Legionis II Augustae*, Cardiff

Casey, P. J. and Hoffmann, B. 1995: 'Excavations at Alstone Cottage, Caerleon, in 1970', *Britannia* **26**, 63–106

Cătinaş, A. 1996: 'Lampes à estampille de Potaissa', *Rei Cretariae Romanae Fautorum acta* **33**, 63–74

Cătinaş, A. 1997: 'Les antéfixes découverts dans le camp de la legio V Macedonica de Potaissa', *Rei Cretariae Romanae Fautorum acta* **35**, 233–8

Ceska, J. and Hosek, R. (eds.) 1967: *Inscriptiones Pannoniae Superioris in Slovacia Transdanubiana Asservatae*, Brno

Chantraine, H. 1968: *Die antiken Fundmünzen der Ausgrabungen in Neuss*, Limesforschungen **8**, Berlin

Chantraine, H. 1982: *Die antiken Fundmünzen der Ausgrabungen in Neuss. Gesamtkatalog der Ausgrabungen 1955–1978*, Limesforschungen **20**, Berlin

Chantraine, H., Gechter, M., Horn, H.-G., Müller, G., Rüger, C.B., and Tauch, M. 1984: *Das römische Neuss*, Stuttgart

Chapman, E. 2002: 'Evidence of an armamentarium at Caerleon? The Prysg Field rampart buildings', in Aldhouse-Green, M. and Webster, P. (eds.), *Artefacts and Archaeology, Aspects of the Celtic and Roman World*, Cardiff, 33–43

Chapman, E.M. 2005: *A Catalogue of Roman Military Equipment in the National Museum of Wales*, BAR **388**, Oxford

Chapot, V. 1907: *Le Frontière de Euphrate, de Pompée à la conquête arabe*, Paris

Charlesworth, D. 1980: 'The south gate of a Flavian fort at Carlisle', in Hanson and Keppie 1980, 201–10

Chiarucci, P. 1988: *Albano Laziale*, ed. 2, Albano Laziale

Chiarucci, P. 1999: 'Le necropoli della II Legione Partica in Albano', in Dal Covolo E. and Rinaldi G. (eds.), *Gli imperatori Severi: storia, archeologia, religione*, Roma, 68–116

Chiarucci, P. 2006: *Settimio Severo e la Legione Seconda Partica*, Albano Laziale

Chmelar, W. and Helgert, H. 1998: 'Die römischen Kasernen unter dem Judenplatz', *Fundort Wien* **1**, 20–7

Ciugudean, D. and Ciugudean, H. 2000: 'Un mormânt de militar roman de la Apulum (Un tombeau militaire romain d'Apulum)', *Apulum* **37**, 341–9

Coarelli, F. 1981: *Guide archeologhe Laterza – Dintorni di Roma*, Roma-Bari

Cobbett, R.E. 2008: 'A dice tower from Richborough', *Britannia* **39**, 219–35

Collingwood, R.G. 1921: 'The purpose of the Roman Wall', *Vasculum* **8**, 4–9

Cool, H.E.M., Lloyd-Morgan, G. and Hooley, A.D. 1995: *Finds from the Fortress*, Archaeology of York **17/10**, York

Cotton, M.A. and Frere, S.S. 1968: 'Ivinghoe Beacon excavations 1963–1965', *Records of Buckinghamshire* **18**, 187–260

Coulston, J.C.N. 1995: 'The sculpture of an armoured figure at Alba Iulia, Romania', *Arma* **7**, 13–17

Coulston, J.C.N. 1998: 'Gladiators and soldiers: personnel and equipment in ludus and castra', *JRMES* **9**, 1–17

Coulston, J.C.N. 2000: '"Armed and belted men": the soldiery in imperial Rome', in Coulston, J.C.N. and Dodge, H. (eds.) *Ancient Rome: the Archaeology of the Eternal City*, Oxford University School of Archaeology Monograph **54**, Oxford, 76–118

Crow, J. 1986: 'A review of the physical remains of the frontier in Cappodocia', in Freeman and Kennedy 1986, 77–91

Crummy, N.C. 1983: *The Roman Small Finds from Excavations in Colchester 1971–9*, Colchester Archaeological Report **2**, Colchester

Crummy, N.C. (ed.) 1987: *The Coins from Excavations in Colchester 1971–9*, Colchester Archaeological Report **4**, Colchester

Crummy, N.C. and Winter, M.J. 1987: 'Coin hoards from Colchester', in Crummy, N.C. 1987, 69–76

Crummy, P. 1974: *Colchester Recent Excavations and Research*, MISCAT Report **2**, Colchester <http://cat.essex.ac.uk/reports/MISCAT-report-0002.pdf> accessed 13.1.10

Crummy, P. 1977: 'Colchester: the Roman fortress and the development of the colonia', *Britannia* **8**, 65–105

Crummy, P. 1984: *Excavations at Lion Walk, Balkerne Lane, and Middleborough, Colchester, Essex*, Colchester Archaeological Report **3**, Colchester

Crummy, P. 1988: 'Colchester (Camulodunum) – Colonia Victricensis', in Webster 1988a, 24–47

Crummy, P. 1990: 'Metrological analysis', *Current Archaeology* **11**, 91–3

Crummy, P. 1992: *Excavations at Culver Street, Gilberd School and Other Sites in Colchester*, Colchester Archaeological Report **6**, Colchester

Crummy, P. 1993a: 'The development of Roman Colchester', in Greep 1993, 34–45

Crummy, P. 1993b: 'Metrological analysis of Roman fortresses and towns in Britain', in Greep 1993, 111–19

Crummy, P. J. 1987: 'The coins as dating evidence', in Crummy N.C. 1987, 5–14

Cunliffe B.W. 1968: *Fifth Report on the Excavations of the Roman Fort at Richborough, Kent*, Reports of the Research Committee of the Society of Antiquaries of London **23**, Oxford

Dabrowa, E. 2000: 'Legio X Fretensis', in Le Bohec and Wolff 2000, 317–25

Daszkiewicz, M., Bobryk, E., Schneider, G., and Dyczek, P. 2000: 'Chemical and mineralogical composition of Roman amphorae from Novae and some other sites in Bulgaria – first results', *Novensia* **12**, 23–42

Davison, D.P. 1989: *The Barracks of the Roman Army from the 1st to 3rd Centuries AD. A Comparative Study of the Barracks from Fortresses, Forts and Fortlets with an Analysis of Building Types and Construction, Stabling and Garrisons*, BAR International Series **472**, Oxford

Dawson, M. 1990: 'Roman military equipment on civil sites in Roman Dacia', in *Journal of Roman Military Equipment Studies* **1**, 7–15

Decker, K.-V. and Selzer, W. 1976: 'Mainz von der Zeit des Augustus bis zum Ende der römischen

Herrschaft', in Temporini, H. and Haase, W. (eds.), *Aufstieg und Niedergang der römischen Welt* **II.5.1**, 457–559

Deckers, J.G. 1979: 'Die Wandmalereien im Kaiserkultraum von Luxor', *Jahrbuch des Deutschen Archäologischen Instituts* **94**, 600–52

Dentzer, J.-M., Blanc, P.-M., and Fournet, T. 2002: 'Le développement urbain de Bosra de l'époque nabatéenne à l'époque byzantine: bilan des recherches françaises 1981–2002', *Syria* **79**, 75–154

De Pachtère, F. 1916: 'Les camps de la IIIe légion en Afrique au Ier siècle de l'Empire', *Comptes Rendus des séances de l'Académie des Inscriptions et Belles-Lettres* **60**, 273–84

Derda, T., Dyczek, P., and Kolendo, J. (eds.) 2008: *Novae: Legionary Fortress and Late Antique Town, vol. I: A Companion on the Study of Novae*, Warsaw

Deschler-Erb, E. 1996: 'Vindonissa: Ein Gladius mit reliefverzierter Scheide und Gürtelteilen aus dem Legionslager', *Gesellschaft Pro Vindonissa. Jahresbericht*, 13–31

Deschler-Erb, E., Fellmann-Brogli, R., and Kahlau, T. 2004: 'Ein "Fellhelm" aus Vindonissa', *Gesellschaft Pro Vindonissa, Jahresbericht*, 3–12

Dessau, H. 1892–1916: *Inscriptiones Latinae Selectae*, Berlin

Detten, D. von 1999: 'Vetera Castra I. Römischer Basisstützpunkt für die militärischen Operationen im rechtsrheinischen Germanien zur Zeit des Augustus', in Schlüter and Wiegels 1999, 401–17

Dickinson, B. and Webster, P.V. 2002: 'A group of Flavian samian from Caerleon', in Genin, M. and Vernhet, A. (eds.), *Céramiques de la Graufesenque et autres productions d'époque romaine. Nouvelles recherches. Hommages à Bettina Hoffmann*, Montagnac, 247–57

Diego Santos, F. 1986: *Inscripciones Romanas de la Provincia de León*, León

Dietz, K. 1984: 'Die älteste Weihinschrift aus dem Regensburger Legionslager', *Bayerische Vorgeschichtsblätter* **49**, 79–85

Dietz, K. 2000: 'Legio III Italica', in Le Bohec and Wolff 2000, 133–43

Dietz, K. and Fischer, T. 1996: *Die Römer in Regensburg*, Regensburg

Dietz, K., Osterhaus, U., Rickhoff-Pauli, S., and Spindler, K. 1979: *Regensburg zur Römerzeit*, Regensburg

Dilke, O.A.W. 1974: 'Archaeological and epigraphic evidence of Roman land survey', in Temporini, H. (ed.), *Aufstieg und Niedergang der römischen Welt* **II.1**, 573–80

Dimitrova-Milčeva, A. 1990: 'Untersuchungen am befestigten Limessystem an der unteren Donau auf dem Territorium der VR Bulgarien', in Vetters and Kandler 1990, 863–74

Dimitrova-Milceva, A. 1991: 'Zum Problem der Datierung der frühesten Perioden des Militärlagers Novae', in Maxfield and Dobson 1991, 271–6

Dimitrova-Milceva, A. 2006: *Die Bronzefunde aus Novae, Moesia Inferior*, Warszawa

Dobrowolski, K. and Piasecki, K. 2003: 'Identifying the species of birds depicted on the funerary stela from Novae (Bulgaria)', *Novensia* **14**, 59–66

Dobson, M. 2008: *The Army of the Roman Republic: The Second Century BC, Polybius and the Camps at Numantia, Spain*, Oxford

Domaszewski, A. von 1921: *Geschichte der römischen Kaiser. Bd. 2*, ed. 3, Leipzig

Domaszewski, A. von, Hauser, A., and Schneider, R. 1886: 'Ausgrabungen in Carnuntum 1885', *Archaeologisch-Epigraphische Mittheilungen* **10**, 32–41

Domaszewski, A. von, Hauser, A., and Schneider, R. 1887: 'Ausgrabungen in Carnuntum', *Archaeologisch-Epigraphische Mittheilungen* **11**, 1–18

Doms, A. 1970: 'Die Entdeckung des Römerlagers in Anreppen im Jahre 1968', *Westfalen* **48**, 160–70

Donevski, P. 1990a: 'Durostorum. Lager und Canabae der Legio XI Claudia', in Vetters and Kandler 1990, 931–9

Donevski, P. 1990b: 'Zur Topographie von Durostorum', *Germania* **68**, 236–45

Donevski, P. 1991: 'Durostorum, Municipium Aurelium und das Lager der Legio XI Claudia', in Maxfield and Dobson 1991, 277–80

Donevski, P. 1998: 'Inner arrangement of the camp at Novae', *Novensia* **10**, 13–15

Donevski, P. 2004: 'Some notes about the legionary fortress at Durostorum (Lower Moesia)', *Novensia* **15**, 15–18

Donevski, P. 2009: 'Archaeological investigations in Silistra (Durostorum)', *Buletinul Muzeului Judeţean Teleorman* **1**, 105–30

Dragovejic-Josifovska, B. 1982: *Les Inscriptions de la Mesie Superieure*, Vol. VI, Beograd, 25–8

Drahor, M.G., Berge, M.A., and Kurtulmuş, T.Ö. 2004: *The Final Report on Large-Scale Geophysical Studies in.the Satala (Legio XV Apollinaris) in 2004*, Doku6z Eylül University Center for Near Surface Geophysics and Archaeological Prospection (CNSGAP), Report **04–03**, İzmir <http://www.mavors.org/PDFs/GeoSatala04.pdf> accessed 4.5.11

Drahor, M.G., Kurtulmuş, T.Ö., Berge, M.A., Hartmann, M., and Speidel, M.A. 2008: 'Magnetic imaging and electrical resistivity tomography studies in a Roman military installation found in Satala archaeological site, northeastern Anatolia, Turkey', *Journal of Archaeological Science* **35**, 259–71

Driel-Murray, C. van 1988: 'A fragmentary shield cover from Caerleon', with contributions by Evans, E.M. and Pickett-Baker, J., in Coulston, J.C. (ed.), *Military Equipment and the Identity of Roman Soldiers. Proceedings of the Fourth Roman Military Equipment Conference*, BAR International Series **394**, Oxford, 51–66

Driel-Murray, C. van and Gechter, M. 1984: 'Funde aus der Fabrica der *Legio I Minervia* am Bonner Berg', in *Beiträge zur Archäologie des römischen Rheinlands 4*, Rheinische Ausgrabungen **23**, Köln, 1–83

Driessen, M. 2009: 'The early Flavian timber *castra* and the Flavian-Trajanic stone legionary fortress at Nijmegen (The Netherlands)', in Morillo et al. 2009, 1245–56

Dunn, G. 2006: 'Roman baths beyond the walls', *Past Uncovered*, 1–2

Dunnett, B.R.K. 1971: 'Excavations in Colchester 1964–8', *Transactions of the Essex Archaeological Society* 3 ser. **3**, 1–10

Dunnett. B.R.K. 1967: 'Excavations on North Hill, Colchester', *Archaeological Journal* **123**, 27–61

Durman, A. 1992: 'O geostrate škom polo žaju Siscije (Sur la position géostratégique de Siscia)', *Opuscula archaeologica* **16**, 117–31

Durry, M. 1938: *Les cohortes prétoriennes*, Bibliothèque des Écoles françaises d'Athènes et de Rome **146**, Paris

Dušanić, S. 1997: 'Three diploma fragments from Viminacium', *Starinar* **48**, 63–71

Dussaud, R. 1927: *Topographie historique de la Syrie antique et médiévale*, Paris

Dussaud, R. 1929: 'La Palmyrène et l'exploration de M. Alois Musil', *Syria* **10**, 52–62

Duval, N. 1982: 'Topographie et urbanisme d'Ammaedara (actuellement Haïdra, Tunisie)', in Temporini, H. (ed.), *Aufstieg und Niedergang der römischen Welt* **II.10.2**, 633–71

Dyczek, P. 1997: 'The Valetudinarium at Novae – New Components', in Groenman-van Waateringe et al. 1997, 199–204

Dyczek, P. 1999: 'A sacellum Aesculapii in the valetudinarium at Novae', in Gudea 1999, 495–500

Dyczek, P. 2001: *Novae – 40 lat wykopalisk*, Warsaw

Dyczek, P. 2007: *Everyday Life in the Fortress of the First Italic Legion at Novae. Exhibition at Warsaw University*, Warsaw

Dyczek, P., Ładomirski, A., and Sarnowski, T. 1993: 'Novae – Western Sector, 1991. Preliminary report on the excavations of the Warsaw University archaeological expedition', *Archeologia* **44**, 81–94

Dyer, J. and Wenham, L.P. 1967: 'Excavations and discoveries in a cellar in Messrs. Chas. Hart's premises, Feasgate, York, 1956', *Yorkshire Archaeological Journal* **39**, 419–25

Ebnoether, C. and Schucany, C. 1998: 'Vindonissa und sein Umland. Die Vici und die ländliche Besiedlung', *Gesellschaft Pro Vindonissa. Jahresbericht*, 67–98

Eck, W. 2009: 'Revision lateinischer Inschriften aus Jerusalem', *ZPE* **169**, 213–29

Eck, W. and Tepper, Y. 2001: 'A dedication to Silvanus near the camp of the Legio VI Ferrata near Lajjun', *Scripta Classica Israelica* **20**, 85–8

Eckhart, L. 1969: *Das Donaukastell Schlögen in Oberösterreich (die Ausgrabungen 1957–1959)*, Der Römische Limes in Österreich **25**, Wien, 1–70

Eckhart, L. 1984: 'Lagerbau und Kommandobereich der Legio II Italica am Donaulimes', *Römisches Österreich* **11/12**, 1983/84, 17–40

Ehmig, U. 2000: *Die römischen Amphoren aus Mainz*, Möhnesee

Ehmig, U. 2010: *Dangstetten IV – Die Amphoren. Untersuchungen zur Belieferung einer Militäranlage in augusteischer Zeit*, Forschungen und Berichte zur Vor- und Frühgeschichte in Baden-Württemberg **117**, Stuttgart

Eisenmenger, U. and Eleftheriadou, E. 2000: 'Ein neues Schlangengefäß aus dem Legionslager Vindobona', *Fundort Wien* **3**, 34–9

Elefterescu, D. and Muşeţeanu, C. 1990: 'Céramique sigillée à Durostorum', *Dacia* **34**, 235–44

El-Saghir, M., Golvin, J.-C., Reddé, M., Hegazy, E., and Wagner, G. 1986: *Le camp romain de Louqsor (avec une étude des graffites gréco-romains du temple d'Amon)*, Mémoires publiés par les membres de l'IFAO **83**, Cairo

Enckevort, H. van, 1997: 'Die Belegerung des frührömischen Lagers auf dem Kops Plateau. Römer, Gallier, Bataven und Keltiberiker in Nijmegen', in Groenman-van Waateringe et al. 1997, 555–64

Enckevort, H. van, Haalebos, J.K., and Thijssen, J. 2000: *Nijmegen. Legerplaats in het achterland van de Romeinse limes*, Abcoude/Nijmegen

Enckevort, H. van and Thijssen, J. 2001–2: 'Militaria from the Roman urban settlements at Nijmegen', *Journal of Roman Military Equipment Studies* **12–13**, 35–41

Enckevort, H. van and Willems, W.J.H. 1994: 'Roman cavalry helmets in ritual hoards from the Kops Plateau at Nijmegen, The Netherlands', *Journal of Roman Military Equipment Studies* **5**, 125–37

Enckevort, H. van and Zee, K. 1996: *Het Kops Plateau. Prehistorische grafheuvels en een Romeinse legerplaats in Nijmegen*, Abcoude/Nijmegen

Enckevort, H. van and Zee, K. 1999: 'Militaria und Belegung des frührömischen Lagers auf dem Kops Plateau in Nijmegen (Niederlande)', in Schlüter and Wiegels 1999, 191–205

Ertel, C. 1999: 'Zur Rekonstruktion der Porta Praetoria des Legionslagers Aquincum', in Gudea 1999, 397–403

Esser, K.H. 1972: 'Mogontiacum', *Bonner Jahrbücher* **172**, 212–27

Ettlinger, E. 1961: 'Vindonissa', *Paulys Realencyclopädie der classischen Altertumswissenschaft* **9A**, 82–105

Ettlinger, E. 1983: *Die italische Sigillata von Novaesium*, Limesforschungen **21**, Berlin

Ettlinger, E. 1998: 'Noch einmal zur Keramik der 11. Legion in Vindonissa', *Gesellschaft Pro Vindonissa. Jahresbericht*, 37–46

Ettlinger, E. and Doppler, H.W. 1986: 'Nochmals Schwertscheiden-Fragmente und verwandte Stücke aus Vindonissa', *Gesellschaft Pro Vindonissa. Jahresbericht*, 5–28

Ettlinger, E. and Fellmann, R. 1955: 'Ein Sigillata-Depotfund aus dem Legionslager Vindonissa', *Germania* **33**, 364–73

Ettlinger, E. and Gonzenbach, V. von 1955–56: 'Die Grabung am Schutthügel 1952', *Gesellschaft Pro Vindonissa. Jahresbericht*, 35–52

Ettlinger, E. and Hartmann, M. 1984: 'Fragmente einer Schwertscheide aus Vindonissa und ihre Gegenstücke vom Grossen St Bernhard', *Gesellschaft Pro Vindonissa. Jahresbericht*, 5–46

Ettlinger, E. and Simonett, C. 1952: *Römische Keramik aus dem Schutthügel von Vindonissa*, Veröffentlichungen der Gesellschaft Pro Vindonissa, Basel

Evans, D.R. and Metcalf, V. 1989: 'Excavations at 10 Old Market Street, Usk', *Britannia* **20**, 23–68

Evans, D.R. and Metcalf, V.M. 1992: *The 'Roman Gates' Site in the Fortress of the Second Augustan Legion at Caerleon, Gwent: The Excavations of the Roman Buildings and Evidence for Early Medieval Activity*, Oxbow Monograph **15**, Oxford

Evans, D.T. 1998: 'Excavations at the former Daveygate Centre', *Interim: the Archaeology of York* **22**(4), 5–9

Evans, D.T. 2000: 'The former Primitive Methodist chapel, 3 Little Stonegate', *Interim: the Archaeology of York* **23**(2), 24–8

Evans, E.M. 1991: 'Excavations at "Sandygate", Cold Bath Road, Caerleon, Gwent', *Britannia* **22**, 103–36

Evans, E.M. 2000: *The Caerleon Canabae: Excavations in the Civil Settlement 1984–90*, Britannia Monograph **16**, London

Evans, E.M. and Maynard, D.J. 1997: 'Caerleon Lodge Hill cemetery, the Abbeyfield Extra Care Society site', *Britannia* **28**, 169–243

Facsády, A.R. 1976: 'Előzetes jelentés a későrómai kori erőd déli védművének feltárásáról (Preliminary Report on the Excavation of the Southern Defensive Works of the Late Roman Fort)', *Budapest Régiségei* **24**, 145–51

Farnum, J.H. 2005: *The Positioning of the Roman Imperial Legions*, BAR International Series **1458**, Oxford

Fellmann, R. 1953/54: 'Die Grabungen im Legionslager Vindonissa im Jahre 1953', *Jahresbericht der Gesellschaft Pro Vindonissa*, 5–60

Fellmann, R. 1954/55: 'Die Grabungen im Legionslager Vindonissa im Jahre 1954/55', *Jahresbericht der Gesellschaft Pro Vindonissa*, 5–66

Fellmann, R. 1956/57: 'Die Principia des Legionslagers Vindonissa, B. 1. Die Principia der 13. Legion', *Jahresbericht der Gesellschaft Pro Vindonissa*, 12ff

Fellmann, R. 1958: *Die Principia des Legionslagers Vindonissa und das Zentralgebäude der römischen Lager und Kastelle*, Brugg

Fellmann, R. 1976: 'Le camp de Dioclétien à Palmyre et l'architecture millitaire du Bas-Empire', in *Mélanges d'histoire ancienne et d'Archéologie offerts à Paul Collart*, Cahiers d'archéologie romande de la Bibliothèque historique vaudoise 5, , 173–91

Fellmann, R. 1989: *Principia – Stabsgebäude*, Kleine Schriften zur Kenntnis der römischen Besetzungsgeschichte Südwestdeutschlands Nr. **31**, Aalen

Filtzinger, P. 1962–63: 'Zur Lokalisierung der Zweilegionenfestung apud aram Ubiorum', *Kölner Jahrbuch* **6**, 23–57

Filtzinger, P. 1972: *Die römische Keramik aus dem Militärbereich von Novaesium*, Limesforschungen **11**, Berlin

Filtzinger, P. 1980: 'Der westliche Umfassungsgraben und das rückwärtige Lagertor (porta decumana) des Zweilegionenlagers der 1. und 20. Legion apud Aram Ubiorum in der Richmodstraße in Köln', *Kölner Jahrbuch* **17**, 59–75

Fingerlin, G. 1970–1: 'Dangstetten, ein augusteisches Legionslager am Hochrhein. Vorbericht über die Grabungen 1967–69', *BRGK* **51-2**, 197–232

Fingerlin, G. 1977: 'Die Tore des frührömischen Lagers von Dangstetten (Hochrhein)', *Fundberichte aus Baden-Württemberg* **3**, 278–85

Fingerlin, G. 1981: 'Eberzahnanhänger aus Dangstetten', *Fundberichte aus Baden-Württemberg* **6**, 417–32

Fingerlin, G. 1986a: 'Küssaberg–Dangstetten. Lager für eine größere Truppeneinheit', in Planck, D. (ed.), *Die Römer in Baden-Württemberg*, Stuttgart, 156–8

Fingerlin, G. 1986b: *Dangstetten I. Katalog der Funde (Fundstellen 1 bis 603)*, Forschungen und Berichte zur Vor- und Frühgeschichte in Baden-Württemberg **22**, Stuttgart

Fingerlin, G. 1998: *Dangstetten II. Katalog der Funde (Fundstellen 604 bis 1358)*, Forschungen und Berichte zur Vor- und Frühgeschichte in Baden-Württemberg **69**, Stuttgart

Fingerlin, G. 1999: 'Römische und keltische Reiter im Lager der 19. Legion von Dangstetten am Hochrhein', *Archäologische Nachrichten aus Baden* **60**, 3–18

Fink, J. 1885: 'Römische Ausgrabungen bei Regensburg (Kumpfmühl) und die Porta Praetoria im Bischofshof', *Korrespondenzblatt der deutschen Geschichts- und Altertumsvereine* **33**, 76

Fink, R.O. 1971: *Roman Military Records on Papyrus*, Cleveland

Finke, H. 1927: 'Neue Inschriften', *BRGK* **17**, 1–107 and 198–231

Fischer, F. 2005: 'Zur historischen Datierung frührömischer Militärstationen. Walenseetürme, Zürich-Lindenhof und Dangstetten', *Germania* **83**, 45–52

Fitz, J. (ed.) 1977: *Limes. Akten des XI Internationalen Limeskongresses, Székesfehérvár, 30.8.–6.9. 1976*, Budapest

Flutur, A. 1999–2000: 'Săpăturile arheologice din castrul Bersobis – campaniile din anii 1998–1999', *Analele Banatului* NS **7–8**, 365–72

Flutur, A. 2001a: 'Săpăturile arheologice din principia legiunii a IV-a Flavia Felix de la Bersobis – 2000–2001', *Analele Banatului* NS **9**, 131–46

Flutur, A. 2001b: 'Tile-Stamps of Legio IV Flavia Felix from Bersobies', in *Die Archäologie und Geschichte der Region des Eisernen Tores zwischen 106–275 n.Chr., Kolloquium in Drobeta-Turnu Severin (1.–4. Oktober 2000)*, Rumänisch-Jugoslawische Kommision fur die Erforschung der Region des Eisernen Tores – Archaologische Abteilung **4**, Bucureşti, 29–33

Flutur, A. 2002–2003: 'Stampilele tegulare ale legiunii a IV-a Flavia Felix de la Bersobis', *Analele Banatului* NS **10–11**, 157–62

Flutur, A. 2006: 'Castrul Berzobis din perspectiva cercetărilor recente', in *Dacia Augusti Provincia.*

Crearea provinciei. Actele simpozionului desfăşurat în 13–14 octombrie 2006 la Muzeul Naţional de Istorie a României, Bucuresti, 165–9

Förtsch, R. 1995: 'Villa und Praetorium. Zur Luxusarchitektur in frühkaiserzeitlicher Legionslager', *Kölner Jahrbuch* **28**, 617–34

Forrer, R. 1927: *Strasbourg-Argentorate, préhistorique, gallo-romain et mérovingien*, Strasbourg

Fortis, A. 1778: *Voyage en Dalmatie par M. l'Abbé Fortis, traduit de l'Italien*, Berne

Fox, A. 1940: 'The legionary fortress at Caerleon, Monmouthshire: Excavations in Myrtle Cottage Orchard 1939', *Archaeologia Cambrensis* **95**, 101–52

Fox, A. 1952: *Roman Exeter (Isca Dumnoniorum): Excavations in the War-Damaged Areas, 1945–7*, Manchester

Fox, A. 1966: 'Roman Exeter (Isca Dumnoniorum), origins and early development', in Wacher, J.S. (ed.), *The Civitas Capitals of Roman Britain*, Leicester, 46–51

Fox, G.E. and St John Hope, W.H. 1901: 'Excavations on the site of the Roman city of Silchester, Hants. in 1900', *Archaeologia* **57**, 229–56

Fox, S. 1995: 'Caerleon, Gwent College of Higher Education: Rathmell extension', *Archaeology in Wales* **35**, 54

Franzen, P. 2009: 'The Augustan legionary fortress at Nijmegen. Legionary and auxiliary soldiers', in Morillo et al. 2009, 1257–69

Freeman, P.W.M. 2007: *The Best Training-Ground for Archaeologists. Francis Haverfield and the Invention of Romano-British Archaeology*, Oxford

Freeman, P., Bennett, J., Fiema, Z.T., and Hoffmann, B. (eds.) 2002: *Limes XVIII. Proceedings of the 18th International Congress of Roman Frontier Studies held in Amman, Jordan (September 2000)*, BAR International Series **1084**, Oxford

Fremersdorf, F. 1954: 'Frankengräber des 7./8. Jahrhunderts in Köln-Poll und Untersuchungen im spätrömischen Kastell Deutz', in Marschall, A., Narr, K.J., and Uslar, R. v. (eds.), *Die vor- und frühgeschichtliche Besiedlung des Bergischen Landes*, Neustadt, 153–62

French, D. 1994: 'Legio III Gallica', in Dabrowa, E. (ed.), *The Roman and Byzantine Army in the East. Proceedings of a Colloquium Held at the Jagiellonian University, Kraków in September 1992*, 29–46

Frere, S.S. 1980: 'Hyginus and the First Cohort', *Britannia* **11**, 51–60

Frere, S.S. 1983: 'Roman Britain in 1982. I. Sites explored', *Britannia* **14**, 280–335

Frey, P. and Pauli-Gabi, T. 2006: 'Priorité à la sécurité, le camp romain de Vindonissa (Windisch) et les fortifications modernes du canton d'Argovie', *Archäologie Schweiz* **29:2**, 16–25

Friesinger, H. and Krinzinger, F. (eds.) 1997: *Der römische Limes in Österreich, Führer zu den archäologischen Denkmälern*, Wien

Fulford, M. and Timby, J. 2000: *Late Iron Age and Roman Silchester: Excavations on the Site of the Forum-Basilica 1977, 1980–86*, Britannia Monograph **15**, London

Gabriel, A. 1940: *Voyages archéologiques dans le Turquie orientale*, Paris, 264–8

Gaisbauer, I. and Mosser, M. 2001: 'Befunde im Legionslager Vindobona. Teil II: Altgrabungen im Bereich der Principia', *Fundort Wien* **4**, 114–57

Galsterer, B. and Galsterer, H. 2010: *Die römischen Steininschriften aus Köln. IKöln, 2. Auflage*, Mainz

Gansser-Burckhardt, A. 1942: *Das Leder und seine Verarbeitung im römischen Legionslager Vindonissa*, Veröffentlichungen der Gesellschaft Pro Vindonissa **1**, Basel

Gansser-Burckhardt, A. 1947–48: 'Die Lederfunde von Vindonissa Jahres 1947', *Gesellschaft Pro Vindonissa. Jahresbericht*, 34–41

Gansser-Burckhardt, A. 1948–49: 'Neue Lederfunde von Vindonissa', *Gesellschaft Pro Vindonissa. Jahresbericht*, 29–52

Gansser-Burckhardt, A. 1952: 'Die Lederfunde aus dem Schutthügel von Vindonissa 1951', *Gesellschaft Pro Vindonissa. Jahresbericht*, 57–65

Garcia y Bellido, A. 1968: *Nueve estudios sobre la legión VII Gemina y su campamento en Leon*, León

Garcia y Bellido, A. 1970a: 'Estudios sobre la Legio VII Gemina y su campamento en León', *Legio VII Gemina*, León, 569–99

Garcia y Bellido, A. 1970b: 'Nacimiento de la Legio VII Gemina', in *Legio VII Gemina*, León, 303–29

García-Bellido, A. (ed.) 2006: *Los campamentos romanos en Hispania (27 a. C.–192 d. C.). El abastecimiento de moneda*, Anejos de Gladius **9**, Madrid

García-Bellido, A., Fernández de Avilés, A., Balil, A., and Vigil, M. 1962: *Herrera de Pisuerga*, Excavaciones Arqueológicas en España **2**, Madrid

García Bellido, M. P. 1996: 'Las monedas hispanicas de los campamentos del Lippe. Legio Prima (antes Augusta) en Oberaden?', *Boreas* **19**, 247–60

García Marcos, V. 2002: 'Novedades acerca de los campamentos romanos de León', in Morillo, Á. (ed.), *Arqueología militar romana en Hispania*, Anejos de Gladius **5**, Madrid, 167–212

García Marcos, V. and Miguel, F. 1997: 'A new view on the military occupation in the North-West of Hispania during the first century: the case of León', in Groenman-van Waateringe 1997, 355–60

García Marcos, V. and Morillo, A. 2000/1: 'El campamento de la legio VII gemina en León. Noveda – des sobre su planta y sistema defensivo', *Lancia* **4**, 103–26

García Marcos, V. and Morillo, A. 2002: 'The legionary fortress of VI Victrix at León (Spain). The new evidence', in Freeman et al. 2002, 791–800

Gardner, A. and Guest, P. 2007: *Caerleon Excavations at Golledge's Field and Priory Field, 2007: Interim Report*, <http://www.cf.ac.uk/hisar/archaeology/crc/files/caerleon_07_interim.pdf> retrieved 13.11.09

Gardner, A. and Guest, P. 2009: 'Fortress Isca', *Current Archaeology* **226**, 31–7

Gardner, A. and Guest, P. 2010: 'Exploring Roman Caerleon. new excavations at the legionary fortress of Isca', *Archaeology International* **12**, 47–51

Gauer, W., 1981: 'Castra Regina und Rom. Zu Ursprung und Erneuerung der europäischen Stadt', *Bonner Jahrbücher* **181**, 1–88

Gawlikowski, M. 1968: 'Die polnischen Ausgrabungen in Palmyra 1959–1967', *Archäologischer Anzeiger*, 289–307

Gawlikowski, M. 1970: *Obóz Dioklecjana w Palmyrze*, Prace Komisji Archeologicznej Oddziału PAN w Krakowie IX, 37–53

Gawlikowski, M. 1974: 'Les défenses de Palmyre', *Syria* **51**, 231–42

Gawlikowski, M. 1976a: 'Palmyre 1973', *Chronique des fouilles* **9**, 273–81

Gawlikowski, M. 1976b: 'Le Camp de Dioclétien: bilan préliminaire', in Frezouls, E. (ed.), *Palmyre. Bilan et perspectives. Colloque de Strasbourg 1973*, Strasbourg, 153–63

Gawlikowski, M. 1977: 'Le temple d'Allat à Palmyre', *Revue Archéologique*, 253–74

Gawlikowski, M. 1978: 'Palmyre 1974', *Chronique des fouilles* **10**, 421–2

Gawlikowski, M. 1979a: 'Palmyre 1975', *Chronique des fouilles* **11**, 267–70

Gawlikowski, M. 1979b: 'Palmyre 1976', *Chronique des fouilles* **11**, 271–3

Gawlikowski, M. 1983: 'Palmyre (Mission polonaise)', *Chronique Archéologique* **60**, 297

Gawlikowski, M. 1984: *Palmyre VIII: Les principia de Dioclétien. Temple des Enseignes*, Warszawa

Gawlikowski, M. 1985a: 'Les principia de Dioclétien à Palmyre', in *Le Dessin d'Architecture dans les Sociétés Antiques: Actes du Colloque de Strasbourg (26–28 Janvier, 1984)*, 283–7

Gawlikowski, M. 1985b: 'Świątynia Allat w Palmyrze. Wstępny raport z wykopalisk 1974–1976', *Studia palmyrénskie* **8**, 5–25

Gawlikowski, M. 1986: 'Palmyre (Mission polonaise)', *Chronique Archéologique* **63**, 397–9

Gawlikowski, M. 1987a: 'Das Horreum-Gebäude in Diokletianslager. Vorbericht über die 26. Ausgrabungskampagne (September–Oktober 1985)', in Ruprechtsberger, E. (ed.), *Palmyra. Geschichte, Kunst und Kultur der syrischen Oasenstadt*, Linz, 249–52

Gawlikowski, M. 1987b: 'Polnische Ausgrabungen in Palmyra: das Diokletianslager', in Ruprechtsberger, E. (ed.), *Palmyra. Geschichte, Kunst und Kultur der syrischen Oasenstadt*, Linz, 253–4

Găzdac, C. 2009: 'An unknown battle? Military artefacts and coin finds', in Busch and Schalles 2009, 109–13

Gechter, M. 1979a: 'Die Anfänge des Niedergermanischen Limes', *Bonner Jahrbücher* **179**, 106–10

Gechter, M. 1979b: 'Grabungen im Legionslager Bonn', *Rheinische Ausgrabungen '78*, 73–5

Gechter, M. 1980: 'Das spätantike Bonner Legionslager', in Hanson and Keppie 1980, 531–9

Gechter, M. 1984: 'Neue Untersuchungen an der Nord- und Ostseite des Bonner Legionslagers', in *Beiträge zur Archäologie des römischen Rheinlands 4*, Rheinische Ausgrabungen **23**, Köln, 85–90

Gechter, M. 1985: 'Ausgrabungen im Bereich des Neusser Legionslagers in den Jahren 1983 und 1984', *Ausgrabungen im Rheinland 1983/84*, 115–20

Gechter, M. 1985: 'Ausgrabungen in Bonn in den Jahren '83/84', in *Ausgrabungen in Rheinland 1983/84*, 121–8

Gechter, M. 1986: 'Neue Untersuchungen im Bonner Legionslager', in *Unz* 1986, 155–8

Gechter, M. 1987: 'Bonn', in Horn, H.G. (ed.), *Die Römer in Nordrhein-Westfalen*, Stuttgart, 364–76

Gechter, M. 1989: 'Das Legionslager Bonn als Modell', in *Archäologie im Rheinland 1988*, Köln, 68–9

Gechter, M. 1989: *Castra Bonnensia – das römische Bonn*, Donauwörth

Gechter, M. 1991: 'Zur Überlieferung der Bauinschrift des Kastells Divitia (Deutz)', *Kölner Jahrbuch* **24**, 377–80

Gechter, M. 2001: 'Das römische Bonn', Rey, M. van (ed.), *Geschichte der Stadt Bonn, Bd. 1 von der Vorgeschichte bis zum Ende der Römerzeit*, Bonn, 35–180

Gechter, M. 2002: 'Die Legionslager Vetera I und II', in Horn, H.-G. (ed.), *Die Römer in Nordrhein-Westfalen*, Hamburg, 619–25

Gechter, M. 2005: 'Neues aus dem römischen Bonn', in Horn, H.G., Hellenkemper, H., and Isenberg, G. (eds.), *Von Anfang an. Archäologie in Nordrhein-Westfalen, Begleitbuch zur Landesausstellung Köln 13. März – 28. August 2005*, Schriften zur Bodendenkmalpflege in Nordrhein-Westfalen **8**, Köln, 423–6

Gechter, M. 2007a: 'Der römische Militärplatz Neuss (Novaesium)', in Uelsberg, G. (ed.), *Krieg und Frieden – Kelten, Römer und Germanen. Begleitbuch zur gleichnamigen Ausstellung im Rheinischen Landesmuseum Bonn 21.6.2007–6.1.2008*, Bonn, 207–13

Gechter, M. 2007b: 'Der römische Militärplatz Bonn im 1. Jahrhundert n. Chr.', in Uelsberg, G. (ed.), *Krieg und Frieden – Kelten, Römer und Germanen. Begleitbuch zur gleichnamigen Ausstellung im Rheinischen Landesmuseum Bonn 21.6.2007–6.1.2008*, Bonn, 214–17

Gechter, M. and Wentscher, J. 1989: 'Römische Militärgebäude außerhalb des Bonner Legionslagers', in *Archäologie im Rheinland 1988*, Köln, 31–2

Genčeva, E. 1998a: 'Zapinki rzymskie i póznoantyczne z Novae', *Novensia* **11**, 7–80

Genčeva, E. 1998b: 'Drobne przedmioty metalowe z odcinka IV w Novae. Sprzaczki, aplikacje kolczyki', *Novensia* **11**, 81–98

Genčeva, E. 2000: 'Metalowe części wyposażenia żołnierskiego z Novae', *Novensia* **12**, 49–98

Genčeva, E. 2003: 'Le premier camp militaire à Novae', *Novensia* **14**, 21–37

Genser, K. 1986: *Der österreichische Donaulimes in der Römerzeit. Ein Forschungsbericht*, Der römische Limes in Österreich **33**, Wien

Gentry, A. P. 1976: *Roman Military Stone-Built Granaries in Britain*, BAR British Series **32**, Oxford

Georgetti, D. 1983: 'Ratiaria and its territory', in Poulter, A.G. 1983: *Ancient Bulgaria: the Proceedings of the International Conference on the Archaeology and Ancient History of Bulgaria 1981*, **2**, Nottingham, 19–39

Gerov, B. 1977: 'Zum problem der Entstehung der romischen Stadte am unteren Donaulimes', *Klio* **2**, 98–304

Gerov, B. 1989: *Inscriptiones Latinae in Bulgaria repertae*, Sofia

Geva, H. 1984: 'The camp of the Tenth Legion in Jerusalem: an archaeological reconsideration', *Israel Exploration Journal* **34**, 239–54

Geva, H. 1994, 'The Tenth Legion did camp on the south-west hill', *Cathedra* **73**, 194

Gietl, R., Kronberger, M., and Mosser, M. 2004: 'Rekonstruktion des antiken Geländes in der Wiener Innenstadt', *Fundort Wien* **7**, 32–53

Gilliver, C.M. 1993a: 'Hedgehogs, caltrops and palisade stakes', *Journal of Roman Military Equipment Studies* **4**, 49–54

Gilliver, C.M. 1993b: 'The *de munitionibus castrorum*: text and translation', *Journal of Roman Military Equipment Studies* **4**, 33–48

Ginella, F. et al. 1999: 'Ein Beitrag zur Nahrungswirtschaft und zur Verpflegung römischer Truppen im Legionslager Vindonissa/Windisch (CH). Archäozoologische Auswertung der Tierknochen aus der Grabung Vindonissa-Feuerwehrmagazin 1976', *Gesellschaft Pro Vindonissa. Jahresbericht*, 3–26

Gissinger, B. 2002: *Recherches sur le site fortifié de Strasbourg durant l'Antiquité tardive. Le castrum d'Argentoratum*, BAR **S1024**, Oxford

Glüsing, P. 2000: 'Ergänzende Anmerkungen zur Enddatierung der frührömischen Lippelager Anreppen und Haltern. Erweiterter Diskussionsbeitrag', in Wiegels, R. (ed.), *Die Fundmünzen von*

Kalkriese und die frühkaiserzeitliche Münzprägung, Osnabrücker Forschungen zu Altertum und Antike-Rezeption Bd. **3**, Möhnesee

Göbl, R. 1987: *Grabungen im Legionslager Carnuntum 1968–1978*, Veröffentlichungen der Numismatischen Kommission **18**, Wien

Goffart, W. 1977: 'The date and purpose of Vegetius' *De Re Militari*', *Traditio* **33**, 65–100

Goguey R., 1967: 'Le camp romain de Mirebeau', *Bulletin de la Société Nationale des Antiquaires de France*, 159–70

Goguey, R. 1971: 'Mirebeau: les fouilles de 1970 sur les thermes', *Mémoires de la Commission des Antiquités de Côte-d'Or* **27**, 14–20

Goguey, R. 1973: 'Le site légionnaire de Mirebeau, d'après les recherches de 1971–1972', *Mémoires de la Commission des Antiquités de Côte-d'Or* **28**, 99–12

Goguey, R. 1977: 'Mirebeau', *Mémoires de la Commission des Antiquités de Côte-d'Or* **30**, 54–9

Goguey, R. 2008: 'Légionnaires romains chez les Lingons: la VIIIème Avgvsta à Mirebeau (Côte-d'Or)', *Revue archéologique de l'Est*, **57**, 227–51 <http://rae.revues.org/index2833.html> accessed 27.11.09

Goguey, R. and Reddé, M. 1995: *Le camp légionnaire de Mirebeau*, Monographien des Römisch-Germanisches Zentralmuseum zu Mainz **36**, Mainz

Gojković, M.V. 2009: 'Early development of Poetovio', in Morillo et al. 2009, 1461–4

Golvin, J.-C. and Janon, M. 1978: 'L'amphithéâtre de Lambèse (Numidie) d'après des documents anciens', *Bulletin archéologique du Comité des travaux historiques et scientifiques* **12–14**, 169–94

Golvin, J.-C. and Reddé, M. 1986: 'L'enceinte du camp militaire romain de Louqsor', in Unz 1986, 594–9

González Echegaray, J. and Solana, J.M. 1975: 'La Legión Macedónica en España', *Hispania Antiqua* **5**, 151–203

Gonzenbach, V. von 1963: 'Die Verbreitung der gestempelten Ziegel der im 1. Jahrhundert n. Chr. in Vindonissa liegenden römischen Truppen', *Bonner Jahrbücher* **163**, 76–150

Gonzenbach, V. von 1965: 'Schwertscheidenbleche von Vindonissa aus der Zeit der 13. Legion', *Gesellschaft Pro Vindonissa. Jahresbericht*, 5–35

Gonzenbach, V. von 1966: 'Tiberische Gürtel- und Schwertscheidenbeschläge mit figürlichen Reliefs', in *Helvetia Antiqua, Festschrift Emil Vogt*, Zürich, 183–208

Gonzenbach, V. von 1976: 'Ein Heiligtum im Legionslager Vindonissa', in *Mélanges d'histoire ancienne et d'archéologie offerts à Paul Collart*, Cahiers d'archéologie romande **5**, Paris, 205–22

Grec, M. 1998: 'Urme de încălțăminte pe materialul tegular din castrul de la Potaissa (Shoe-prints on tegular material from Roman camp at Potaissa)', *Analele Banatului* **6**, 241–50

Green, C. 1942: 'Glevum and the Second Legion', *JRS* **32**, 39–52

Greep, S. J. 1993: *Roman Towns: the Wheeler Inheritance. A Review of 50 Years' Research*, CBA Research Report **93**, York

Gregory, S. 1989: 'Not "why not playing cards?" but "why playing cards in the first place?"', in French, D.H. and Lightfoot, C.S. (eds.), *The Eastern Frontier of the Roman Empire. Proceedings of a Colloquium held at Ankara in September 1988*, BAR **S553**, Oxford, 169–75

Gregory, S. 1995–97: *Roman Military Architecture on the Eastern Frontier*, 3 vols, Amsterdam

Gregory, S. and Kennedy, D. 1985: *Sir Aurel Stein's Limes Reports: The Full Text of M. A. Stein's Unpublished Limes Reports (his Aerial and Ground Reconnaissances in Iraq and Transjordan in 1938–9)*, BAR Int. Ser. **272**, Oxford, 385–91

Grewe, K. 2001: 'Die Wasserleitung für das Legionslager Bonn', in Rey, M. von (ed.), *Geschichte der Stadt Bonn, Bd. 1: Bonn von der Vorgeschichte bis zum Ende der Römerzeit*, Bonn, 181–98

Grewe, K. 2002: 'Aquaeductus Bonnensis. Die Wasserleitung für das römische Legionslager Bonn', *Antike Welt* **33**, 163–74

Gręzak, A. and Piątkowska-Małecka, J. 2006: 'Faunal remains from *principia* of the 1st century A.D. in Novae. Second group', *Novensia* **17**, 39–44

Grimes, W.F. 1930: *Holt, Denbighshire, the Works-Depôt of the Twentieth Legion at Castle Lyons*. Y Cymmrodor **41**, London

Grimes, W.F. 1935: 'The Roman legionary fortress at Caerleon in Monmouthshire: Report on the excavations carried out in the Town Hall Field in 1930', *Archaeologia Cambrensis* **90**, 112–22

Groenman-van Wateringe, W., van Beek, B.L., Willems, W.J.H., and Wynia, S.L. (eds.) 1997: *Roman Frontier Studies 1995. Proceedings of the XVIth International Congress of Roman Frontier Studies*, Oxbow Monograph **91**, Oxford

Groller, M. von 1900: 'Das Standlager von Carnuntum', *Der römische Limes in Österreich* **1**, 19–46

Groller, M. von 1901: 'Das Lager von Carnuntum', *Der römische Limes in Österreich* **2**, 15–84

Groller, M. von 1902: 'Grabungen im Lager von Carnuntum', *Der römische Limes in Österreich* **3**, 31–116

Groller, M. von 1903: 'Grabungen im Lager von Carnuntum', *Der römische Limes in Österreich* **4**, 53–122

Groller, M. von 1904: 'Grabungen im Legionslager von Carnuntum', *Der römische Limes in Österreich* **5**, 33–92

Groller, M. von 1905: 'Das Lager Carnuntum', *Der römische Limes in Österreich* **6**, 63–114

Groller, M. von 1906a: 'Das Legionslager Carnuntum', *Der römische Limes in Österreich* **7**, 47–82

Groller, M. von 1906b: 'Das Legionslager Lauriacum', *Der Römische Limes in Österreich* **7**, 41–6

Groller, M. von 1907a: 'Die Grabungen im Kastell Albing', *Der Römische Limes in Österreich* **8**, 1907, 157–72

Groller, M. von 1907b: 'Die Grabung im Lager Lauriacum', *Der Römische Limes in Österreich* **8**, 119–56

Groller, M. von 1908a: 'Die Grabung im Lager Lauriacum', *Der Römische Limes in Österreich* **9**, 87–116

Groller, M. von 1908b: 'Die Grabungen in Carnuntum', *Der römische Limes in Österreich* **9**, 1–80

Groller, M. von 1909a: 'Die Grabungen in Carnuntum', *Der römische Limes in Österreich* **10**, 1–78

Groller, M. von 1909b: 'Die Grabungen in Lauriacum', *Der Römische Limes in Österreich* **10**, 79–114

Groller, M. von 1910: 'Die Grabungen im Lager Lauriacum und dessen nächster Umgebung im Jahre 1908', *Der Römische Limes in Österreich* **11**, 1–60

Groller, M. von 1919a: 'Grabung im ager Lauriacum im Jahre 1911', *Der Römische Limes in Österreich* **13**, 1–32

Groller, M. von 1919b: 'Die Grabungen im Lager Lauriacum in den Jahren 1912 und 1913', *Der Römische Limes in Österreich* **13**, 117–264

Groller, M. von 1924a: 'Die Grabungen im Lager Lauriacum im Jahre 1914 und 1915', *Der Römische Limes in Österreich* **14**, 1–54

Groller, M. von 1924b: 'Die Grabungen im Lager Lauriacum im Jahre 1916', *Der Römische Limes in Österreich* **14**, 121–64

Groller, M. von 1925a: 'Die Grabungen im Lager Lauriacum im Jahre 1917', *Der Römische Limes in Österreich* **15**, 1–58

Groller, M. von 1925b: 'Die Grabungen im Lager Lauriacum im Jahre 1918', *Der Römische Limes in Österreich* **15**, 99–136

Groller, M. von 1925c: 'Die Grabungen im Lager Lauriacum im Jahre 1919', *Der Römische Limes in Österreich* **15**, 175–200

Grossmann, P., Jones, M., Noeske, H. -C., Le Quesne, C., and Sheehan, P. 1988: 'Zweiter Bericht über die britisch-deutschen Grabungen in der römischen Festung von Babylon-Alt-Kairo', *ArchAnz*, 173–207

Grossmann, P., Le Quesne, C., and Sheehan, P. 1994: 'Zur römischen Festung von Babylon-Alt-Kairo', *ArchAnz*, 271–87

Grote, K. 2004: 'Stützpunkt der römischen Expansionspolitik. Das Römerlager bei Hedemünden an der Werra. Ein Vorbericht', *Göttinger Jahrbuch* **52**, 5–12

Grote, K. 2005a: 'Römer an der Werra. Das Militärlager bei Hedemünden im südlichen Niedersachsen', *Archäologie in Niedersachsen* **8**, 113–17

Grote, K. 2005b: *Römerlager Hedemünden. Vor 2000 Jahren: Römer an der Werra*, Sydekum-Schriften zur Geschichte der Stadt Münden **34**, Hann-Münden

Grote, K. 2006a: 'Das Römerlager im Werratal bei Hedemünden (Ldkr. Göttingen). Ein neuentdeckter Stützpunkt der augusteischen Okkupationsvorstöße im rechtsrheinischen Germanien', *Germania* **84**, 27–59

Grote, K. 2006b: 'Die Römer an der Werra. Das Militärlager aus der Zeit der augusteischen Germanienfeldzüge bei Hedemünden', in Rohde, D. and Schneider, H. (eds.), *Hessen in der Antike. Die Chatten vom Zeitalter der Römer bis zur Alltagskultur der Gegenwart*, Kassel, 70–87

Grote, K. 2006c: 'Neue Forschungen und Funde im augusteischen Römerlager bei Hedemünden (Werra)', *Göttinger Jahrbuch* **54**, 5–19

Grote, K. 2007: 'Der römische Militärstützpunkt an der Werra bei Hedemünden', in Uelsberg, G. (ed.), *Krieg und Frieden. Kelten – Römer – Germanen. Begleitbuch zur gleichnamigen Ausstellung im Rheinischen Landesmuseum Bonn 21.6.2007–6.1.2008*, Bonn, 218–22

Grote, K. 2007a: 'Das Römerlager Hedemünden (Werra). Die archäologischen Arbeiten bis Jahresende 2007. 3. Vorbericht', *Göttinger Jahrbuch* **55**, 5–17

Grote, K. 2008: 'Der römische Stützpunkt bei Hedemünden an der Werra/Oberweser. Aspekte seiner logistischen Ausrichtung im Rahmen der augusteischen Germanienvorstöße', in Kühlborn, J.S. (ed.), *Rom auf dem Weg nach Germanien: Geostrategie, Vormarschtrassen und Logistik. Internationales Kolloquium in Delbrück-Anreppen vom 4. bis 6. November 2004*, Bodenaltertümer Westfalens **45**, Mainz, 323–43

Grünewald, M. 1981: *Die Kleinfunde des Legionslagers Carnuntum mit Ausnahme der Gefäßkeramik (Grabungen 1968–1974)*, Der römische Limes in Österreich **31**, Wien

Grünewald, M. 1983: *Die Funde aus dem Schutthügel des Legionslagers von Carnuntum . Die Baugrube Pingitzer*, Römische Limes in Österreich **32**, Wien

Grünewald, M. 1986: *Keramik und Kleinfunde des Legionslagers von Carnuntum: Grabungen 1976–1977*, Römische Limes in Österreich **34**, Wien

Gschwind, M. 2006: 'Raphaneae', *Jahresbericht 2005 des Deutschen Archäologischen Instituts. Archäologischer Anzeiger*, 285

Gschwind, M. 2007: 'Raphaneae', *Jahresbericht 2006 des Deutschen Archäologischen Instituts. Archäologischer Anzeiger*, 321–3

Gschwind, M. 2008a: 'Raphaneae (Syrien)', *Deutsches Archäologisches Institut, Orient-Abteilung. Aktuelle Forschungsprojekte*, 84–5

Gschwind, M. 2008b: 'Raphaneae', *Jahresbericht 2007 des Deutschen Archäologischen Instituts. Archäologischer Anzeiger*, 265–7

Gschwind, M. and Hasan, H. 2008: 'Raphaneae: Geophysical Survey Work conducted by the Syrian-German Cooperation Project in 2007', *Chronique Archéologique en Syrie* **3**, 203–16

Gschwind, M. and Hasan, H. (in press): 'The Legionary Fortress and Roman City Raphaneae: Topographical, Archaeological and Geophysical Survey Work conducted in 2005–2007', in Bartl, K. and al-Maqdissi, M. (eds.), *New Archaeological Prospections in the Middle Orontes Region. First Results of Archaeological Fieldwork. Orient-Archäologie*

Gschwind, M., Hasan, H., Grüner, A. and Hübner, W. 2009: 'Raphaneae. Report on the 2005 and 2006 Survey', *Zeitschrift für Orient-Archäologie* **2**, 234–89

Gschwind, M., Hasan, H. and Ramadan, J. (in press): 'Investigating the castra hiberna of legio III Gallica: Ground Penetrating Radar Surveys conducted in Raphaneae in 2008', *Chronique Archéologique en Syrie* **4**

Gudea, N. 1979: 'The defensive system of Roman Dacia', *Britannia* **10**, 63–87

Gudea, N. (ed.) 1999: *Roman Frontier Studies: Proceedings of the XVIIth International Congress of Roman Frontier Studies*, Zalău

Guest, P. and Gardner, A. 2008: *Caerleon Excavations in Priory Field, 2008: Interim Report*, <www.cf.ac.uk/hisar/archaeology/crc/files/Caerleon08_interimWEB.pdf> retrieved 13.11.09

Guest, P. and Young, T. 2006: 'Mapping Isca: geophysical investigation of Priory Field, Caerleon', *Archaeologia Cambrensis* **155**, 117–33

Gugl, C. and Kastler, R. (eds.) 2007: *Legionslager Carnuntum: Ausgrabungen 1968–1977*, Römische Limes in Österreich **45**, Wien

Haalebos, J.K. (ed.) 1995: *Castra und Canabae. Ausgrabungen auf der Hunerberg in Nijmegen*, Libelli Noviomagenses **3**, Nijmegen

Haalebos, J.K. 1991: 'Das grosse augusteische Lager auf dem Hunerberg in Nijmegen', in Aßkamp, R. and Berke, S. (eds.), *Die römische Okkupation nördlich der Alpen zur Zeit des Augustus: Kolloquium Bergkamen 1989*, Münster, 97–107

Haalebos, J.K. 1999: 'Das große Lager auf dem Hunerberg in Nijmegen (NL)', in Schlüter and Wiegels 1999, 381–99

Haalebos, J.K. 2002: 'Die fruheste Belegung des Hunerberges in Nijmegen', in Freeman et al. 2002, 403–14

Haalebos, J.K. 2006: 'Le grand camp sur le Hunerberg', in Reddé, M., Brulet, R., Fellmann, R., Haalebos, J.K., and Schnurbein, S. von (eds.), *Les fortifications militaires, l'architecture de la Gaule romaine*, Documents d'archéologie française **100**, Paris/Bordeaux, 350–2

Haensch, R. 2003: 'Mogontiacum als "Hauptstadt" der Provinz Germania superior', in Klein 2003, 71–86

Hall, R.A. 1997: *Excavations in the Praetentura: 9 Blake Street*, Archaeology of York AY**3/4**, York

Handendorn, A. 1998: 'Neues zum Lagerzentrum von Vindonissa – Ausgrabungen in der Breite 1996–1998', *Gesellschaft Pro Vindonissa. Jahresbericht*, 23–36

Hanel, N. 1995: *Vetera I. Die Funde aus den römischen Lagern auf dem Fürstenberg bei Xanten*, Rheinische Ausgrabungen **35**, Köln

Hanel, N. 2002: 'Zur Datierung der frühkaiserzeitlichen Militärlager von Novaesium (Neuss)', in Freeman et al. 2002, 497–50

Hanel, N. 2007: 'Military camps, *canabae*, and *vici*. The archaeological evidence', in Erdkamp, P. (ed.), *A Companion to the Roman Army*, Oxford, 395–416

Hanel, N. 2008: 'Die Militärlager von Vetera I und ihre Lagersiedlungen', in Müller et al. 2008, 93–107

Hanel, N. and Song, B. 2007: 'Neue Ergebnisse der Luftbildarchäologie zu den römischen Militärlagern Vetera Castra I auf dem Fürstenberg bei Xanten', *Germania* **85**, 349–58

Hanel, N., and Verstegen, U. 2005: 'Gestempelte Ziegel aus dem spätantiken Militärlager Köln-Deutz (Divitia)', *Rei Cretariae Romanae Fautores Acta* **39**, 187–91

Hanel, N., and Verstegen, U. 2006: 'Gestempelte Ziegel aus dem spätrömischen Kastell Divitia (Köln-Deutz)', *Kölner Jahrbücher* **39**, 2006, 213–52

Hanson, W.S. and Oltean, I.A. 2003: 'The identification of Roman buildings from the air: recent discoveries in Western Transylvania', *Archaeological Prospection* **10**, 101–17

Hanson, W.S. and Keppie, L.J.F. (eds.) 1980: *Roman Frontier Studies XII*, BAR International Series **71**, Oxford

Harl, O. 1979: *Vindobona. Das römische Wien*, Wiener Geschichtsbücher **21/22**, Wien

Harl, O. 1986: 'Wien/innere Stadt – Vindobona' in Kandler and Vetters 1986, 177–84

Harnecker, J. 1997: *Katalog der römischen Eisenfunde von Haltern*, Bodenaltertümer Westfalens **35**, Mainz

Hartmann, M. 1973a: 'Der Gesamtplan der Holzbauten von Vindonissa', *Jahresbericht der Gesellschaft Pro Vindonissa*, 43ff

Hartmann, M. 1973b: 'Untersuchungen am Keltengraben von Vindonissa', *Archäologische Korrespondenzblatt* **3**, 329–34

Hartmann, M. 1979/80: 'Vindonissa. Stand der Erforschung', *Jahresbericht der Gesellschaft Pro Vindonissa*, 5–22

Hartmann, M. 1980: 'Der augusteische Militärposten von Vindonissa', in Hanson and Keppie 1980, 553–66

Hartmann, M. 1982: 'Ein Helm vom Typ Weisenau aus Vindonissa', *Gesellschaft Pro Vindonissa. Jahresbericht*, 5–9

Hartmann, M. 1983: *Das römische Legionslager von Vindonissa*, Archäologische Führer der Schweiz **18**, Brugg

Hartmann, M. 1986: *Vindonissa. Oppidum – Legionslager – Castrum*, Brugg

Hartmann, M. and Speidel, M.A. 1991: 'Die Hilfstruppen des Windischer Heeresverbandes. Zur Besatzungsgeschichte von Vindonissa im 1. Jahrhundert n. Chr.', *Gesellschaft Pro Vindonissa. Jahresbericht*, 3–33

Hartmann, M. and Speidel, M.A. 2001: 'Zeugma am Euphrat', in *Schweizer Grabungen im Ausland*, Veröffentlichung der Schweizer Arbeitsgemeinschaft für Klassische Archäologie, 62–6

Hartmann, M. and Speidel, M.A. 2002: 'Roman Military Forts at Zeugma. A preliminary report', in Freeman et al. 2002, 259–68

Hartmann, M. and Speidel, M.A. 2003: 'The Roman army at Zeugma: recent research results', in Early, R., Crowther, C., Nardi, R., Önal, M., Abadie, C., Darmon, J.-P., Hartmann, M., and Speidel, M.A.,

Zeugma: Interim Reports, Rescue Excavations, Journal of Roman Archaeology Supplementary Series **51**, Portsmouth, 101–26

Hartmann, M. and Speidel, M.A. forthcoming a: 'Roman Military Forts at Zeugma IV', in *Kazi Sonuçlari Toplantisi* **24**

Hartmann, M. and Speidel, M.A. forthcoming b: 'The Roman army and its military installations at Zeugma', in Aylward, W. (ed.), *The Zeugma Publication of the Packard Humanities Institute*

Hartmann, M., Speidel, M.A., and Ergeç, R. 1999: 'Roman military forts at Zeugma', *Kazi Sonuçlari Toplantasi* **20**, 417–23

Hartmann, M., Speidel, M.A., Rüger, C., and Ergeç, R. 2000: 'Roman military forts at Zeugma II', *Kazi Sonuçlari Toplantisi* **21**, 337–40

Hartmann, M., Speidel, M.A., Rüger, C., and Ergeç, R. 2001: 'Roman military forts at Zeugma III', *Kazi Sonuçlari Toplantisi* **22**, 255–8

Hartmann, T. 1991: 'Die Firmalampen von Vindonissa', *Gesellschaft Pro Vindonissa. Jahresbericht*, 50–64

Hassall, M. 2000: 'Pre-Hadrianic legionary dispositions in Britain', in Brewer 2000, 51–67

Hassall, M.W. and Rhodes, J.F. 1974: 'Excavations at the New Market Hall, Gloucester, 1966–7', *Transactions of the Bristol and Gloucestershire Archaeological Society* **93**, 15–100

Hatt, J.-J. 1949a: 'Découverte de vestiges d'une caserne romaine dans l'angle du Castrum d'Argentorate: rapport provisoire sur les fouilles de l'église Saint-Etienne à Strasbourg (été 1948)', *Cahiers d'archéologie et d'histoire d'Alsace* **9**, 257–76

Hatt, J.-J. 1949b: 'Les récentes fouilles de Strasbourg (1947–1948), leurs résultats pour la chronologie d'Argentorate', *Comptes-rendus des séances de l'Académie des Inscriptions et Belles-Lettres* **93**, 40–6

Hatt, J.-J. 1949c: 'L'incendie d'Argentorate en 96–97 ap. J.-C., une révolte militaire ignorée dans les Champs Décumates, sous Nerva', *Comptes-rendus des séances de l'Académie des Inscriptions et Belles-Lettres* **93**, 132–6

Hatt, J.-J. 1953: 'Les fouilles de la ruelle Saint-Médard à Strasbourg', *Gallia* **11**, 225–48

Hatt, J.-J. 1956: 'Fouilles romaines sous l'église Saint-Étienne à Strasbourg et à Mackwiller', *Comptes-rendus des séances de l'Académie des Inscriptions et Belles-Lettres* **100**, 476–83

Hatt, J.-J. 1980: *Strasbourg romain*, Strasbourg

Hatt, J.-J. 1993: *Strasbourg-Argentorate*, Lyon

Haupt, D. and Horn, H.-G. (eds.) 1977: *Studien zu den Militärgrenzen Roms: Vorträge des 10. internationalen Limeskongresses in der Germania Inferior*, Bonner Jahrbücher **38**, Köln/Bonn

Hauser, A. 1884: 'Ausgrabungen in Carnuntum', *Archaeologisch-Epigraphische Mittheilungen* **8**, 55–9

Hauser, A., Schmidel, E., and Bormann, E. 1888: 'Ausgrabungen in Carnuntum', *Archaeologisch-Epigraphische Mittheilungen* **12**, 146–74

Hawkes, C. 1930: 'The Roman legionary fortress at Caerleon in Monmouthshire: Report on the excavations carried out in the eastern corner in 1929', *Archaeologia Cambrensis* **85**, 144–96

Heierli, J. 1905: *Vindonissa, Quellen und Literatur*, Argovia **31**, Aarau

Heighway, C. 1983: *The East and North Gates of Gloucester and Associated Sites: Excavations 1974–81*, Western Archaeological Trust Excavation Monograph **4**, Bristol

Heising, A. 2007: *Figlinae Mogontiacenses. Die römischen Töpfereien von Mainz*, Ausgrabungen und Forschungen **3**, Remshalden

Hejl, E. and Mosser, M. 2005: 'Ein Farbmörser aus dem Legionslager Vindobona', *Fundort Wien* **8**, 154–61

Helbaek, H. 1964: 'The Isca grain, a Roman plant introduction in Britain', *New Phytologist* **63**, 158–64

Hellenkemper, H. 1972–73: 'Oppidum und Legionslager in Köln. Überlegungen zur frührömischen Topographie', *Kölner Jahrbuch* **13**, 59–64

Hellenkemper, H. 1983: 'The Roman defences of Cologne – Colonia Claudia Ara Agrippinensium', in Maloney, J. and Hobley, B. (eds.), *Roman Urban Defences in the West*, CBA Research Report **51**, London, 20–8

Henderson, C.G. 1984: *Exeter Archaeology 1983/4*, Exeter

Henderson, C.G. 1988: 'Exeter (Isca Dumnoniorum)' in Webster 1988a, 91–119

Henderson, C.G. 1991: 'Aspects of the planning of the Neronian fortress of *legio II Augusta* at Exeter', in Maxfield and Dobson 1991, 73–83

Hernandez Guerra, L. 1994: *Inscripciones romanas en la provincia de Palencia*, Valladolid

Herrmann, F.X. 1992: 'Das Römerlager bei Marktbreit', *Gymnasium* **99**, 546–64

Héron de Villefosse, A. 1908: 'Le camp romain de Mirebeau', *Bulletin du Comité des Travaux Historiques et Scientifiques*, 133–5

Heuberger, S. 1909: *Aus der Baugeschichte Vindonissas und vom Verlauf ihrer Erforschung*, Argovia **33**, Aarau

Heydendorff, W. 1950: 'Zur Baugeschichte der römischen Legionslager Albing und Lauriacum', *Unsere Heimat* **21**, 72–6

Hild, F. 1968: *Supplementum epigraphicum zu CIL III: das pannonische Niederösterreich, Burgenland und Wien 1902–1968*, Wien

Hill, P. 2006: *The Construction of Hadrian's Wall*, Stroud

Hintermann, D. 1998: 'Gräber von Soldaten und Zivilistinnen im Umfeld des Legionslagers von Vindonissa', *Gesellschaft Pro Vindonissa. Jahresbericht*, 55–62

Hirschfeld, O. 1877: 'Ausgrabungen in Carnuntum', *Archaeologisch-Epigraphische Mittheilungen* **1**, 130–44

Hirschfeld, O. 1878: 'Ausgrabungen in Carnuntum', *Archaeologisch-Epigraphische Mittheilungen* **2**, 176–89

Hobley, B. 1967: 'An experimental reconstruction of a Roman military turf rampart', in Applebaum, S. (ed.), *Roman Frontier Studies 1967: Proceedings of the 7th International Congress, Tel Aviv*, Tel Aviv, 21–33

Hodgson, N. 2002: '"Where did they put the horses?" revisited: the recent discovery of cavalry barracks in the Roman forts at Wallsend and South Shields on Hadrian's Wall', in Freeman et al. 2002, 887–94

Hoffiller, V. and Saria, B. 1938: *Antike Inschriften aus Jugoslawien. 1: Noricum und Pannonia Superior*, Zagreb

Hoffmann, B. 1995: 'The quarters of legionary centurions of the Principate', *Britannia* **26**, 107–51

Hoffmann, B. 1997: 'Zenturionenquartiere in römischen Legionslagern', in Groenman-van Wateringe et al. 1997, 195–9

Hoffmann, B. 2002a: 'Some thoughts on the presence and absence of soldiers in fourth-century Chester', in Carrington 2002a, 79–88

Hoffmann, B. 2002b: 'The rampart buildings of Roman legionary fortresses', in Freeman et al. 2002, 895–900

Holbrook, N. and Bidwell, P.T. 1991: *Roman Finds from Exeter*, Exeter Archaeological Reports **4**, Exeter

Holbrook, N. and Bidwell, P.T. 1992: 'Roman pottery from Exeter 1980–1990', *Journal of Roman Pottery Studies* **5**, 35–80

Holbrook, N. and Fox, A. 1987: 'Excavations in the legionary fortress at Bartholomew Street East, Exeter 1959', *Devon Archaeological Society Proceedings* **45**, 23–57

Honigmann, E. 1931: 'Sura (1)', in *Paulys Realencyclopädie der classischen Altertumswissenschaft* **4A**, 953–960

Horváth, M. 1985: *Aquincum*, Budapest

Houben, P. 1839: *Denkmaeler von Castra Vetera und Colonia Traiana in Ph. Houben's Antiquarium zu Xanten*, Xanten

Howard-Davies, C. 2009: *The Carlisle Millennium Project. Excavations in Carlisle, 1998–2001. Volume 2: The Finds*, Lancaster Imprints **15**, Lancaster

Howell, R. 2000: 'The demolition of the roman tetrapylon in Caerleon: an erasure of memory?', *Oxford Journal of Archaeology* **19**, 387–95

Hurst, H. 1972: 'Excavations at Gloucester, 1968–71: first interim report', *Antiquaries Journal* **52**, 24–69

Hurst, H. 1974: 'Excavations at Gloucester, 1971–73: second interim report', *Antiquaries Journal* **54**, 8–52

Hurst, H. 1976: 'Glevum, a colonia in the west country', in Branigan, K. and Fowler, P. (eds.), *The Roman West Country*, London, 63–80

Hurst, H. 1986: *Gloucester: The Roman and Later Defences*, Gloucester Archaeological Reports **2**, Gloucester

Hurst, H. 1988: 'Gloucester (Glevum)', in Webster 1988a, 48–73

Ilakovac, B. 1984: *Burnum II. Der römische Aquadukt Plavno Polje – Burnum, Bericht über die Forschungen 1973 und 1974*, Wien

Ilisch, P. 1999: 'Die Münzen aus den römischen Militäranlagen in Westfalen', in Schlüter and Wiegels 1999, 279–91

Illarregui, E. 1999: 'La Legio IIII Macedonica a través de los materiales arqueológicos', *Regio Cantabrorum*, 179–84

Illarregui, E. 2002: 'Asentamientos militares de Herrera de Pisuerga y su entorno', *Arqueología Militar*, 155–66

Isaac, B. and Roll, I. 1979: 'Legio II Traiana in Judaea ', *ZPE* **33**, 149–56

Ivanišević, V. and Nikolić-Đorđević, S. 1997: 'Novi tragovi antičkih fortifikacija u Singidunumu – lokalitet Knez Mihailova 30 (New traces of Roman fortification in Singidunum: 30 Knez Mihailova Street site)', *Singidunum* **1**, 65–150

Ivanov, R. 1993: 'Zur Frage der Planung und der Architektur der romischen Militarlager', *Bulgarian Historical Review* **1**, 3–4

Ivanov, T. 1998: *Ulpia Oescus = Ulpiia Eskus: rimski i rannovizantiiški grad*, Sofia

Jacobi, H. 1996: *Mogontiacum – Das römische Mainz*, Mainz

James, S. 2004: *The Excavations at Dura-Europos Conducted by Yale University and the French Academy of Inscriptions and Letters, 1928 to 1937. Final Report VII: the Arms and Armour and Other Military Equipment*, London

Jandl, M. and Mosser, M. 2008: 'Befunde im Legionslager Vindobona. Teil IV: Vallum, fabrica und Kasernen in der westlichen retentura – Vorbericht zu den Grabungen Am Hof im Jahr 2007', *Fundort Wien* **11**, 4–35

Janon, M. 1973: 'Recherches à Lambèse', *Antiquités Africaines* **7**, 193–254

Janon, M. 2005: *Lambèse – Capitale militaire de l'Afrique romaine*, Nantes

Jilek, S. 1991: 'Die Kleinfunde aus dem Auxiliarkastell von Carnuntum', in Maxfield and Dobson 1991, 230–1

Jilek, S. 1994: 'Ein Zerstörungshorizont aus der 2. Hälfte des 2. Jhs. n. Chr. im Auxiliarkastell von Carnuntum', in Friesinger, H., Tejral, J., and Stuppner, A. (eds.), *Markomannenkriege – Ursache und Wirkungen*, Brno, 387–406

Jilek, S. 2005: 'Militaria aus einem Zerstörungshorizont im Auxiliarkastell von Carnuntum', *Carnuntum Jahrbuch 2005*, 165–80

Jobst, W. 1983: *Provinzhauptstadt Carnuntum. Österreichs größte archäologische Landschaft*,Wien

Johnson, J.S. 1970: 'The date of the construction of the Saxon Shore fort at Richborough', *Britannia* **1**, 240–8

Johnson, J.S. 1979: *The Roman Forts of the Saxon Shore*, ed. 2, London

Johnson, J.S. 1981: 'The construction of the Saxon Shore fort at Richborough', in Detsicas, A. (ed.), *Collectanea Historica: Essays in Memory of Stuart Rigold*, Maidstone, 23–31

Johnson, P. and Haynes, I. 1996: *Architecture in Roman Britain*, CBA Research Report **94**, York

Jones, A. 2003–4: 'Some unusual Roman antefixes from Chester', *Journal of the Chester Archaeological Society* **78**, 23–47

Jones, B. 1982: 'Scapula, Paullinus or Agricola?', *Popular Archaeology* **3:7**, 16–21

Jones, M. 1988: 'Lincoln (Lindum)', in Webster 1988a, 145–66

Jones, M.J. 1975: *Roman Fort Defences to A.D.117*, BAR British Series **21**, Oxford

Jones, M.J. 1980: *The Defences of the Upper Roman Enclosure*, The Archaeology of Lincoln **7.1**, Lincoln

Jones, M.J. and Gilmour, B. 1980: 'Lincoln, *principia* and forum: a preliminary report', *Britannia* **11**, 61–72

Jones, M.J., Stocker, D., and Vince, A. 2003: *The City by the Pool: Assessing the Archaeology of the City of Lincoln*, Lincoln Archaeology Studies **10**, Oxford

Kaba, M. 1986: 'Die "Thermae Maiores" in Aquincum', in Unz 1986, 336–40

Kaba, M. 1991: 'Die rekonstruierten und restaurierten "Thermae Maiores" der legio II Adiutrix', in Maxfield and Dobson 1991, 232–6

Kaba, M. and Szentpétery, T. 1987: *Thermae maiores. Das große Bad des Legionslagers von Aquincum, Budapest III*, Budapest

Kabakcieva, G. 1999: 'Neue Angaben zum frührömischen Legionslager am Oescus-Fluss (Nordbulgarien). Grabungsergebnisse 1995–1996', in Gudea 1999, 487–94

Kaiser, M. 1994: 'Neuere Forschungsergebnisse zur Geschichte der römischen Militäranlagen in Neuss', in *Fund und Deutung. Neuere archäologische Forschungen im Kreis Neuss*, Veröffentlichungen des Kreisheimatbundes Neuss e.V. **5**, Neuss, 64–72

Kaiser, M. 2005: 'Ein Satyrkopf aus dem römischen Legionslager von Neuss', in Horn, H.G., Hellenkemper, H., and Isenberg, G. (eds.), *Von Anfang an. Archäologie in Nordrhein-Westfalen, Begleitbuch zur Landesausstellung Köln 13. März – 28. August 2005*, Schriften zur Bodendenkmalpflege in Nordrhein-Westfalen **8**, Köln, 437

Kalinka, E. 1906: *Antike Denkmäler in Bulgarien*, Wien

Kandler, M. 1974: 'Die Ausgrabungen im Legionslager Carnuntum 1968–1973. Eine vorläufige Zusammenfassung', *AnzWien* **111**, 27–40

Kandler, M. 1976: 'KG Bad Deutsch-Altenburg, Gem. Bad Deutsch-Altenburg, BH Bruck an der Leitha', *FÖ* **15**, 250–252, 257, 260

Kandler, M. 1977: 'Legionslager und canabae von Carnuntum', in Temporini, H. (ed.), *Aufstieg und Niedergang der römischen Welt* **II.6**, 626–60

Kandler, M. 1978: 'Zu den Innenbauten des Legionslagers', in *Vindobona – die Römer im Wiener Raum. 52. Sonderausstellung des Historischen Museums der Stadt Wien*, Wien, 90–100

Kandler, M. 1979: 'Zu den Grabungen F. Lorgers im Legionslager Ločica (=Lotschitz)', *Arheološki Vestnik* **30**, 172–207

Kandler, M. 1980: 'Archäologische Beobachtungen zur Baugeschichte des Legionslagers Carnuntum am Ausgang der Antike', in Wolfram, H. and Daim, F. (eds.), *Die Völker an der mittleren und unteren Donau im fünften und sechsten Jahrhundert, Berichte des Symposions der Kommission für Frühmittelalterforschung, Zwettl 1978*, Wien, 83–92

Kandler, M. 1986: 'Bad Deutsch-Altenburg – Carnuntum', in Kandler and Vetters 1986, 213–20

Kandler, M. (ed.) 1997: *Das Auxiliarkastell Carnuntum 2. Forschungen seit 1989*, Sonderschriften des Österreichischen Archäologischen Instituts **30**, Wien

Kandler, M. 1999: 'Neues zum Carnuntiner Auxiliarkastell', in Gudea 1999, 379–95

Kandler, M. 2006: 'Römische Reitereinheiten und ihr Lager in Carnuntum', in Humer, F. (ed.), *Legionslager und Druidenstab – Vom Legionslager zur Donaumetropole. Sonderausstellung Archäologisches Museum Carnuntinum, Bad Deutsch-Altenburg (2006)*, Bad Deutsch-Altenburg, 261–9

Kandler, M. and Vetters, H. (eds.) 1986: *Der römische Limes in Österreich. Ein Führer*, Wien

Kapusta, A.A. and Underwood, J. H. 2000: *A Fractographic Study of a Circa AD 83 Roman Nail*, Army Armament Research Development and Engineering Center, Close Combat Armaments Center, Benét Laboratories Memorandum Report ARCCB-MR-00007 <http://handle.dtic.mil/100.2/ADA387460> accessed 11.1.10

Kayser, F. 1994: *Recueil des inscriptions grecques et latines (non funéraires) d'Alexandrie impériale*, Cairo

Kemkes, M. and Scheuerbrand, J. (eds.) 1999: *Fragen zur römischen Reiterei. Kolloquiumsbericht zur Ausstellung 'Reiter wie Statuen aus Erz. Die römische Reiterei am Limes zwischen Patrouille und Parade' im Limesmuseum Aalen am 25./26.02.1998*, Stuttgart 1999

Kemmers, F. 2005: 'The coin finds from the Augustan legionary fortress at Nijmegen (The Netherlands): Coin circulation in the Lower Rhine area before Drusus' campaigns', in Alfaro, C., Marcos, C., and Otero, P. (eds.), *XIII Congreso Internacional de Numismática. Madrid 2003. Actas-Proceedings-Actes*, Madrid, 987–90

Kennedy, D.L. 1978: 'Some observations on the Praetorian Guard', *Ancient Society* **9**, 275–301

Kennedy, D. (ed.) 1998a: *The Twin Towns of Zeugma on the Euphrates. Rescue Work and Historical Studies*, JRA Supplementary Series **27**, Ann Arbor

Kennedy, D. 1998b: 'Miscellaneous artefacts', in Kennedy 1998a, 129–38

Kennedy, D.L. 2000: *The Roman Army in Jordan*, London

Kennedy, D. and Falahat, R. 2008: '*Castra Legionis VI Ferratae*: a building inscription for the legionary fortress at Udruh near Petra', *Journal of Roman Archaeology* **21**, 150–69

Kennedy, D.L. and Riley, D.N. 1990: *Rome's Desert Frontier from the Air*, London

Kenward, H.K., Hall, A.R., and Jones, A.K.G. 1986: *Environmental Evidence from a Roman Well and Anglian Pits in the Legionary Fortress*, Archaeology of York **14/5**, York

Keppie, L. 1984: *The Making of the Roman Army from Empire to Republic*, London

Kerdő, K. 1990: 'Forschungen im nördlichen Teil des retentura des Legionslagers des 2-3. Jh..s von Aquincum in den Jahren 1983-84', in Vetters and Kandler 1990, 703-7

Kermorvant, A., Leblanc, J., and Lenoir, M. 2000: 'Bosra (Syrie): le camp de la légion IIIe Cyrénaïque. Chronique', *Mélanges de l'école française de Rome* **112**, 496-502

Killick, A.C. 1982: 'Udruh, 1980 and 1981 seasons', *Annual of the Department of Antiquities of Jordan* **26**, 415-16

Killick, A.C. 1983a: 'Udruh, 1980, 1981, 1982 seasons, a preliminary report', *Annual of the Department of Antiquities of Jordan* **27**, 231-44

Killick, A.C. 1983b: 'Udruh. The frontier of an empire: 1980 and 1981 seasons, a preliminary report', *Levant* **15**, 110-31

Killick, A.C. 1986a: 'Udruh and the southern frontier', in Freeman, P.W.M. and Kennedy, D.L. (eds.), *The Defence of the Roman and Byzantine East*, BAR **S297**, Oxford, 431-46

Killick, A.C. 1986b: 'Udruh – eine antike Statte vor den Toren Petras', in Lindner, M. (ed.), *Petra: neue Ausgrabungen und Entdeckungen*, Bad Windsheim, 44-57

Killick, A.C. 1989: 'Udhruh', in Homes-Fredericq, D. and Hennessy, J.B. (eds.), *Archaeology of Jordan* **II.2**, Leuven, 576-80

Klein, M.J. (ed.) 2003: *Die Römer und ihr Erbe. Fortschritt durch Innovation und Integration*, Mainz

Knight, J.K. 1964: 'Excavations in Cold Bath Road, Caerleon', *Archaeologia Cambrensis* **113**, 41-7

Knight, J.K. 2003: *Caerleon Roman Fortress*, ed.3, Cardiff

Knörzer, K.-H. 1970: *Römerzeitliche Pflanzenfunde aus Neuss*, Limesforschungen **10**, Berlin

Kocsis, L. 1986: 'Ein neugefundener römischer Helm aus dem Legionslager von Aquincum', in Unz 1986, 350-4

Kocsis, L. 1989: 'Inschriften aus dem Mithras-Heiligtum des Hauses des tribunus laticlavius im Legionlager von Aquincum aus dem 2.-3. Jahrhundert', *Acta Archaeologica Academiae Scientiarum Hungarica* **41**, 81-92

Kocsis, L. 1990: 'Zur Periodisierung des Hauses des tribunus laticlavius im Legionslager von Aquincum', in Vetters and Kandler 1990, 709-14

Kocsis, L. 1991: 'A tribunus laticlaviusok háza az aquincumi 2-3. sz-i legiotáborban (Előzetes jelentés) (Das Haus der tribuni laticlavii aus dem Legionslager von 2-3. Jh. in Aquincum (Vorbericht))', *Budapest Régiségei* **28**, 117-97

Kocsis, L. 2001: 'Die Südostecke des Legionslagers von Aquincum aus dem 2.-3. Jahrhundert und der daran angrenzende Mauerabschnitt der spätrömischen Festung (Bericht)', *Budapest Régiségei* **34**, 71-8

Koenen, C. 1904: 'Beschreibung von Novaesium', *Bonner Jahrbücher* **111/112**, 97-242

Koepp, F., Ritterling, E., Schuchhardt, C., Loeschcke, S., and Dahm, D. 1909: Die römische Niederlassung bei Haltern, Mitteilungen der Altertumskommission für Westfalen **2**, Münster

Kolbe, H.-G. 1974: 'Die Inschrift am Torbau der Principia im Legionslager von Lambaesis', *Römische Mitteilungen* **81**, 281-300

Kolendo, J. 1980: 'Le rôle du primus pilus dans la vie religieuse de la légion. En rapport avec quelques inscriptions des principia de Novae', *Archeologia* **31**, 49-60

Kolendo, J. 1988: 'Les nouvelles inscriptions des primi pili de Novae', *Archeologia* **39**, 91-103

Kolendo, J. 2001: 'Inscription d'un soldat originaire de Clunia découverte à Novae (Mésie Inférieure)', *Gerión* **19**, 525-31

Kolendo, J. 2002: 'Trzy stele z napisami malowanymi z Novae', *Novensia* **13**, 35-48

Kolendo, J. 2003: 'Images d'oiseaux sur une stèle de Novae. Remarques préliminaires', *Novensia* **14**, 67-76

Kolendo, J. and Bozilova, V. 1997: *Inscriptions grecques et latines de Novae (Mésie inférieure)*, Bordeaux

Kondić, V. 1961: 'Singidunum – Castra Tricornia', *Limes u Jugoslaviji* **1**, 117-23

Konrad, M. 2005: *Die Ausgrabungen unter dem Niedermüster zu Regensburg*, Münchner Beiträge zur Vor- und Frühgeschichte **57**, München

Konrad, M. 2006: 'Regensburg. Vom römischen Militärlager zur mittelalterlichen Stiftskirche. Archäologie unter dem Niedermünster zu Regensburg', *Akademie Aktuell, Zeitschrift der Bayerischen Akademie der Wissenschaften* **18**, 38-45

Konrad, M. 2009: 'Aspekte der Kontinuität im Legionslager Regensburg', in Morillo et al. 2009, 1297–1308

Korać, M. and Pavlović, R. 2004: 'Application of remote sensing in the Roman Town and Legionary Camp of Viminacijum', MECEO, Beograd

Koščević, R. 2003: 'Antičke staklene posude iz Siscije (Antique glass vessels from Siscia)', *Prilozi* **20**, 89–93

Kovács, P. and Szabó, Á. (eds.) 2009a: *Studia Epigraphica Pannonica 2*, Budapest

Kovács, P. and Szabó, Á. 2009b: *Tituli Aquincenses*, Budapest

Kovalevskaja, L.A., Tomas, A., and Sarnowski, T. 2000: 'Flasze gliniane z principia w Novae', *Novensia* **12**, 107–26

Kowalski, S.P. 1994: 'The Praetorium of the Camp of Diocletian in Palmyra', *Studia palmyreńskie* **9**, 39–70

Kowalski, S.P. 1998: 'The camp of legio I Illyricorum in Palmyra', *Novensia* **10**, 189–209

Kropatscheck, G. 1909: 'Mörserkeulen und Pila Muralia', *Jahrbuch des Kaiserlich Deutschen Archäologischen Instituts* **23**, 79–93

Krüger, M.-L. 1967: *Die Rundskulpturen des Stadtgebietes von Carnuntum*, CSIR Österreich **1.2**, Wien

Krüger, M.-L. 1970: *Die Reliefs des Stadtgebietes von Carnuntum I*, CSIR Österreich **1.3**, Wien

Krüger, M.-L. 1972: *Die Reliefs des Stadtgebietes von Carnuntum II*, CSIR Österreich **1.4**, Wien

Krunić, S. 2005: 'Roman lamps from Singidunum', *Singidunum* **4**, 45–104

Kucan, D. 1981: 'Pflanzenreste aus dem Römerlager Oberaden', *Zeitschrift für Archäologie* **15**, 149–62

Kucan, D. 1984: 'Der erste römerzeitliche Pfefferfund – nachgewiesen im Legionslager Oberaden (Stadt Bergkamen)', *Ausgrabungen und Funde in Westfalen-Lippe* **2**, 51–6

Kucan, D. 1992: 'Die Pflanzenfunde aus dem römischen Militärlager Oberaden', in Kühlborn 1992, 237–65

Kühlborn, J.-S. 1989: 'Oberaden', in Trier, B. (ed.), *2000 Jahre Römer in Westfalen. Ausstellungskatalog*, Mainz, 44–51

Kühlborn, J.-S. 1990: 'Die augusteischen Militärlager an der Lippe', in Horn, H.-G. (ed.), *Archäologie in Nordrhein-Westfalen. Geschichte im Herzen Europas*, Mainz, 169–86

Kühlborn, J.-S. 1991: 'Die Lagerzentren der römischen Militärlager von Oberaden und Anreppen', in Asskamp, R. and Berke, S. (eds.), *Die römische Okkupation nördlich der Alpen zur Zeit des Augustus: Kolloquium Bergkamen 1989*, Bodenaltertümer Westfalens **26**, Münster, 129–40

Kühlborn, J.-S. 1992: *Das Römerlager in Oberaden III. Die Ausgrabungen im nordwestlichen Lagerbereich und weitere Baustellenuntersuchungen der Jahre 1962–1988*, Bodenaltertümer Westfalens **27**, Münster

Kühlborn, J.-S. 1995: 'Die Grabungen in den westfälischen Römerlagern Oberaden und Anreppen', in Horn, H.-G. (ed.), *Ein Land macht Geschichte. Archäologie in Nordrhein-Westfalen*, Mainz, 203–9

Kühlborn, J.-S. 1999: 'Antike Berichte durch Ausgrabungen bestätigt', *Archäologie in Deutschland* **3**, 6–12

Kühlborn, J.-S. 2000: 'Schlagkraft. Die Feldzüge unter Augustus und Tiberius in Nordwestdeutschland', in Wamser et al. 2000, 27–37

Kühlborn, J.-S. 2005: 'Die Grabungen in den westfälischen Römerlagern', in Horn, H.-G., Hellenkemper, H., and Isenberg, G. (eds.), *Von Anfang an. Archäologie in Nordrhein-Westfalen, Begleitbuch zur Landesausstellung Köln 13. März – 28. August 2005*, Schriften zur Bodendenkmalpflege in Nordrhein-Westfalen **8**, Köln, 119–27

Kühlborn, J.-S. 2006: 'Delbrück/Anreppen', in Reddé, M. et al. (eds.), *L'architecture de la Gaule romaine. Les fortifications militaires*, Paris/Bordeaux, 261–3

Kühlborn, J.-S. 2007: 'Zwischen Herrschaft und Integration. Die Zeugnisse der Archäologie', in Wiegels, R. (ed.), *Die Varusschlacht. Wendepunkt der Geschichte?*, Stuttgart, 65–94

Kühlborn, J.-S. 2008: *Oberaden, Stadt Bergkamen, Kreis Unna, und Beckinghausen, Stadt Lünen, Kreis Unna*, Römerlager in Westfalen **3**, Münster

Künzl, E. 2005: 'Aesculapius im Valetudinarium', *Archäologisches Korrespondenzblatt* **35**, 55–64

Kütter, J. 2008: *Graffiti auf römischer Gefäßkeramik aus Neuss*, Aachen

Kütter, J. and Pause, C. 2006: *Geritzt und gestempelt. Schriftzeugnisse aus dem römischen Neuss, Begleitband zur Ausstellung im Clemens-Sels-Museum Neuss 2006*, Neuss

Kunisz, A. 1987: *Le trésor d'antoniniens et de folles des principia de la légion de Novae*, Warszawa

Kuzmová, K. 1999: 'Brigetio und sein Brückenkopf vom Aspekt der Sigillata Versorgung', in Gudea 1999, 699–704

LaBaume, P. 1973: 'Oppidum Ubiorum und Zweilegionslager in Köln', *Gymnasium* **80**, 333–47

LaBaume, P. 1980: 'Zur Lage von Oppidum Ubiorum und Zweilegionslager', in *Führer zu vor- und frühgeschichtlichen Denkmälern 37/1: Köln I,1: Einführende Aufsätze*, Mainz, 53–61

Ladenbauer-Orel, H. 1984: 'Mittelalterliche Quellen zur römischen Lagermauer von Vindobona', *Wiener Geschichtsblätter* **39**/2, 75–9

Lambert, P. 2001: *Fortifications and the Synagogue: The Fortress of Babylon and the Ben Ezra Synagogue, Cairo*, ed.2, Chicago

Lander, J. and Parker, S. T. 1982: 'Legio IV Martia and the legionary camp at El-Lejjun', *Byzantinische Forschungen* **8**, 185–210

Laur-Belart, R. 1959: *Limes-Studien: Vortrage des 3. Internationalen Limes-Kongress in Rheinfelden/Basel, 1957*, Basel

Lazar, I. 2006: *Ilovica pri Vranskem*, Ljublijana

Le Bohec, Y., 1977: 'Le pseudo-camp des auxiliaires à Lambèse', in *Armée romaine et Provinces* **1**, 71–85

Le Bohec, Y. 1989: *La Troisième Légion Auguste*, Paris

Le Bohec, Y, 1994: *The Imperial Roman Army*, London

Le Bohec Y. 1999: 'Recherches sur les terrains d'exercice de l'armée romaine sous le Haut-Empire', *Bulletin des Antiquités Luxembourgeoises* **27**, 79–95

Le Bohec, Y. (ed.) 2003: *Les discours d'Hadrien à l'armée d'Afrique*, Paris

Le Bohec, Y. 2008: 'L'architecture militaire à Lambèse (Numidie)', *Archäologisches Korrespondenzblatt* **38:2**, 247–62

Le Bohec, Y. and Wolff, C. (eds.) 2000: *Les légions de Rome sous le Haut-Empire. Actes du IIème congrès de Lyon (17–19 septembre 1998) sur l'armée romaine*, Paris

Leblanc, J. and Lenoir, M. 1999: 'Le camp de la légion IIIe Cyrénaïque. Chronique', *Mélanges de l'école française de Rome* **111**, 527–9

Leckebusch, J. 1998: 'Die Herkunft der Kochtöpfe von Dangstetten', *Fundberichte aus Baden-Württemberg* **22**, 377–427

Lee, J.E. 1862: *Isca Silurum, Or, An Illustrated Catalogue of the Museum of Antiquities at Caerleon*, London

Legionslager Vindobona <http://www.archaeologie-wien.at/roemer/legionslager.htm> accessed 26.11.09

Lehner, H. 1904: 'Die Einzelfunde von Novaesium', *Bonner Jahrbücher* **111/112**, 243–418

Lehner, H. 1918: *Die antiken Steindenkmäler des Provinzialmuseums in Bonn*, Bonn

Lehner, H. 1926: *Das Römerlager Vetera bei Xanten. Ein Führer durch die Ausgrabungen des Bonner Provinzialmuseums*, Bonn

Lehner, H. 1927: 'Ausgrabung in Vetera bei Xanten 1926', *Gnomon* **3**, 612–16

Lehner, H. 1930: *Vetera. Die Ergebnisse der Ausgrabungen des Bonner Provinzialmuseums bis 1929*, Berlin & Leipzig

Lehner, H. 1936: *Vetera bei Xanten*, Düsseldorf

Lenoir, M. 1998: 'Bosra (Syrie): le camp de la légion IIIe Cyrénaïque. Chronique', *Mélanges de l'école française de Rome* **110**, 523–8

Lenoir, M. 2002: 'Le camp de la légion IIIe Cyrenaica a Bostra. Recherches recentes', in Freeman et al. 2002, 175–84

Lepper, F. and Frere, S. 1988: *Trajan's Column: A New Edition of the Cichorius Plates*, Gloucester

Le Quesne, C. 1999: *Excavations at Chester. The Roman and Later Defences, Part 1: Investigations 1978–1990*, Archaeological Service Excavation and Survey Report **11**, Chester

Lewis, B. 1891: 'The Roman antiquities of Augsburg and Ratisbon', *Archaeological Journal* **48**, 137–61, 396–415

Lewis, C.T. and Short, C. 1879: *A Latin Dictionary. Founded on Andrews' Edition of Freund's Latin Dictionary*, Oxford <http://www.perseus.tufts.edu/hopper/text?doc=Perseus:text:1999.04.0059>

Lewis, J.M. 1957: 'A centurial stone from Caerleon', *Archaeologia Cambrensis* **106**, 121–2

Lieb, H. 1998: 'Vindonissa und die römischen Lagerstädte', *Gesellschaft Pro Vindonissa. Jahresbericht*, 63–6

Lightfoot, C.S. 1990a: 'Roman legions at Satala, a frontier fortress in north-east Turkey', *Image* **29**, 26–7

Lightfoot, C.S. 1990b: 'Satala survey, 1989', *Anatolian Studies* **40**, 13–16

Lightfoot, C.S. 1998: 'Survey work at Satala, A Roman legionary fortress in north-east Turkey', in Matthews, R. (ed.), *Ancient Anatolia. Fifty Years' Work by the British Institute of Archaeology at Ankara*, London, 273–84

Liz, J. and Amaré, M.T. 1993: *Necrópolis tardorromana del Campus de Vegazana y las producciones latericias de la Legio VII Gemina*, León

Lloyd-Morgan, G. 1987: 'Professor Robert Newstead and finds of Roman military metalwork from Chester', in Dawson, M. (ed.), *Roman Military Equipment: the Accoutrements of War. Proceedings of the Third Roman Military Equipment Research Seminar*, BAR International Series **336**, Oxford, 85–97

Lőrincz, B. 1975: 'Zur Erbauung des Legionslagers von Brigetio', *Acta Archaeologica Academiae Scientiarum Hungarica* **27**, 347–52

Lőrincz, B. 2000a: 'Legio I Adiutrix', in Le Bohec and Wolff 2000, 151–8

Lőrincz, B. 2000b: 'Legio II Adiutrix', in Le Bohec and Wolff 2000, 159–68

Lőrincz, B. 2000c: 'Legio II Italica', in Le Bohec and Wolff 2000, 145–9

Lőrincz, B. 2001: *Die römischen Hilfstruppen in Pannonien während der Prinzipatszeit. I: Die Inschriften*, Wien

Loeschcke, S 1909: 'Keramische Funde in Haltern', *Mitteilungen der Altertumskommission für Westfalen* **5**, 101–322

Loeschcke, S. 1919: *Lampen aus Vindonissa*, Zurich

Lorger, F. 1919: 'Vorläufiger Bericht über Ausgrabungen nächst Lotschitz bei Cilli', *Jahreshefte des Österreichischen archäologischen Institutes in Wien* **19–20** (Beiblatt), 107–34

Ludowici, W. 1927: *Stempel-Namen und Bilder römischer Töpfer, Legions-Ziegel-Stempel, Formen von Sigillata- und anderen Gefassen aus meinen Ausgrabungen in Rheinzabern 1901–1914, Katalog 5*, Speyer

Lugli, G. 1969: *Studi e ricerche su Albano archeologica 1914–1967*, ed. 2, Albano Laziale

Lyne, M. 1994: 'Late Roman helmet fragments from Richborough', *JRMES* **5**, 97–105

Lyne, M. 1999: 'Fourth century Roman belt fittings from Richborough', *JRMES* **10**, 103–13

MacAdam, H.I. 1989: 'Fragments of a Latin building inscription from Aqaba, Jordan', *ZPE* **79**, 163–72

MacGregor, A. 1976: *Finds from a Roman Sewer and an Adjacent Building in Church Street*, Archaeology of York **17/1**, York

Mackensen, M. 1997: 'Die castra hiberna der legio III Augusta in Ammaedara/Haïdra', *Römische Mitteilungen* **104**, 321–34

Macnab, N. 2000: 'More on the Roman fortress: a lift-pit excavation behind 3 Little Stonegate', *Interim: the Archaeology of York* **23(3)**, 31–46

McPeake, J.C., Bulmer, M., and Rutter, J.A. 1998: 'Excavations in the garden of No 1 Abbey Green, Chester, 1975–77: interim report', *Journal of the Chester Archaeological Society* **73**, 15–37

Madarassy, O. 1999: 'Canabae legionis II Adiutricis', in Gaál, A. (ed.), *Pannoniai kutatások. A Soproni Sándor emlékkonferencia előadásai. Bölcske, 1998. október 7*, Szekszárd, 69–75

Maier, F.B. 1993: 'Vindonissa: Rückblick auf die Feldarbeiten zwischen Herbst 1992 und Herbst 1993', *Gesellschaft Pro Vindonissa. Jahresbericht*, 59–66

Maier, F.B. 1995: 'Vindonissa: Rückblick auf die Feldarbeiten im Jahr 1995', *Gesellschaft Pro Vindonissa. Jahresbericht*, 29–35

Maier, F.B. 1996: 'Vindonissa: Rückblick auf die Feldarbeiten im Jahr 1996', *Gesellschaft Pro Vindonissa. Jahresbericht*, 39–46

Maier, F.B. 1997: 'Vindonissa: Rückblick auf die Feldarbeiten im Jahr 1997', *Gesellschaft Pro Vindonissa. Jahresbericht*, 77–86

Maier, F.B. 1998: 'Vindonissa: Rückblick auf die Feldarbeiten im Jahr 1998', *Gesellschaft Pro Vindonissa. Jahresbericht*, 99–110

Maier, F.B. 1999: 'Vindonissa: Rückblick auf die Feldarbeiten im Jahr 1999', *Gesellschaft Pro Vindonissa. Jahresbericht*, 73–9

Maier-Osterwalder, F.B. and Widmer, R. 1990: 'Die sogenannte "ältere" oder "frühere" römische Wasserleitung zum römischen Legionslager Vindonissa', *Gesellschaft Pro Vindonissa. Jahresbericht*, 43–56

Manning, W.H. 1975: 'Roman military timber granaries in Britain', *Saalburg-Jahrbuch* **32**, 105–29

Manning, W.H. 1977: 'Usk Roman legionary fortress', *Current Archaeology* **6**, 71–7

Manning, W.H. 1981: *Report on the Excavations at Usk Volume II: The Fortress Excavations 1968–1971*, Cardiff

Manning, W.H. 1997: 'The legionary fortress at Usk', *The Monmouthshire Antiquary* **13**, 37–42

Manning, W.H. 2000: 'The fortresses of Legio XX', in Brewer 2000, 75–6

Manning, W.H. 2002: 'Roman fortress studies: present questions and future trends', in Carrington 2002a, 1–6

Manning, W.H. and Scott, I.R. 1979: 'Roman timber military gateways in Britain and on the German frontier', *Britannia* **10**, 19–61

Manning, W.H. and Scott, I.R. 1989: *Report on the Excavations at Usk Volume IV. The Fortress Excavations 1972–1974 and Minor Excavations on the Fortress and Flavian Fort*, Cardiff

Mapelli, C., Nicodemi, W., Riva, R.F., Vedani, M., and Garibold, E. 2009: 'Nails of the Roman legionary at Inchtuthil', *La Metallurgia Italiana* (January), 51–8

Marcos Herran, F.J. 2002: *Vidrios romanos de Herrera de Pisuerga (Palencia)*, Palencia

Martin, C. 1995: 'The legionary hospital at Inchtuthil', *Britannia* **26**, 309–12

Martin Valls, R., Romero Carnicero, M.V. and Carretero Vaquero, S. 2002: 'Marcas militares en material de construcción de Petavonium', in Morillo Cerdán, A. (ed.), *Arqueología Militar Romana en Hispania*, Gladius Anejos **5**, Madrid, 137–54

Martinez Garcia, A.B. 1999: *El vidrio en el campamento romano del Ala II Flavia Hispanorum Civium Romanorum en Petavonium (Rosisnos de Vidriales)*, Zamora

Marvell, A. 1990: 'Recent work on the Neronian fortress at Usk, 1986–1988', *Trivium* **25**, 19–26

Marvell, A. 1996: 'Excavations at Usk 1986–1988', *Britannia* **27**, 51–110

Marvell, A.G. and Maynard, D.J. 1998: 'Excavations south of the legionary fortress at Usk, Gwent, 1994', *Britannia* **29**, 247–67

Marvell, A.G., Webster, P.V., Wilkinson, J.L., and Greep, S. 1998: 'Salvage finds from The Orchard, Usk', *Archaeology in Wales* **38**, 64–7

Mary, G.T. 1967: *Die südgallische Terra sigillata aus Neuss*, Limesforschungen **6**, Berlin

Mason, D.J.P. 1982: 'A group of Roman hypocaust pilae at the Keeper's Cottage, Oakmere', *Cheshire Archaeological Bulletin* **8**, 6–9

Mason, D.J.P. 1987: 'Chester: the canabae legionis', *Britannia* **18**, 143–68

Mason, D.J.P. 1988: '"Prata Legionis" in Britain', *Britannia* **19**, 163–90

Mason, D.J.P. 1996: 'An elliptical peristyle building in the fortress of Deva' in Johnson and Haynes 1996, 77–92

Mason, D.J.P. 2000: *Excavations at Chester. The Elliptical building: an Image of the Roman world? Excavations 1939 and 1963–4*, Archaeological Service Excavation and Survey Report **12**, Chester

Mason, D.J.P. 2001: *Roman Chester, City of the Eagles*, Stroud

Mason, D.J.P. 2002a: 'The construction and operation of a legionary fortress: logistical and engineering aspects', in Carrington 2002a, 89–112

Mason, D.J.P. 2002b: 'The foundation of the legionary fortress: Deva, the Flavians and imperial symbolism', in Carrington 2002a, 33–51

Mason, D.J.P. 2005: *Excavations at Chester: the Roman Fortress Baths, Excavation and Recording 1732–1998*, Archaeological Service Excavation and Survey Report **13**, Chester

Mason, H. and Macdonald, P. 1997: *The Roman Legionary Fortress at Caerleon in Gwent: Report on the Excavations of the Southern Defences Carried out in 1982*, Cardiff Studies in Archaeology Specialist Report No.**5**

Matthews, K.J. 1995: *Excavations at Chester. The Evolution of the Heart of the City: Investigations at 3–15 Eastgate Street 1990/1*, Archaeological Service Excavation and Survey Report 7, Chester

Maxfield, V.A. and Dobson, M.J. (eds.) 1991: *Roman Frontier Studies 1989. Proceedings of the XVth International Congress of Roman Frontier Studies*, Exeter

Medeleț, F. and Petrovszky, R. 1974: 'Cercetări arheologice în castrul roman de la Berzovia', *Tibiscus* **3**, 133–6

Meiggs, R. 1973: *Roman Ostia*, Oxford

Metcalf Dickinson, V.M. 1983: 'Salvage work at Caerleon, Gwent', *Glamorgan-Gwent Archaeological Trust Ltd Annual Report*, 64

Meyer-Freuler, C. 1989: *Das Praetorium und die Basilika von Vindonissa. Die Ausgrabungen im südöstlichen Teil des Legionslagers (Grabungen Scheuerhof 1967/68, Wallweg 1979 und Koprio 1980)*, Veröffentlichungen der Gesellschaft Pro Vindonissa **9**, Brugg

Meyer-Freuler, C. 1998: *Vindonissa Feuerwehrmagazin: die Untersuchungen im mittleren Bereich des Legionslagers*, Brugg

Meyer-Freuler, C. 2003: 'Vindonissa – Italische Terra Sigillata-Importe der Vorlagerzeit und frühen Lagerzeit aus der Sicht der Töpferstempel', *Rei Cretariae Romanae Fautorum Acta* 38, 357–60

Michałowski, K. 1960: *Palmyre, fouilles polonaises, 1959*, Warszawa-Paris

Michałowski, K. 1962: *Palmyre, fouilles polonaises, 1960*, Warszawa-Paris

Michałowski, K. 1963: *Palmyre, fouilles polonaises, 1961*, Warszawa-Gravenhage

Michałowski, K. 1964: *Palmyre, fouilles polonaises, 1962*, Warszawa-Gravenhage

Michałowski, K. 1966: *Palmyre, fouilles polonaises, 1963 et 1964*, Warszawa-Gravenhage

Mihailov, G. 1958–1970: *Inscriptiones Graecae in Bulgaria repertae, 1–4*, Sofia

Miletić, Ž. 2010a: 'Burnum. A military centre in the province of Dalmatia', in Radman-Livaja, I. (ed.), *Finds of the Roman Military Equipment in Croatia*, Zagreb, 113–41

Miletić, Ž. 2010b: 'The catalogue of finds', in Radman-Livaja, I. (ed.), *Finds of the Roman Military Equipment in Croatia*, Zagreb, 143–76

Miller, S. 1925: 'Roman York: excavations of 1925', *JRS* **15**, 176–94

Miller, S. 1928: 'Roman York: excavations of 1926–1927', *JRS* **18**, 61–99

Millett, M. 1982: 'Distinguishing between the Pes Monetalis and the Pes Drusianus: some problems', *Britannia* **13**, 315–20

Milner, N.P. 1996: *Vegetius: Epitome of Military Science*, Liverpool

Mirković, M. 1961: 'Fragmenti iz istorije rimskog Singidunuma', *Limes u Jugoslaviji* **1**, 109–15

Mirković, M. 1971: 'Sirmium – its history from the I century A.D. to 582 A.D.', *Sirmium* **1**, 5–90

Mirković, M. 1976: 'Singidunum et son territoire: introduction historique', in Mirković, M. and Dušanić, S., *Inscriptions de la Mésie Supérieure* 1, Beograd, 23–41

Mirković, M.B. 1997: 'Tri nova natpisa iz Singidunum (Three new inscriptions from Singidunum)', *Singidunum* **1**, 57–64

Mirković, M. 1999: 'New fragments of military diplomas from Viminacium', *ZPE* **126**, 249–54

Mirković, M.B. 2000: 'Ein Praefectus Castrorum (?) legionis IV Flaviae in Singidunum (Jedan praefectus castrorum (?)legije IV Flavia u Singidunumu)', *Singidunum* **2**, 7–10

Mirković M.B. 2005a: 'Bricks of the VI Herculia legion in Singidunum', *Singidunum* **4**, 111–15

Mirković M.B. 2005b: 'Legion IV Flavia and Alexander Severus', *Singidunum* **4**, 105–9

Mitford, T.B. 1974a: 'Bilotti's excavations at Satala', *Anatolian Studies* **24**, 221–44

Mitford, T.B. 1974b: 'Some inscriptions from the Cappadocian limes', *JRS* **64**, 160–75

Mitford, T.B. 1997: 'The Inscriptions of Satala (Armenia Minor)', *ZPE* **115**, 137–67

Mitford, T.H. 1980: 'Cappadocia and Armenia Minor', in Temporini, H. (ed.), *Aufstieg und Niedergang der römischen Welt* II.7.2, 169–228

Mócsy, A. 1962: 'Pannonia', *Paulys Realencyclopädie der classischen Altertumswissenschaft* Suppl. **9**, 515–776

Mócsy, A. 1974: *Pannonia and Upper Moesia*, London

Moga, M. 1971: 'Castrul Berzobis', *Tibiscus* **1**, 51–8

Moga, V. 1994: 'Castrul roman Apulum', *Apulum* **31**, 131–7

Moga, V. 1997: *Un secol de la debutul investigațiilor în Castrul roman de la Apulum*, Alba Iulia

Moga, V. 1999a: *Apulum – porta principalis dextra – a castrului Legiunii XIII Geminae*, Alba Iulia

Moga, V. 1999b: 'Descoperiri arheologice din poarta castrului Apulum', *Apulum* **36**, 215–24

Moga, V. 2002: 'Castrul roman de la Apulum, Editura Casa Cărții de Știință, Cluj, 1998', *Studii de Istorie a Banatului* **23–5** (1999–2001), 44–70

Monaghan, J. 1993: *Roman Pottery from the Fortress: 9 Blake Street*, Archaeology of York **16/7**, York

Monaghan, J. 1997: *Roman Pottery From York*, Archaeology of York **16/8**, York

Moore, D. 1970: *Caerleon: Fortress of the Legion*, Cardiff

Morgan, O. 1866: *Notice of a Tessellated Pavement Discovered in the Churchyard, Caerleon; Together with an Essay on Mazes and Labyrinths by Edward Trollope*, Monmouthshire & Caerleon Antiquarian Assoc., Newport

Morgan, O. 1877: 'Discovery of a tessellated pavement in the town of Caerleon, Monmouthshire', *Proceedings of the Society of Antiquaries of London*, 2nd ser., **7**, 219–23

Morillo, Á. 1992: *Cerámica romana de Herrera de Pisuerga (Palencia, España): las lucernas*, Santiago de Chile

Morillo, Á. 1996: 'Campamentos romanos en la Meseta Norte y el Noroeste: ¿un limes sin frontera?' in Fernández Ochoa, C. (ed.), *Los finisterres atlánticos en la antigüedad, época prerromana y romana (Coloquio internacional): homenaje a Manuel Fernández-Miranda*, Gijón, 77–84

Morillo, Á. 1999: *Lucernas romanas en la región septentrional de la Península Ibérica. Contribución al conocimiento de la implantación romana en Hispania*, Monographies Instrumentum **8**, Montagnac

Morillo, Á. 2000: 'La legio IIII Macedonica en la península ibérica. El campamento de Herrera de Pisuerga (Palencia)', in Le Bohec and Wolff 2000, 609–24

Morillo, Á. 2002: 'Conquista y estrategia: el ejército romano durante el periodo augusteo y julio-claudio en la región septentrional de la península ibérica', in Morillo, Á. (ed.), *Arqueología militar romana en Hispania*, Anejos de Gladius **5**, Madrid, 67–94

Morillo, Á. 2003: 'Los campamentos romanos de Astorga y León', *Espacio, tiempo y forma*, Serie II, Historia Antigua **16**, 83–110

Morillo, Á. 2007: 'Los campamentos romanos de Astorga y León', in Navarro, M. and Palao, J.J. (eds.), *Ville et territoire dans le bassin du Douro á l'époque romaine (2004)*, Bordeaux, 59–90

Morillo, Á. and Ángeles Sevillano, M. 2006: 'Astorga legionary fortress and Roman town', in Morillo and Aurrecoechea 2006, 290–8

Morillo, A. and Aurrecoechea, J. (eds.) 2006: *The Roman Army in Hispania. An Archaeological Guide*, León

Morillo, Á. and Fernández Ibáñez, C. 2001/2: 'Un aplique decorativo con inscripción militar procedente de Herrera de Pisuerga (Palencia, España)', *JRMES* **12/13**, 47–51

Morillo, Á. and García-Marcos, V. 2003: 'Legio VII Gemina and its Flavian fortress at León', *Journal of Roman Archaeology* **16**, 275–87

Morillo, Á. and García-Marcos, V. 2004: 'Arqueología romana en la ciudad de León: balance de dos décadas de excavaciones', in Blánquez, J. and Pérez Ruiz, M. (eds.), *Antonio García y Bellido. Miscelánea*, serie varia **5**, Madrid, 263–91

Morillo, Á. and García-Marcos, V. 2005: 'The defensive system of the legionary fortress of *VII gemina* at León (Spain). The *porta principalis sinistra*', in Visy 2005, 569–83

Morillo, Á. and García-Marcos, V. 2006a: 'Legio (León). Introducción histórica y arqueológica', in García-Bellido, M.P. (ed.), *Los campamentos romanos en Hispania (27 a. C.-192 d. C.). El abastecimiento de moneda*, Anejos de Gladius **9**, Madrid, 225–43

Morillo, Á. and García-Marcos, V. 2006b: 'León legionary fortress', in Morillo and Aurrecoechea 2006, 327–38

Morillo, Á. and García-Marcos, V. 2009: 'The Roman camps at León (Spain): state of the research and new approaches', in Morillo et al. 2009, 389–405

Morillo, Á., García-Marcos, V., and Fernández Ochoa, C. 2002: *Imágenes de Arqueología leonesa. Antonio García y Bellido y el Noroeste peninsular en la Antigüedad*, Valladolid

Morillo, Á. and Gómez Barreiro, M. 2006a: 'Herrera de Pisuerga (Palencia). Catálogo abreviado de monedas', in García-Bellido 2006, 422–40

Morillo, Á. and Gómez Barreiro, M. 2006b: 'Herrera de Pisuerga (Palencia). Circulación monetaria en Herrera de Pisuerga', in García-Bellido 2006, 338–421

Morillo, Á. and Gómez Barreiro, M. 2006c: 'Legio (León). Circulación monetaria en los campamentos romanos de León', in García-Bellido 2006, 258–98

Morillo, Á, Hanel, N., and Martin, E. 2009: *Limes XX. XXth International Congress of Roman Frontier Studies León (España), Septiembre, 2006*, Anejos de Gladius **13**, Madrid

Morillo, Á., Pérez-González, C. and Illarregui, E. 2006: 'Herrera de Pisuerga (Palencia). Cronologías estratigráficas', in García-Bellido 2006, 324–37

Moritz, B. 1889: *Zur antiken Topographie der Palmyrene*, Berlin

Morris, P. 1933–6: 'Report of the Exeter Excavation Committee', *Proceedings of the Devon Archaeological Exploration Society* **2**, 227–31

Mosser, M. 1998: 'Das Legionslager Vindobona – EDV-gestützt Erfassung neuer und alter Grabungen', *Fundort Wien* **1**, 74–88

Mosser, M. 1999: 'Befunde im Legionslager Vindobona. Teil I: Altgrabungen im Judenplatz und Umgebung', *Fundort Wien* **2**, 48–85

Mosser, M. 2001: 'Die Porta Principalis Dextra im Legionslager von Vindobona', in *Akten des 8. Österreichischen Archäologentag, 1999*, 145–52

Mosser, M. 2002a: 'Zivile und militärische Aspekte in der Nutzung des Legionslagerareals von Vindobona', in Borhy, L. (ed.), *Die norisch-pannonischen Städte und das römische Heer im Lichte der neuesten archäologischen Forschungen: II. Internationale Konferenz über Norisch-Pannonische Städte, Budapest-Aquincum, 11–14. September 2002*, Aquincum nostrum **2,3**, 159–80

Mosser, M. 2002b: 'Zur Präsentation des Legionslagers Vindobona im Rahmen der Science Week 2002', *Forum Archaeologiae* <http://homepage.univie.ac.at/~trinkle5/forum/forum0902/24lager.htm> accessed 26.11.09

Mosser, M. 2003: *Die Steindenkmäler der legio XV Apollinaris*, Wiener Archäologische Studien **5**, Wien

Mosser, M. 2004: 'Befunde im Legionslager Vindobona. Teil III: Das Lagergrabensystem', *Fundort Wien* **7**, 212–23

Mosser, M. 2005a: 'Die römischen Truppen in Vindobona', *Fundort Wien* **8**, 126–53

Mosser, M. 2005b: 'Das Legionslager von Vindobona', in Krinzinger, F. (ed.), *Vindobona. Beiträge zu ausgewählten Keramikgattungen in ihrem topographischen Kontext*, Archäologische Forschungen **12**, 11–18

Al-Mougdad, R., Blanc, P.-M., and Dentzer, J.-M. 1990: 'Un amphithéâtre à Bosra', *Syria* **67**, 201–4

Mouterde, R. 1949/50: 'A travers l'Apamene', *Mélanges de l'Université Saint-Joseph* **28**, 1–42

Mráv, Z. and Harl, O. 2008: 'Die trajanische Bauinschrift der porta principalis dextra im Legionslager Vindobona – Zur Entstehung des Legionslagers Vindobona', *Fundort Wien* **11**, 36–55

Müller, G. 1979: *Ausgrabungen in Dormagen, 1963–1977*, Rheinische Ausgrabungen **20**, Köln

Müller, G. et al. 1979: 'Grabungen im Legionslager Novaesium', in *Ausgrabungen im Rheinland*, Sonderheft des Rheinischen Landesmuseums Bonn, Bonn

Müller, M. 2002: *Die römischen Buntmetallfunde von Haltern*, Bodenaltertümer Westfalens **37**, Mainz

Müller, M., Schalles, H.-J., and Zieling, N. (eds.) 2008: *Colonia Ulpia Traiana. Xanten und sein Umland in römischer Zeit*, Mainz

Murray Threipland, L. 1965: 'Caerleon: Museum Street site 1965', *Archaeologia Cambrensis* **114**, 130–45

Murray Threipland, L. 1967: 'Excavations at Caerleon 1966: Barracks in the north corner', *Archaeologia Cambrensis* **116**, 23–56

Murray Threipland, L. 1969 'The Hall, Caerleon 1964: Excavations on the site of the legionary hospital', *Archaeologia Cambrensis* **118**, 86–123

Murray Threipland, L. and Davies, W.J. 1959: 'Excavations at Caerleon 1956', *Archaeologia Cambrensis* **108**, 126–43

Murray, J. 1880: *Handbook for Travellers in Lower and Upper Egypt*, London

Nagy, T. 1976: 'Aquincum. Stadt und Lager im 4. Jh.', *Acta Antiqua Academiae Scientiarum Hungaricae* **24**, 369–82

Nagy, T. 1977: 'Das zweite Lager der legio II adiutrix in Aquincum (Obuda)', in Haupt and Horn 1977, 359–66

Nash-Williams, V.E. 1929: 'The Roman legionary fortress at Caerleon in Monmouthshire. Report on the excavations carried out in Jenkins's Field 1926', *Archaeologia Cambrensis* **84**, 237–307

Nash-Williams, V.E. 1930: 'Note on the bath-building outside the south-eastern defences', in Hawkes 1930, 147–9

Nash-Williams, V.E. 1931 'The Roman legionary fortress at Caerleon in Monmouthshire: Report on the excavations carried out in the Prysg Field 1927–9. Part I', *Archaeologia Cambrensis* **86**, 99–157

Nash-Williams, V.E. 1932a: 'Further excavations within the Roman legionary fortress at Caerleon, Monmouthshire', *Archaeologia Cambrensis* **87**, 394–5

Nash-Williams, V.E. 1932b: 'The Roman legionary fortress at Caerleon. Report on the excavations carried out in the Prysg Field, 1927–9. Part II. The Finds (pottery excepted)', *Archaeologia Cambrensis* **87**, 48–104

Nash-Williams, V.E. 1932c: 'The Roman legionary fortress at Caerleon in Monmouthshire. Report on the excavations in the Prysg Field 1927–9. Part III. The pottery', *Archaeologia Cambrensis* **87**, 265–349

Nash-Williams, V.E. 1932d: 'A new centurial stone from Caerleon', *Bulletin of the Board of Celtic Studies* **6**, 291

Nash-Williams, V.E. 1933: 'Further excavations within the Roman legionary fortress at Caerleon, Monmouthshire', *Archaeologia Cambrensis* **88**, 111–14

Nash-Williams, V.E. 1936: 'Caerleon excavations, 1936', *Archaeologia Cambrensis* **91**, 107–8

Nash-Williams, V.E. 1939: 'White Hart Lane, Caerleon, 1938', *Archaeologia Cambrensis* **94**, 107–8

Nash-Williams, V.E. 1951: 'Bronze bracelet from Caerleon (Mon.)', *Bulletin of the Board of Celtic Studies* **14**, 252

Nash-Williams, V.E. 1953: 'Caerleon: Prysg Field II site', *Bulletin of the Board of Celtic Studies* **15**, 236–42

Nash-Williams, V.E. 1969: *The Roman Frontier in Wales*, 2nd ed., Jarrett, M.G. (ed.), Cardiff

Németh, E. 1998: 'Două antefixe romane de la Berzovia / Zwei in Berzovia endeckte römische Antefixe', *Analele Banatului* NS **6**, 227–31

Németh, M. 1976: 'Archaeological observations near the north-eastern corner of the camp', *Budapest Régiségei* **24**, 61–9

Németh, M. 1986: *Denkmäler des Legionslagers von Aquincum*, Budapest

Németh, M. 1990: 'Forschungen im Alenkastell von Aquincum', in Vetters and Kandler 1990, 675–81

Németh, M. 1991: 'Stand der Forschungen in den Militärlagern von Aquincum', *Carnuntum Jahrbuch*, 81–7

Németh, M. 1993: 'Kutatások az aquincumi alatábor területén (Forschungen im Gebiet des Ala-Lagers von Aquincum), *Budapest Régiségei* **30**, 55–9

Németh, M. 1994: 'Roman military camps in Aquincum', in Gábor, H. (ed.), *La Pannonia e l'Impero Romano*, Annuario dell' Accademia d'Ungheria, Roma, 139–53

Németh, M. 2003: 'Contra Aquincum fortress', in Visy 2003, 201–3

Németh, M. 2005: 'Zur Funktion der thermae maiores von Aquincum in 4. Jahrhundert', in Visy 2005, 667–79

Németh, M. and Kerdő, K. 1986: 'Zur Frage der Besatzung von Aquincum im 1. Jahrhundert', in Unz 1986, 384–8

Nesselhauf, H. 1937: 'Neue Inschriften aus dem römischen Germanien und den angrenzenden Gebieten', *BRGK* **27**, 51–134

Nesselhauf, H. and Lieb, H. 1959: 'Dritter Nachtrag zu CIL XIII: Inschriften aus den germanischen Provinzen und dem Trevererebiet', *BRGK* **40**, 120–228

Neuffer, E. 1951: 'Grabstein des Tiberius Iulius Pancuius', *Bonner Jahrbücher* **151**, 192–4

Neumann, A. 1967: *Forschungen in Vindobona 1948 bis 1967. Lager und Lagerterritorium*, Der römische Limes in Österreich **23**, Wien

Newstead, R. 1899: 'Discovery of Roman Remains in Bridge Street 1899', *Journal of the Chester Archaeological Society* **6**, 395–9

Newstead, R. and Droop, J.P. 1932a: 'The Roman Amphitheatre at Chester', *Journal of the Chester Archaeological Society* **29**, 1–40

Newstead, R. and Droop, J.P. 1932b: 'The south-east corner of the Roman fortress, Chester', *Journal of the Chester Archaeological Society* **29**, 41–4

Newstead, R. and Droop, J.P. 1935: 'The Roman fortress at Chester: a newly-discovered turret and rampart building', *Annals of Archaeology and Anthropology* **22**, 19–30

Newstead, R. and Droop, J.P. 1940: 'Excavations at Chester 1939: the Princess Street clearance area', *Journal of the Chester Archaeological Society* **34**, 5–47

Nibby, A. 1848: *Analisi storico-topografico-antiquaria della carta de' dintorni di Roma*, vol. I, ed. 2, Roma

Nikolić-Đorđević, S. 2005: 'Antička keramika Singidunuma. Oblici posuda (Antique pottery from Singidunum. Forms of vessels)', *Singidunum* **4**, 11–244

Nissen, H. 1904: 'Geschichte von Novaesium', *Bonner Jahrbücher* **111/112**, 1–96

Noelke, P. 1975a: 'Militärlager und Siedlungen in Neuss', in *Kölner Römer-Illustrierte* **2**, Köln, 112–14

Noelke, P. 1975b: 'Soldatengrabstein aus Neuss', in *Kölner Römer-Illustrierte* **2**, 114

Noelke, P. 1977: 'Grabsteine aus dem römischen Neuss', *Neusser Jahrbuch*, 5–21

Nowotny, E. 1914: 'Die Grabungen im Standlager zu Carnuntum 1908–1911', *Der römische Limes in Österreich* **12**, 1–222

Nuber, H.U. 2008: 'P. Quinctilius Varus, Legatus Legionis XIX. Zur Interpretation der Bleischeibe aus Dangstetten, Lkr. Waldshut', *Archäologisches Korrespondenzblatt* **38**, 223–31

O'Neil, H.E. 1966: 'Excavations in the Kings's School gardens, Gloucester', *Transactions of the Bristol and Gloucestershire Archaeological Society* **84**, 15–27

O'Sullivan, D. 1987: 'The reconservation of two mosaics from Caerleon', *Conservation News* **32**, 14–17

Oates, D. 1956: 'The Roman frontier in Northern Iraq', *The Geographical Journal* **122**, 190–9

Oates, D. 1968: *Studies in the Ancient History of Northern Iraq*, Oxford

Ohlenschlager, F. 1874: 'Das römische Militärdiplom von Regensburg', *Sitzungsberichte der philologischen und historischen Classe der K. b. Akademie der Wissenschaften zu München* **2**, 193–230

Ohlenschlager, F., 1885: 'Die Porta Praetoria in Regensburg', *Westdeutsche Zeitschrift für Geschichte und Kunstgeschichte – Korrespondenzblatt* **4**, 123

Oldenstein, J. 2001: 'Mogontiacum', in *Reallexikon der Germanischen Altertumskunde* **20**, 144–53

Opreanu, C. 1998: 'Castrul legiunii I Adiutrix de la Apulum în timpul lui Traian. Consecinţe asupra urbanismului roman la Apulum', *Apulum* **35**, 121–34

Opreanu, C. 1999: 'Legio I Adiutrix in Dacia. Military Action and its Place of Garnison During Trajan's Reign', in Gudea 1999, 571–84

Opreanu, C. H. 2006: 'Activitatea constructivă a legiunii IIII Flavia Felix la nordul Dunării, în anii 101–107 d. Ch.', in Teodor, E. and Ţentea, O. (eds.), *Dacia Avgvsti Provincia. Crearea provinciei*, Bucureşti, 51–74

Osterhaus, U. 1972: 'Beobachtungen zum römischen und frühmittelalterlichen Regensburg', *Verhandlungen des historischen Vereins für Oberpfalz und Regensburg* **112**, 7–17

Osterhaus, U. 1974: 'Baubeobachtungen an der Via Principalis im Legionslager von Regensburg', *Bayerische Vorgeschichtsblätter* **39**, 160–80

Ottaway, P. 1985: '7–9 Aldwark', *Interim: the Archaeology of York* **10**, 13–15

Ottaway, P. 1991: 'The Roman fortress: planning for the future', *Interim: the Archaeology of York* **16(3)**, 3–13

Ottaway, P. 1992: *The English Heritage Book of Roman York*, London

Ottaway, P. 1996: *Excavations and Observations on the Defences and Adjacent Sites: 1971–90*, Archaeology of York 3/3, York

Ottaway, P. 1997: 'The sewer trenches in Low Lane, Petergate', *Interim: the Archaeology of York* **22(3)**, 15–23

Ottaway, P. 2004: *Roman York*, ed. 2, Stroud

Oxé, A. 1925: 'Ein römischer Inschriftenstein aus Neuss (Oclatiusstein)', *Die Heimat* **4**, 162

Päffgen, B. and Zanier, W. 1995: 'Überlegungen zur Lokalisierung von Oppidum Ubiorum und Legionslager im frühkaiserzeitlichen Köln', in Czysz, W. et al. (eds.), *Provinzialrömische Forschungen. Festschrift für Günter Ulbert zum 65. Geburtstag*, Espelkamp, 111–29

Päffgen, B. and Zanier, W. 1998: 'Zur Deutung der Alteburg als spätaugusteisch-frühtiberisches Militärlager', *Kölner Jahrbuch* **31**, 299–315

Pahič, S. 1996: 'Uničujoča Drava', *Ptujski zbornik* **6**, 139

Panter, A. 2007: *Der Drususstein in Mainz und dessen Einordnung in die römische Grabarchitektur seiner Erbauungszeit*, Mainzer Archäologische Schriften **6**, Mainz

Parker, H.M.D. 1958: *The Roman Legions*, revd ed., Oxford

Parker, S.T. 1986: *Romans and Saracens. A History of the Arabian Frontier*, Winona Lake

Parker, S.T. (ed.) 1987: *The Roman Frontier in Central Jordan: Interim Report on the Limes Arabicus Project, 1980–1985*, BAR International Series 340, Oxford

Parker, S.T. 1988: 'Preliminary Report on the 1985 Season of the Limes Arabicus Project', *Bulletin of the American Schools of Oriental Research. Supplementary Studies* **25**, 131–74

Parker, S.T. 1990: 'Preliminary Report on the 1987 Season of the "Limes Arabicus" Project', *Bulletin of the American Schools of Oriental Research. Supplementary Studies* **26**, 89–136

Parker, S.T. 1991: 'Preliminary Report on the 1989 Season of the Limes Arabicus Project', *Bulletin of the American Schools of Oriental Research. Supplementary Studies* **27**, 117–54

Parker, S.T. 1996: 'The Roman Aqaba Project: the economy of Aila on the Red Sea', *Biblical Archaeologist* **59**, 182

Parker, S.T. 1997: 'Preliminary report on the 1994 season of the Roman Aqaba Project', *Bulletin of the American Schools of Oriental Research* **305**, 19–44

Parker, S.T. 1998: 'An early church, perhaps the oldest in the world, found at Aqaba', *Near Eastern Archaeology* **61**, 254

Parker, S.T. 2000: 'Roman legionary fortresses in the East', in Brewer 2000, 121–38

Parker, S.T. 2006: *The Roman Frontier in Central Jordan: Final Report on the Limes Arabicus Project, 1980–1989*, Washington

Parnicki-Pudełko, S. 1990: *The Fortifications in the Western Sector of Novae. Novae-sektor zachodni*, Poznań

Pascher, G. 1949: *Römische Siedlungen und Straßen im Limesgebiet zwischen Enns und Leitha*, Der römische Limes in Österreich **19**, Wien

Pauli-Gabi, T. 2002: 'Ausgrabungen in Vindonissa im Jahr 2002', *Gesellschaft Pro Vindonissa. Jahresbericht*, 37–50

Pauli-Gabi, T. 2005a: 'Sondierungen am Schutthügel und im Vorgelände des Nordtores von Vindonissa', *Gesellschaft Pro Vindonissa. Jahresbericht*, 53–60

Pauli-Gabi, T. 2005b: 'Vindonissa – ein Offizierhaus mit grosser Küche Ausgrabung Römerblick 2002–2004', in Visy 2005, 595–608

Pauli-Gabi, T. 2007: 'Ausgrabungen in Vindonissa im Jahr 2007', *Gesellschaft Pro Vindonissa. Jahresbericht*, 81–99

Pauli-Gabi, T., Benguerel, S., and Trumm, J. 2004: 'Ausgrabungen in Vindonissa im Jahr 2004', *Gesellschaft Pro Vindonissa. Jahresbericht*, 109–20

Pauli-Gabi, T., Berger, D., Schucany, C., and Trumm, J. 2005: 'Ausgrabungen in Vindonissa im Jahr 2005', *Gesellschaft Pro Vindonissa. Jahresbericht*, 61–75

Pauli-Gabi, T. and Trumm, J. 2003: 'Ausgrabungen in Vindonissa im Jahr 2003', *Gesellschaft Pro Vindonissa. Jahresbericht*, 45–55

Paulovics, S., 1934: 'Újabb kutatások a brigetioi (szőnyi) római táborban és annak környékén (Neuere Forschungen im Legionslager und in der Umgebung von Brigetio)', *Archaeologia Értesítő* **47**, 134–40

Paulovics, S., 1941: 'Funde und Forschungen in Brigetio (Szőny)', in *Laureae Aquincenses 2*, Dissertationes Pannonicae **II,11**, Budapest, 11–164

Pearson, A. 2002: *The Roman Shore Forts. Coastal Defences of Southern Britain*, Stroud

Pearson, N. 1986: 'The Purey Cust Nuffield Hospital', *Interim: the Archaeology of York* **11**, 15–18

Pearson, N.F. 1990: 'Swinegate excavation', *Interim: the Archaeology of York* **15(1)**, 2–10

Pekáry, T. 1971: *Die Fundmünzen von Vindonissa von Hadrian bis zum Ausgang der Römerherrschaft*, Brugg

Pelgen, S. 2004: *Aquädukt-Ansichten – Aus der Denkmalgeschichte der Wasserversorgung für das römische Mainz*, Archäologische Ortsbetrachtungen **5**, Mainz

Pérez-González, C. 1989: *Cerámica romana de Herrera de Pisuerga (Palencia): la terra sigillata*, Santiago de Chile

Pérez-González, C. 1996: 'Asentamientos militares de Herrera de Pisuerga', in Fernández Ochoa, C. (ed.), *Los finisterres atlánticos en la antigüedad, época prerromana y romana (Coloquio internacional): homenaje a Manuel Fernández-Miranda*, Gijon, 91–102

Pérez-González, C. and Illarregui, E. 1992: 'Aproximación al conocimiento del conjunto arqueológico de Herrera de Pisuerga', *Papeles Herrerenses* **1**, 15–90

Pérez-González, C. and Illarregui, E. 1994: 'Un taller de útiles óseos de la Legión IIII Macedónica', *Trabalhos de Antropologia e Etnologia* **34** (3–4) (*I Congreso de Arqueología Peninsular IV, Porto 1993*), 259–67

Pérez-González, C. and Illarregui, E. 2006: 'Herrera de Pisuerga camp and forts', in Morillo and Aurrecoechea 2006, 322–7

Petch, D.F. 1962: 'Excavations in Lincoln, 1955–58', *Archaeological Journal* **117**, 40–70

Petch, D.F. 1968: 'The praetorium at Deva', *Journal of the Chester Archaeological Society* **55**, 1–5

Petch, D.F. 1970–71: 'Excavations on the site of the Old Market Hall, Chester: second summary report 1968–1970', *Journal of the Chester Archaeological Society* **57**, 3–26

Peters, W.J.T. 1970: 'Mural painting fragments found in the Roman legionary fortress at Nijmegen II', *Bericht van de Rijksdienst Oudheidkundig Bodemonderzoek (Amersfoort)* **19**, 51–71

Petolescu, C.C. 1996–: *Inscriptiones Daciae Romanae. Inscriptiones extra fines Daciae repertae*, Bucharest

Petolescu, C.C. 2005: *Inscriptii latine din Dacia (ILD) – Inscriptiones latinae Daciae*, Bucharest

Pető, M. 1976: 'Feltárások a II–III. századi aquincumi legiostábor retenturájában (Excavations in the retentura of the 2–3rd century A.D. legionary camp of Aquincum)', *Budapest Régiségei* **24**, 113–23

Petrikovits, H. von 1958: 'Vetera', *Paulys Realencyclopädie der classischen Altertumswissenschaft* **8A**, 1801–34

Petrikovits, H. von 1959: 'Die Legionsfestung Vetera II', *Bonner Jahrbücher* **159**, 89–133

Petrikovits, H. von 1960: *Das römische Rheinland*, Köln

Petrikovits, H. von 1961: 'Die Ausgrabungen in Neuß (Stand Ende 1961)', *Bonner Jahrbücher* **161**, 449–85

Petrikovits, H. von 1970: 'Die Spezialgebäude römischer Legionslager', *Legio VII Gemina*, León, 227–52

Petrikovits, H. von 1974: 'Militärische Fabricae der Römer', in Pippidi 1974, 399–407

Petrikovits, H. von 1975: *Die Innenbauten römischer Legionslager während der Prinzipatszeit*, Abhandlungen der Rheinisch-Westfälischen Akademie der Wissenschaften **56**, Opladen

Phillips, E.J. 1975: 'The gravestone of M. Favonius Facilis at Colchester', *Britannia* **6**, 102–5

Phillips, A.D. and Heywood, B. 1995: *Excavations at York Minster, vol. I: Roman to Norman, The Headquarters of the Roman Legionary Fortress at York and Its Exploitation in the Early Middle Ages (71–1070 A.D.)*, (Carver, M.O.H., ed.), London

Philp, B. 1981: 'Richborough, Reculver and Lympne: a reconsideration of three of Kent's late-Roman shore-forts', in Detsicas, A. (ed.), *Collectanea Historica: Essays in Memory of Stuart Rigold*, Maidstone, 41–9

Pietsch, M. 1989: 'Die Untersuchungen 1989 im frührömischen Legionslager bei Marktbreit, Landkreis Kitzingen, Unterfranken', *Das Archäologische Jahr in Bayern*, 108–14

Pietsch, M. 1990: 'Marktbreit – ein neues Augusteisches Legionslager bei Würzburg, Unterfranken', *Antike Welt* **21**, 118

Pietsch, M. 1991a: 'Marktbreit – ein neues augusteisches Legionslager bei Wurzburg, Unterfranken', in Maxfield and Dobson 1991, 196–202

Pietsch, M. 1991b: 'Die Untersuchungen 1991 im augusteischen Legionslager bei Marktbreit, Landkreis Kitzingen, Unterfranken', *Das Archäologische Jahr in Bayern*, 107–13

Pietsch, M. 1992: 'Abschliessende Untersuchungen im augusteischen Legionslager Marktbreit: die zentralen Verwaltungsgebäude', *Das Archäologische Jahr in Bayern*, 93–6

Pietsch, M. 1993: 'Die Zentralgebäude des augusteischen Legionslagers von Marktbreit und die Principia von Haltern', *Germania* **71**, 355–68

Pietsch, M. 2003: 'Das augusteische Legionslager Marktbreit', in Wiegels, R. and Woesler, W. (eds.), *Arminius und die Varusschlacht*, Paderborn, 41–66

Pietsch, M., Timpe, D., and Warmser, L. 1991: 'Das augusteische Truppenlager Marktbreit. Bisherige archäologische Befunde und historische Erwägungen', *BRGK* **72**, 263–324

Pippidi, M. (ed.) 1974: *Actes du IXe congrès international d'études sur les frontières romaines, Mamaia, 6–13 September 1972*, Bucharest

Pîslaru, M. 2001: 'Ein Aureus aus dem Legionslager von Potaissa', *Acta Musei Napocensis* **38:1**, 135–6

Pîslaru, M. 2004: 'Ritrovamenti monetari nei principia del castrum legionario di Potaissa (Dacia)', *Rivista italiana di numismatica e scienze affini* **105**, 93–133

Piso, I. 2006: *Le forum vetus de Sarmizegetusa I*, Bucureşti

Pitts, L.F. and St Joseph, J.K. 1985: *Inchtuthil. The Roman Legionary Fortress*, Britannia Monograph Series **6**, London

Platner, S.B. and Ashby, T. 1929: 'Castra Praetoria', *A Topographical Dictionary of Ancient Rome*, London, 106–8

Póczy, K. 1976a: 'A porta praetoria feltárása az aquincumi legiostáborban (The excavation of Porta Praetoria in the Aquincum legionary camp)', *Budapest Régiségei* **24**, 79–86

Póczy, K. 1976b: 'Az aquincumi legiostábor és katonaváros romjainak a feltárása és a műemléki bemutatása (The investigation of the Aquincum legionary camp and the restoration of its ruins)', *Budapest Régiségei* **24**, 11–26

Póczy, K. 1977: 'Beiträge zur Baugeschichte des 3. und 4. Jahrhunderts im Legionslager Aquincum. Vorbericht über die Grabungen 1973–1974', in Haupt and Horn 1977, 373–8

Póczy, K. 1983: 'Az aquincumi canabae utcahálózata és fontosabb épületei a II. és a III. században', *Archeológia Értesítő* **110**, 252–73

Póczy, K. 1984: 'Aquincum – castra, canabae, colonia. (Az 1976–1980. közötti idõszak ásatási eredményeinek összefoglalása.) (Aquincum – castra, canabae, colonia. (Zusammenfassung der Grabungsergebnisse der Periode 1976–1980))', *Budapest Régiségei* **25**, 15–34

Póczy, K. 1986: 'Die Militarstadt von Aquincum im 2. und 3. Jahrhundert', in Unz 1986, 404–8

Póczy, K. 1990: 'Zur Baugeschichte des Legionslagers von Aquincum zwischen 260 und 320', in Vetters and Kandler 1990, 689–702

Póczy, K., Németh, M., Szirmai, K., and Kocsis, L. 1986: 'Das Legionslager von Aquincum', in Unz 1986, 398–403

Póczy, K. and Zsidi, P. 1992: *Römische Keramik in Aquincum. Ausstellung des Aquincum-Museums, August 1992 – Februar 1993 im Burgmuseum von Buda*, Budapest

Poidebard, A. 1934: *La trace de Rome dans le désert de Syrie. Le Limes de Trajan à la conquête arabe, recherches aériennes (1925–1932)*, Bibliothèque archéologique et historique **18**, Paris

Polenz, H. 1986: *Das römische Budapest. Neue Ausgrabungen und Funde in Aquincum*, Katalog zur Ausstellung des Westfälischen Museums für Archäologie, Münster/Lengerich

Pollak, M. 1992: 'Ein spätantiker Fundkomplex vom Wildpretmarkt in Wien', *Beiträge zur Mittelalterarchäologie in Österreich* **8**, 117–57

Popović, M. 1997: 'Antički Singidunum: dosadašnja otriča i mogućnost daljih istraživanja (Ancient Singidunum: discoveries and possibilities of further research', *Singidunum* **1**, 1–20

Poulter, A. 1986: 'The Lower Moesian limes and the Dacian Wars of Trajan', in Unz 1986, 519–28

Precht, G. 1971: 'Die Ausgrabungen um den Kölner Dom. Vorbericht über die Untersuchungen 1969/70', *Kölner Jahrbücher* **12**, 52–64

Precht, G. 2002: 'Köln-Deutz. Römisches Kastell', in Horn, H.-G. (ed.), *Die Römer in Nordrhein-Westfalen*, Hamburg, 513–16

Precht, H. 1972/3: 'Die Ausgrabungen im Bereich des castellum Divitia; Vorbericht über die Kastellgrabungen', *Kölner Jahrbuch* **13**, 120–7

Prentice, W.K. 1908: *Publications of the Princeton University Archaeological Expedition to Syria 3. Greek and Latin Inscriptions B: Northern Syria*, New York

Press, L. and Sarnowski, T. 1987: 'Novae, rzymska twierdza legionowa i miasto wczesnobizantyjskie nad Dolnym Dunajem', *Novaensia* **1**, 289–322

Pro Austria Romana 7, 1957, 35; **24**, 1974, 20; **27**, 1977, 23

Probst, P. 2007: Review of Farnum 2005, *Bryn Mawr Classical Review* 2007.09.52 <http://bmcr.brynmawr.edu/2007/2007-09-52.html> accessed 12.12.09

Protase, D. and Petculescu, L. 1975: 'Coiful roman de la Berzovia', *Banatica* **3**, 85–90

Rabanal Alonso, M.A. and García Martínez, S.M. 2001: *Epigrafía romana de la provincia de León: revisión y actualización*, León

Radley, J. 1966: 'A section of the Roman fortress wall at Barclay's Bank, St Helen's Square, York', *Yorkshire Archaeological Journal* **41**, 581–4

Radley, J. 1970: 'Two interval towers and new sections of the fortress wall, York', *Yorkshire Archaeological Journal* **42**, 399–402

Radley, J. 1972: 'Excavations on the defences of the city of York in an early medieval stone tower and the successive earth ramparts', *Yorkshire Archaeological Journal* **44**, 38–64

Radman-Livaja, I. 2004a: *Militaria Sisciensia. Nalazi rimske vojne opreme iz Siska u fundusu Arheoloskoga muzeja u Zagrebu, Musei Archaeologici Zagrabiensis, Catalogi et Monographiae* **1**, Zagreb

Radman-Livaja, I. 2004b: 'Historical survey', in Radman-Livaja 2004a, 15–22

Radman-Livaja, I. 2010a: 'Siscia as a Roman military stronghold', in Radman-Livaja, I. (ed.), *Finds of the Roman Military Equipment in Croatia*, Zagreb, 179–201

Radman-Livaja, I. 2010b: 'The catalogue of finds', in Radman-Livaja, I. (ed.), *Finds of the Roman Military Equipment in Croatia*, Zagreb, 203–11

Rahmani, L.Y. 1981: 'A Roman patera from Lajjun', *Israel Exploration Journal* **31**, 190–6

Rakob, F. 1971–74: 'Le "Torsaal" des principia du camp romain de Lambèse', *Bulletin d'Archéologie Algérienne* **5**, 35–42

Rakob, F. 1979: 'Das Groma-Nymphaeum Legionslager von Lambaesis', *Römische Mitteilungen* **86**, 379–89

Rakob, F. 2001: 'Die Bauphasen des Groma-Gebäudes im Legionslager von Lambaesis', *Römische Mitteilungen* **108**, 7–40

Ralegh Radford, C.A. and Morris, P. 1933–6: 'Report of the Exeter Excavation Committee: the defences of Roman Exeter', *Proceedings of the Devon Archaeological Exploration Society* **2**, 181–7

Ramm, H.G. 1956: 'Roman York: excavations of 1955', *JRS* **46**, 76–90

Rankov, N.B. 1982: 'Roman Britain in 1981. I. Sites explored', *Britannia* **13**, 328–95

Rasbach, G. and Becker, A. 2000: 'Neue Forschungsergebnisse der Grabungen in Lahnau-Waldgirmes in Hessen', in Wamser et al. 2000, 38–40

Reddé, M. 1995: 'Sur quelques tuiles de la VIIIe légion à Xanten', *Caesarodunum* **29**, 205–12

Reddé, M. 1996: 'Le camp légionnaire de Mirebeau', in Reddé, M. (ed.), *L'armée en Gaule romaine*, Paris, 191–201

Reddé, M. 1997: 'Réflexion sur l'occupation militaire de Strasbourg et de Mirebeau au 1er siècle après J.-C', *Gesellschaft Pro Vindonissa. Jahresbericht*, 5–12

Reddé, M. 2006: 'Mirebeau', in Aupert, P. (ed.), *L'architecture de la Gaule romaine*, Document d'Archéologie Française **100**, Paris, 331–4

Reddé, M. and Schnurbein, S. von 1997: 'Les Nouvelles fouilles d'Alesia', in Groenman-van Waateringe et al. 1997, 175–85

Redžić, S. 2008: 'Vtere Felix belt sets on the territory of Viminacium', *Starinar* **58**, 155–62

Reinecke, P. 1958: 'Die Porta principalis dextra in Regensburg', *Germania* **36**, 89–96

Reisch, E. 1913: 'Das Standlager in Burnum', *Osterreichische Jahreshefte* **16**, 112–35

Ricci, C. 2000: 'Legio II Parthica: una messa punto', in Le Bohec and Wolff 2000, 397–406

Ricci, G.A. 1787: *Memorie storiche dell'antichissima città di Alba Longa e dell'Albano moderno*, Roma

Rice, W. 1719: 'An account of an ancient Roman inscription found at Caerleon upon Usk. With some conjectures thereon by John Harris', *Philosophical Transactions of the Royal Society of London* **30**, 945–6

Richardson, A. 2004: *Theoretical Aspects of Roman Camp and Fort Design*, BAR **S1321**, Oxford

Richardson, A. 2005: 'The orientation of Roman camps and forts', *Oxford Journal of Archaeology* **24**, 415–26

Richmond, I.A. 1927: 'The relation of the praetorian camp to Aurelian's wall', *Proceedings of the British School at Rome* **10**, 12–22

Richmond, I.A. 1959: 'The Agricolan legionary fortress at Inchtuthil', in Laur-Belart 1959, 152–5

Rippon, S. 1996: *Gwent Levels: The Evolution of a Wetland Landscape*, CBA Research Report **105**, York

Ritterling, E. 1925: 'Legio', in *Paulys Realencyclopädie der classischen Altertumswissenschaft* **12**, 1211–1829

Roach Smith, C. 1850: *The Antiquities of Richborough, Reculver and Lympne in Kent*, London

Rómer, F. 1861: 'Az újabb Ó-Szőnyön kiásott régiség Rómer Flóristól', *Archaeologiai Közlemények* **2**, 158–9

Rómer, F. 1862: 'Római várnák. Bregetio (Ó-Szőny)', *Archaeologiai Közlemények* **3:2**, 45–9

Romero Carnicero, M.V. and Carretero Vaquero, S. 1999: 'Los campamentos y la ciudad de Petavonium', in *Congreso de Los Orígenes de la Ciudad en el Noroeste Hispánico, Lugo, 1996*, Lugo, 1077–1108

Romero Carnicero, V. and Carretero Vaquero, S. 2006: 'Rosinos de Vidriales camp, fort and vicus', in Morillo and Aurrecoechea 2006, 347–56

Roth-Rubi, K. 2004: 'Das Militärlager von Dangstetten und seine Rolle für die spätere Westgrenze Raetiens', in Hüssen, C.-M. (ed.), *Spätlatènezeit und frühe römische Kaiserzeit zwischen Alpenrand und Donau*, Kolloquien zur Vor- und Frühgeschichte **8**, Bonn, 133–48

Roth-Rubi, K. 2005: 'Bilderwelt und Propaganda im frühaugusteischen Lager von Dangstetten', in Visy 2005, 919–30

Roth-Rubi, K. 2006: *Dangstetten III. Das Tafelgeschirr aus dem Militärlager von Dangstetten*, Forschungen und Berichte zur Vor- und Frühgeschichte in Baden-Württemberg **103**, Stuttgart

Roth-Rubi, K. (ed.) 2006: *Varia Castrensia. Haltern, Oberaden, Anreppen*, Bodenaltertümer Westfalens 42, Mainz

Royal Commission on Ancient and Historical Monuments (England) 1962: *Eburacum*, vol. 1, London

Rudnick, B. 1995: *Die verzierte Arretina aus Oberaden und Haltern*, Mainz

Rudnick, B. 2001: *Die römischen Töpfereien von Haltern*, Bodenaltertümer Westfalens **36**, Mainz

Rüger, C.B. 1981: 'Inschriftenfunde der Jahre 1975–1979 aus dem Rheinland', *ES* **12**, 287–307

Rüger, C.B. 1984: 'Eine kleine Garnisonsgeschichte des römischen Neuss', in Chantraine et al. 1984, 9–52

Rüger, C.B., Precht, G., and Wegner, H.-H. 1979: 'Ein Siegesdenkmal der legio VI Victrix', *Bonner Jahrbücher* **179**, 187–200

Ruprechtsberger, E.M. 1985: 'Fundbeobachtungen im Legionslager von Albing, G. St. Pantaleon/NÖ', *Pro Austria Romana* **35**, 13–15

Ruprechtsberger, E.M. 1986a: 'Lorch/Enns – Lauriacum. 1. Legionslager' in Kandler and Vetters 1986, 92–101

Ruprechtsberger, E.M. 1986b: 'Die Legionslager in Albing/NÖ. und Lauriacum/Lorch-Enns', in *Ausstellungskatalog Oberösterreich – Grenzland des römischen Reiches*, Kataloge des Oberöstreichen Landesmuseums N.F. **7**, 71–8

Ruprechtsberger, E.M. 1996: 'Lauriacum unter römischer Herrschaft', in Katzinger, W., Ebner, J., and Ruprechtsberger, E.M. (eds.), *Geschichte von Enns*, Enns, 11–62

Ruprechtsberger, E.M. 2006: 'Elmar Tscholl (1919–2002) und seine Forschungen im antiken Wallsee', *Carnuntum Jahrbuch 2006*, 11–20

Salvatore, J.P. 1996: *Roman Republican Castrametation: A Reappraisal of Historical and Archaeological Sources*, BAR **S630**, Oxford

Sanader, M. 1998: 'Tilurij – rimski vojni logor. Prethodno izvješće s arheoloških istraživanja u 1997. i 1998', *Opuscula Archaeologica* **22**, 243–55

Sanader, M. 2000: 'Tilurij – rimski vojni logor', *Obavijesti Hrvatskog arheološkog društva* **32/1**, 51–62

Sanader, M. 2001: 'Tilurij – rimski vojni logor. Prethodno izvješće o arheološkim istraživanjima u sezoni 2000', *Opuscula archaeologica* **25**, 183–94

Sanader, M. 2002: 'Tilurij – arheološka istraživanja u godini 2002', *Obavijesti Hrvatskog arheološkog društva* **34/3**, 87–97

Sanader, M. 2003a: 'Grabsteine der Legio VII aus Tilurium. Versuch einer Typologie', in Noelke, P. (ed.), *Akten des VII. Internationalen Colloquiums über Probleme des provinzialrömischen Kunstschaffens*, Mainz, 501–10

Sanader, M. 2003b: 'Rimske legije i njihovi logori u hrvatskom dijelu panonskog limesa', *Opuscula Archaeologica* **27**, 463–8

Sanader, M. 2003c: *Tilurium I. Forschungen 1997–2001*, Zagreb

Sanader, M. 2006: 'The Roman legionary fortress at Tilurium – state of research,' in Davison, D., Gaffney, V., and Marin, E. (eds.), *Dalmatia. Research in the Roman Province 1970–2001*, BAR **S1576**, Oxford, 56–66

Sanader, M. 2009: 'Mannschaftsbaracken mit Strebepfeilern aus Tilurium', in Morillo et al. 2009, 1507–14

Sanader, M., Milićević Bradač, M., and Demicheli, D. 2007: 'A "poet" in the military camp at Tilurium', <http://ciegl.classics.ox.ac.uk/html/webposters/Tilurium.jpg> accessed 6.1.11

Sanader, M. and Tončinić, D. 2003: 'Tilurij – arheološka istraživanja u godini 2003', *Obavijesti Hrvatskog arheološkog društva* **35/3**, 87–99

Sanader, M. and Tončinić, D. 2005: 'Das Projekt Tilurium. Die Wehrmauer', in Visy 2005, 685–8

Sanader, M. and Tončinić, D. 2009: 'Das Projekt Tilurium. Waffendarstellungen auf Steindenkmälern aus Tilurium', in Busch and Schalles 2009, 199–202

Sanader, M. and Tončinić, D. 2010a: 'Gardun – the ancient *Tilurium*', in Radman-Livaja, I. (ed.), *Finds of the Roman Military Equipment in Croatia*, Zagreb, 33–53

Sanader, M. and Tončinić, D. 2010b: 'The catalogue of finds', in Radman-Livaja, I. (ed.), *Finds of the Roman Military Equipment in Croatia*, Zagreb, 55–111

Saria, B. 1974: 'Pregled topografije Poetovio', *Časopis za zgodovino in narodopisje* **10:45**, Maribot, 225

Sarnowski, T. 1977: 'Fortress of the Legio I Italica at Novae', in Fitz 1977, 415–24

Sarnowski, T. 1979a: 'La destruction des principia à Novae vers 316/317 de notre ere. Révolte militaire ou invasion gothique?', *Archeologia* **30**, 149–63

Sarnowski, T. 1979b: 'Une tête de Caracalla découverte à Novae', *Archeologia* **30**, 149–63

Sarnowski, T. 1980: 'Mramorna glava na Karakalla ot Novae', *Arheologija (Sofia)* **3**, 35–43

Sarnowski, T. 1981: 'The legionary defences of Novae', *Archeologia* **32**, 29–46

Sarnowski, T. 1983a: 'Die Ziegelstempel aus Novae', *Archeologia* **34**, 17–61

Sarnowski, T. 1983b: 'La fortresse de la legion I Italica et le limes du sud-est de la Dacie', *Eos* **71**, 265–76

Sarnowski, T. 1984: 'Początki legionowego budownictwa w Novae i wojny dackie Domicjana i Trajana', *Balcanica Posnaniensia* **1**, 143–69

Sarnowski, T. 1985: 'Bronzefunde aus dem Stabsgebaude in Novae und Altmetalldepots in den römischen Kastellen und Legionslagern', *Germania* **63**, 521–40

Sarnowski, T. 1989: 'Zur Statuenausstattung der römischen Stabsgebäude', *Bonner Jahrbücher* **189**, 97–120

Sarnowski, T. 1991: 'The headquarters building of the legionary fortress at Novae (Lower Moesia)', in Maxfield and Dobson 1991, 303–7

Sarnowski, T. 1992: 'Das Fahnenheiligtum des Legionslagers Novae', in Lipska, A., Niezgoda, E., and Ząbecka, M. (eds.), *Studia Aegaea et Balcanica in honorem Lodovicae Press*, Warszawa, 221–33

Sarnowski, T. 1993a: 'Nova Ordinatio im römischen Heer des 3. Jh. und eine neue Primus pilus-Weihung aus Novae in Niedermoesien', *ZPE* **95**, 197–204

Sarnowski, T. 1993b: 'Primi ordines et centuriones legionis I Italicae und eine Dedikation an Septimius Severus aus Novae in Niedermoesien', *ZPE* **95**, 205–19

Sarnowski, T. 1993c: 'Wykopaliska w Novae', in *Dzieje archeologii na Uniwersytecie Warszawskim*, Warszawa, 331–5

Sarnowski, T. 1995: 'Another legionary groma gate hall? The case of Novae in Lower Moesia', in *Novae. Studies and Materials I*, Poznań, 37–40

Sarnowski, T. 1996a: 'Die römische Anlegestelle von Novae in Moesia Inferior', in Petrović, P. (ed.), *Roman Limes on the Middle and Lower Danube*, Cahiers des Portes de Fer Monographies **2**, Belgrade, 195–203

Sarnowski, T. 1996b: 'Promotio ex nova ordinatione eines künftigen Centurio. Zur Inschrift aus Novae in ZPE 95, 1993', *ZPE* **111**, 289–90

Sarnowski, T. 1999: 'Die Principia von Novae im späten 4. und frühen 5. Jh.', in Bulow, G. von and Milceva, A. (eds.), *Der Limes an der unteren Donau von Diokletian bis Heraklios. Vorträge der internationalen Konferenz, Svishtov, Bulgarien (1.–5. September 1998)*, Sofia, 57–63

Sarnowski, T. 2000: 'Novae – western sector, 1998–1999. Preliminary report on the excavations of the Warsaw University archaeological expedition', *Archeologia* **51**, 79–87

Sarnowski, T. 2002: 'Headquarters building (principia) of legio I Italica at Novae', in Dyczek, P. (ed.), *Novae – 40 Years of Excavations*, Warszawa, 31–7

Sarnowski, T. 2003: 'Novae – Western Sector (Principia), 2000–2002. Preliminary report on the excavations of the Warsaw University archaeological expedition', *Archeologia* **54**, 65–75

Sarnowski, T. 2005: 'Drei spätkaiserzeitliche Statuenbasen aus Novae in Niedermösien', in Mirkovic, M. (ed.), *Römische Städte und Festungen an der Donau. Akten der regionalen Konferenz, 16–19 Oktober 2003*, Beograd, 223–30

Sarnowski, T. and Gacuta, W. 1982: 'Skarb brązów z zachodniego aerarium komendantury w Novae', *Archeologia* **33**, 125–42

Sarnowski, T. and Kaniszewski, J. 2007: 'Roman and early Byzantine defences of Novae in Lower Moesia. North-eastern corner', in Vagalinski, L. (ed.), *The Lower Danube in Antiquity*, Sofia, 227–30

Sarnowski, T., Kovalevskaya, L., and Kaniszewski, J. 2005: 'Novae – Castra Legionis, 2003-2005. Preliminary report on the excavations of the Warsaw University archaeological expedition', *Archeologia* **56**, 141–52

Sarnowski, T. and Press, L. 1990: 'Novae. Römisches Legionslager und frühbyzantinische Stadt an der unteren Donau', *Antike Welt* **21**, 225–43

Sarnowski, T. and Trynkowski, J. 1990: 'Stemple "okrętowe" legionu I Italskiego na cegłach i dachówkach z Novae', *Balcanica Posnaniensia* **5**, 251–63

Sarre-Herzfeld, F.P.T. 1911: *Archaeologische Reise im Euphrat- und Tigris-Gebiet*, Berlin

Šašel Kos, M. 1995: 'The 15th legion at Emona – some thoughts', *ZPE* **109**, 227–44

Šašel Kos, M. 1998: 'Je bila Emona nekdanji tabor 15. legije in veteranska kolonija? (Was Emona ever a camp of the 15th legion and a veteran colony?)', *Zgodovinski časopis* **52/53**, 317–29

Sauer, E.W. 2005: 'Inscriptions from Alchester: Vespasian's base of the Second Augustan Legion(?)', *Britannia* **36**, 101–33

Schaer, A. 2005: 'Aktuelle Ausgrabungsergebnisse aus den römischen Legionsziegeleien von Hunzenschwil (AG)', *Gesellschaft Pro Vindonissa, Jahresbericht*, 41–51

Schaffhausen, H., Veith, C. von, and Klein, J. 1888: *Das römische Lager in Bonn. Festschrift zu Winkelmanns Geburtstage am 9. December 1888*, Bonn

Schalles, H.-J. 1994a: 'Frühkaiserzeitliche Militaria aus einem Altrheinarm bei Xanten-Wardt', *Journal of Roman Military Equipment Studies* **5**, 155–65

Schalles, H.-J. 1994b: 'Ein neuer Schildfesselbeschlag aus Xanten?', *Arma* **6**, 18–19

Schalles, H.-J. 1996: 'Corona Civica oder Girlande? Ein neues Motiv auf einem tiberischen Schwertscheidenblech mit Reliefverzierung sowie Nachträge zu den Schwertscheidenblechen des 1. Jahrhunderts n. Chr. aus Xanten', *Archäologisches Korrespondenzblatt* **26**, 463–73

Schalles, H.-J. 1999: 'Beutegut oder Kampfplatzzeugnis? Ergänzende Überlegungen zu den frühkaiserzeitlichen Militaria aus Xanten-Wardt', in Schlüter and Wiegels 1999, 207–25

Schalles, H.-J. and Schreiter, C. 1993: *Geschichte aus dem Kies. Neue Funde aus dem Alten Rhein bei Xanten*, Xantener Berichte **3**, Köln

Scheithauer, A. and Wesch-Klein, G. 1990: 'Von Köln-Deutz nach Rom? Zur Truppengeschichte der legio II Italica Divitensium', *ZPE* **81**, 229–36

Schenk, D. 1930: *Flavius Vegetius Renatus: die Quellen der Epitoma Rei Militaris*, Klio Beiheft **22**, Leipzig

Schillinger-Häfele, U. 1977: 'Vierter Nachtrag zu CIL XIII und zweiter Nachtrag zu Fr. Vollmer, Inscriptiones Baivariae Romanae. Inschriften aus dem deutschen Anteil der germanischen Provinzen und des Treverergebiets sowie Raetiens und Noricums', *BRGK* **58**, 452–603

Schlüter, W. and Wiegels, R. (eds.) 1999: *Rom, Germanien und die Ausgrabungen von Kalkriese*, Osnabrücker Forschungen zu Altertum und Antike-Rezeption **1**, Osnabrück

Schmidts, T. 2001: 'Ein Hallenbau im Legionslager Castra Regina-Regensburg', *Bayerische Vorgeschichtsblätter* **66**, 95–140

Schmitz, D. 2008: 'Das Lager Vetera II und seine Legionen', in Müller et al. 2008, 141–170

Schneider, G. and Wirz, E. 1991: 'Chemische Analysen von Firmalampen aus Vindonissa', *Gesellschaft Pro Vindonissa. Jahresbericht*, 35–49

Schnitzler, B. and Kuhnle, G. 2010: *Strasbourg–Argentorate – un camp légionnaire sur le Rhin (Ier au IVe siècle après J-C)*, Strasbourg

Schnurbein, S. von 1974: *Die römischen Militäranlagen bei Haltern*, Bodenaltertümer Westfalens **14**, Münster

Schnurbein, S. von 1981: 'Untersuchungen zur Geschichte der römischen Militärlager an der Lippe', *BRGK* **62**, 5–101

Schnurbein, S. von 2000: 'The organization of the fortresses in Augustan Germany', in Brewer 2000, 29–39

Schnurbein, S. von 2002: 'Neue Grabungen in Haltern, Oberaden und Anreppen', in Freeman et al. 2002, 527–33

Schnurbein, S. von 2004: 'Germanien in römischer Sicht. Germania Magna und die römischen Provinzbezeichnungen', in Beck, H., Greuenich, D., Steuer, H., and Hakelberg, D. (eds.), *Zur Geschichte der Gleichung 'germanisch-deutsch'. Sprache und Namen, Geschichte und Institutionen*, Ergzbd. RGA **34**, Berlin/New York, 25–36

Schulten, A. 1894: 'Das Territorium Legionis', *Hermes* **29**, 481–516

Schulten, A. 1927: *Numantia: die Ergebnisse der Ausgrabungen 1905-19. Bd.3. Die Lager des Scipio*, München

Schulten, A. 1929: *Numantia: die Ergebnisse der Ausgrabungen 1905-19. Bd.4. Die Lager bei Renieblas*, München

Schultze, R. 1925: 'Die römischen Legionslazarette in Vetera und anderen Legionslagern', *Bonner Jahbücher* **139**, 54–63

Schumacher, L. 2003: 'Mogontiacum. Garnison und Zivilsiedlung im Rahmen der Reichsgeschichte', in Klein 2003, 1–28

Schwanzar, C. 1989: 'Schlögen – Ioviacum', in Kandler and Vetters 1986, 74–80

Schwemin, F. 1998: *Die Römer in Oberaden*, Werne

Seeck, O. 1962: *Notitia Dignitatum: Accedunt Notitia Urbis Constantinopolitanae et Latercula Provinciarum*, Frankfurt am Main

Selkirk, A. 1987: 'Usk', *Current Archaeology* **10**, 184–6

Selzer, W., Decker, K.-V., and Do Paco, A. 1988: *Römische Steindenkmäler. Mainz in römischer Zeit*, Mainz

Septilici, R.-M. and Truican, A. 2006: 'New accidental finds of roman coins around the village of Berzovia (Caras-Severin county)', *Analele Banatului* NS **14**, 271–5

Sheehan, P. 1996: 'The Roman fortress of Babylon in Old Cairo', in Bailey, D.M. (ed.), *Archaeological Research in Roman Egypt*, JRA Supplement **19**, Ann Arbor, 95–7

Sheehan, P. 2001: 'The Roman fortification', in Lambert 2001, 49–6

Shirley, E.A.M. 1996: 'The building of the legionary fortress at Inchtuthil', *Britannia* **27**, 111–28

Shirley, E.A.M. 2000: *The Construction of the Roman Legionary Fortress at Inchtuthil*, British Archaeological Reports S**298**, Oxford

Shirley, E. 2001: *Building a Roman Legionary Fortress*, Stroud

Simonett, C. 1935: 'Eine verzierte Schildbuckelplatte aus Vindonissa', *Anzeiger für Schweizerische Altertumskunde* **37**, 176–81

Simonett, C. 1937: 'Grabungen der Gesellschaft Pro Vindonissa in den Jahren 1935 und 1936 auf der Breite', *Anzeiger fur schweizerische Altertumskunde* **39**, 81–92, 201–17

Simonett, C. 1939: 'Grabungen der Gesellschaft Pro Vindonissa im Jahre 1938', *Zeitschrift für Schweizerische Archäologie und Kunstgeschichte* **1**, 106–13

Simonett, C. 1940: 'Grabungen der Gesellschaft Pro Vindonissa', *Zeitschrift für Schweizerische Archäologie und Kunstgeschichte* **2**, 1–9

Simonett, C. 1941: 'Grabungen der Gesellschaft Pro Vindonissa im Jahre 1940', *Zeitschrift für Schweizerische Archäologie und Kunstgeschichte* **3**, 170–5

Simpson, G. 2000: *Roman Weapons, Tools, Bronze Equipment and Brooches from Neuss: Novaesium Excavations 1955-1972*, BAR S**862**, Oxford

Smith, N.A. 1982: 'Culver Street continues…', *Catalogue* **10**, 2–6

Sölter, W. 1977: 'Das Ende einer Ausgrabung. Die Ausgrabungen im römischen Legionslager Bonn', *Rheinische Ausgrabungen* '76, 116

Sölter, W. 1983: *Das römische Germanien aus der Luft*, ed. 2, Bergisch Gladbach

Sölter, W. 2005: *Römische Kalkbrenner im Rheinland*, Reihe Rheinische Kunststätten im Rheinland **490**, Köln

Sommer, C.S., 2006: 'Canabae et vici militaires', in Aupert, P. (ed.), *L'architecture de la Gaule romaine*, Document d'Archéologie Française 100, Paris, 331–4

Sommer, S. 1999: 'Wohin mit den Pferden? Stallbaracken sowie Aufmarsch- und Übungsplätze in römischer Zeit', in Kemkes and Scheuerbrand 1999, 84–90

Speidel, M.A. 1996: *Die römischen Schreibtafeln von Vindonissa*, Baden

Speidel, M.A. 1998: 'Legio IV Scythica: its movements and men', in Kennedy 1998a, 163–204

Speidel, M.A. 2000: 'Legio IV Scythica', in Le Bohec 2000, 328–37

Speidel, M.A. 2001: 'Legio operosa felix', in Dabrowa, E. (ed.), *Roman Military Studies*, Electrum **5**, 153–6

Speidel, M.A. 2010: 'Auf kürzestem und gut verpflegt an die Front. Zur Versorgung pannonischer Expeditionstruppen während der severischen Partherkriege', in Eich, A. (ed.), *Die Verwaltung der kaiserzeitlichen römischen Armee*, Stuttgart, 133–48

Speidel, M.P. 1992: *The Framework of an Imperial Legion: The Fifth Annual Caerleon Lecture In Honorem Aquilae Legionis II Augustae*, Caerleon

Speidel, M.P. 1994: *Die Denkmäler der Kaiserreiter. Equites singulares Augusti*, Köln

Speidel, M.P. 2006: *Emperor Hadrian's Speeches to the African Army: A New Text*, Mainz

Speidel, M.P. and Dimitrova-Milčeva, A. 1978: 'The cult of genii in the Roman army and a new military deity', in Temporini, H. (ed.), *Aufstieg und Niedergang der römischen Welt* **II.16.2**, 1542–55

Speidel, M.P. and Reynolds, J. 1985: 'A veteran of *legio I Parthica* from Carian Aphrodisias', *Epigraphica Anatolica* **5**, 31–5

Spence, K., Sheehan, P., and Le Quesne, C. 2001: 'Archaeological survey drawings of the fortress of Babylon', in Lambert 2001, 40–7

Spindler. K., 1978: 'Die Römermauer in Regensburg', in Strobel, R. (ed.), *Regensburg. Die Altstadt als Denkmal*, München, 113–17

Stead, I.M. 1958: 'Excavations at the south corner of the Roman fortress at York, 1956', *Yorkshire Archaeological Journal* **39**, 515–38

Stead, I.M. 1968: 'An excavation at King's Square, York, 1957', *Yorkshire Archaeological Journal* **42**, 151–64

Steane, K. 2006: *The Archaeology of the Upper City and Adjacent Suburbs*, Lincoln Archaeology Studies **3**, Oxford

Steinby, E.M. 1993: *Lexicon topographicum urbis Romae*, Vol. I, Roma

Steinmetz, W.-D. 2006: 'Berichtsstand 26.Oktober 2006. Der Burgwall von Isingerode – archäologische Ausgrabungen 2006', <http://www.fabl.de/isingerode.htm> accessed 24.2.11

Stephens, G.R. 1986: 'The Roman aqueduct at Chester', *Journal of the Chester Archaeological Society* **68**, 59–69

Stieren, A. (ed.) 1943: *Die Funde von Haltern seit 1925*, Bodenaltertümer Westfalens **6**, Münster

Stiglitz, H. (ed.) 1997: *Das Auxiliarkastell Carnuntum 1*, Sonderschriften des Österreichischen Archäologischen Institutes **29**, Wien

Stockwell, M. 1990: 'Sorry about the smell but …', *Interim: the Archaeology of York* **15**(1), 20–5

Storz, S. and Rakob, F. 1974: 'Die Principia des römischen Legionslagers in Lambaesis. Vorbericht über Bauaufnahme und Grabungen', *Römische Mitteilungen* **81**, 253–80

Straker, V., Robinson, M., and Robinson, E. 1984: 'Biological investigation of waterlogged deposits in the Roman fortress ditch at Exeter', *Proceedings of the Dorset Archaeological and Natural History Society* **42**, 59–69

Straub, S. 1879: 'Rapport sur les antiquités découvertes à Koenigshoffen près Strasbourg, notamment en mars et avril 1878', *Bulletin de la Société pour la Conservation des Monuments Historiques d'Alsace* **10**, 330–46

Strickland, T.J. 1980: 'First century Deva: some evidence reconsidered in the light of recent archaeological discoveries', *Journal of the Chester Archaeological Society* **63**, 5–13

Strickland, T.J. 1982a: 'Chester: excavations in the Princess Street/Hunter Street area 1978–1982. A first report on discoveries of the Roman period', *Journal of the Chester Archaeological Society* **65**, 5–24

Strickland, T.J. 1982b: 'The defences of Roman Chester: a note on discoveries made on the north wall, 1982', *Journal of the Chester Archaeological Society* **65**, 25–36

Strickland, T.J. 1983: 'The defences of Roman Chester: discoveries made on the east wall, 1983', *Journal of the Chester Archaeological Society* **66**, 5–11

Strickland, T.J. 1984: 'The Roman heritage of Chester: the survival of the buildings of Deva after the Roman period', *Journal of the Chester Archaeological Society* **67**, 17–36

Strickland, T. 1993: 'Gifford and Partners Archaeological Service, 1991–2', *Cheshire Past* **2**, 22

Strickland, T.J. 1996: 'Recent research at the Chester legionary fortress: the curtain wall and the barrack veranda colonnades', in Johnson and Haynes 1996, 104–19

Strobel, R. 1965: 'Beobachtungen in den principia von Castra Regina', *Bayerische Vorgeschichtsblätter* **30**, 176–88

Stroh, A. 1953: 'Neue Beobachtungen im römischen Regensburg', *Germania* **31**, 217–19

Stroh, A. 1958: 'Untersuchung an der Südostecke des Lagers der Legio III Italica in Regensburg', *Germania* **36**, 78–89

Stroh, A. 1963: 'Fortsetzung der Untersuchung an der Südostecke des Lagers der Legio III Italica in Regensburg', *Germania* **41**, 131–3

Stroh, A. 1971: 'Untersuchungen an der Ostseite des Lagers der Legio III Italica in Regensburg', *Saalburg-Jahrbuch* **28**, 52–5

Sumpter, A.B. and Coll, S. 1977: *Interval Tower SW5 and the South-West Defences: Excavations 1972–75*, Archaeology of York **3/2**, York

Swoboda-Milenovic, R.M. 1956: 'Grabungen 1956', *Carnuntum Jahrbuch 1956*, 45–64

Swoboda-Milenovic, R.M. 1957: 'Grabung 1957', *Carnuntum Jahrbuch 1957*, 21–47

Syme, R. 1978: 'Antonius Saturninus', *JRS* **68**, 12–21

Számadó, E. and Borhy, L. 2003: 'Brigetio castra legionis', in Visy 2003, 75–7

Szilágyi, M. 1986: 'Zur Rangordnung der rheinischen Legionen im 1. Jahrhundert n. Chr.', in Unz 1986, 787–91

Szirmai, K. 1976: 'Előzetes beszámoló az óbudai legiostábor principiáján és közvetlen környékén végzett kutatásokról (Preliminary report on the excavations conducted at the principia of the Obuda legionary camp and its immediate vicinity)', *Budapest Régiségei* **24**, 91–107

Szirmai, K. 1980: 'Kutatások az aquincumi II–III. századi legióstábor északi részén 1973–77-ben. (Forschungen im nördlichen Teil der Praetentura des Legionslagers im 2–3. Jh. zu Aquincum 1973–1977)', *Archeológia Értesítő* **107**, 187–200

Szirmai, K. 1984a: 'Az aquincumi II–III. századi legióstábor praetenturája (Die Praetentura des Legionslagers in Aquincum)', *Budapest Régiségei* **25**, 135–79

Szirmai, K. 1984b: 'Újabb adatok az aquincumi legióstábor falfestészetéhez (Neuere Angaben zur Wandmalerei des Legionslagers von Aquincum)', *Budapest Régiségei* **25**, 247–53

Szirmai, K. 1985: 'Kutatások a II–III. századi aquincumi legióstábor keleti védmůveinél (1974–1980)', *Communicationes Archeologicae Hungaricae 1985*, 49–68

Szirmai, K. 1986: 'Das Straßennetz des Legionslagers von Aquincum im und 3. Jahrhundert', in Unz 1986, 426–839

Szirmai, K. 1990: 'Zur Chronologie des Auxiliarkastells und des Legionslagers des 2.-3. Jh.', in Vetters and Kandler 1990, 683–7

Szirmai, K. 1991a: 'Barrack-blocks in the praetentura of the legionary fortress in Aquincum (1987–1988)', in Maxfield and Dobson 1991, 259–62

Szirmai, K. 1991b: 'Régészeti adatok az aquincumi I. századi legióstáborhoz, valamint a II-III. századi legióstábor retenturájához (Archäologische Beiträge zum Legionslagers von Aquincum aus den 1. Jh., sowie zur Retentur des Legionslagers vom 2–3. Jh.)', *Budapest Régiségei* **27**, 105–37

Szirmai, K. 1991c: 'Újabb adatok az aquincumi II–III. századi legiostábor principiájának nyugati traktusához (Neue Angaben zum westlichen Trakt der Prinzipia in Aquincum aus dem 2–3. Jahrhundert.)', *Budapest Régiségei* **28**, 107–16

Szirmai, K. 1996: 'Verzierte Schwertscheidenbeschläge aus dem Legionslager von Aquincum', in Bauchhenß, G. (ed.), *Akten des 3. internationalen Kolloquiums über Probleme des provinzialrömischen Kunstschaffens, Bonn 1993*, Köln-Bonn, 199–202

Szirmai, K. 1997: 'Kaszárnyák az aquincumi 2-3. századi legiotábor retenturájában (1987–1988) (Barrack-blocks in the praetentura of the legionary fortress in Aquincum (1987–1988))', *Budapest Régiségei* **31**, 273–80

Szőnyi, E. 2003: 'Arrabona castellum', in Visy 2003, 68–9

Taylor, D.J.A. 1999: 'A Note on "The Building of the Legionary Fortress of Inchtuthil"', *Britannia* **30**, 297–9

Tepper, Y. 2002: 'Lajjun–Legio in Israel: results of a survey in and around the military camp area', in Freeman et al. 2002, 231–42

Tepper, Y. 2007: 'The Roman legionary camp at Legio, Israel: results of an archaeological survey and observations on the Roman military presence at the site', in Lewin, A.S. and Pellegrini, P. (eds.), *The Late Roman Army in the Near East from Diocletian to the Arab Conquest. Proceedings of a Colloquium Held at Potenza, Acerenza and Matera, Italy (May 2005)*, BAR **S1717**, Oxford, 57–72

Tepper, Y. and Di Segni, L. 2005: *A Christian Prayer Hall of the Third Century CE at Kefar 'Othnay (Legio). Excavations at the Megiddo Prison*, Jerusalem

Terenzio, A., Trovalusci, G.B., Lugli, G., Mathiae, G., Galletti, A., and Bellagamba, G. 1972: *Il tempio di Santa Maria della Rotonda*, ed. 2, Albano Laziale

Thompson, F.H. 1959: 'Excavations in Weaver Street, 1956', *Journal of the Chester Archaeological Society* **46**, 69–72

Thompson, F.H. 1962: 'Excavations in Nicholas Street 1957', *Journal of the Chester Archaeological Society* **49**, 5–8

Thompson, F.H. 1967a: 'Excavations in Bolland's Court, Chester, 1954 and 1959', *Journal of the Chester Archaeological Society* **54**, 1–3

Thompson, F.H. 1967b: 'Excavations on the Site of Woolworth's Chester 1959', *Journal of the Chester Archaeological Society* **54**, 9–19

Thompson, F.H. 1967c: 'Notes on Two Building Sites in Chester', *Journal of the Chester Archaeological Society* **54**, 21–2

Thompson, F.H. 1969: 'Excavations at Linenhall Street, Chester, 1961–2', *Journal of the Chester Archaeological Society* **56**, 1–21

Thompson, F.H. and Whitwell, J.B. 1973: 'The gates of Roman Lincoln', *Archaeologia* **104**, 129–207

Thompson, F.H., Sunter, N.J., and Weaver, O.J. 1976: 'The excavation of the Roman amphitheatre at Chester', *Archaeologia* **105**, 127–239

Tomlin, R.S.O. 1992: 'The Twentieth Legion at Wroxeter and Carlisle in the first century: the epigraphic evidence', *Britannia* **23**, 141–58

Tomlin, R.S.O. 2000: 'The legions in the Late Empire', in Brewer 2000, 159–81

Tortorici, E. 1975: *Castra Albana, Forma Italiae XI*, Roma

Tragau, C. 1897: 'Die Befestigungsanlagen von Carnuntum', *Archaeologisch-Epigraphische Mittheilungen* **20**, 173–203

Tragau, K. 1909: 'Eine Dolchscheide aus Poetovio', *Jahrbuch für Altertumskunde* **3**, 117–20

Tscholl, E. 1977/78: 'Ein Römisches Limeskastell in Wallsee. 10 Jahre Beobachtungen zum Limeskastell von Wallsee (1966–1976)', *Römisches Österreich* **5/6**, 109–22

Tscholl, E. 1986: 'Wallsee – Ad Iuvense?' in Kandler and Vetters 1986, 113–17

Tscholl, E. 1989: 'Ausgrabungen im römischen Wallsee (Kastell und Vicus)', *Jahrbuch des Oberösterreichischen Musealvereines* **134**, 63–77

Tscholl, E. 1990: 'Das spätantike Restkastell von Wallsee', *Jahrbuch des Oberösterreichischen Musealvereines* **135**, 35–81

Tscholl, E. 2002, 'Archäologische Mosaiksteine aus Wallsee. Beobachtungen, Feststellungen, Fundbergungen und Grabungen im Bereich des Donau-Auxiliarkastells. Teil B: Neue Funde aus dem Kastellbereich Wallsee, 1979–1999. Hannsjörg Ubl zum 65. Geburtstag', *Römisches Österreich* **23/24**, 113–203

Tsuk, T. 1988/9: 'The aqueduct to Legio and the location of the camp of the VIth Roman Legion', *Tel Aviv* **15–16**, 92–7

Ulbert, G. 1962: 'Silbertauschierte Dolchscheiden aus Vindonissa', *Gesellschaft Pro Vindonissa. Jahresbericht*, 5–18

Unz, C. 1972: 'Zu den Schwertscheidenmedaillons aus Vindonissa', *Gesellschaft Pro Vindonissa. Jahresbericht*, 43–8

Unz, C. 1973: 'Römische Funde aus Windisch im ehemaligen Kantonalen Antiquarium Aarau', *Gesellschaft Pro Vindonissa. Jahresbericht*, 11–42

Ulbert, G. 1984: *Cáceres el Viejo. Ein spätrepublikanisches Legionslager in Spanisch-Extremadura*, Madrider Beiträge **11**, Mainz

Unz, C. 1972: 'Zu den Schwertscheidenmedaillons aus Vindonissa', *Gesellschaft Pro Vindonissa. Jahresbericht*, 43–8

Unz, C. 1973: 'Römische Funde aus Windisch im ehemaligen Kantonalen Antiquarium Aarau', *Gesellschaft Pro Vindonissa. Jahresbericht*, 11–42

Unz, C. (ed.) 1986: *Studien zu den Militärgrenzen Roms III. 13. internationaler Limeskongreß Aalen 1983 Vorträge*, Forschungen und Berichte zur Vor- und Frühgeschichte in Baden-Württemberg **20**, Köln

Unz, C. and Deschler-Erb, E. 1997: *Katalog der Militaria aus Vindonissa. Militärische Funde, Pferdegeschirr und Jochteile bis 1976*, Veröffentlichungen der Gesellschaft Pro Vindonissa **14**, Brugg

Vega, M. 1966: 'Die römischen Lampen von Neuss', in *Novaesium II*, Limesforschungen **7**, Berlin, 63–127

Vega, M. 1975: 'Die augusteische Gebrauchskeramik von Neuss', in *Novaesium VI*, Limesforschungen **14**, Berlin, 3–76

Velkov, V. 1973: 'Die Stadt Transmarisca (Moesia Inferior)', *Archaeologia Polona* **14**, 263–8

Vetters, G. 2001: 'Wandmalereien aus dem Legionslager von Vindobona – Altfunde vom Judenplatz', *Fundort Wien* **4**, 64–77

Vetters, H. 1963: 'Zur Spätzeit des Lagers Carnuntum', *Österreichische Zeitschrift für Kunst und Denkmalpflege* **17**, 157–63

Vetters, H. 1969: 'Die Grabungen der Limeskommission im Legionslager von Carnuntum', *Anzeiger der phil.-hist. Klasse der Österreichischen Akademie der Wissenschaften* **106**, 369–73

Vetters, H. 1986: 'Albing', in Kandler and Vetters 1986, 105–9

Vetters, H. and Kandler, M. (eds.) 1990: *Akten des 14. internationalen Limeskongresses in Bad Deutsch-Altenburg/Carnuntum, 14.–21. September 1986*, Römische Limes in Österreich Sonderband, Wien

Vičič, B. 2002: 'Early Roman Settlement under Grajski grič (Castle Hill) in Ljubljana. Gornji trg 3 (Frührömische Siedlung unter dem Schloßberg in Ljubljana. Gornji trg 3)', *Arheološki Vestnik* **53**, 193–221

Vičič, B. 2008: 'Ljubljana-Tribuna, izvrtana preteklost', <http://www.arhej.com/images/pdf/ljubljana-tribuna_1.pdf> accessed 27.1.11

Victoria Romero Carnicero, M. and Carretero Vaquero, S. 2006: 'Rosinos de Vidriales camp, fort and vicus', in Morillo and Aurrecoechea 2006, 347–56

Vidal, J. 1986: 'Arqueología urbana en León: precedentes y aportaciones recientes', *Archivos Leoneses* **79/80**, 365–80

Vidal, J. and García-Marcos, V. 1996: 'Novedades sobre el origen del asentamiento romano de León y de la Legio VII Gemina', in Fernández Ochoa, C. (ed.), *Los finisterres atlánticos en la antigüedad, época prerromana y romana (Coloquio internacional): homenaje a Manuel Fernández-Miranda*, Gijon, 147–56

Visy, Z. (ed.) 2003: *The Roman Army in Pannonia. An Archaeological Guide of the Ripa Pannonica*, Pécs

Visy, Z. (ed.) 2005: *Limes XIX. Proceedings of the XIXth International Congress of Roman Frontier Studies (Pécs, 2003)*, Pécs

Voişan, V. 1997: 'In Ulpia Traiana Sarmizegetusa entdeckte Bestandteile militärischer Ausrüstung', *Acta Musei Napocensis* **34**, 201–11

Volken, M. and Volken, S. 2005: 'Drei neu interpretierte Lederfunde aus Vindonissa: Kopfstück einer Pferdedecke, Sitzfläche eines Klappstuhls und Schreibtafeletui', *Gesellschaft Pro Vindonissa. Jahresbericht*, 33–9

Vollmer, F. 1915: *Inscriptiones Baivariae Romanae, sive inscriptiones provinciae Raetiae, adiectis aliqvot Noricis Italicisqve*, München

Vorbeck, E. 1954: *Militärinschriften aus Carnuntum*, Römische Forschungen in Niederösterreich **2**, Wien

Vorbeck, E. 1980a: *Militärinschriften aus Carnuntum 2*, Wien

Vorbeck, E. 1980b: *Zivilinschriften aus Carnuntum*, Wien

Wagner, F. 1956/57: 'Neue Inschriften aus Raetien', *BRGK* **37/38**, 215–64

Waldherr, G.H. 2001: *Auf den Spuren der Römer – ein Stadtführer durch Regensburg*, Regensburg

Walthew, C.V. 1981: 'Possible standard units of measurement in Roman military planning', *Britannia* **12**, 15–35

Walthew, C.V. 1988: 'Length-units in Roman military planning: Inchtuthil and Colchester', *Oxford Journal of Archaeology* **7**, 81–98

Wamser, L. 1991: 'Marktbreit, ein augusteisches Truppenlager am Maindreieck', in Trier, B. (ed.), *Die römische Okkupation nördlich der Alpen zur Zeit des Augustus. Kolloquium Bergkamen 1989*, Münster, 109–27

Wamser, L., Flügel, C., and Ziegaus, B. (eds.) 2000: *Die Römer zwischen Alpen und Nordmeer. Zivilisatorisches Erbe einer europäischen Militärmacht*, Mainz

Ward, M. 1998: 'A collection of samian from the legionary works-depot at Holt', in Bird, J. (ed.), *Form and Fabric: Studies in Rome's Material Past in Honour of B. R. Hartley*, Oxford, 133–43

Ward, S.W. 1988: *Excavations at Chester: 12 Watergate Street 1985: Roman Headquarters Building to Medieval Row*, Chester

Ward, S.W. and Strickland, T.J. 1978: *Excavations on the Site of the Northgate Brewery, Chester, 1974–5: a Roman Centurion's Quarters and Barrack*, Chester

Ward, T. 1975: 'Excavations in Goss Street, Chester, 1971', *Journal of the Chester Archaeological Society* **58**, 47–51

Warry, P. 2010: 'Legionary tile production in Britain', *Britannia* **41**, 127–47

Watermann, R. 1978: *Valetudinarium. Das römische Legionskrankenhaus, Ausstellungskatalog des Clemens-Sels-Museums*, Neuss

Watkins, T.H. 1983: 'Roman legionary fortresses and the cities of modern Europe', *Military Affairs* 47:1, 15–25

Weber-Hiden, I. 1996: *Die reliefverzierte Terrasigillata aus Vindobona. Teil 1, Legionslager und Canabae*, Wiener Archäologische Studien **1**, Wien

Webster, G. 1949: 'The legionary fortress at Lincoln', *JRS* **39**, 57–78

Webster, G. 1952: 'Excavations on the legionary defences at Chester, 1948–52 (Part I)', *Journal of the Chester Archaeological Society* **39**, 21–8

Webster, G. 1953: 'Excavations on the legionary defences at Chester, 1948–52 (Part II)', *Journal of the Chester Archaeological Society* **40**, 1–23

Webster, G. 1955: 'A section through the legionary defences on the west side of the fortress', *Journal of the Chester Archaeological Society* **42**, 45–7

Webster, G. 1956: 'Excavation of the Roman Remains East of Trinity Street 1950–1953', *Journal of the Chester Archaeological Society* **43**, 27–33

Webster, G. 1962: 'The defences of Viroconium (Wroxeter)', *Transactions of the Birmingham Archaeological Society* **78**, 27–39

Webster, G. 1969: 'Wroxeter', *Current Archaeology* **2**, 82–6

Webster, G. 1977–8: 'Wroxeter', *Current Archaeology* **9**, 364–8

Webster, G. 1980: *The Roman Invasion of Britain*, London

Webster, G. 1985: *The Roman Imperial Army of the First and Second Centuries A.D.*, ed. 3, London

Webster, G. (ed.) 1988a: *Fortress into City. The Consolidation of Roman Britain, First Century* AD, London

Webster, G. 1988b: 'Wroxeter (Viroconium)', in Webster 1988a, 120–44

Webster, G. 1991: 'The defences of the legionary fortress at Viroconium (Wroxeter) c.AD 55–90', in Maxfield and Dobson 1991, 125–31

Webster, G. and Chadderton, J. (ed.) 2002: *The Legionary Fortress at Wroxeter. Excavations by Graham Webster, 1955–85*, English Heritage Archaeological Report **19**, London

Webster, J. 1990: 'An Unusual Brooch from Caerleon', *Britannia* **21**, 297–99

Wellner, I. 1973: 'Az aquincumi katonaváros nyugat–keleti irányú vízvezetékrendszere', *Budapest Régiségei* 23, 179–86

Wellner, I. 1980: 'Das Legionslager von Aquincum und die vermutete Principia', *Alba Regia* **18**, 349–55

Wellner, I. 1990: 'Die Militärlager Aquincums in spätrömischer Zeit und im Mittelalter (Aquincum und das Nibelungenlied)', in Vetters and Kandler 1990, 715–21

Wells, C.M. 1970: 'The supposed Augustan base at Augsburg-Oberhausen: a new look at the evidence', *Saalburg-Jahrbuch* **27**, 63–72

Wells, C.M. 1972: *The German Policy of Augustus: An Examination of the Archaeological Evidence*, Oxford

Wenham, L.P. 1961: 'Excavations and discoveries adjoining the south-west wall of the Roman legionary fortress in Feasgate, York, 1955–57', *Yorkshire Archaeological Journal* **40**, 329–50

Wenham, L.P. 1962: 'Excavations and discoveries within the legionary fortress in Davygate, York, 1955–58', *Yorkshire Archaeological Journal* **40**, 507–87

Wenham, L.P. 1968: 'Discoveries in King's Square, York, 1963', *Yorkshire Archaeological Journal* **42**, 165–8

Wenham, L.P. 1972: 'Excavations in Low Petergate, York, 1957–8', *Yorkshire Archaeological Journal* **44**, 65–113

Werz, U. 2008: 'Zur Datierung des Römerlagers bei Hedemünden, Ldkr. Göttingen, durch gegengestempelte Fundmünzen', in Zelle, M. (ed.), *Terra incognita? Die nördlichen Mittelgebirge im Spannungsfeld römischer und germanischer Politik um Christi Geburt. Akten des Kolloquiums im Lippischen Landesmuseum Detmold vom 17. bis 19. Juni 2004*, Mainz, 187–90

Wesch-Klein, G. 2000: 'Die Legionsziegeleien von Tabernae', in Le Bohec and Wolff 2000, 459–63

Wheeler, M. and Nash-Williams, V.E. 1970: *Caerleon Roman Amphitheatre and Prysg Field Barrack Buildings, Monmouthshire. Caerllion Sir Fynwy*, London

Wheeler, R.E.M. and Wheeler, T.V. 1928: 'The Roman amphitheatre at Caerleon, Mon', *Archaeologia* **18**, 111–218

Whitcomb, D. 1990: 'Diocletian's miṣr at Aqaba', *Zeitschift des deutschen Palastina-Vereins* **106**, 156–61

Whitcomb, D. 1993: 'Aqaba, 1989–90', *Syria* **70**, 239–44

Whitwell, J.B. 1967: *Lindum Colonia: A Brief Account of Excavations on the Northern Defences and the East Gate of the Roman Legionary Fortress and Town at Lincoln*, Lincoln

Whitwell, J.B. 1976: *The Church Street Sewer and an Adjacent Building*, Archaeology of York **3/1**, York

Wiegels, R. 1989: 'Zwei Bleimarken aus dem frührömischen Truppenlager Dangstetten', *Fundberichte aus Baden-Württemberg* **14**, 427–56

Wilkes, J.J. 2000: 'Roman legions and their fortresses in the Danube lands (first to third centuries AD)', in Brewer 2000, 101–19

Willems, W.J.H. 1991: 'Een Romeins viziermasker van het Kops Plateau te Nijmegen', *Jaarboek Numaga* 9–18

Willems, W.J.H. 1994: 'Roman face masks from the Kops Plateau, Nijmegen, The Netherlands', *Journal of Roman Military Equipment Studies* **3**, 57–66

Willems, W.J.H. 1996: 'Een Romeins legerkamp op het Kops Plateau te Nijmegen / Ein römisches Militärlager auf dem Kops Plateau in Nijmegen', in Swinkels, L.J.F. (ed.), *Een leven te paard. Ruiters uit de Lage Landen in het Romeinse leger / Reiten für Rom. Berittene Truppen an de römischen Rheingrenze*, Nijmegen-Köln, 28–31

Willems, W.J.H. and Enckevort, H. van 1996: 'Roman cavalry helmets in ritual hoards from the Kops Plateau at Nijmegen, the Netherlands', *Journal of Roman Military Equipment Studies* **5**, 125–37

Willems, W.J.H. and Enckevort, H. van, 2009: *Vlpia Noviomagvs – Roman Nijmegen. The Batavian Capital at the Imperial Frontier*, JRA Supplement **73**, Portsmouth

Willems, W.J.H. and Kooistra, L.I. 1991: 'Early Roman camps on the Kops Plateau at Nijmegen (NL)', in Maxfield and Dobson 1991, 210–14

Wilmanns, G. 1884: *Étude sur le camp et la ville de Lambèse*, Paris

Wilmott, T., Garner, D., and Ainsworth, S. 2006: 'The Roman amphitheatre at Chester: an interim account', *English Heritage Historical Review* **1**, 6–23

Wilson, D.R. 1977: 'A first-century fort near Gosbecks, Essex', *Britannia* **8**, 185–7

Wilson, D.R. 1984: 'Defensive outworks of Roman forts in Britain', *Britannia* **15**, 51–61

Winkler, G., 1971: 'Legio II Italica. Geschichte und Denkmäler', *Jahrbuch des oberösterreichischen Musealvereines* **116/I**, 85–138 <http://www.limes-oesterreich.at/php/site.php?ID=378> accessed 26.11.2009

Witteyer, M. 1999: 'Mogontiacum – Militärbasis und Verwaltungszentrum. Der archäologische Befund', in Dumont, F., Scherf, F., and Schütz, F. (eds.), *Mainz – Die Geschichte der Stadt*, 2. Auflage, Mainz, 1021–59

Wolff, C. 2000: 'Legio I Parthica', in Le Bohec and Wolff 2000, 247–9

Wolff, G. 2000: 'Das Deutzer Kastell', in Wolff, G., *Das Römisch-Germanische Köln. Führer zu Museum und Stadt*, ed. 5, Köln, 260–2

Wood, I. 1995: 'Turning a fortress into a cathedral', *British Archaeology* **7**, 7

Wright, R.P. 1976: 'Tile stamps of the sixth legion found in Britain', *Britannia* **7**, 224–35

Wright, R.P. 1978: 'Tile stamps of the ninth legion found in Britain', *Britannia* **9**, 379–82

Wuilleumier, P. 1963: *Inscriptions Latines des trois Gaules*, Paris

Young, T.P. 2006: *Geophysical Investigation of the Priory Field, Caerleon, 2006* <http://www.cf.ac.uk/hisar/archaeology/crc/files/priory_field_survey.pdf> retrieved 13.11.09

Zabehlicky, S., Schaffenegger, S., and Kandler, M. 1979: *Das Standlager in Burnum I. Erster Bericht über die Kleinfunde der Grabungen 1973 und 1974 auf dem Forum*, Schriften der Balkankomission **14**, Wien

Zaninović, M. 1968: 'Burnum: castellum, municipium', *Diadora* **4**, 119–29

Zienkiewicz J.D. 1990: 'The early development of the legionary fortress of Caerleon-Isca and consequences for Flavian policy in Britain', in Burnham, B.C. and Davies, J.L. (eds.), *Conquest, Co-existence and Change. Recent Work in Roman Wales*, Trivium **25**, Lampeter, 27–34

Zienkiewicz, J.D. 1984a: 'Caerleon', *Archaeology in Wales* **24**, 55–7

Zienkiewicz, J.D. 1984b: 'Great Bulmore', *Archaeology in Wales* **24**, 57–8

Zienkiewicz, J.D. 1986a: *The Legionary Fortress Baths at Caerleon vol I: The Buildings*, Cardiff

Zienkiewicz, J.D. 1986b: *The Legionary Fortress Baths at Caerleon vol II: The Finds*, Cardiff

Zienkiewicz, J.D. 1987a: 'Caerleon, Isca, British Telecom site, Museum Street', *Archaeology in Wales* **27**, 47–8

Zienkiewicz, J.D. 1987b: *Roman Gems from Caerleon*, Cardiff

Zienkiewicz, J.D. 1992a: 'Pottery from excavations on the site of the Roman Legionary Museum, Caerleon, 1983–5', *Journal of Roman Pottery Studies* **5**, 81–109

Zienkiewicz, J.D. 1992b: 'Roman glass vessels from Caerleon: Excavations at the Legionary Museum Site 1983–5', *The Monmouthshire Antiquary* **8**, 1–9

Zienkiewicz, J.D. 1993: 'Excavations in the Scamnum Tribunorum at Caerleon: the Legionary Museum Site 1983–5', *Britannia* **24**, 27–140

Ziethen, G. 1999: 'Mogontiacum. Vom Legionslager bis zur Provinzhauptstadt', in Dumont, F., Scherf, F., and Schütz, F. (eds.) 1999, *Mainz – Die Geschichte der Stadt*, 2. Auflage, Mainz, 39–71

Zmeev, R. 1969: 'Kasteiüt Transmariska (Le castel Transmariska)', *Archeologija* **11**, 45–54

Index

Occurrences in line illustrations have the page number *italicized* whilst plate numbers are **emboldened**